I0831124

Towards a Cultural History of the Mamluk Era

BEIRUTER TEXTE UND STUDIEN

HERAUSGEGEBEN VOM
ORIENT-INSTITUT BEIRUT

BAND 118

Towards a Cultural History of the Mamluk Era

Edited by

Mahmoud Haddad, Arnim Heinemann,
John L. Meloy and Souad Slim

BEIRUT 2010

ERGON VERLAG WÜRZBURG
IN KOMMISSION

Umschlaggestaltung: Taline Yozgatian
Druckbetreuung: Sara Binay

Umschlagfoto: Screen of Abū Sargā, Cairo, detail of the geometric decoration. Photography by Adeline Jeudy.

Bibliografische Information der Deutschen Bibliothek

Die Deutsche Bibliothek verzeichnet diese Publikation
in der Deutschen Nationalbiografie;
detaillierte biografische Daten sind im Internet
über http://dnb.d-nb.de abrufbar.

Bibliographic information published by the Deutsche Nationalbibliothek

The Deutsche Nationalbibliothek lists this publication
in the Deutsche Nationalbibliografie;
detailed bibliographic data are available in the Internet
at http://dnb.d-nb.de.

ISBN 978-3-89913-734-7

 Gedruckt mit Unterstützung des Orient-Instituts Beirut, gegründet von der Deutschen Morgenländischen Gesellschaft, aus Mitteln des Bundesministeriums für Bildung und Forschung und mit Mitteln der Universität Balamand.

Ergon-Verlag, Dr. H.J. Dietrich
Keesburgstr. 11, D-97074 Würzburg

Universität Balamand,
El-Koura, North Lebanon

Druck: Dergham sarl
Gedruckt auf alterungsbeständigem Papier

Erratum

It has come to our notice that a paper by Professor Doris Behrens-Abouseif, entitled 'Craftsmen and upstarts in the late Mamluk period' has been reproduced in this volume without the authorisation of the author and copyright owner.

The Orient-Insitut Beirut regrets this oversight on its part, and apologises to Professor Behrens-Abouseif for any inconvenience experienced by her as a result. We confirm that the material cited is an original work of authorship created by Professor Behrens-Abouseif, and that copyright in the material concerned is vested in the School of Oriental and African Studies (SOAS).

A modified and updated version of Professor Behrens-Abouseif's paper, entitled 'Craftsmen, upstarts and Sufis in the late Mamluk period', which supersedes the version in this volume, has been accepted for publication in the *Bulletin of the School of Oriental and African Studies*.

TABLE OF CONTENTS

INTRODUCTION

This volume gathers papers first presented at a conference on Mamluk history held at the University of Balamand from May 4-7, 2005, convened under the auspices of the University and the Orient-Institut Beirut. The title of the conference, "Towards a Cultural History of Bilād al-Shām during the Mamluk Era: Prosperity or Decline, Tolerance or Prescrvation," indicated two main objectives: to consider the cultural history, broadly conceived, of the era of the Mamluk Sultanate and, more particularly, to investigate the relations of the state to various social groups within Bilād al-Shām.

In assembling the contributions to be published it became evident that the conference title should be adjusted to reflect more accurately the results of the conference. In particular, our original purview expanded, perhaps inevitably, to include Egypt, but certainly not to the exclusion of geographical Syria. It is our hope that this project will to some extent draw attention to topics relating to Bilād al-Shām, a region too often neglected in Mamluk Studies. The papers assembled here have been divided into five parts, reflecting the major issues addressed in the conference: the interaction among religious communities within the Sultanate; fields of cultural production in the visual arts, sciences, and literature; and the cultural contexts of political practice and social relations.

The first part of this volume, and to a great extent the heart of the conference proceedings, includes contributions on the interaction among religious groups, dealing primarily with the situation of the Christians in Syria and Egypt, but also dealing with the Druzes, Nusayris, and Shi'a during the Mamluk period. The dire state of these communities, which included being subjected to military assault, systematic discrimination through confiscations and removal from office, and suppression of religious and cultural expression, stands in contrast to other positive developments in Mamluk society. The depredations against these communities are well known to scholars of the Mamluk period. Jørgen Nielsen's suggestive paper, which also served as the keynote presentation of the conference, reviews scholarship on the participation of Christians and Jews in the state apparatus. Nielsen's remarks remind us of the necessity to recognize the common cultural context of all the religious communities in an effort to provoke discussion and prompt new questions for future research.

The authors of these papers met that challenge. Seldom do we see so clearly delineated the religious, political, economic, social and (including the two articles on Christian art) artistic manifestations of non-majoritarian groups in Mamluk society. In particular, these contributions shed significant light on modes of determined response and resistance to state ideology. Ray Mouawwad explores valuable Aramaic and Karshuni sources rarely, if ever, used in her examination of the role of martyrdom as expressed in religious books and popular songs which were suppressed by the state authorities. Elias al-Qattar transfers our view to rural regions of Lebanon to show how these mountain populations adopted a defensive posture to await the withdrawal of state forces. Contributions by Ahmad Hutait and André Nassar show how members of the Christian urban communities achieved considerable influence and a certain degree of integration in their respective societies, at times succumbing to conversion and identified as such. David Thomas examines an early fourteenth century theological correspondence between Christians in Cyprus and Muslims in Damascus. He concludes that in the context of the deterioration of the status of Christians and the residual tension in the wake of the Crusader retreat from the region these efforts at inter-faith dialogue were hindered by the deployment of their respective scriptural models and the lack of a common discourse.

The examination of these communities is partly continued in the second part of the volume, devoted to cultural production in the visual arts. In two papers, Elyas al-Zayyat and co-authors Mat Immerzeel and Adeline Jeudy examine the production of Christian art in the Mamluk Sultanate. Al-Zayyat addresses the issue of determining identifiable Christian elements in the context of the Mamluk period art production in Bilād al-Shām. Immerzeel and Jeudy extend the field of vision to Egypt in an effort to document changes in Christian art production from earlier periods into the Mamluk era, pointing to a cessation of art production in Syria soon after the Mamluk takeover while in Egypt Christian art production diminished later, during the middle of the fourteenth century. The other three papers examined other aspects of the production of art of architecture. Doris Behrens-Abouseif examines the role of craftsmen and perceptively demonstrates the increasing social recognition of this class of individuals and their work over the course of the Mamluk period. Howayda al-Harithy switches our view from artisan to product in her case study of inscriptions on religious monuments in Tripoli, demonstrating the distinct political function of these messages.

Anis Shaya traces the development of urban structures and fortifications of Tripoli in order to explain the shift of the city's core inland from the port area.

The investigation of cultural production is continued in Part Three, concerning historical literature. Antoine Doumit directs our view to the first half of the fifteenth century with his study of Taqī al-Dīn al-Maqrīzī's method of writing history. Doumit identifies characteristics of "renewal" in al-Maqrīzī's writing about basic elements of information, behaviour and knowledge within the Mamluk state, stressing his creativity (*ibdāᶜ*) at the level of form (*shakl*) and of content/meaning (*maḍmūn*), showing that the historian's point of view serves as the driving force of the work. Our view shifts to the end of the Mamluk period with the paper by Axel Havemann, which explores the culture of common people in an assessment of Ibn Iyās's *Badāʾiᶜ al-zuhūr*. Ibn Iyās reveals multiple layers of Cairene society, including those rarely, if ever, discussed in other sources. Since many of his reports are linked to events ranging from the criminal to the scandalous, as well as amusing gossip and beggar's tales, Havemann shows how this example of Mamluk literature proves itself essential as a source for doing "history from below."

An often neglected area in Mamluk Studies concerns developments in the history of sciences and in Part Four of this volume George Saliba and Floréal Sanagustin make considerable headway in rectifying that deficiency, while placing these developments in their cultural and cross-cultural contexts. Saliba reviews the accomplishments of mathematical astronomy during the Mamluk period in the context of scientific developments before and after. The achievements of the fourteenth century Damascene astronomer Ibn al-Shāṭir stand out in particular by forming the essential mathematical groundwork that enabled the subsequent formulation of Copernican astronomy in Europe. Sanagustin shifts our view to transformations within the Islamic tradition in an examination of the codification of "prophetic" medicine (*al-ṭibb al-nabawī*) during the Mamluk period. He advances the hypothesis that this intellectual effort constituted in effect the construction of an origin narrative, which allowed for the re-reading of an idealized mythical past.

In the last part, the contributors explored, at different scales, political practice and social relations in Mamluk society and culture. The paper of Albrecht Fuess to some extent takes up the broad view of cultural relations in Mamluk society, offered by Nielsen with regard to religious communities at the outset of the volume, in an examination of relations between the Mamluk military elite and the Arabic-speaking populace. Fuess explores the contradictory attitudes of the latter toward the former, ranging from antipathy to admiration. At a more focused level, Ahmad Abdelsalam and Aliya Saidi examine particular dimensions of Mamluk politics and society. Abdelsalam examines a fundamental governmental institution, that of the *ḥisba,* in an effort to track a shift from religious and legal appointments to civil and administrative appointments. The final paper directs our attention to the more particular level of marital relations within the Mamluk elite. Saidi examines the high incidence of mental illness among women in polygamous marriages, set within the prevailing tolerance within Mamluk culture toward divorce and serial monogamy.

Together these contributions investigate new lines of research and raise new questions. Many of these papers explore the Mamluk past of Bilād al-Shām and, more particularly, Tripoli and Mount Lebanon, localities that have received comparatively little attention compared to that of the Sultanate's capital and Egypt more generally. It is our hope that these will serve as a reminder of the communal diversity of late medieval Syria and Egypt and the importance of a firm appreciation of the cultural dimensions of the Mamluk Era.

The Editors

Due to the frequent usage of local place names, which become virtually unrecognizable when rendered in transliterated classical Arabic, in editing the text we have chosen to allow the contributing authors to use their preferred systems of transliteration, while retaining uniformity for commonly used terms. We have also allowed authors some latitude with regard to citation style. Our goal has been to ensure consistency within each contribution. Although these decisions may not conform to the usual standard of scholarly practice, we feel that the results will be no less useful, and perhaps even more accessible, to our readers.

Part One

Religious Communities and their Interaction

The Participation of Christians and Jews in the Ayyubid and Mamluk State: A Historiographical Reflection

JØRGEN S. NIELSEN

The title given to this paper has deliberately emphasized the participation of *dhimmīs* in the Ayyubid and Mamluk state and society, so as to distinguish it from the more traditional question of their place and role. This was intended to be a discussion not of the status of the *ahl al-kitāb* nor of the institutional place of their institutions but of their participation. At first this could be thought to represent a current political and institutional agenda with little regard for historical contexts. But as many of the papers in this volume suggest, there is little of such contemporary apologetic dimensions behind it, although the term 'participation' has certainly been used for apologetic purposes. As one example one could cite a scholar such as Abdullah Schleifer, who might be considered a Muslim nostalgic medievalist (Schleifer 1987, 165). On the other hand, it is over four decades since Prof. S. D. Goitein used the phrase 'Jewish participation in the medieval civilization of the Middle East' in a chapter subtitle (Goitein 1974, 125). More recently, the concept has been discussed even though not explicitly named by a number of scholars, including Jewish ones (Sharot 1996, Cohen 1996). In fact, the present papers suggest that a significant reorientation has recently taken place among scholars, by which a rather wider view than the traditional ones has developed, one in which the participation of the *ahl al-kitāb* in Muslim societies is regarded as encompassing rather more than those comparatively limited aspects where their role was circumscribed by the *dhimma*.

It has, of course, been one of the tenets of Arab nationalism, especially as it developed in geographical Syria – *Bilād al-Shām* – that traditional Arab-Islamic society was characterised by a harmonious collective interaction between and mutual recognition of various linguistic and religious communities. Unfortunate incidents in breach of this were exceptions, as were the situations at particular times and places, e.g. Almohad Spain or the oppressed status of Jews in Yemen. We are obviously not dealing with a subject which is innocent of contemporary reference. In fact, one is sometimes tempted to exasperation at the extent to which the current agendas of various interest groups determine which particular aspects of the historical record are to be given emphasis, not to mention how commonly cited sources and incidents are interpreted in contradictory manner – and it has to be accepted that this paper and its author writing elsewhere will find it difficult to avoid falling into the same sin.

Recent writings about the situation of Christians or Jews in the Arab world in this century have tended to have an almost obligatory historical introduction. It is not always a simple matter to relate the interpretation of such summaries to the main work. There seem to be two approaches, both of which paint the medieval circumstances in a sombre light. Robert Betts, writing before the outbreak in 1975 of the Lebanese civil war, compresses the period 633-1798 CE into a dozen pages under the title 'The Dark Millennium' significantly followed by a 'Revival' starting in 1798 (Betts 1978, 7-19). Here, the generally negative experience of the medieval period is set to contrast with the more positive potentials introduced by the western impact symbolised by Napoleon's landing in Egypt. And this is a generally optimistic work compared to a number of more recent works written under the impact of the Lebanese war and the rise of Islamic political activism.

A particular trend of current analysis tends to seek out the most negative interpretation of our theme. There is here an almost 'unholy alliance' between Jewish and Christian propagandists against Islam, wilfully seeking to distort the historical record. One might cite works by John Laffin, Bat Ye'or and Joan Peters as being outstanding examples of this genre (Cohen 1996, 51f. and Mitri 1998).

This is not to say that the other side is innocent. One has long been familiar with Muslim apologetics according to which everything under Islamic rule was good and all Islamic teaching represents an ideal solution. Thus Schleifer:

> Yet in the particularities of its claim to archetype, Islamic Jerusalem in contrast to Mecca and Medina – cities of the homogeneric Arabian homeland – stands as a model for much of the Middle East that traditionally contains a mosaic of religious, ethnic and linguistic communities within the unifying field of a broadly defined Islamic civilization: a civilization that drew its characteristic qualities as a social order from the overwhelmingly Muslim character of the population without restricting participation in that civilization to Muslims (Schleifer 1987, 164f).

When this view is confronted with the historical record of Muslim writers in Arabic, the response tends, in the writings of such as Mawdūdī and

Sayyid Qutb, to be on the line: 'but that is not Islam; do not judge Islam by the mistakes of oppressive rulers'.

It is worth noting, on the other hand, that there is movement from within both these 'camps'. There are evangelical Christians who now are taking a more balanced view of the past, as there are Muslims. This coincides with a revisiting among western writers of the Crusades, a process which has taken place over many decades but which only recently has begun to filter into public media expression, such as in a highly entertaining and historically very clever four-part TV serial on the Crusades by Terry Jones and the BBC.

What all of this indicates is that the role of Jews and Christians in premodern Middle Eastern history is one which is difficult to analyze without running against expectations and biases deriving from our own time, even more strongly so than is the case usually in most historiography.

The term participation itself, as already indicated, suggests a contemporary agenda. Is the theme therefore, as an anachronism, historiographically invalid? Fortunately, the recent attention which has been given to the concept of 'civil society' suggests that we can still explore the idea of 'participation' before either of the two terms become locked into the status of being technical terms or discipline jargon which require esoteric definitions in each instance before we are allowed to use them.

The idea of 'civil society', introduced by contemporary political science, has drawn attention to the shift of the concentration of students of Arab society away from the role of government and official institutions. This shift had already started some decades ago with the growing interest in court records and other archives indicative of the life of the broader population and has been complemented, for earlier periods, by the extensive work on the wealth of information available in, above all, the Geniza documents. The scholars of these archives have not used the term 'civil society' in any technical sense in the way it has come to be used for contemporary political science analysis, exemplified particularly in the 'Civil Society Project' (Norton 1995). But even here any technical sense still remains so loose that 'civil society' can still be a useful perspective on pre-modern Middle Eastern society. This was done very effectively for a generalist audience by HRH Prince al-Ḥasan of Jordan (Hassan 1997).

The idea that Christians and Jews in medieval Islam had an autonomous status as *dhimmīs* with a degree of internal communal self-government in the general context of second-class status is standard. Equally, it is not new that individual Christians and, less often, Jews occupied significant government posts. However, little has been done to look beyond the place of *dhimmīs* in such narrow terms. On the other hand, social and urban studies of the medieval Middle East have experienced significant advances in recent years and have gone some way towards opening up the question of the extent of participation by the Muslim majority in various aspects of the social, cultural and political environment. What needs to be done now is to look at *dhimmī* participation in the rather more complex terms of participation of the subject populations in general. After all, if we are to assess levels of participation it must be done in terms of the epoch being studied rather than in terms of our own.

The scholarly context in which I would suggest that such a review should take place is that of the burgeoning field of urban studies. The first phase of this field among western scholars was represented by people such as Jean Sauvaget whose studies of Damascus (Sauvaget 1932) and Aleppo (Sauvaget 1941) concentrated on the physical geography of those cities, to which was soon added an institutional dimension which focused on the role of the *Sharīʿa* and its institutions. A significant part of the purpose of those scholars was to identify the nature of the Islamic city and to discover how it could be differentiated from the European city. Both were clearly imaginary ideal types. The entry into the field of scholars with a social sciences bias posed new questions of the source material and in the process discovered new source material, or rather discovered that known sources could be used in previously unsuspected ways. Here the wealth of information available in biographical dictionaries came into its own, especially when the sorting and analytical power of computers was applied to it. The imaginative synthesizing work of Ira Lapidus (1967) had led the way in applying a social scientific approach, integrating detailed studies such as those of Claude Cahen and constructing an overall picture of a complex city. Significantly he also undermined the ideal type approach, talking of ‘Muslim cities’ rather than ‘the Islamic city’. The impression given is now one of complex social networks relating to each other in processes both of mutual exclusion and inclusion. Urban geographers have continued to study individual cities incorporating the findings and approaches of such theoretical developments, a process which might be exemplified by the magisterial study of Aleppo by Gaube and Wirth (1984). More recently, the whole field has been subjected to an extensive critical survey by a group of Japanese scholars (Haneda and Miura 1994) who represent the full swing of the pendulum from the ideal type approach of the pre-1940 period to a stance which takes as its starting point the assumption that each city (read: community) is different.

My own view would tend towards a middle way between the two extremes of the pendulum. Of course, every city is different and the differences must be taken seriously, seriously enough to raise substantial doubts about an ideal type approach. On the other hand, the common Islamic character cannot just be one of external expression. The expectations created by Islamic norms as discussed and developed by the *ʿulamāʾ* were a constant measure against which realities were tested, in the breach as much as in the observance: they functioned like a magnet counteracting the centrifugal forces of local particularities whatever their natures. This magnet was constantly renewed and reinforced by the mobility of the *ʿulamāʾ* both physically and intellectually within a professional structure which was close to having the character of a transregional guild. In this connection I would suggest that social anthropologists attracted by the views of such as Clifford Geertz (1968) are led to push the argument for particularity to extremes by the very nature of their discipline.

So how can we revisit the question of assessing the nature of *dhimmī* participation in medieval Islamic society? As a start one might test this by looking at the question from the point of view of different *dhimmī* perspectives. How might the community and its leaders as a whole have experienced their place in the wider local and regional society? The same question might be asked from the point of view of individuals. There is also a matter of how they fitted into the institutional structures and the extent to which they participated or were simply dependent clients. More amorphous, but probably of deeply psychological significance, was the extent to which there was a sense of a shared culture. Finally, as I turn attention more explicitly to the Ayyubid and early Mamluk period, we have to consider the changing context which might have led to the situation as between the beginning and end of the period being changed.

Considering the question at the communal level does require reiteration of formal institutional positions, which particularly have to do with how the state chose to interpret and work with *dhimmī* status. There is little point here in going into this in any detail beyond to remind ourselves of the published syntheses ranging from Tritton (1930) through Fattal (1958) to more recent works. There is ample published evidence of the formal relationships between the organs of state and the hierarchical leaders of the *dhimmī* communities, such as that of al-Qalqashandī (Bosworth 1972). What is more interesting is the point, which is being made with increasing strength, that urban society in general was characterised by its autonomy from the state. Charles Beckingham stated the case succinctly, firstly summarising the oft-repeated statement of *dhimmī* autonomy but then putting it into a general context:

> Even in regard to its Muslim subjects, however, a traditional Muslim government almost always practised what one might term minimal government, something that is now very much out of fashion. (Beckingham 1976, 610)

This general distancing of the state from direct involvement with the subject population provides the space for a host of local community organisation which could be argued to be common to all regardless of religion. The work of Cahen, Lapidus and others on forms of community control through the *aḥdāth* and *zuᶜār* makes it clear that a variety of different collective labels could be mobilised in various circumstances. In Baghdad and Damascus at certain times the clashes were between Sunni *madhāhib*, especially Shafiᶜis and Hanbalis. At other times, for example in Aleppo it could be between Sunnis and Shiᶜis, or between Arabs and Turcomans. It should come therefore as no surprise that occasionally it was also Jews or Christians, or less often *dhimmīs* as a whole, who were identified as a group in urban clashes.

Equally it was in the nature of the case that the state sought to use such communal divisions as a means to retain overall control. If this meant playing on rivalries and prejudices, so be it. Lapidus has a telling passage which throws light on this:

> The working population, the common people proper, indulged in looting only when authorized by the Mamluks in circumstances of civil wars. Their pillaging was almost entirely directed against defeated amirs, and the markets and property in general were safe. Occasionally hunger would lead to the looting of bread shops in time of famine; other social stresses might provoke attacks on Christians and foreigners. But even religious and social resentments which resulted in the plunder and destruction of churches and synagogues never went so far as pillage of non-Muslims generally for the sake of robbery alone. (Lapidus 1984, 169)

In other words, the state set one community on another when it suited its purposes, but all communities could become victims. The development of community-based city quarters was both an effect and a cause of such phenomena: mutual support and common defence were inextricably two sides of the same coin. The European concept of the ghetto is totally inappropriate as an analogy to this situation. If the circumstances were right communities could just as well cooperate, even in the countryside where the divisions tended to be more deeply set, as when Jews and Muslims jointly harassed Frankish remnants after Ṣalāḥ al-Dīn's reconquest of Galilee (Kedar 1990, 155).

Scholars in this field have made much of the continuing employment by the Ayyubid and Mamluk governments of administrative officials from among particularly the Coptic community (e.g. Little 1976). One notices, of course, repeated appeals by the native Muslim elites to the government to rid itself of these people who were alleged to make decisions in favour of their own. But ample other evidence suggests that this was a case of special pleading: all government officials were wont to use their positions in favour of whomsoever they might consider their own.

More complex is how to understand the position of the Copts and the Muslim establishment's perception of them. As both Little (1976) and, for a later period, Petry (1981) show, Coptic conversion to Islam among the bureaucratic classes was common. But conversion appears not to have allowed them to avoid the accusations of partisanship which may have been an incentive for the conversion. Indeed conversion seems not to have granted them or their children, and often not even their grandchildren, access to the estate of *ʿulamāʾ*. A principle of 'once a Copt, always a Copt' seems to have operated, regardless of religion. At the risk of interfering in a contemporary Egyptian debate, is one not possibly entitled to consider the Copts an ethnic, as much as, if not more than, a religious community at least in this period? The contrast is marked with the sons of Mamluk officers who, excluded from entry into their fathers' profession, moved in numbers into Islamic scholarship and positions identified for the *ʿulamāʾ*. Here, at least, is evidence that the traditional perception of the primacy of religious difference as a criterion of level of status needs moderation.

A number of scholars have stressed the factor of a common cultural environment contributing to a relationship among communities and a self-perception of those communities which distinguishes their situation sharply from that of religious minorities, particularly Jews, in medieval Europe. This point has been made both by Sharot and Cohen (in Deshen and Zenner 1996) and has been substantiated in detail by Goitein's massive study of the Geniza materials (1967-1983). At the popular cultural levels religious practices showed little respect for the borders imposed by the religious professionals of all communities.

At the other end of the scale was a political culture which one could argue was also held in common. The state tended to reinforce the authority of the religious community leaderships, most formally through its ratification, and sometimes appointment, of patriarchs and gaons. But in principle this could be argued to have been but a variation of the role of the state in appointing senior Muslim clerics. In fact the state had a closer degree of self-interest in the latter appointments than in the former. So the chief *qāḍīs* become key figures in state ceremonial and key mediators between foreign rulers and the native population (Escovitz 1984 and Nielsen 1985, 123ff), but by that very token they became pawns in the manipulations of the state in a way which was hardly the case with Christian or Jewish hierarchs.

Finally, there is a time dimension. The period we are dealing with coincides with the decline and disappearance of the Frankish states and the new threat of the Mongols. Of the two the latter would seem to have been the major psychological disaster for the Muslim learned communities, especially with the massacre of the Abbasid caliphal family in 1258. But to what extent were the *ʿulamāʾ* the 'chattering classes' of the time, and to what extent did they represent the ordinary people or the secular governing elite? In other words, are historians, by relying on the written record produced primarily by *ʿulamāʾ*, being led into a limited picture of a whole, much of which is to be found elsewhere? To judge by the nature of urban street clashes – riots – events linked to the successive defeats of Frankish princes and garrisons were much more prevalent than any such events linked to Mongol advances and retreats. This could suggest that for this particular region the Franks were the present and constant danger.

This would also account for the progressive deterioration in the social standing of the Christian communities. I stress social, because while the 7th/14th century is one of steady tightening of restrictions against Christians in particular, and thence *dhimmīs* in general, usually expressed in repeated reaffirmations of the application of the terms of the so-called Covenant of ʿUmar, the evidence of earlier periods would suggest that the scope for increasing formal restrictions was consistently determined by the general social status of the Christians. In other words, and this is nothing new, the Christians of the Middle East were the main long-term victims of the Crusades. But at the same time, this trend must not be excessively generalised, for we know that there were often specific circumstances in which the rulers and the *ʿulamāʾ* quite explicitly distinguished between the Christianity of the Franks and that of their own subjects and neighbours.

As I have warned at the outset, this paper is rather a provocation to discussion, as much for myself as for any wider audience at this stage, than an attempt to develop a theory fully or to marshal all the evidence for it. But I think I have given enough evidence to suggest that an approach to the subject is justified which does not reiterate, in however a refined and differentiated manner, the traditional analyses in which religious differences are the primary terms of reference. There are other ways of looking at the subject, ways which might be more loyal to the perspectives of the people themselves, within the constraints and horizons which determined their daily lives.

References

Beckingham, C. (1976). 'Misconceptions of Islam: Medieval and modern', *JRAS*, 124, pp. 606-611.

Bosworth, C.E. (1972). 'Christian and Jewish dignitaries in Mamluk Egypt and Syria (II)', *IJMES*, 3, pp. 199-216.

Cohen, M. (1996). 'Islam and the Jews: Myth, counter-myth, history', in Deshen and Zenner (1996), pp. 50-63.

Deshen, S. and Zenner, W.P., eds. (1996). *Jews among Muslims: Communities in the precolonial Middle East*, London: Macmillan.

Escovitz, J.H. (1984). *The office of qāḍī al-quḍāt in Cairo under the Bahrī Mamlūks*, Berlin: Klaus Schwarz.

Fattal, A. (1958). *Le statut légal des non-Musulmans en pays d'Islam*, Beyrouth: Imprimerie catholique.

Gaube, H. and Wirth, E. (1984): *Aleppo*, Wiesbaden: Ludwig Reichert.

Goitein, S.D. (1955): *Jews and Arabs: Their contacts through the ages*. New York: Schocken.

Goitein, S.D. (1967-83): *A Mediterranean society*, 5 vols., Berkeley: University of California.

Haneda, M. and Miura, T., eds. (1994): *Islamic urban studies: Historical review and perspectives*, London: Kegan Paul International.

Kedar, B.Z. (1990): 'The subjected Muslims of the Frankish Levant', in Powell (1990), pp. 135-174.

Lapidus, I.M. (1967): *Muslim Cities in the Later Middle Ages*, Cambridge, Mass.: Harvard University Press.

Little, D.P. (1976): 'Coptic conversion to Islam under the Bahri Mamluks, 692-755/1293-1354', *BSOAS*, 39, pp. 552-569.

Mitri, T. (1998): 'Views on Arab Christians between Past and Present', *Islam and Christian-Muslim Relations*, 9, pp. 115-120.

Nielsen, J.S. (1985): *Secular justice in an Islamic state: Mazalim under the Bahri Mamluks*, Leiden: Nederlands historisch-archaeologisch instituut te Istanbul.

Norton, A.R. (1995): *Civil society in the Middle East*, 2 vols. Leiden: E.J.Brill.

Petry, C.F. (1981): *The civilian elite of Cairo in the later Middle Ages*, Princeton: Princeton University Press.

Powell, J.M. ed. (1990): *Muslims under Latin rule 1100-1300*, Princeton: Princeton University Press.

Sauvaget, J. (1932): *Les monuments historiques de Damas*, Beirut: Imprimerie catholique.

Sauvaget, J. (1941) : *Alep: Essai sur le développement d'une grande ville syrienne des origines au milieu du XIXe siècle*, Paris: Paul Geuthner.

Schleifer, A. (1987): 'Islamic Jerusalem as archetype of a harmonious urban environment', in *The Middle East city: Ancient traditions confront a modern world*, New York: Paragon House.

Sharot, S. (1996): 'Jewish acculturation in premodern societies', in Deshen and Zenner (1996), pp. 35-49.

Talal, al-Hassan bin, Crown Prince (1997): 'Islam and civil society', *Islam and Christian-Muslim Relations*, 8, pp. 99-103.

Tritton, A.S. (1930): *The Caliphs and their non-Muslim subjects*, Oxford University Press.

Christian-Muslim Misunderstanding in the Fourteenth Century: The Correspondence between Christians in Cyprus and Muslims in Damascus

DAVID THOMAS

In the early years of the fourteenth century a letter containing a strikingly original defence of Christianity was composed in Cyprus. It was ostensibly intended to invite Muslims to agree that the major doctrines and liturgical observances of Christianity were all explicitly supported by the Qur᾽ān, that in effect Christianity is confirmed in Muslim scripture as the supreme revelation from God. In 1316 this letter was sent to the Ḥanbalī scholar Taqī al-Dīn Aḥmad Ibn Taymiyya in Damascus, and again in 1321 it was sent in a slightly different form to another Damascus celebrity Muḥammad Ibn Abī Ṭālib. They responded with the two longest and most vehement refutations of Christianity that have survived from Muslim authors, restating the traditional teaching about the relationship between the two faiths, and showing up the fallacies they detected in this upstart piece of apologetic. The substantial correspondence which the three authors completed provides a prime example of the misunderstanding that bedevilled Christians and Muslims in their relations at the time, the lack of sympathy they exhibited, and the lack of intellectual tolerance shown by both sides.

The story begins about a century before this correspondence, with the letter written by the Melkite bishop of Sidon to a Muslim friend.[1] This purported to relate a meeting between the bishop and some Christian experts while he was on a journey in Europe, and the reasons they give for not converting to Islam. He employs a series of arguments based on the text of the Qur᾽ān and upon reason to show that Muslim scripture speaks affirmatively about Christian beliefs and worship, that Christian doctrine is rational, and that the proclamation brought by Muḥammad was intended only for Arabs and not the whole of humankind. His letter has the appearance of being a polite and reasonable defence of Christianity and for its continuing validity in the presence of a faith that claims to supersede it. But, in fact, it is an

[1] Paul Khoury, *Paul d'Antioche, évêque melkite de Sidon (XIIe s.)*, Beirut: Imprimerie Catholique, 1964, 59-83 (Arabic text), 169-87 (French translation).

aggressive diatribe that devalues Islam to the point of worthlessness and treats its scripture as no better than an incomplete pastiche of the Bible. When, in the invented dialogue between Paul and the experts, he reminds them that if they accept parts of the Qurʾān to support their position the Muslims might require them to accept it all, they say:

The issue is not in this form. In effect, if a man held a bill against another with a debt of a hundred dinars, and the bill stated that it had been redeemed and the one to whom the debt was owed showed the bill and demanded the hundred dinars from the debtor, then if the debtor argued that in the bill it stated it was redeemed, could the person owed the debt justifiably say to him, 'As you accept this, accept the hundred dinars and pay them'? Surely not! He is acquitted of the hundred dinars in the bill by what the bill also contains that it has been redeemed.[2]

Effectively, their argument is that the particular verses of the Qurʾān which they select for their purposes have force by themselves, without need to refer to less supportive or contrary teachings. This renders the Qurʾān an incomplete scripture and implies that its true message can only be discovered by reading it in the light of the Bible.

The net effect of Paul's exegesis of Muslim scripture is that Islam is discredited by having its prophet reduced to a local missionary of monotheism and its scripture diminished to an encoded copy of the Gospels. This kind of argument would hardly lead to cooperative dialogue between Christians and Muslims, but it would rather set Muslims on the defensive as they saw the threat posed to the integrity of Islam and its claims to universality and finality.

Paul's letter, which can probably be dated to the end of the twelfth century, became sufficiently well-known in the years following its composition for the Egyptian jurist Aḥmad Ibn Idrīs al-Qarāfī (d. 1285) to refute it, and for Ibn Taymiyya in the fourteenth century to recall seeing old copies of it and to remember Christians making use of it a number of times.[3] Sometime in the early years of the fourteenth century an unknown Christian in Cyprus obtained a copy and reworked it, presumably for the express purpose of sending it to leading Muslim intellectuals he knew of, in order to persuade them to see the value and continuing integrity of Christianity and to accept it alongside Islam. This reworked version suggests high ideals on the part of its author, but shows totally unrealistic expectations that betray arrant misunderstanding of Islam that verges on intolerance.

---

2 Khoury, *Paul d'Antioche*, 76/181-2, § 45.

3 Ibn Taymiyya, *Jawāb al-ṣaḥīḥ li-man baddala dīn al-Masīḥ*, 4 vols, Cairo: Maṭbaʿa al-Nīl, 1905, vol. 1, 19-20. He names it as *Kitāb al-manṭīqī al-dawla khānī al-mubarhan ʿan al-ʾitiqāl al-ṣaḥīḥ wa-l-raʾy al-mustaqīm*.

Comparison of this reworked Cyprus *Letter* and Paul of Antioch's original shows that the Cypriot author took great pains to remove many arguments that could only annoy Muslim readers.[4] Thus, where Paul cavalierly omitted phrases from Qurʾān verses to suit the point he was making, this author restores the text and makes his point another way; where Paul argued too offensively, this author simply removes the passage altogether; and where Paul employed risky arguments based on rational foundations, this author prefers arguments based on scripture. The net result is a work that is much less acerbic in tone and more persuasive in contents, as though the author wishes to encourage his Muslim readers to see the validity of his points rather than compel them grudgingly to concede the value of what they read, as Paul does.

It is a moot point whether the *Letter from Cyprus* should be regarded as an edited version of Paul of Antioch's *Letter to a Muslim Friend* or a new composition that is loosely based on the earlier form. There is good reason to regard it as the latter, because it changes the whole direction of the argument and appears to be searching for grounds upon which Muslims will agree, rather than points they might only reluctantly allow or vehemently reject. In order to do this, the author relies primarily upon Christian and Muslim scripture to make his case, and removes as many reason-based arguments as he can, with the evident though undisclosed intention of replacing what can be questioned and refuted by easy counter-arguments with what is God-given and so incontrovertible. But in order to do this, he introduces a long and forceful defence of the integrity and continuing validity of the Bible:

If the book which they have in the one language of Arabic and is in one location cannot have been altered and not one letter of it substituted, how can our books which are written in seventy-two languages be altered? In each one of them there are thousands of copies, which were accepted for six hundred years before the coming of Muḥammad. They came into people's hands, and they read them in their different languages despite the size of their countries and the distance between them. Who can speak seventy-two languages? Or who could take the decision to collect them from the four corners of the earth in order to change them? If some of them were changed and some were left - this was not possible because they are all one message, all the languages. So such a thing cannot ever be said.[5]

---

4 Cf. D. Thomas, 'Paul of Antioch's *Letter to a Muslim Friend* and *The Letter from Cyprus*', in D. Thomas, ed., *Syrian Christians under Islam, the first thousand years*, Leiden: Brill, 2001, 203-21, and further R. Ebied and D. Thomas, eds, *Muslim-Christian Polemic during the Crusades, the Letter from the People of Cyprus and Ibn Abī Ṭālib al-Dimashqī's Response*, Leiden: Brill, 2005, 1-12.

5 Ebied and Thomas, *Muslim-Christian Polemic*, 71-3, §§ 15-16.

Here he refutes any possibility that there has been alteration to the original Bible text. Added to verses from the Qurʾān which appear to affirm the soundness of the Bible, this opens the way for using texts from the Bible alongside verses from the Qurʾān to support points and to make points.

But if the general impression created by the imaginative recasting by the anonymous Christian from Cyprus is to present arguments in favour of the validity of Christianity, the implications of this inviting defence are momentous. For the very logic of the author's position demands him to rank Christianity above Islam: as he says at the end of the *Letter*, the climax of God's communication with his creatures was the grace he gave to complete the gift of the Law through Moses. The only way he could do this was by uniting with a perfect human in order to communicate directly with humankind. This was perfection, and after it nothing more was needed.[6] He does not say anything about Islam here, but his argument, which weaves in Qurʾān verses that can be interpreted to exalt Jesus to the highest position, renders the later religion unnecessary in God's plan for his creatures. Islam is certainly not superior to Christianity, and it adds nothing to what Christianity has already given.

If at this sensitive closing position of the *Letter* the author does not explicitly place Islam below Christianity or reject it as surplus to requirements, he comes close to doing exactly this near the start. At that point, the narrator asks the experts who make the defence of Christianity (they are Cypriots and not, as in Paul's letter, Europeans) why they have not accepted the Qurʾān after reading it. And they reply that according to its own words it is intended for Arabic-speakers and not for them, and indeed Muḥammad was sent to the Arab tribes who, unlike the Christians, had been sent no warner beforehand.[7] In other words, the prophet of Islam was a local preacher sent to one particular location, and even a pre-evangelist who directed his monotheistic proclamation at pagans in an effort to bring them towards true faith in its Christian fullness. This directly contradicts what Islam has always taught.

The efforts that the Cypriot editor put into toning down Paul of Antioch's original letter produced a result that is hardly less unacceptable to Muslim readers. It certainly makes a case for validating Christianity on the grounds of Qurʾanic teaching and Biblical teaching, which itself is proven authoritative. But in consequence Islam is rendered superfluous as a faith purporting to complete and correct Christianity, and though acknowledged

6 *Ibid.*, 139-47, §§ 59-63.

7 *Ibid.*, 57-61, §§ 4-7.

as God-given is relegated to the status of a local revelation intended for a particularly resistant group of pagan tribes for whom the full Gospel might prove indigestible.

It is difficult to imagine that the author of this *Letter* ever seriously hoped for a sympathetic response from the Muslim scholars to whom his neat but inflammatory work was sent. He may have hoped to win their acknowledgement on the coherence of the arguments he constructed, but did he realistically think he would win their agreement to his overall claim that Christianity was the supreme God-given faith, with all it implied about Islam? This may well have been the case, because he concludes with the words:

Praise and blessing be to God, for he has brought unanimity of view and put an end to suspicion between his servants the Christians and Muslims, may God protect them all![8]

It is as though he is celebrating his achievement in finding a place for the two dispensations side by side, oblivious to what he may have instigated. He does show a hint of realism in a final addendum:

If he has found anything different from this, may our master the revered teacher – may God eternally protect him and prolong his existence – point it out so that I may inform them about it and determine what views they have on it.[9]

But this seems an invitation to raise minor points that can be settled by quick negotiation. Little could the author have thought about the reactions he was encouraging. Two mighty replies were fired off by his brief epistle, which if they ever reached him must have dismayed him and silenced him for ever.

The author's true intentions as not disclosed in the *Letter*, though since he took pains to tone down Paul's brutally direct points to a more persuasive form, as we have said, and clearly hoped to obtain agreement from leading Muslim scholars to the arguments he so carefully laid out, it is not unlikely that he really thought he could create some consensus about the continuing validity of Christianity. If so, one must wonder at the breadth of his miscalculation, and his misunderstanding of the Muslim perception of the relationship between Christianity and Islam.

It may be possible to gather a little more about the author's intention from the *Letter* itself, and from the political and religious background against which he wrote. First, evidence from within the *Letter*: the author was clearly at home in Arabic, which he wrote with facility; he knew the text of the Qurʾān well enough to complete the partial quotations in Paul's

---

8 *Ibid.*, 147, § 64.

9 *Ibid.*, 147, § 64.

letter, and to name each *sūra* when he quoted from it – in fact, he quotes accurately from the Qurʾān, while he often appears less confident with parts of the Bible; he knew of two of the leading intellectual celebrities of Damascus in his day, and ensured that the *Letter* reached them. This all points to a background within the Arab world, and maybe the Islamic empire and the vicinity of Damascus. If so, the author could have been one of the Christians from the mainland who sought refuge in Cyprus when the Crusader possessions were taken by the Mamluks in the closing decades of the thirteenth century. His thorough knowledge of the Qurʾān may even identify him as a former Muslim, in which case he would have fled his homeland with all the more urgency when it was returned to Muslim rule and reprisals against apostates became likely. If there is any measure of probability in these inferences, one can imagine the author seeking to open avenues of dialogue with his old faith on the understanding that the faith into which he has moved is accepted as authentic, and continuing in force.

It is even possible to push this supposition further. In arguing that Christianity had not only not been superseded by Islam, but was in fact endorsed by the Qurʾān and shown to be the climax of God's acts of revelation in the world, and in showing that Muḥammad had a place in God's plan as a prophet of simple monotheism sent to the stubborn pagans of Arabia, the Cypriot author was maybe answering a question that fellow-Christians asked with particular urgency at that time. For when the Muslim state appeared to be in the ascendant and the hard-won possessions of Christendom had failed, many Christians who lived under Muslim rule must have wavered in their allegiance, and almost all would have asked why the faith claimed to derive from God's Son himself would have been forced into decline by a faith that directly denied its cardinal claims. This author may have been intimating that this was not the case, but that attentive reading of the Qurʾān and understanding of the Prophet Muḥammad's true role proved the continuing authority and veracity of Christianity. Hence his intention in writing was both to open dialogue with Muslims and to reassure fellow-Christians.

These rather lofty ambitions carried with them high risk, and they eventually failed. But in the atmosphere of the time, the author may easily be forgiven for harbouring them. This is because whenever Christians appear to have contemplated Islam, they imagined its end and the triumph of Christianity.

This was the time of Ramon Llull (who died in 1316, the year in which the *Letter* was sent to Ibn Taymiyya), and his calls to the great throughout Europe for intellectual engagement with Muslims. He perfected what he thought was a rational means of proving Christianity right, which during his visit to Cyprus in 1302 may have sown a seed that flowered in the decision to re-edit Paul's letter and send it off. It was also a time when plans for new Crusades were repeatedly drafted, many with Cyprus as the main starting-point. Despite the complete loss of all Crusader strongholds on the mainland by 1291, hopes of regaining lost possessions remained high, frequently fuelled by expectations that the Mongol invaders from the east would unite with European Christians in a pincer movement to crush the Mamluks. And it was also a period when prophecies and predictions about the extinction of Islam circulated widely throughout Europe. In 1267 the English Franciscan Roger Bacon referred to calculations from Arab scientists that Islam would end 693 years after its beginning and thus it must collapse before 1300, while William of Tripoli in 1271 and the author of *De statu Saracenorum* in 1273, both knew accounts from Muslims that foretold the imminent demise of their faith. In such an atmosphere of buoyant expectation it is easy to imagine a Christian in Cyprus, especially one who yearned for his Syrian homeland, exuberantly writing to invite Muslims to see the truth of Christianity confirmed in their own faith, and to reassure Christians of the continuing validity of what they held onto.

With a general background of hope such as this, it is plausible, though strictly hypothetical, to see the *Letter* in just these terms. And at a remove of nearly seven hundred years it is possible to perceive the utter miscalculation involved and the misunderstanding of its author. For where he may have imagined Muslims ready to fulfil hopes and enter into discussion about the relation between the Qurʾan and Christianity, or the authenticity of the Bible, or the true stature of the Prophet Muḥammad, he met with complete rejection, and what amounts to a dismissal of his careful arguments and a denial of his aims. The two Muslim authors replied with refutations that on their part show equal misunderstanding of an opportunity, and what amounts to intolerance of an outmoded faith.

In 1316 a version of the *Letter* was sent to Ibn Taymiyya in Damascus. This is known from what he himself says in his reply, nothing being stated about how it reached him or why he was chosen as recipient (though his reputation must be the explanation for this). If the senders of the *Letter* knew more than a little about the person they hoped would engage with its contents and return a moderate reply, they might have thought again. Ibn Taymiyya thundered back with his voluminous *Jawāb al-ṣaḥīḥ li-man baddala dīn al-masīḥ*, in which he not only refuted the contents of the *Letter,* but also took the opportunity to demonstrate the total bankruptcy of Christianity.

Whatever the Cypriot Christians who sent the *Letter* had hoped for, they met with blank rejection. Ibn Taymiyya's attitude towards Christianity is based firmly upon familiar teachings of the Qurʾān, and embodies all the features which the *Letter* was in effect subverting. It is possible to see clearly what he actually thought about Christianity from an earlier letter which he wrote to Cyprus, known as *al-Risāla al-Qubruṣiyya*. As Yahya Michot has shown in his edition and French translation, this letter was written to sire Johan, Lord of Gibelet, to ask for sympathetic treatment of Muslim prisoners on the island.[10] Since it refers to the Mongol leader Ghāzān as though he is living, it cannot have been written after 1304, the year in which he died. Thus, it preceded the *Letter from Cyprus* by at least ten years.[11]

As a sort of preface to his main argument in this *Risāla*, Ibn Taymiyya outlines the history of God's communication with his creatures, and speaks in such a forthright way about the true form of Christianity and the errors committed by its followers that a reader might suppose he ran a serious risk of offending his Cypriot addressee.

He sets the tone at the very start. After his introduction, he explains that God made his creatures to worship him on the basis of knowing him and loving him. Thus, to those whom he guides God gives mercy, knowledge and understanding of his beautiful names and most high attributes; he provides the means for them to draw near him and to fear at the mention of him, to submit to him and to acknowledge his divinity; on their part, his creatures do not associate any other being with God or worship any other in his place.[12] It is not difficult to see here an emphatically different doctrine from Christianity: humans have a stature that enables them to know God accurately and relate to him appropriately, very unlike the Christian belief that because of sin human perceptions of God are flawed and any possibility of approaching him is ruled out. From the very beginning of this request for clemency, Ibn Taymiyya makes plain his understanding that Islam reinstates the correct view of human nature that Christianity has distorted.

He goes on to explain why God sent his messengers. Idolatry crept in after Adam, so God sent Noah, and among other messengers Abraham, Moses and David, all calling humankind back to true worship. Then he sent Jesus

---

10 J.R. Michot, *Ibn Taymiyya, Lettre à un roi croisé*, Louvain-la-Neuve: Bruylant-Academia, and Lyons: Tawhid, 1995.

11 T. Michel, *A Muslim Theologian's Response to Christianity, Ibn Taymiyya's Al-Jawab al-Sahih*, Delmar NY: Caravan Books, 1984, 78, suggests that this *risāla* was the ultimate reason why the *Letter from Cyprus* was sent to Ibn Taymiyya. But since there is no obvious relation between the contents of the letters, it cannot be taken as a cause, and if there is a connection between them this can only lie in Ibn Taymiyya's name being known in Cyprus. This suggestion does not explain why the *Letter* was sent to al-Dimashqī.

12 Michot, *Lettre à un roi croisé*, 601-3 (Arabic text).

with many signs, and made him gentle and compassionate among a hard and cruel generation. But the Jews rejected him as a liar and held onto the Law, while the Christians took him as divine, saying that God had come down to be crucified as a sacrifice for the sin of Adam, and they also said that God was three, dividing into sects over their beliefs, disagreeing over things that no rational person would say nor any revelation has reported apart from ambiguous references in the Bible.[13] Ibn Taymiyya makes quite plain here that the vocation of Jesus was as a messenger of God, and he has no qualms about pointing out the doctrinal errors of Christians. But he goes further than this.

He continues to say that Christian belief is both contrary to the natural disposition according to which God created humans, and to revelation. Consequently, whenever a priest achieves a position of eminence he denies his beliefs, and more often takes an interest in science than Christianity. Furthermore, monks resort to all manner of tricks in order to fool the masses that miracles occur. They also abandon all divine laws and introduce innovations in conduct and worship that neither Christ, nor his Apostles instituted, and they split into sects about the nature of Jesus. By contrast, the Muslims follow the way of the prophets, keeping to the middle course without any exaggeration in belief.[14]

This depiction is uncompromising in its emphasis upon the Qurʾanic account of true religion and in its criticism of the distortions that crept into Christianity as a result of abandoning true belief. Ibn Taymiyya explains that he presents it to Sire Johan as a gesture of true regard, because the best thing he can give him is instruction about true religion.[15] But his direct denial of what the Christian noble presumably believes lacks pragmatism, for he places such a high premium on setting out the status of Christianity that he risks losing his reader's sympathy. His approach, although intended to set out the true situation in religion and to show what is right and what is not, actually exhibits a degree of intolerance towards Christianity that can only be explained as total indifference to actual relations between the followers of the two faiths.

If in this *Risāla*, which was intended to appeal for clemency towards Muslim prisoners in Cyprus, Ibn Taymiyya shows scant regard for Christianity, it is little wonder that in the *Jawāb al-ṣaḥīḥ* he shows no sympathy for the *Letter from Cyprus* at all. In his earlier *Risāla* he implies insistently that any deviation from the faith that is given both in reason and revelation is culpable. In the *Jawāb* he accepts, as proven, that Christianity is such a

---

13 *Ibid.*, 603-8.

14 *Ibid.*, 608-15.

15 *Ibid.*, 616.

dire distortion of the truth that any engagement in argument with Christians is unnecessary, and even beneath the attention of a reasonable person. In fact, he uses the arrival of the *Letter* as an opportunity to expand the theological structure he sketches in *al-Risāla al-Qubruṣiyya*, on the importance of true believe and the consequences of abandoning it, speaking as much to Muslims as to Christians.

This purpose is evident from the very beginning of the *Jawāb*. At the start Ibn Taymiyya lists errors committed by the Jews and Christians, and adds that some Muslims are guilty of them, themselves. He explains that, like the Christians and Jews, some Muslims either declare that God indwells every place or has united with one of the Prophet's family or a particular individual, and he names extreme Shīʿī and Ṣūfī groups. Part of his purpose is thus to compare:

Through an understanding of the real nature of the religion of the Christians and its falsity one can also know the falsity of those views which resemble theirs – that is, the views of the perpetrators of apostasy and innovation.[16]

Thus, the attack on Christianity is in reality a demonstration to fellow Muslims of the errors that result from abandoning the straight path of true Islam. This is why the work is addressed to Muslims, and Christians are referred to in the third person.

It is only at this point that the *Letter from Cyprus* is introduced. Ibn Taymiyya says he will answer it section by section, 'in order that thinking people will benefit thereby', and will show that its arguments can be turned back on its authors as instances of 'the corrupt nature of their teaching'. In what they do these Christians resemble all innovators who make use of scripture, but they can be answered by showing that the very texts they select can be used against them.[17]

It is clear at this early point that the contents of the *Letter* have no appeal at all for Ibn Taymiyya. He approaches it with the strong conviction – already formed – that all Christians are wrong, and his purpose in composing this reply is both to show this on the basis of what the Cypriot author has written, and also to widen it out to include those within Islam who have departed from the truth in the same way as Christians. With this as his stated position, it is no surprise that he is not open to what the *Letter* might be trying to say, or that he does not respond to it in any constructive manner. His presuppositions about Christianity lead him to a coldness that verges on intolerance.

---

[16] Michel, *Response*, 139-40.

[17] *Ibid.*, 140-2.

This attitude is evident throughout the *Jawāb*, and it leads Ibn Taymiyya to categorise Christians as religious extremists who culpably commit errors about religion. At one point in this vast and discursive work he sums up the reasons for religious error as: preferring complex and ambiguous statements from the prophets to straightforward ones; taking wonderful occurrences as signs from God when they are in fact demonic; accepting information received as true when it is plainly false. He turns to the resurrection of Christ to illustrate what he means:

Among the Christians it is handed down in the Gospels that the one who was crucified and buried in the grave was seen by some of the apostles and others after he was buried. He rose from the grave two or three times. He showed them the place of the nails and said, 'Do not suppose that I am a demon'. If this [report] is sound, then that was a demon who claimed he was Christ and thereby deceived them.[18]

This is a sweeping judgement. The fact that he can cite as demonic the very event upon which Christianity is founded speaks eloquently of his distance from this other faith and his intolerance of what he perceives as a whole structure of error.

This dismissive attitude is symptomatic of Ibn Taymiyya's approach to Christianity throughout the *Jawāb*. His starting point is his stern theological analysis of the faith as a distortion of Christ's original teaching, and the result is what emerges as a general survey of the points contained in the *Letter from Cyprus*, and little close engagement with its contents.

Did Ibn Taymiyya understand the *Letter* to which it was hoped he would offer a more positive reply? In many ways one could say that he understood it all too well. He recognised it as another example of the way in which Christians express their error by appearing to seek recognition for their doctrines and observances from the Qur'ān, while in reality they try to reverse the proper relationship between the two faiths by demoting the status of the Prophet Muḥammad and his scripture. From the context of his Qur'anic theology, such a construction bears the most glaring flaws that make it unworthy of a detailed response. Nevertheless, one must wonder whether the *Jawāb* represents a missed opportunity. Given the opposition between the two sides, the Cypriot author must be recognised as trying, however clumsily, to set Christianity and Islam in some positive relationship. His reduction of Islam in order to fit it into this relationship would inevitably be distasteful to any Muslim, but he does offer grounds for debate, disagreement and reassessment. Other Muslims before Ibn Taymiyya frequently sought to show where Christianity was a distortion of basic truths, and held up some possibility of

18 *Ibid.*, 199-200.

revision and correction no matter how theoretical. But Ibn Taymiyya makes no such offer. He dismisses Christianity as an error from the start, and holds out no possibility of redemption. He offers only renunciation and repentance of the systematic errors in this other faith.

The brutality of this approach might be considered as misunderstanding, and it certainly shows itself in intolerance: where the Cypriot author implicitly recognises Muḥammad and the Qurʾān as God-sent, albeit to one location, here there is no recognition and no restraint in condemning Christianity wholesale. Ibn Taymiyya impatiently dismisses the gesture because it conflicts with his strict dogmatic line, and reveals that no attempt at rapprochement will succeed, in fact nothing less than a complete admission of error from the Christians.

So the idealistically mis-intended *Letter* from the Christians of Cyprus met with a forthright rejection from the master in Damascus. It hardly seems likely that they could have achieved anything more, given their misunderstanding of what was at stake (or maybe they understood it all too well, but hoped they could secure agreement from Muslims who might be convinced by their selection of scriptural passages), and it is clear that Ibn Taymiyya would concede little, given his stern insistence from years beforehand that only his version of Qurʾanic theology and salvation history was valid. The two sides did not come near to meeting, because they harboured entirely different expectations of one another.

Four or five years after the *Letter from Cyprus* was sent to Ibn Taymiyya, it was sent in a slightly amended version to another Damascus master, Muḥammad Ibn Abī Ṭālib al-Dimashqī. Whether or not this second version was sent because Ibn Taymiyya had replied so coldly or had not bothered to return his reply (there is no evidence that the *Jawāb* reached Cyprus) remains a mystery. And it is not at all clear why al-Dimashqī was identified as a suitable recipient. Maybe the Cypriot author knew of him, because he was locally famous for the breadth of his knowledge.

Al-Dimashqī received his copy of the *Letter* in March 1321, and says that he composed his *Risāla ilā ahl jazīrat Qubruṣ* within a few months, probably by June of the same year.[19] He acknowledges that Ibn Taymiyya had earlier been sent a copy, though it is not clear that he had actually read the *Jawāb* before composing his own *Response*.[20] Whatever the case, he

---

19 Ebied and Thomas, *Muslim-Christian Polemic*, 151.

20 Al-Dimashqī certainly employs a number of arguments and examples that appear in both the *Jawāb* and the *Risālat al-Qubruṣiyya*. Close examination will show whether he copied them from one of these works or a common source, or was simply repeating the same popular traditions as Ibn Taymiyya.

adopted rather a different approach in his reply, although his tone is not so different from that of his contemporary.

Like Ibn Taymiyya, al-Dimashqī answers the *Letter* by quoting sections in turn and replying to the arguments as they appear. And he is almost as discursive in the range of illustrations and examples he gives, although he tends to stay closer to the points made by the Christians. But he differs greatly in one central feature, for his reply is addressed *seriatim* to the Christians and takes up their arguments directly, presenting counter-arguments that refute the particular points made in the *Letter* and meeting the Cypriot's claims head on. Thus, where Ibn Taymiyya's *Jawāb* proceeds from a set of doctrinal principles that effectively prohibit the Christians' arguments from being treated as anything other than examples of failed thinking to be given as warnings to fellow-Muslims, al-Dimashqī's *Response* considers each of the Christians' arguments in detail and shows whether they are factually correct or rationally coherent. There is certainly refutation here, but it is more closely geared to the contents of the *Letter*. It would therefore, have more urgently demanded a reply from the Christians, though as with the *Jawāb* there is no evidence that this *Response* ever reached Cyprus, nor indeed that it circulated widely at all.[21]

Al-Dimashqī gives an indication of the approach he adopts at the outset. After commenting that the *Letter from Cyprus* is 'exemplary in politeness but alien in intention and shocking in purpose',[22] he goes on to relate how he detected its true intention and set about answering it:

When this poor soul read it and reflected upon it, he realised they were looking for a response to what it contained. For they were opening up means of seeking a confrontation through it, under the impression that they had mastered what they had been assured was teaching, or that this might lead straight to their religion by the mention of it. But this poor soul found that everything they clutched at was dust, or 'as a mirage in a desert, which the thirsty one supposeth to be water'. So I thought it right to send back responses to what they had written, and to provide a proof that what they believed was false.[23]

He clearly saw the danger and reacted accordingly.

The general character of the *Response* can be seen from its first substantive argument.[24] This is a reply to the opening of the *Letter* in which the

21 It survives in only two MSS, Utrecht Codex No. 40 [1449] dated 1371, and Bodleian Marsh 40 [Uri Arab. Moh. 124 (2)] dated 1645. Comparison shows that the later MS is a slavish copy of the earlier.

22 Ebied and Thomas, *Muslim-Christian Polemic*, 155.

23 *Ibid.*, 157.

24 *Ibid.*, 159-227.

Christians claim that because Muḥammad had appeared among the Arabs and was sent with a revelation in Arabic, they themselves do not regard his proclamation as directed at them or feel any compulsion to abandon their Christian faith. Al-Dimashqī's argument is long and elaborate, amassing a rich variety of points that demand detailed response.

He begins by citing references from the Old Testament and Gospels that can be taken to predict Muḥammad's coming.[25] These include a number of verses well-known in the polemical tradition, such as 'God came from Sinai and shone out from Seir and towered over the mountains of Paran' from Deuteronomy 33.2, in which he equates Sinai as the mountain of the Law with Moses, identifies Seir as Nazareth and equates it with Jesus, and identifies Paran as the Ḥijāz and equates it with Muḥammad;[26] the riders on asses and on camels of Isaiah 21.7 (here attributed to Jeremiah), whom he conventionally identifies as Jesus followed by Muḥammad;[27] and the Paraclete verses from the Gospel of John, which he follows Muslim convention in identifying as references to Muḥammad.[28] Should Christians complain at the interpretations he gives, he could point to a long exegetical tradition within Islam for validation, and so open up a discussion on method in scriptural interpretation.

Not content with these Biblical replies to this opening point about the Prophet Muḥammad, al-Dimashqī adds a series of arguments that one must assume are derived from the anecdotal history of Muslim apologetic and interfaith debate. He tells how a Muslim flotilla landed in Sicily during the caliphate of ʿUthmān and the sailors were brought five likenesses treasured by the king, which they were able to identify as the Prophet and the Rightly-Guided Caliphs; he briefly recounts the story of the monks Baḥīrā and Nestorius recognising the boy Muḥammad as prophet; he describes how the people of Jerusalem surrendered when they recognised the Caliph ʿUmar, something they would only have done if they already knew about the universal mission of Muḥammad; and he tells more definitely Islamic stories such as the portentous events of the cracking of the arch of Ctesiphon, the drying up of lake Sāwa and the flooding of the valley of Sihāwa at Muḥammad's birth, and the experiences of the soothsayer Sawād Ibn Qārib who was warned by the jinn that Muḥammad had come and so went to find him, and converted.[29] Each of these serves as a historical witness to the general expectation about Muḥammad and the acclaim at his arrival,

---

25 *Ibid.*, 163-75.

26 *Ibid.*, 163.

27 *Ibid.*, 171.

28 *Ibid.*, 167.

29 *Ibid.*, 175-83.

and it demands either acceptance as it is presented or good counter-arguments to deny its validity. They provide strong evidence, to those who accept them, that Muḥammad did not arrive without forewarning or expectation, but was widely looked for and attended by scriptural predictions and supernatural signs.

Al-Dimashqī concludes this richly-textured reply to the first point made by the Cypriot scholars who lead the debate in the *Letter* by demonstrating that the Qurʾān verses they cite by do not mean what they think. For example, the Christians read Q 9.128 in a restricted way: 'By sending unto them a messenger of their own, *min anfusihim*', suggesting that this messenger was from and for the Arabs alone. But al-Dimashqī counters by following another reading, *min anfasihim*, taking the word as the elative of *nafīs*, 'excellent', instead of *anfusihim*, the plural of *nafs*, 'self'. This renders the meaning as 'from the most distinguished among them', suggesting that Muḥammad was the most noble of all those to whom he was sent, and freeing the verse from the restrictions read in it by the Christians. In a similar way he argues that Q 32.3, 'That thou mayest warn a folk unto whom no warner came before thee', does not refer to the Arabs alone, as the Christians contend, because 'a folk' refers to all who were living at the time he was sent.[30] It is fascinating to see his ingenuity displayed here, and he is not by any means isolated in his exegesis, for regarding the first of these two examples there is evidence in al-Zamakhsharī that the vocalisation *min anfasihim* was the one preferred by the Prophet Muḥammad himself, his daughter Fāṭima and his wife ʿĀʾisha.[31]

Al-Dimashqī's *Response* continues in this colourful and detailed manner to refute the *Letter* point by point. But he does not stop at replying to the Christians' arguments, for he gradually unfolds a whole ecclesiastical history that provides an explanation for the errors of Christianity and the refusal to accept Islam or acknowledge Muḥammad as prophet. This becomes the background to his argument, and although not systematically presented but inserted piecemeal at various points, forms the logical basis upon which his reply to the Christians rests.

At the heart of this history is the emperor Constantine. Al-Dimashqī identifies him as initiating the historical faith of Christianity and unwittingly causing the corruption of the original faith imparted by Jesus. After his conversion, it was he who made enquiries about the Christians, collected the Gospel 'from the mouths of the four transmitters', and accepted that

30 *Ibid.*, 225-7.

31 Al-Zamakhshari, *Al-kashshāf ʿan ḥaqāʾiq ghawāmiḍ al-tanzīl wa-ʿuyūn al-aqāwīl fī wujūh al-taʾwīl*, *ad loc*.

the Paraclete was the Holy Spirit rather than a person who would come.[32] Since he had been a Ṣābian, he found it easy to acknowledge more than one divine being, and so readily accepted the atonement story, which involved a Divinity in heaven and a Divinity on earth.[33] He had the Gospels compiled and Christian law codified,[34] and introduced many innovations into the original faith.[35]

By inserting these references at various points, and by adding references to doctrinal corruptions introduced by St Paul who is represented as Constantine's contemporary,[36] al-Dimashqī brings into his work the history of Christian deviation that he claims led to the false doctrines held by Christians and the refusal to appreciate the Prophet Muḥammad.

This approach is markedly different from that of Ibn Taymiyya. The latter simply articulates a Qurʾanic systematic in which the Christians deviate from the truth given by Christ, and leaves it at that. Al-Dimashqī, however, roots his assessment of Christian deviation in the contingencies of history, and the familiar culprits Constantine and Paul. His explanation is therefore more open to Christian understanding, and does not pre-empt debate by claiming the unquestionable authority of scripture. Though while in principle it may be less peremptory, in practice it is just as impervious to challenge.

It will be clear that al-Dimashqī's versions of events, whether incidents attending the coming of Muḥammad or the history of the church and his interpretations of the Bible and the Qurʾān carry no more weight than any other versions. They just happen to be what suits him in this argument, and one suspects he might favour other versions should the circumstances change. His is an Islamically coloured Christianity that invites disagreement and quibbling over facts and large and small details. In effect, he rejects the attempt made in the *Letter* as drastically as Ibn Taymiyya, and with as little tolerance. For, where the latter suggests that Islamic revelation is the unimpeachable authority, he suggests that the Islamic account of history and Muslim interpretation of scripture are final. Intolerance is built into every argument.

In one respect, al-Dimashqī's method in recasting the faith of his opponents resembles that of the Cypriot Christian. The latter turns Islam into a local religious phenomenon and a pre-evangelistic proclamation, and can thus explain it as God-given and bring it into relation with Christianity. In turn, al-Dimashqī employs the traditional figures of Constantine and Paul

32 Ebied and Thomas, *Muslim-Christian Polemic*, 183-5, 277.

33 *Ibid.*, 211-13.

34 *Ibid.*, 259, 267.

35 *Ibid.*, 289, 429.

36 *Ibid.*, 397-401.

to refashion Christianity into a deviation from the original proclamation of Jesus, so that he can explain why it no longer agrees with Islam, as Islamic teachings have always held. Both authors make their own version of what happened in order to fit it into their scheme of divine economy. But they can only assert that their version is the correct one, and they risk the inevitable consequences of disagreement and refusal. Consequently, they are setting out events as dictated by their respective religious beliefs, and are really engaged in apologetic rather than a debate that holds out promise of agreement.

In this respect both the Cypriot and the Damascus scholar agree with the dogmatist Ibn Taymiyya. He staunchly sets out a scheme directly indebted to the Qurʾān account of revelation history, without acknowledgement that he may have to defend this to Christians who did not accept it. His apologetic stance is, therefore, more obvious. But at the end he is shown to be no less flexible than the other two participants in this large correspondence.

In insisting upon their own respective versions of the other faith and of the sequence of historical events, the three correspondents all exhibit a curious form of myopia about the practicalities of dialogue. It is almost as though each of them had no serious regard for members of the other faith, and could thus refashion beliefs and the historical record at will, according to a convenient theological scheme. They had ceased to talk the same language, and had receded into the structures of thought that were dictated by the implications of their respective revelations, on the Christian side turning Islam into a primitive form of itself, and on the Muslim side turning Christianity into a deviant form of itself. This lack of coherent common discourse contrasts starkly with the communication of a bygone era.

Five hundred years before this early fourteenth-century correspondence, Arabic-speaking theologians of both Christianity and Islam conversed in a common tongue within a common conceptual framework. This was the time of the early ʿAbbasid caliphate, when Muslim theologians debated the precise nature of the character of God. On one side the Muʿtazila, who upheld the strict unity of God, said that any description of his being must be treated as external to God himself because if the qualities predicated of him were thought to derive from real attributes located in his essence then he would become a multiple being. Their opponents within the theological community insisted that precisely this was the case: the qualities predicated of God in the Qurʾān and by reason were accurate descriptions of him because they derived from attributes that were real within his essence. The first side conceded agnosticism about God in order to safeguard his absolute unity and distinctiveness, while the other conceded a degree of pluralism in order to allow him stable, unchanging characteristics.

This was one of the most heated theological debates of the ninth century. But it was not restricted to Muslims. Theologians in the Arabic-speaking churches within the Islamic empire entered the debate by articulating the doctrine of the Trinity in terms of the divine attributes. Thus, to take the example of a certain ʿAmmār al-Baṣrī, a Nestorian who was probably a contemporary of leading early ninth century Muʿtazilites, said that God must necessarily have the qualities of living and knowing, otherwise he would be dead and ignorant and therefore not divine. His being living and knowing entailed his possessing the two attributes of life and knowledge within his essence as stable sources of these abiding qualities. Hence it followed that the Godhead comprised the Possessor, who is the Father, Life, who is the Holy Spirit, and Knowledge, who is the Son.[37]

This account of the Trinity was given in terms that both Muslims and Christians could understand, and to some extent accept. And it offered opportunity for debate, because the obvious response from the Muslim side was that if one accepts this logic, one has to allow that because God has more qualities than these two he must have many more attributes. The triune God thus becomes multiple and the Christian case is lost. To this the Christians replied that the two attributes of Life and Knowledge were uniquely integral to God's essence, and other attributes derived from them. And so the debate went on, in fact for a few hundred years, in terms which the two sides could understand and accept, and therefore debate.

By the time of this fourteenth century correspondence this common grammar of discourse had receded into the past (although Ibn Taymiyya was more than content in the Jawāb to quote earlier Muslims who employed it), but had evidently not been replaced by any updated forms to which all might subscribe. Rather, the respective scriptural models of relations had been reasserted, with the resultant lack of mutual understanding that can be discerned in this correspondence. There is almost a tragic element in the amount of effort so carefully applied by the Cypriot Christian in order to demonstrate how the Qurʾān can be made to endorse Christianity, and something almost heroic in the elaborate arguments massed together by Ibn Taymiyya and Muḥammad Ibn Abī Ṭālib. But it was all to no avail. There was no reciprocal acceptance of the religious models upon which each side was building, and so inevitably no meeting of minds. Misunderstanding and intolerant rejection were the inevitable outcome.

---

[37] Cf. Sidney Griffith, 'The Concept of *al-Uqnūm* in ʿAmmār al-Baṣrī's Apology for the Doctrine of the Trinity', in: *Actes du premier congrès international d'etudes arabes chrétiennes (Goslar, Septembre 1980)*, ed. Khalil Samir, Rome: Pontificium Institutum Studiorum Orientalium, 1982, 169-91.

Christian Martyrs in Tripoli in the Mamluk Era

Ray Mouawwad

Introduction

One of Tripoli's Christian martyrs encountered in the course of this research asked his executioner to allow him to pray before his beheading. He then turned his face toward the East, leaned down to the ground and took up some soil for communion, as if it was the body and the blood of Christ, then he stood up, raised his hands to the sky and offered a prayer.

The words he said and the whole scene were recorded in one of the main sources on such events: Church books which recorded the life of the saints of the day for every day of the year, the *synaxārs*. Another of such religious sources, known as the *Menaon* in the Greek orthodox tradition and the *Teshmeshtō* for the Maronite one, are liturgical texts containing special prayers sung to honor a specific saint on his commemoration day. These prayers, usually in a poetic form, recall the life of the saint, adding further details about his life and praising his example. During the Mamluk era, from 1289 to 1516, the two main Churches of the province of Tripoli were the Maronite and the Greek Orthodox ones. They sanctified their martyrs according to their own liturgical tradition and the memory of these saints was perpetrated for centuries to come through their yearly celebration.

Is it relevant nowadays to inquire about these cases of martyrdom? The issue is whether they were exceptional events in the course of Mamluk rule in the province of Tripoli, or if they reflected the general policy of a ruling elite towards its Christian subjects at the time. Moreover this study uses local sources often ignored by historians, either because they are not in Arabic, or because they are not purely "historical". These sources were written mostly in the Syriac Aramaic language or in Arabic with Syriac characters (*Karshūnī*). According to some Greek Orthodox sources, they were prayers and biographies primarily destined to be read by local Christians and not by Arab Muslims.

I- Christians' Reaction to Mamluk Rule in the Niyāba of Tripoli

I– To address the fundamental question of wether these martyrdoms were isolated events or the consequence of a general policy one should recall the circumstances in which Mamluk rule was established in Mount Lebanon. It occurred between 1283 and 1305 in several stages: in June 1283 Mamluk soldiers came from the ᶜAkkār plain north of Tripoli and climbed the mountains towards the Maronite villages of Iḥdin, Ḥaṣrūn and Ḥadath. Within a month, they secured and controlled the whole upper area overlooking Tripoli[1]. According to the chronicles of a Mamluk secretary in Cairo at that time[2], the expedition was done with the apparent consent of the Franks of Tripoli, led by prince Bohemond VII, who seemingly was on hostile terms with a Maronite patriarch who controlled the region. This patriarch, whose name is not mentioned, was made prisoner by the Mamluks and, according to our Arab chronicler, "his capture was like the conquest of a fortress". Therefore after mid-1283 the Mamluks held the mountain overlooking Tripoli, and the Franks were on the coast. Their total eviction from these territories was only a question of time.

The second episode occurred five years later on April 27, 1289 when the Mamluk sultan Qalāwūn conquered Tripoli after a one-month siege. The whole province fell into his hands.

A poet called Sulaymān of Ashlūᶜ of the Melkite community wrote in colloquial Arabic a poem on the fall of Tripoli, expressing his sorrow in emotional terms[3]:

Woe on me! How my soul is distressed! What fire of affliction devours me!

In Tripoli is born the expression "woe on me!" as pain consumed me before I even composed this poem,

---

1 A contemporary Maronite bishop, Ibrāhīm from Ḥadath, gave a brief account of this expedition, cf. Isṭifān al-Duwayhī, *Taʾrīkh al-Azmina*, ed. Buṭrus Fahd, Bayrūt: Dār Laḥd Khātir 1983, 261. The expedition was well studied by Fadi Barudi, « La grotte de ᶜAsi-l-Hadath », in: *Momies du Liban, Rapport préliminaire sur la découverte archéologique de ᶜAsi-l-Hadath*, Liban: Édifra, Antélias 1994, 82-145; before him by Kamal Salibi, *Maronite Historians of Medieval Lebanon*, Beirut: American University of Beirut, Oriental Series No. 34, 1959, 59-66.

2 The chronicler is Ibn ᶜAbd al-Ẓāhir, *Tashrīf al-ayyām wa-l-ᶜuṣūr fī sīrat al-malik al-Manṣūr*, ed. Murād Kāmil, al-Qāhira: 1961, 47.

3 See the edition of this poem and its translation in my article "Un témoin melkite de la chute de Tripoli aux mains des Mamluks (27 avril 1289)", in: *Studies on the Christian Arabic heritage*, eds. Rifaat Ebied, Herman Teule, Louvain: Peeters 2004, 133-161. This poem came down to us in three *Karshūnī* versions transcribed by Maronite copyists.

On Christians and what happened to them and their children!

Christians, their glory was on the whole earth, and nothing remains of them, no mention neither work,

They dispersed in the countries in Egypt, Damascus, Gaza and the Ḥawrān,

Baʿlbak until Hims, Aleppo, al-Maʿarra and to the distant countries,

The sun cries on them every time it rises and the moon and the stars are cold and distant.

... People told me: "Unfortunate man why are you crying?" I answered: "My brothers I cry for the Christians, I cry for what happened to them, on Tuesday, a day of misfortune,

The Turks entered the suqs attacking by land and by sea, and they encircled them with those they encountered

They brandished swords that cut rocks when they are used and piled victims on the soil.

How many knights were killed? After their assault they were dead, naked, weeping on their children!

You wouldn't have recognized them, saying while turning them: "What is this? A man's cadaver?"...

What happened next is generally less known or documented. Maronite clerical sources together with Mamluk records and a later Druze historian, Ṣāliḥ Ibn Yaḥyā, confirm that after the Franks' departure resistance against the new conquerors was organized in Mount Lebanon. It was not exclusively Christian, but included other groups, Shiites and Druzes. Fights extended from the Jubayl area to the Kisrawān, which included at the time what we call nowadays the Metn province overlooking Beirut. The Mamluks made several counteroffensives against Mount Lebanon, one of them in which the famous Muslim theologian Ibn Taymiyya took part, in 1305. In this major attack, troops from Damascus and Tripoli were gathered and others from Egypt were sent by sea. The Mamluks fought ferociously against the mountaineers, destroying everything from crops and trees to houses and churches. Men were slaughtered or imprisoned, women raped and taken as slaves with their children. The Kisrawān (including the Metn), apparently at the heart of the rebellion, was devastated. Important transfers of population occurred in Mount Lebanon: the Maronites completely abandoned these areas for at least two hundred years, until they were able to resettle there under Ottoman rule in the course of the 16th century. Shiites took refuge in the upper summits of Mount Lebanon in Fārayya-Hrājil and the ᶜĀqūrā districts; they also returned to the Biqāᶜ, in the Baᶜlbak area and around Jizzīn in the South. The clan of ᶜAssāf, a Sunni Turkish tribe, was settled by the Mamluk rulers in the heart of Kisrawān where they were given fiefdoms with the mission of controlling the area and patrolling the Lebanese coastline from Ṣaydā to Tripoli[4].

After this military expedition of 1305, Mamluk order finally prevailed even if tensions remained high. As Ibn al-Qilāᶜī a 15th century Maronite author states[5]:

ملكوا كل مارونياً...
استعبدوهم وكادوهم وكنايسهم هدموهم
الصلبان والقون احرقوهم ولا عجايب ولا برهان

> *They ruled over each Maronite...*
> *They made them slaves and deceived them, their churches they destroyed*
> *The crosses and the icons they burnt, and there were neither miracles nor proof.* [6]

Meanwhile, the Franks who had left Lebanon and fled to Cyprus made plans to come back. Projects of new crusades to the Holy Land circulated in the royal courts of the West and in circles close to the pope. One of these was submitted to pope Clement V in 1307 by a nephew of the King of Armenia called Hayton who was very close to the Franks, as he later retired in a Franciscan monastery in Cyprus. In his project of a new Crusade, after analyzing the political and military situation of the Mamluks he concludes that the Franks together with the local Christians could free the city of Tripoli. "There is", says Hayton, "in the mounts of Lebanon around 40.000 Christians, good fighters, who could be of great help to the pilgrims; they rebelled against the sultan several times, inflicting losses to his army[7]. Once the city of Tripoli is freed, the Christians could hold it until the arrival of the main troops and

---

4 The Mamluk expedition on the Kisrawān in 1305 has been studied by more than a historian; the main research remains the one of Henri Laoust, « Remarques sur les expéditions du Kasrawan sous les premiers Mamluks », *Bulletin du Musée de Beyrouth* tome IV (1940), 92-115; see also Kamal Salibi for the Maronite account of this expedition in *Maronite Historians of Medieval Lebanon*, 72-75.

5 Buṭrus Jumayyil, *Zajaliyyāt Jibrāʾīl Ibn al-Qilāᶜī,* Bayrūt: Dār Laḥd Khātir 1982, 108.

6 Proof of God's help because of their sins. The discourse of Ibn al-Qilāᶜī, a major Maronite author of the 15th century, is usually not historical but has a theological purpose.

7 It is an interesting confirmation from a western source of the resistance that occurred in Mount Lebanon to Mamluk occupation in the aftermath of the crusades.

could take over the whole county; this would be very helpful because the main army would find a secured port where it could land."[8]

This mood in the West was behind the many attempts by Frankish troops to land on the Lebanese coast in the 14th and 15th centuries. Such attempts have been recorded by several Arab authors and the one Druze author from Mount Lebanon already mentioned, Ṣāliḥ Ibn Yaḥyā[9]: the Franks tried to come back to their former possessions as soon as they left, using Cyprus as a platform for their attacks; these occurred with remarkable regularity during the two centuries that followed their eviction from the East.

This state of affairs explains the Mamluks' nervousness towards any contacts between their Christian subjects of Mount Lebanon and Western pilgrims, missionaries or merchants, and their distrust towards them. These feelings were reciprocal as the Christians witnessed the destruction of many of their churches in Tripoli and the Kisrawān districts in the aftermath of the Mamluks' conquest of Tripoli (1289) and Beirut (1291).

During the following two centuries of Mamluk rule in the Beirut-Tripoli area some episodes of persecution of Christians are recorded, apart the cases of martyrdom. In 765/1363-4 an edict of the governor (*nāʾib*) of Tripoli sent to the governor of Ḥisn al-Akrād recommended that the *nawāqīs*[10] of the Christians should not be allowed to be seen. About the same period, sometime after 1395 and before 1432, the Melkite church dedicated to Saint Barbara in Beirut was seized and transformed into a mosque[11]. And finally in 1440, the Mamluk soldiers upon the orders of the governor of Tripoli plundered the Maronite patriarchal seat of Mayfūq (Jubayl) and arrested several monks while the patriarch Yuḥannā al-Jājī took refuge in the inaccessible monastery of Qannubīn in the Qadisha Valley which became the permanent seat of the Maronite patriarchs up to the 19th century. The circumstances of this violent incident are still not clear as the pretext of the military intervention was the visit to the patriarch of two Franciscan missionaries. They were coming back from an important

8 Prince Hayton, « La Fleur des histoires de la terre d'Orient », in: *Croisades et Pèlerinages Récits, Chroniques et Voyages en Terre Sainte XIIe-XVIe siècle*, directed by Danielle Régnier-Bohler, Paris: Robert Laffont 1997, 803-878, here 876.

9 Ṣāliḥ ibn Yaḥyā, *Tārīkh Bayrūt*, eds. Francis Hours s.j., Kamāl S. Sālibī, Bayrūt: Dār al-Mashriq 1969, with a French translation by Francis Hours, Beirut: Université Saint Joseph, *Annales d'Histoire et d'Archéologie* vol. 6, 1995, 1-64; vol. 7, 1996, 83-168.

10 Device in wood or metal traditionally used by Oriental Christians for the call for prayer.

11 According to Bertrand de la Brocquière a French merchant who came to Beirut in 1432, Ṣāliḥ Ibn Yaḥyā who writes about the same time, and Franciscan sources.

Church council held in Florence, Italy, in 1439 and were carrying a message from the pope[12].

II- A Maronite Martyr: Gabriel of Ḥjūla

Setting the context in the previous section allows us to better understand the first known case of a Christian martyr in Tripoli after the establishment of Mamluk rule. It occurred in 1367 and the martyr was no less than a Maronite patriarch called Gabriel of Hjūlā, a village in the mountain not far from Jubayl and the sea and today entirely inhabited by a Shiite population.

The event is first told by the Maronite author, Gabriel Ibn al-Qilāʿī who mentions in one of his *Zajaliyyas* (poems in colloquial language traditional to Mount Lebanon) "a patriarch from Hjūla who died a martyr, burnt into flames"[13]; the explanation he gives to what happened is theological: basically that it reflects God's punishment of the Maronites because they failed to be faithful to the Church of Rome[14]. According to the following verses, the patriarch was not executed without some sort of a trial, as

"Forty Christians testified against him, that he went against his original faith

And they accused him of things from which he was innocent about demands and women".

These verses have been quoted by patriarch Isṭifān al-Duwayhī, a later Maronite author of the 17th century. According to Duwayhī, the arrest of the Maronite patriarch occurred in a general context of terror for the Christians of Bilād al-Shām as a whole. The reason for that persecution, he says, was the expedition in 1365 of the Frankish king of Cyprus Peter of Lusignan to Alexandria, a major Mamluk port in northern Egypt; Duwayhī cites here a small note written by a contemporary Maronite bishop of Iḥdin fleeing persecution. The note is found at the end of a Syriac gospel the bishop copied from the Greeks on March 14, 1677 (1366 A.D.). It was in Syriac Aramaic and could therefore only be understood by members of his own Church[15]:

---

12 For more details, my article on the monastery of Mayfūq," Mayfūq revisité, le couvent de l'épée et du fourreau", *Parole de l'Orient* (USEK) 26, (2001), 159-199.

13 Jumayyil, *Zajaliyyāt Jibrāʾīl Ibn al-Qilāʿī*, 108. It seems that Ibn al-Qilāʿī has also written a *Zajaliyya* about patriarch Gabriel of Hjūla's martyrdom that is lost. As a reminder, all Ibn al-Qilāʿī's work came down to us in *Karshūnī*, a system of writing Arabic that barely the clergy alone could read in 15th century Mount-Lebanon,

14 Ibn al-Qilāʿī who was born a Maronite, studied twenty years in Italy and became a Franciscan Friar.

15 Isṭifān al-Duwayhī, *Tārīkh al-Ṭāʾifa al-Mārūniyya*, ed. Rashīd Shartūnī, Beirut: Imprimerie catholique 1890, 386. Duwayhī provides the Syriac text with its translation in Arabic.

> "On this day the king of Cyprus attacked Alexandria, plundered it, killed its men and took the weakest as prisoners. The sultan of the Muslims[16] got angry against the Christians; he seized the leaders of the clergy and threw them in prison in Damascus. As for me, miserable Yaᶜqūb who is called bishop, I fled and left them. The Lord Christ helped me and I write this as I am fleeing."

The attack and plundering of Alexandria, in October 1365 by the Frankish king of Cyprus and the following reaction of Mamluk authorities against local Christians in Egypt and other provinces like Bilād al-Shām are otherwise confirmed by independent sources, like Ibn Kathīr from Damascus, a contemporary of the events (d.1372), and al-Maqrīzī (d.1441), a later Egyptian chronicler. According to them, Christian clergymen in Egypt were arrested and required to collect money for the release of the prisoners who had been taken by the king Peter of Lusignan. In addition, Damascus' governor received official orders to arrest all high ranking Christian clergy on his territory. Around four hundred people were seized. Duwayhī confirms that an official order had been issued and continues his interpretation of what happened that led to patriarch Gabriel of Hjūlā's martyrdom:

"The *ᶜulamāʾ* (doctors of law) did not issue a *fatwā* (a religious opinion) to kill members of the clergy only because of the attack of Alexandria by the king of Cyprus. But in the year 757/1356 the Franks had attacked Ṣaydā[17], as Ibn Sbāt[18] informs us; they killed a lot of its inhabitants and took a great number of prisoners who were bought back for a sum of 30.000 *dirhams* taken from the prisoner's *dīwān* (office). And three years before, a huge fire had occurred in Damascus… another one had occurred in 740/1339 in which the *sūq* (market) al-Daḥsha, the *sūq* of the swords and the *qayṣariyyah*[19] of the spears and archery burnt and there were many losses. And fifty years earlier, the boats of the Genoese had entered Beirut's port and fights had occurred in Beirut's small streets for two days." Finally Duwayhī adds:

> "because of these and other similar events of which Christians were held responsible, an order was issued to arrest their leaders and imprison them in Damascus. Some of the Maronite heads of the clergy

16 This refers to the Mamluk sultan al-Ashraf Nāṣir ad-Dīn Shaᶜbān II (764/1363-778/1376).

17 They apparently attacked also Tripoli before as certified by a chronicler from Aleppo, Ḥabib al-Ḥalabī, who was present at the time.

18 A 16th century Druze author from Mount Lebanon who was a major source of Duwayhī's Chronicle.

19 A building specialized in stocking and selling a specific merchandize or product.

> were sized like Yaᶜqūb, Iḥdin's bishop, and others were able to flee, as bishop Ḥunayn who crossed the sea to Cyprus[20]; others went into hiding ... Patriarch Gabriel of Ḥjūla was one of those."

The patriarch was arrested because while he was hiding near his village, Damascus' governor wrote to the governor of Tripoli pressing him to take action. Tripoli's *nāʾib* then seized forty men from the village of Hjūlā as hostages in exchange for information on the patriarch's whereabouts. The patriarch finally came out and delivered himself to Mamluk authority. He was burnt alive outside Tripoli at Taylān on April 1st (1367), says Duwayhī, "as it is recorded in the funerary poem dedicated to him by his nephew"[21]. Taylān was a mosque that can still be seen today, built by one of Tripoli's Mamluk governor in 1336.[22]

A Maronite calendar of saints gives a very brief account of Patriarch Ḥjūla's martyrdom on March 26. It is difficult to explain the difference of dates, but Duwayhī seems to be a more reliable source as he specifically refers to the funerary poem of the patriarch's nephew.

His account of the events provides two main reasons as to what happened at the time: A direct one linked to the attack and plunder of Alexandria, the richest port of the Mamluk sultanate, by the King of Cyprus that provoked the ire of Mamluk authorities against their Christian subjects and induced them to take legal action for the arrest of their higher clergy in Egypt as well as in Bilād al-Shām. Duwayhī clearly states that the governor of Tripoli acted in conformity with those official directives and not on his own authority. But he also suggests indirect causes for the patriarch's martyrdom through his own analysis of the events. He links it to previous attacks by the Franks on Ṣaydā and Beirut, suggesting that the Mamluks' hostility towards their Christian subjects in Damascus and in Tripoli was due to the frequent attacks by the Franks and their constant threat to Muslims. Duwayhī also suggests that there was a general climate in Bilād al-Shām in which blame was cast on Christians for other catastrophes as well. He also mentions a fire that destroyed Damascus' markets, for which two monks from Constantinople were

---

20 The first Maronite bishop of Cyprus is mentioned in 1340, as a consequence of the importance of Maronites migration from Lebanon to the island in Mamluk's time, but the Maronite community on the island precedes the Crusades.

21 Isṭifān al-Duwayhī, *Tārīkh al-Ṭāʾifa al-Mārūniyya*, 387. This funerary poem seems to be lost.

22 Amir Ṣaif al-Din Taylān, twice governor of Tripoli (1326-1333; 1333-1340) built a many-domed mosque on the emplacement of Tripoli's Carmelite Church. This church had been built by the Crusaders outside their walled city and, after the fall of Tripoli in 1289, stood deserted and in ruins.

accused in 1339[23]. The two monks escaped arrest through Beirut's port and, according to Duwayhī, a lot of Christians who were employed in the Mamluk administration were arrested, and money taken from them: fourteen among them were crucified and displayed in the surrounding country on camelback. He finally adds that the governor of Damascus (Tankiz), who was responsible for these abuses, was later arrested by the authorities in Cairo, thrown into prison there, and then transferred to Alexandria. Therefore the second indirect cause of patriarch Ḥjūla's martyrdom was, according to Duwayhī's analysis, a tendency by local governors in Bilād al-Shām to blame local catastrophes on the Christians and therefore to direct popular anger against them, requesting their dismissal from their posts in the administration apparatus and extorting money from them.

A last explanation of Patriarch Gabriel of Ḥjūla's martyrdom has been provided recently by a Lebanese historian, based on an event ignored by Duwayhī. In August 1367, thc Franks attacked Tripoli as mentioned by several Mamluk chroniclers[24]. According to these sources this particular attack, which failed, would explain the patriarch's arrest. But there is a problem concerning the date here, since the patriarch died on March 26 or April 1st, a few months before this particular attack. Nevertheless it adds a further argument to the fact that local Christians in the province of Tripoli paid for a virtual state of war existing at the time between Franks and Mamluks.

III- Greek Orthodox Martyrs

The other Christian martyrs in Tripoli were Greek Orthodox. For some of them only the name and day of martyrdom are known, but not the circumstances, or the year of martyrdom. There is, for example, the case of a saint called Mar Yaᶜqūb al-Ḥāmatūrī, whose name is mentioned in the *synaxār* of Saint Georges' monastery of Ḥāmatūrā, in the Kūra district east of Tripoli. He was a monk of the monastery and, according to the notice mentioning him in the *synaxār*, "on October the 13th the Mamluks took him to the city of Tripoli and there he was beheaded and burnt"[25].

---

23 This episode by Duwayhī is based on more than one account by Mamluk chroniclers like Ibn Kathīr, al-Maqrīzī, and al-Dhahabī.

24 Ibn Kathīr, *Al-ijtihād fī ṭalab al-jihād* (769 H. events) quoted by ᶜUmar ᶜAbd al-Salām Tadmurī, *Tārīkh Ṭarāblus al-siyāsī wal-ḥaḍārī ᶜibr al-ᶜusūr*, part 2, Lubnān: Al-Muʾassasah al-ᶜArabiyyah Lil-Dirāsāt wal-Nashr 1981, 149 n. 54; He also quotes for the same event al-Nuwayri, *Al-ilmām bi- aᶜlām*, p. 150 no. 58.

25 *Ms. Balamand* 149 (previously 432) copied in the village of Btarrām in the Kūra district in 7064 of Adam's year (1556 A.D.) by the deacon David for the church "of the leader of the angels Mīkhāʾīl (Michael) that is in the city of Tripoli in the quarter of al-Naṣr".

Another such martyr was Yaᶜqūb of Ḥims who, while he was flogged, was asked to renounce Christ, then "they took him to a place called Bab al-Halqa in Tripoli and he was crucified, then thrown into an immense fire". He died on June 27, year unknown[26].

The best documented case of the Greek Orthodox martyrs occurred on February 1st, 1477[27]. His name is Rizqallāh Ibn Nabᶜ. According to one version, he was a secretary in the *dīwān* of a Tripoli governor called Azdamar, who liked him dearly, so much that he insisted convert to Islam. Progressively annoyed by Rizqallāh's refusal, Azdamar threw him in jail, and finally ordered his beheading which took place outside Tripoli in a place called "Tell al-Mustaha". It is this Rizqallāh who asked the *sayyāf*, sword holder, to let him pray and take communion with soil. Like all the other martyrs his body was burnt but, adds the narrative in a very interesting passage: "at this very moment the Lord sent a heavy rain, so much which the rivers flooded. Those who were there left the scene and the fire ended without harming the saint's body. At night the believers came, and took the body to Cyprus where they honored it with prayers and buried him properly in one of their holy churches".[28]

This last detail provides us with a clue about why all these martyrs were thrown into fire. It was done so none of their relics would remain and in order to avoid the transformation of their tomb into a sanctuary or a place of worship and pilgrimage.

A more plausible reason for this saint's martyrdom rather than his refusal to convert to Islam is the jealousy of Ibn Jumᶜa, a competitor also employed by the governor, who accused Rizqallāh of having offended Islam on one occasion. The story goes on describing the accusation, the circumstances of his arrest, his prayer before he died and his consecutive death and rain on the fire that did not consume the body that was taken overseas.

This version resembles other cases that occurred in Tripoli and Damascus at different periods which involved Jewish or Christian secretaries

---

26 *Ms. Vatican Arabic* 472, copied in the Kūra district area partly in 1560 A.D. and partly in 1633. The manuscript belonged to the church of Mar Sassīn in the village of ᶜAfsdīq; the saint is mentioned in a note on the margin written on "a Sunday fourth of July of the year 7082 of Adam (1574 A.D.) by the priest Būlus (Paul)", see Tūmā Bīṭār (archimandrite), *Al-Qiddīsūn al-mansiyyūn fī al-turāth al-Antāqī*, Lubnān: Matbaᶜat al-Nūr 1995, 407-409.

27 According to the *Ms. of Dayr ᶜAtiyyah* No. 35. Ḥabīb Zayyāt in his article on the Christian Martyrs in the Muslim era conjectures another date for this saint's martyrdom (1363-1365) but he did not know *Ms. 35* cf. "Shuhadāʾ al-Naṣrāniyya fī al-Islām", *al-Mashriq* 36 (1938), 459-465.

28 The story of this saint can be found in the *Ms. of Dayr ᶜAtiyyah* No. 35, *Ḥims* 19 and 20, and *Paris B.N.* No. 254 (15th century), cf. Tūmā Bīṭār, *Al-Qiddīsūn al-mansiyyūn*, 10.

employed by a governor and who were later accused by jealous amirs of being "infidels" and consequently martyred. There was the case in 1301 of a rich Jew in Tripoli responsible for the trade of the province and whose jealous local opponents accused him of being a *kāfir*, an infidel, enjoying too many privileges. Typically, the governor of Tripoli, Amir Asandmar Karjī did not want to give him away to his enemies; but he was obliged to put him to death in 1305[29].

These last cases of martyrdom shed a light on a persistent cause of persecution towards non-Muslims in general in Bilād al-Shām, besides the first one already mentioned, the accusation of their collusion with the Franks. It was the ambivalent need by the Mamluk administration of these employees in their *dīwāns* in Damascus and in Tripoli that contradicted their ideological discourse directed against the "infidels", Franks or local Christians alike. The ambiguity of the Mamluk attitude is illustrated by the flourishing trade between them and the Franks that made cities like Alexandria, Beirut, Damascus and Tripoli so prosperous at their time. Special quarters in each of those cities were reserved for foreign merchants with their churches, baths and khans. In both Beirut and Tripoli, the Mamluks allowed the Franciscan missionaries, who had left in 1291 with all the Franks of the city, to come back in 1333 in order precisely to provide assistance to foreign merchants and travelers. At the same time the Mamluks had to keep a watchful eye on these foreigners. In times of crisis, the Christian and Jewish holders of offices in the administration couldn't enjoy much protection from the state, and at times their competitors' jealousy caused their eventual martyrdom.

---

29 Events related by Taqi-ad-Dīn Aḥmad b. ʿAlī Al-Maqrīzī, *Al-Sulūk li-maʿrifat duwal al-Mulūk* (events of 704 H.), ed. Muḥammad Muṣṭafā Ziyāda, al-Qāhira: part 2, t.1, 1941, 3, 4, 14.

Part Two

Fields of Cultural Production: Arts

Christian Art in the Mamluk Period

Mat Immerzeel and Adeline Jeudy

There is little doubt about the negative consequences of the Mamluk takeover on the position of the indigenous Christian communities in the Middle East. Visible witnesses of the medieval artistic heritage of those Christians are the many works of art that have survived until present days, in particular wall paintings, icons, liturgical objects, and wooden church furniture. The main question is whether their production continued after the rise of Mamluk power, or came to an end. We will try to answer this question for two regions with a different history: Bilād al-Shām and Egypt. Only wall paintings and some icons have come down to us in Bilād al-Shām, but in Egypt various kinds of objects have survived.

Lebanon and Syria

Compared to other regions in the Eastern Mediterranean, the number of churches decorated with wall paintings in Lebanon (about thirty) and western Syria (about ten) is surprisingly high.[1] Unfortunately, in this matter, the quantity does not live up to the quality; often the images are badly deteriorated and unrecognisable. Some were made as early as the eleventh century, yet the period from the late twelfth century to the fall of Tripoli in 1289 was exceptionally productive. These decorations are exponents of the artistic revival of the indigenous Christian Churches – Byzantine Orthodox (Melkite), Syrian Orthodox (western Syrian) and Maronite – in the aftermath of the crusader presence in the Levant, within crusader territory as well as in the neighbouring Emirate of Damascus. Indications for a pre-

[1] Erica Cruikshank Dodd, *Medieval Painting in the Lebanon*, Wiesbaden: Reichert Verlag 2004 (SKCO 8); Mat Immerzeel, "Medieval Wall Paintings in Lebanon: Donors and Artists", *Chronos* 10 (2004), 7-47; Levon Nordiguian and Jean-Claude Voisin, *Châteaux et Eglises du Moyen Age au Liban*, Beirut: Editions Terre du Liban 1999; Stephan Westphalen, "Wandmalereien in syrischen und libanesischen Kirchen", *Antike Welt* 31,5 (2000), 487-502.

Mamluk dating of these wall paintings follow from a combination of different arguments: dates mentioned in inscriptions, chronological clues in written sources, art-historical analyses (style and iconography), and the use of Latin in inscriptions. A few examples illustrate this approach.

So far, the only monument with inscriptions informing us about the date of completion of the mural paintings on which they are applied is Dayr Mār Mūsā al-Ḥabashī near Nebk in Syria (the Monastery of St Moses the Ethiopian). Here three different layers can be distinguished, the oldest one dates back to A.D. 1048-1088, the second to 1095, and the third to 1192/93 or 1208.[2] An instance of a documented historical incident furnishing a *terminus ante quem* for paintings is the attack in 1266 on Qārah and the neighbouring Monastery of St James (Dayr Mār Yāqūb), ca 10 km north of Nebk. When accused of selling Muslims to the crusaders as slaves, Sultan Baybars' troops killed a number of monks and deported the village's Melkite inhabitants. Evidently, the wall paintings preserved in Qārah's Church of St Sergius and St Bacchus and in the monastery must have been fashioned prior to this event.[3]

Another example is that of the decoration of the Church of Mār Sharbil in Maʿad, in the mountains between Jbayl and Batrūn. Erica Cruikshank Dodd refers to the seventeenth-century Maronite patriarch Stephan al-Duwayhī, who writes that its porch was reconstructed with Frankish help in 1243, on which occasion the interior was decorated as well. She believes that this remark concerns the second layer of paintings in this church, executed in the local 'Syrian' style of the thirteenth century.[4] The hand of the same indigenous artist has been recognized in the murals of the Church of Mār Tādrus (St Theodore) in nearby Biḥdaydāt. Here we also find some interesting iconographical clues relating these paintings to the crusaders. Two supplicant donors are represented next to two mounted saints; the first depicted kneeling in front of St Theodore and dressed as a knight. The second person stands below the belly of St George's horse; he wears a western

---

[2] Erica Cruikshank Dodd, *The Frescoes of Mar Musa al-Habashi. A Study in Medieval Painting in Syria*, Toronto: Pontifical Institute for Mediaeval Studies 2001. For layer 3, she interprets the date as A.G. 1504 (A.D. 1292/93; 170), Paolo Dall'Oglio, however, as A.H. 604 (A. D. 1208; (P. dall'Oglio, "Storia del Monastero di San Mose' l'Abissino e descrizione degli affreschi della sua chiesa", in *Il restauro del monastero di San Mosé l'Abissino, Nebek, Siria* (Damasco 1998), 11-22, on 16).

[3] Andrea Schmidt and Stephan Westphalen, *Mar Yakub, Christliche Wandmalereien in Syrien: Qara und das Kloster Mar Yakub*, Wiesbaden: Reichert Verlag 2005 (SCKO 14), 34-37, 120-131.

[4] Cruikshank Dodd, *Medieval Painting*, 317-323, Pls 18.1-27; LXIX-LXXVII; N. Hélou; "La fonction de l'annexe sud de l'église de Maad ", *Tempora* 10-11 (1999-2000), 139-162; Immerzeel, "Medieval Wall Paintings", 12-13, 16, 25, 28-29, Pls 4, 5.

mi-parti garment, consisting of red and blue halves (Pl. 1). Both donors must have belonged to the Latin upper class of the County of Tripoli.[5] As in Maᶜad, the church was refurbished with support of Latins, who, as an enduring memorial to their involvement had themselves represented near their favourite saints.

Mounted soldier saints were an extremely popular subject in Bilād al-Shām. In some cases they are depicted carrying red-crossed white banners, e.g. in the Church of Mār Mtanios in Diddih near Tripoli, and the Church of Mār Sābā in Eddé-Batrūn.[6] This characteristic crusader symbol does not necessarily imply a direct Latin involvement, since this attribute also features in Dayr Mār Mūsā (layer 3; Pl. 2) and the Church of St Sergius and St Bacchus in Qārah (before 1266; Pl. 3), both within the territory of the former Emirate of Damascus.[7] Apparently the banner was adopted by indigenous Christians, as an addition to their traditional iconography of mounted saints. One imagines that such practices were possible under Ayyubid rule, renowned for its relative tolerance towards Christians, but not under the Mamluks.

Stylistic features close to those of Byzantine paintings outside Bilād al-Shām are of great help in estimating the chronology, e.g., for several representations in the Church of St Phocas (Mār Fūqā) in Amyūn, which displays strong Byzantine-Cypriot influences from the late twelfth century.[8] A puzzling case, however, is a detached wall painting representing the Ascension of the Prophet Elijah, with Greek inscriptions, now in a private collection (Pl. 4). Allegedly, it originates from Syria or Lebanon and dates from the fifteenth century, i.e. in the Mamluk period.[9] From a stylistic standpoint, this dating is plausible, but the suggested origin is doubtful because of the unmistakably Byzantine-Cypriot appearance of the scene.[10] One may explain this confusion by suggesting that the mural was actually taken from a church in

---

5 Mat Immerzeel, "Holy Horsemen and Crusader Banners. Equestrian Saints in Wall Paintings in Lebanon and Syria", *ECA* 1 (2004), 29-60, on 43-45, Pls 14-18, idem, "Medieval Wall Paintings", 16-17, Pls 6-10; for Biḥdaydāt: Cruikshank Dodd, *Medieval Painting*, 339-343, Pls LXXVIII-LXXXVI; 19.1-41.

6 Immerzeel, "Holy Horsemen", 47, Pls 21, 22.

7 Idem, passim, Pls 2, 19, 20.

8 Cruikshank Dodd, *Medieval Painting*, 159-163, Pl. I-IX, 1.1-33.

9 Michel van Rijn, *Icons and East Christian Works of Art*, Amsterdam 1980, 80, 173-174.

10 Compare to the fifteenth-century image of Simon of Cyrene carrying the Cross in the Church of St Paraskevi at Geriskipos (Ewald Hein, Andrija Jakovljević and Brigitte Kleidt, *Zypern. Byzantinische Kirchen und Klöster*, Ratingen: Melina-Verlag 1996, 118, Abb. 118).

Cyprus and smuggled away from the island by way of a neighbouring country in the Middle East, to end up on the western art market.

Latin inscriptions are present on the murals inside the Cave of St Marina near the village of Qalamūn near Tripoli,[11] as well as on a scene representing the Presentation in the Temple from Crac des Chevaliers, which includes a donor called SISONIN in Latin.[12] The style of the painting suggests that it should be ascribed not to a westerner, but to a local artist, who worked in this crusader stronghold before its fall in 1271.

When it comes to the production of icons, the situation is more complex because such painted panels could easily be transported. A number of icons in the Monastery of St Catherine at Mount Sinai may originate from the Tripoli area. Recent studies have revealed craftsmanship similar to that of the only thirteenth-century icon in Lebanon, a bilateral masterpiece kept in the Monastery of Our Lady of Kaftūn.[13] The discovery of stylistically comparable wall paintings the Church of St Sergius and St Bacchus outside this convent support this hypothesis.[14] Once more, the workshop that produced these icons and murals was active when the area was still under Latin control. Not only do two of the icons on Mount Sinai represent St Sergius carrying the red-crossed white banner, the formal aspects also suggest dating them roughly to the third quarter of the thirteenth century.[15]

Damage and Destruction

After excluding the possibility of any continuity in church decoration in Bilād al-Shām during the Mamluk period, we have to turn to the matter of what happened to extant wall paintings after the takeover of power. Many of them are severely damaged, but can the Mamluks be held responsible for this?

The decorated churches are divided into two geographical clusters. The first one, in Lebanon, coincides more or less with the borders of the County of Tripoli in its final years. Some churches are situated along the coast; the

---

11 Cruikshank Dodd, *Medieval Painting*, 292-296, Pls LXIV, LXV, 16.1-14.

12 Jaroslav Folda, "Crusader Frescoes at Crac des Chevaliers and Marqab Castle", *DOP* 36 (1982), 177-210, on 182-183; idem, *Crusader Art in the Holy Land, From the Third Crusade to the Fall of Accre, 1187-1291*, New York 2005, 97, Fig. 53 Westphalen, "Wandmalereien", 496, Abb. 27.

13 Nada Hélou, "L'icône bilatérale de la Vierge de Kaftoun au Liban: une oeuvre d'art syro-byzantin à l'époque des croisés", *Chronos* 7 (2003), 101-131; Immerzeel, "Holy Horsemen 49-53", Pls 23, 24; idem, "Medieval Wall Paintings", 25, Pl. 13.

14 Nada Hélou and Mat Immerzeel, "The Wall Paintings", *BAAL*, forthcoming.

15 See note 14.

majority, however, are to be found in the mountains between Tripoli and Jbayl, as far as the Qadisha Valley to the east. One would also have expected more discoveries to the north of this region, e.g. in Antioch, but here the situation is disappointing. There are murals in the crusader strongholds Marqab Castle and Crac des Chevaliers, but these are exceptional.[16] More or less the same phenomenon can be observed across the Lebanese mountain chain. The second cluster encompasses sites in the Qalamūn area, north of Damascus: Dayr Mār Mūsā, the monastery and church in Qārah, some churches in and around Ṣaydnāyā, and the Church of Mar Elian in Homs.[17]

Almost all the sites have in common the fact that they are located in remote places, or, exceptionally, inland cities (e.g. Amyūn and Homs). The absence of paintings in the surviving churches in important coastal cities like Beirut and Jbayl (Byblos) is striking, but it is hard to believe that their walls were always devoid of any decoration. Erica Cruikshank Dodd quotes Wilbrand of Oldenburg, who, in 1211, described the wealthy decoration in John of Ibelin's palace in Beirut, executed by Syrian, Muslim and Greek artists, and supposes that the metropolitan churches must have been decorated likewise.[18] The discovery of a ruined sanctuary with fragmented images in Beirut supports her suggestion.[19] Furthermore, in the early twentieth century, traces were still visible under the whitewash of the Cathedral of John the Baptist in Beirut.[20] Undeniably, the overwhelming presence of decorated sanctuaries in Tripoli's hinterland is a mere shadow of what was once visible in the churches of the main centres.

If we limit our study to the sites where paintings are still preserved, we have to live with the lack of direct or indirect information concerning the building history of these sanctuaries. This also means that we have no indications for holding the Mamluks or their Muslim subjects responsible for any destruction of images. On the contrary, the reasons why so many

16 Folda, "Crusader Frescoes"; idem, *Crusader Art*, 32-34, Figs 5-8; 97-99, Figs 53-57.

17 For Ṣaydnāyā: Mat Immerzeel, "The Decoration of the Chapel of the Prophet Elijah in Maʿarat Saydnaya", in: Schmidt/Westphalen, *Mar Yaqub*, 155-182; for Homs: M. Immerzeel, "The Wall Paintings in the Church of Mar Elian at Homs: A 'Restoration Project' of a Nineteenth-century Palestinian Master", *Eastern Christian Art* 2 (2005), forthcoming. There are also traces of paintings underneath the eighteenth-century programme in the Church of Mar Gabrial in Saddad, in between Homs and Damascus (unpublished).

18 Cruikshank Dodd, *Medieval Painting*, 16.

19 Idem, 375-376, Pls 21.1-3, Figs 31.1-2.

20 Erica Cruikshank Dodd, "Mar Thadros, Bahdeidat. Paintings in a Lebanese Church from the Thirteenth Century", *Journal of the Canadian Society for Syriac Studies* 1 (2001), 61-79, on 69.

representations have disappeared or are reduced to scant traces are numerous. Some general remarks may help to clarify part of the problem.

More than the country side, cities are subject to regular changes in their infrastructure, which makes their ancient buildings extremely vulnerable. Old structures, even sanctuaries, run the risk of being broken down, modernised, or replaced by new constructions. Even village churches and monastic chapels that remained in use for a long time did not escape modernisation, unfortunately at the cost of their artistic heritage. However contradictory it may seem, in this matter the continuation or revival of Christian traditions represents the greatest danger. In the last decades of the twentieth century, many church interiors were 'refreshed'. A sad example of the fashionable preference for bare or smoothly plastered walls is the Monastery of St Sergius and St Bacchus in Maᶜalūla (Syria), where just one small fragment testifies to its artistic past.[21] Dayr Mart Shmūnī in the Qadisha Valley was once decorated as well, but today nothing can be seen. Fortunately, this case was studied prior to modernisation,[22] but other paintings vanished without being photographed or described.

Many medieval wall paintings have survived in a fragmentary state, but this does not necessarily imply intentionally inflicted damage. The preservation of murals depends on what happens to their support. Walls may collapse as a result of earthquakes, erosion or bad maintenance; and humidity and vegetation may affect the fixation of painted plaster layers as well as of the pigments. Once exposed to open air, delicately painted surfaces are extremely vulnerable to weather influences. If buildings remained in use for centuries, or were occupied again, renovations were necessary to tackle the problem of decaying solidity, but also endangered extant decoration. Sometimes images were 'brought back to life again' in a modernized version. In Lebanon, some scenes in Dayr Ḥammāṭūra near Kūsbā were repainted – and damaged again afterwards – but the primitive brushwork does not furnish reliable clues as to when this occurred.[23] A better documented instance is the decoration of the south apse in the Church of Mar Elian in Homs. It has been suggested that the images were painted in the Mamluk period[24], but the mention of the year 1811 in a Greek inscription confirms the outcome of an art-historical analysis: a medieval programme was restored by painters working in the Je-

[21] Immerzeel, "The Decoration", 156.

[22] Cruikshank Dodd, *Medieval Painting* 262-264, Pls XLVI-XLIX, 13.1-14.

[23] Mat Immerzeel, "Le saint cavalier de Deir Saydet Hamatour", *Tempora* x (2005), forthcoming.

[24] Gabriel Saadé, *Saint Eliân de Homs*, Homs 1974, 38-39.

rusalem style of the first half of the nineteenth century.[25] During renovations in the 1970s, some fragments of the original thirteenth-century layer came to light from underneath a layer of undecorated plaster on the south wall, which had therefore escaped the attention of the Palestinian 'restorers'.

In the view of the users of the building, clean, smoothened church interiors were an attractive alternative for a patchwork of poorly preserved and hardly recognisable representations from a distant past. The method of withdrawing damaged, now meaningless, murals from sight with plaster or whitewash, which spared some scenes in Homs from a facelift, was widely applied in Egypt, Lebanon and Syria. To the workers and their commissioners, this approach had the advantage of saving time and money, but a positive side effect was that the covered fragments were also protected from further decay. This widespread working method does not seem to have been inspired by iconoclastic considerations, because more often than not, only part of the decoration was covered. In the church of Dayr al-Sūryān in the Wadi al-Natrūn (Egypt), the well-preserved paintings in its three half-domes remained visible for centuries, while the paintings on the walls had been covered by a layer of white plaster.[26] Bishop Martyros' study of documents in the monastery's library and the abundant graffiti on the plaster has revealed that the renovations took place shortly after 1780.[27] The patron of this refurbishment was a prominent Copt, the later Minister of Finance Ibrāhīm al-Jawharī (d. 1795), who invested a great deal in the restoration of Coptic buildings.

We now have to turn to the matter of recognizing intentional mutilation. Some non-natural damage can easily be discerned. Since paintings are too smooth to hold covering plaster, as a preparatory treatment holes were chiselled into the old surface. A sad example is a scene over the western entrance of the church of Dayr Ḥammāṭūra near Kūsbā (Lebanon). With difficulty one can make out St. George killing his adversary, King Dadianus, or Diocletian (Pl. 5; Fig. 2).[28] A 'pock-marked' appearance of wall paintings results from practical considerations, but the situation is different if faces are damaged. As a matter of fact, in Lebanese and Syrian wall paintings the number of mutilated faces is high, particularly those at eye level, although this mutilation is often limited to the eyes (e.g. the donor in

---

25 Immerzeel, "The Wall Paintings".

26 See the reports on the restoration programmes in the monastery by Karel Innemée (Leiden University) on the website of *Hugoye* (whttp://syrcom.cua.edu/Hugoye).

27 Unpublished; presented at the Seventh International Congress of Coptic Studies, Leiden 2000.

28 Immerzeel, "Le saint cavalier", Fig. 3, Pls 1-3.

Biḥdaydāt; Pl. 1). Apparently, some people felt uncomfortable with these holy figures staring at them, but were they Muslims or superstitious Christians? In this matter Muslims can be given the benefit of the doubt, but the situation changes if crosses, the most marked symbols of Christianity, have been damaged as well (e.g. St Sergius in Qārah; Pl. 3). Nevertheless, even in such cases it is scarcely possible to tell with certainty when and by whom the mutilation was inflicted.

In conclusion, due to the lack of hard evidence, the Mamluks must be cleared of the charge of iconoclasm. Nevertheless, from the case study of the Cave Chapel of the Prophet Elijah at Maᶜarrat Ṣaydnāyā near Ṣaydnāyā, follows that some damage may have been caused during their rule.[29] The walls of the cave were decorated by an artist working in the Cypriot style in about the first half of the thirteenth century. Of the images in a niche cut into the north wall, those of Nicholas and the Virgin Enthroned with the Child are the best preserved (Pl. 6). On the north wall itself, there remain the Ascension of Elijah and three anonymous saints, as well as traces of two bishops and the Virgin from a procession of bishops surrounding the altar. Two more prelates and a deacon are placed on the opposite wall (Pl. 7). Three different kinds of damages can be observed. First, there is the intentional mutilation of, for example, the eyes of the Virgin and Child in the niche, and the crosses on the garments of the bishops (Pl. 7). Second, erosion has resulted in the partial collapse of the decorated south wall and the roof of the cave. Finally, large parts have been affected by water infiltration and vegetation on the natural rock walls. It is difficult to tell whether the mutilations occurred before or after the collapse, but some damage was repaired; in particular the crosses on the bishops' garments and several faces were painted again. The Virgin and Child, however, were left in their deteriorated state (Pl. 6). During later renovations, the chapel's interior was covered with several layers of plaster. In 1962 Maurice Tallon noticed some fragments,[30] but on the restoration of the paintings in the 1990s large surfaces on the north wall were still partly hidden.

In the account of his visit to Ṣaydnāyā in 1737, the British traveller Richard Pococke went into detail about the chapel, though without mentioning any murals.[31] This is the more remarkable since Pococke carefully

---

29 Immerzeel, "The Decoration".

30 Maurice Tallon, "Peintures Byzantines au Liban, inventaire", *MUSJ* 38 (1962), 279-294, on 294; see also Immerzeel, "The Decoration", 157.

31 Richard Pococke, *A Description of the East, and some other Countries* II,1. *Observations on Palaestine or the Holy Land, Syria, Mesopotamia, Cyprus, and Candia*, London 1745, 133.

listed the churches in Ṣaydnāyā in which he had observed the remains of paintings. Presumably he did not notice the chapel's representations because at that point they were hidden by the plaster layers that would be removed more than 250 years later. Apparently, all intentional damage, the collapse and the repainting occurred between the decoration of the chapel and the 1730s, i.e., in the Mamluk or – from 1513 – the Ottoman period. The repainting was executed primitively and in several phases. Drops of paint spoiled the images of the bishops on this wall (Pl. 7), and all this does not say much for the artistic capabilities of those who tried to bring the images back to life. The dilettante brushwork betrays a lack of craftsmanship and can therefore hardly be regarded as proof of a vivid Christian artistic tradition under Mamluk or early Ottoman rule.

Egypt

Unlike the indigenous Christians of Bilād al-Shām, who lived in a territory taken by force and, to judge from the accusations against the people of Qārah, suspicious in Mamluk eyes because of their relations with the Latins and Mongols, their fellow believers in Egypt were already subjects of Mamluk rule from the moment they took power. Though relations between the Copts and the Mamluks, including questions concerning oppression or discriminatory laws, are the subject of other contributions to this volume, it is necessary here to give a brief outline of the Egyptian social context under the Mamluks. Indeed, social factors partly explain the continuity or break witnessed in Christian art from the thirteenth to the sixteenth century.

The urban character of Egyptian society certainly plays a major role in this very different setting. After the Mamluks took over power in 1250 Cairo became once again the intellectual, religious and artistic centre of the Arab world, and a shelter for craftsmen from Iran and Iraq escaping the Mongol invasions.[32] Less tolerant than their predecessors towards the *dhimmīs* (non-Muslims), the Mamluks randomly persecuted religious minorities, especially the Copts, by alternating discriminatory decrees and periods of tolerance. This led to a massive reduction of the number of Christians in the country, many of whom converted to Islam.[33] Though

---

32 Robert Hillenbrand, *Islamic Art and Architecture,* London: Thames and Hudson 1999, 138-166.

33 Richard Irwin, *The Middle East in the Middle Ages, The early Mamluk Sultanate 1250-1382*, London 1986, 98-99; Maqrīzī, *Kitāb aṣ-Ṣulūk li-Maʿrifat Dūwal al-Mulūk,* II, Muḥammad Muṣṭafā Ziyāda (ed.), Cairo 1941, 927. It should also be remembered that the Black Death of 1347 also had consequences in Egypt and decimated the population.

the hostility towards the Copts was reinforced by the crusades which took place in neighbouring countries, the Copts were not bracketed together with the Latins. The periodic persecution they suffered was mainly due to a more general feeling of resentment towards the government; the Copts, as a rather wealthy minority, served as scapegoats.[34]

Contrary to common ideas, the Copts, even in their reduced numbers, still occupied a place of importance in the state's administration, at least until the middle of the fourteenth century.[35] Their influence was considerably weakened and they were victims of sporadic but severe persecution. However, they still preserved a rather comfortable economic position. Essential to the administration, they were perfectly familiar with the way it functioned, the more so because positions were often passed down from one generation to the next.[36] Thus the Mamluk sultans could not afford to annihilate them totally, since the Copts maintained their financial wealth.[37] If the Copts were very often dismissed from office in attempts to calm popular riots, they were always reinstated not long afterwards. Through random persecution, the Turkish sultans also wished to calm the indignation of the fundamentalist *ʿulamāʾ* and the *ṣūfīs*, who appealed to the sultans to respect the Covenant of ʿUmar[38] and envied the Copts' position in the financial administration.[39] Consequently, numerous Copts working in the administration converted to Islam (thereby becoming *musālima*),[40] but they maintained a Christian household, with a Christian wife. After several waves of severe ri-

34 Doris Behrens-Abouseif, "Location of Non-Muslim Quarters in Medieval Cairo", *Annales Islamologiques* 22 (1986), 117-132, on 124; Donald Richards, "The Coptic Bureaucracy under the Mamluks", in *Colloque International sur l'Histoire du Caire*, Cairo, 1974, 377-378; D.P. Little, "Coptic Conversion to Islam under the Bahri Mamluks, 692-755/1293-1354", *Bulletin of the School of Oriental and African Studies* 39 (1976), 552-569, on 553, 561.

35 Richards, "The Coptic Bureaucracy", 374.

36 Idem, 373.

37 Little, "Coptic Conversion", 557.

38 Al-ʿAynī, *ʿIqd*, Ahmet III MS 2912/4, fol. 337a; Al-Nuwayrī, *Nihāyat al-ʿArab*, Dār al-Kutub MS 549 *maʿārif ʿamma*, XXXI, 7.

39 Ibn Ḥajar, *Durar*, II, 429-430; Richards, "The Coptic Bureaucracy", 373-376; Little, "Coptic Conversion", 556. The Covenant of ʿUmar legitimates the status of the *dhimmīs*: they are tolerated but have to pay taxes, among other rules. The famous Karīm al-Dīn al-Kabīr can be quoted as an instance of an influential Coptic official converting to Islam. Two historians mention his role in stories of the destruction of churches: how he convinced the sultan to spare the buildings: Maqrīzī, *al-Sulūk*, II, 182-183; Al-ʿAynī, *ʿIqd*, Ahmet III MS 2912/4, fol. 321a.

40 We can mention the case of Ibn al-Ghanam, a prosperous Coptic secretary, who converted to Islam following persecution in 1293: Little, "Coptic Conversion", 555.

ots during the first half of the fourteenth century, the Coptic community was greatly weakened under the reigns of al-Nāṣir Muḥammad and his successor Baybars al-Jāshankīr, by the second half of the same century. We preserve numerous accounts from different historians on the demolition of churches; most of the time, this destruction occurred in the course of rioting, and not as a result of explicit orders from the sultan to burn or loot churches.[41]

The depletion of the Coptic community leads to questions concerning the consequences for its artistic activities. If we notice an artistic decline, does this imply that the community had been weakened? Due to the constant reuse of pieces and their circulation among churches, to the absence of documentation about the workshops and artists, and to a visual vocabulary shared by Christians and Muslims alike, we lack a reliable methodology that would help to determine the attribution of undocumented objects either to the thirteenth, fourteenth or fifteenth century. Some objects can be positioned in the chronology according to stylistic details, but others have often been dated to the thirteenth or fourteenth century without any convincing evidence. Can we identify specific characteristics of Christian art under the Mamluks which would enable us to securely attribute a Mamluk dating to an undocumented object or a painting? Oleg Grabar has already tried to answer this question in relation to Islamic art.[42] We will try to answer it for Coptic art through some case studies.

Is the commonplace that Christian art declined under the Mamluks a justified one? The weakening of the community would logically lead to lessening liturgical needs and reduced means for decorating places of worship. However, as outlined above, until the middle of the fourteenth century, the Coptic community remained a rather wealthy minority. As a result of persecution, a considerable number of churches were destroyed, but there is nothing to indicate that this persecution arose from any iconoclastic spirit, since the destruction targeted the whole building (or part of the building) and not especially the decoration. We hear of such destruction in the historians' accounts of the popular riots which occurred in the Mamluk period.[43] As for the surviving wall paintings in monasteries and churches,

---

41 Al-ʿAynī, *ʿIqd*, Ahmet III MS 2912/4, fol.334a-7b; Maqrīzī, *Suluq* II, 216-28 et *Khiṭaṭ* II, 425-33; Al-Nuwayrī, *Nihāyat al-ʿArab*, Dār al-Kutub MS 549 *maʿārif ʿāmma*, XXXI, 4-8; Al-Muqrī, *Nathr al-Jumān fī Tarājim al-Aʿyān*, Chester Beatty MS 4113, fols. 141a-7b. These accounts make clear that the destruction was not encouraged by the sultan, but was undertaken by the people out of hatred for the Christians. One such instance is the case of the destruction of the Church of al-Zaharī, told by Maqrīzī: Maqrīzī, *Khiṭaṭ*, IV/2, Aymān Fuʾād (ed.), London 2003, 1066-1067.

42 Oleg Grabar, "Reflections on Mamluk Art", *Muqarnas* 2 (1984), 1-12.

43 See note 40.

these can be dated prior to the mid-thirteenth century.[44] In one case, even fourteenth-century paintings have survived. The church of Dayr Anbā Būlā (the Monastery of St Paul) near the Red Sea was decorated in A.D. 1333/34 (Pl. 8).[45] Since the interior was repainted in the early eighteenth century, just a few elements of the earlier programme are visible in spots where the later paintings have flaked off. They are situated in the upper part of the western wall of the *haykal* of St Antony. If a dedicatory inscription mentioning the date had not survived as well, the fragmented images of several saints would have been regarded as thirteenth century works of art. Another contemporary painted object is even more unique: a shroud or door hanging bearing the painted image of the Archangel Michael was discovered as an adornment in a tomb at Antinoe in 1908. It is provided with a Sahidic Coptic inscription, informing us that it was painted by Philotheus in 1328.[46] Zuzana Skalova suggests that it could have been a shroud, probably dedicated to 'Apa Pshai', which was re-used as a sanctuary door curtain. Its size allows such an hypothesis; the shroud could have hung in front of the entrance to the sanctuary instead of a door, or over the door as is the case nowadays and as it is described in *Tartīb al-Kahānut* (The Order of the Priesthood), an Arabic text attributed to Sāwīrus Ibn al-Muqaffaᶜ, thought to date to the tenth century. The author mentions that 'the door (of the *haykal*) is always covered with a curtain which falls upon it'.[47] With a curtain such as that described above, the entrance to the sanctuary would then be 'guarded' by the archangel painted on the textile, endued with well-known apothropaic value and regarded as an 'icon on linen support'.

On the other hand, a number of objects - sanctuary screens, doors and

---

44 E.g. the monasteries of Wadi Natrun, the Red Sea, Fayyum, Sohag, Esna and some churches in Cairo (Abū Sayfayn, al-Muᶜallaqa). Many the paintings date to the twelfth or thirteenth century; see Gertrud J.M. van Loon and Mat Immerzeel, "Inventory of Coptic Wall-paintings. Part One. Wall-paintings in Monasteries and Churches", *Essays on Christian Art and Culture in the Middle East* 1 (1998), 6-55.

45 Michael Jones, "Conservation of the Cave Church at the Monastery of St. Paul by the Red Sea", *BARCE* 181 (2001-02), 30-32; Paul van Moorsel, *Les peintures du monastère de Saint-Paul près de la Mer Rouge*, Cairo: IFAO 2002 (MIFAO 120); Michael Jones, "Conservation Continues at St. Paul's Monastery", *BARCE* 186 (2004), 10-12. The paintings are also reproduced in: Mahmoud Zibawi, *Images de l'Egypte Chrétienne*, Paris 2003, 191.

46 Zuzana Skalova and Gawdat Gabra, *Icons in the Nile Valley*, Cairo 2003, 210-211.

47 F° 136; translation and edition: Julius Assfalg. See: Julius Assfalg, *Die Ordnung des Priestertums (Tartib al-Kahanut), Eine altes liturgisches Handbuch der koptischen Kirche,* coll. Publications du Centre d'Etudes Orientales de la Custodie Franciscaine de Terre-Sainte, *Coptica* 1, 1955. Assfalg does not attribute the text to Ibn al-Muqaffaᶜ but to an unknown Coptic author from the mid-thirteenth century.

isolated panels – have been preserved, to which a dating to the Mamluk period can be attributed on the basis of stylistic analysis. They are made from precious imported wood (ebony, palisander) and most of them are inlaid with bone or ivory. The continuity in the rich furnishing of church interiors, already testified for several centuries and contrasting with the apparently simple exteriors of the churches, suggests that under the Mamluks, at least in the first century of their domination, there were still Christian patrons or donors rich enough to afford supplying the churches with liturgical furniture of quality. Some of those commissioners or donors could have been members of the intellectual urban elite, such as Copts working in the administration, and their families.[48] The influential al-ʿAssāl family was renowned for commissioning works of art. Manuscripts especially were funded by the fourth brother, al-Amjad; these were copied by the scribe Gabriel, the future patriarch of Alexandria (1268-1271).[49] A statement of this kind echoes the nuances in the situation of the Copts discussed above.

Attribution of works of art to the Mamluk period relies upon stylistic analysis, once more bringing to light a visual culture shared by both Christian and Islamic art, for instance a specific kind of decoration used for flat surfaces. Characteristic of Islamic art and developed since the twelfth century, woodworking and the technique of assembled polygonal pieces became most widespread and reached its most sophisticated level under the Mamluks (Pl. 9). Some earlier items considered paradigms for this technique are the wooden *mirhabs* of the Mausoleums of Sayyida Ruqayya (1133) and Sayyida Nafīsa (1138/45). The masterpiece of this technique is undoubtedly the *minbar* donated by the Sultan Lājīn to the Mosque of Ibn Ṭūlūn in 1296. This shows that the first decades of Mamluk rule witness the final elaboration of a model

48 Although the question concerning patrons in medieval Cairo requires further investigation, it has already come to light that the 'bourgeoisie' certainly played an important role in commissioning works of art, especially under the Ayyubids and the first Mamluk (Grabar, "Reflections", 11). See also: Oleg Grabar, "The Illustrated Maqamat of the Thirteenth Century: The Bourgeoisie and the Arts", in: *The Islamic City*, eds. A.H. Hourani and S. Stern, Oxford 1970, 207-222; Ibn Iyas, *Journal d'un bourgeois du Caire*, trad. Gaston Wiet, Paris, 1955; Eva Baer, *Ayyubid Metalwork with Christian Images*, Leiden: Brill 1989.

49 Al-Amjad was the secretary of the military diwan. The Al-ʿAssāl family is known to have lived rather comfortably, as Al-Amjad owned a house in Ḥārat Zuwaylah in Cairo and another in Damascus, while many works were completed under the family's patronage. Their influence went as far as promoting Gabriel III to the patriarchate. Among the manuscripts written by Gabriel for the family are the *Nomocanon*, al-Asʿad's Arabic Gospel and al-Ṣāfī's Coptic canon laws. See: Khalil Samir, *Al-Safi Ibn al-ʿAssal: brefs chapitres sur la Trinité et l'Incarnation, Patrologia Orientalis* 42.2 (1985), 622-632; Leslie Maccoull, "A note on the career of Gabriel III, scribe and patriarch of Alexandria", *Arabica* XLIII/2 (1996), 357-360.

continuously developed from the end of the Fatimids, now produced *en masse* and applied uniformly to every kind of flat surface (book covers; ceramic tiles; painted ceilings; bronze doors; chests). If the geometric composition, and above all its diffusion, became emblematic of the Mamluk dynasty, this model was so widespread that, as a result, it is difficult to attribute a precise dating to undocumented objects. If we compare such works with better documented Islamic objects (some bearing inscriptions), we note that the decorative patterns did not evolve much from the fifteenth century onwards. The use of this mass-produced model shared with Islamic art is certainly one reason for the general perception of a decline of Christian art under the Mamluks, for the Copts' main works of art no longer seem to bear any specifically Christian identity. Nevertheless, some of the most striking medieval objects made for the Christians do, in fact, date from the Mamluk period. On closer inspection, one may notice that more or less individualized art was still being produced.

Two sanctuary screens can be dated with accuracy. One is preserved in the Church of Ḥārat Zuwaylah in Islamic Cairo (an area continuously inhabited by Copts, Jews, Greeks and Armenians since the foundation of al-Qāhira until the present day) and the second is preserved in a sanctuary dedicated to the Ethiopian saint Thekla Haymanot, in the Church of Al-Muᶜallaqa in Old Cairo. The door of the screen of Ḥārat Zuwaylah (Pl. 10) is not original; it apparently used to be a 'real' door in the Church of Abū Sayfayn in Old Cairo, as is testified by a photograph most probably taken in the beginning of the twentieth century by the Comité de Conservation des Monuments de l'Art Arabe. This door was thus reused in the screen of Ḥārat Zuwaylah, perhaps during a restoration campaign; this choice was rather accurate as the door's geometric decoration matches that of the whole screen. It also contains some animals carved among the inlaid pieces making up the two half rosettes (Pl. 11). The screens of both Ḥārat Zuwaylah and al-Muᶜallaqa show a particular polygonal composition, slightly different from that usually observed on similar flat wooden surfaces of contemporary or later screens, doors and panels.[50] This seems to be a kind of pattern rather popular under the reign of al-Nāṣir Muḥammad ibn Qalāwūn, "made up of pentagons and little polygons shaped

50 The present screen of Ḥārat Zuwaylah cannot be identified with the screen (*maqtaᶜ*) mentioned in a manuscript from the late twelfth or beginning of the thirteenth century, preserved in Munich and attributed to Abū al-Makārim. On folio 3a, the latter states that the church's screen is a "*new one made by ... with ... the archdeacon Gamal al-Kafah Abu Said in the Caliphate of al-Hafiz in the year 547*" (1152). Such a Fatimid dating is too early for the present screen: by 1152 only the very first examples of wooden geometric composition had been elaborated, such as the miḥrābs of Sayyida Ruqayya and the mausoleums of Nafisa, the door of the mosque of al-Aqmar and the minbar of the mosque of Ṣalāḥ Talai. See: Bishop Samuel al-Syriānī, *Abu al-Makarim, History of the Churches and the Monasteries in Lower Egypt in the Thirteenth Century*, Cairo 1992, 1-2.

like wings and propellers (which) is inserted between rosaces".[51] We can compare these screens to the door of the Mosque of Altunbukha al-Maridāni in Islamic Cairo, now displayed in the Louvre Museum.[52] Allegedly, this mosque was erected in 1338-1340 by Ibn al-Siyūfī, official architect of al-Nāṣir. Another object displays a similar pattern: the cover of a Qur'ān made in 1313, again for al-Nāṣir. Such a pattern is also found on the later *minbar* of the Madrasa-Mausoleum of Qā'it Bay, made in 1472-1474, and, in a rougher variation, on that of the Madrasa of al-Ghūrī (ca 1503). However, it seems characteristic for the reign of al-Nāṣir. This allows us to date back the two screens of Ḥārat Zuwaylah and Al-Muᶜallaqa to between the second quarter and the second half of the fourteenth century, making them contemporary with, or later than, the successive reigns of al-Nāṣir.[53] The presence of such a work of art in Ḥārat Zuwaylah could be explained by the establishment of the See of the Coptic Patriarchate in this church in 1303; it would remain here for almost three centuries.[54]

Three other sanctuary screens most probably date back to the fourteenth or fifteenth century, an estimation again indicated by the nature and quality of their decoration. These are the central screens of the churches of al-Muᶜallaqa (Pl. 12), Sitt Barbara and Abū Sargā, in Old Cairo, which have been subjected to numerous restoration campaigns.[55] Various panels reused to form new screens or other objects probably also date from the Mamluk period. They all display the common patterns used as a model for contemporary and later screens.[56] What distinguishes these three 'ancient' screens from others which are quite similar but date from a much later period, is the quality of the materials, the intricate inlay, and the carving of the polygonal pieces, featuring

---

51 Elise Anglade, *Catalogue des boiseries de la section islamique*, Paris 1988, 92. Pieces shaped like 'propellers' can already be seen on the minbar of Qus, dating to the twelfth century.

52 Idem.

53 The sultanate of al-Nāṣir Muḥammad Ibn Qalāwūn lasted through irregular periods: 1293-1294, 1299-1309, 1310-1340. It is arguable whether the screens date to before or after the riots of 1321, which resulted in massive conversion to Islam and large-scale looting and destruction of churches.

54 Myriam Wissa, "Harit Zuweylah", in Aziz Atiya (ed.), *The Coptic Encyclopedia*, IV, New York 1991, 1208: the Patriarchal Seat was settled in Harit Zuweylah from John VIII (1300-1320) to Matthew IV (1660-1675).

55 The main screen of Sitt Barbara is a hybrid object made of several panels reused to complete the central structure which is the original core of the screen. This 'core' is Mamluk, while the other panels date from the Ottoman period.

56 This typical model, so widespread under the Mamluk, is exemplified by all the furnishing coming from contemporary mosques, such as the mosque-madrasa of Umm al-Sultan Shaᶜbān, in the district of Darb al-Aḥmar within Islamic Cairo.

looped stems and vine leaves. Similar features are so commonly found on other objects (mostly doors) that it is not necessary to quote precise examples.[57] One striking, though not innovative, pattern on the screens is the star-shaped piece - sometimes bearing a central 'eye' -, which is very common on doors from the thirteenth century onwards, from Anatolia to Egypt.[58]

When viewed at a distance, the decoration of the above objects does not differ from that of Islamic works of art. The Christian equivalents, on sanctuary screens, of the inlaid diamond-shaped pieces decorating Islamic doors and *minbars*, are, in many cases, strictly the same. So what makes these objects Christian?[59] Obviously, the mere fact that they are sanctuary screens should be sufficient to distinguish them from Islamic works of art. The function and shape of the screens are typically Christian, adapted to use inside churches. Already under the Fatimids, the decoration of the screen of the Church of Sitt Barbara (Old Cairo) did not convey any obvious Christian symbolism through its decoration, borrowed from the popular visual repertory of the sequence known as the Princely Cycle.[60] The use on sanctuary screens of popular patterns shared with Islamic art highlights yet again the artistic symbiosis between Christians and Muslims, for every kind of art, from the period of the Caliphates to the present. Relying on different holy books does not prevent Christians and Muslims from relying on the same techniques and patterns to convey their faith. However, if the sanctuary screens display the contemporary popular geometric composition, they also show a few small crosses carved among the inlaid pieces. This is the case for the five screens discussed above, on which each rosette pattern is adorned with a central Greek cross (Pl. 13). The two small windows in the screens, and the upper part below the row of icons, also display a large

57 A. Lee, "Islamic star pattern", *Muqarnas* 4 (1987), 182-197; G.S. Karnouk, "Form and Ornament of the Cairene Bahri Minbar", *Annales Islamologiques* 17 (1981), 113-139.

58 Examples of doors bearing star-shaped pieces among their decoration include two inlaid doors from Egypt, dated to the fourteenth century (André Raymond (ed), *Le Caire*, Paris 2000, Figs. 302-303-305); the main door of the mosque of Sidi Yussef, dating to the fourteenth century and drawn by Prisse d'Avennes (Etienne Prisse d'Avennes, *Islamic Art in Cairo*, Cairo reprint 1999, 100); and a rather massive wooden door from Anatolia dated to the late thirteenth or early fourteenth century, preserved in the Staatliches Museum Berlin.

59 A similar question has already been raised regarding the Abbassid-like stuccoes decorating the *haykal* in the church of the Virgin in Dayr al-Sūryān: Mat Immerzeel, "The Stuccoes of Deir al-Surian: a Wafq of the Takritans in Fustat?", in: *Coptic Studies on the Threshold of a New Milennium. Proceedings of the Seventh International Congress of Coptic Studies. Leiden, 27 August-2 September 2000*, eds Mat Immerzeel and Jacques van der Vliet, Louvain: Peeters 2004, 1303-1320.

60 Edmond Pauty, *Bois sculptés d'églises coptes (époque fatimide)*, le Caire 1930.

cross in the centre of each square panel. The screen of Ḥārat Zuwaylah even bears icons within this location, said to be of late Paleologan style.[61]

From the previous observations, let us recall that among the mass-produced 'neutral' polygonal pieces, some were carved with crosses, which means that mass-produced objects may also have been customized to meet the requirements of the Coptic community. Still, it is clear that some effort was made to personalize the works of art made for Christians.

Other objects can less easily be attributed to the Mamluk period. Here the need for an adequate methodology prevails. Some of these objects might equally date from the late Ayyubid and others from the Ottoman period. The objects in question are several doors and panels bearing inlaid crosses, preserved in the Coptic Museum and in churches, and also some panels reused as icon frames, e.g., the one preserved in the southern nave of the Church of al-Muᶜallaqa.[62] However, the frame of an icon of St Barbara in the eponymous church seems to be original and also probably dates broadly from the Mamluk period, as no detail indicates a precise dating.[63] Among these various objects, two lecterns have also survived. One of them is thought to come from the Church of al-Muᶜallaqa, but is now in the former Coptic Cathedral of al-Azbakiyya. It was drawn by Alfred Butler and each of its four faces shows a large inlaid cross.[64] This piece has been erroneously dated to the Mamluk period, whereas it is most probably Ottoman. The second lectern can be given a more accurate dating, especially its main panel. It seems to have been re-used in a later (Ottoman?) lectern found in the Church of Ḥārat al-Rūm (Islamic Cairo) and now in the Coptic Museum (Pl. 14). So far, it has

61 Lucy-Anne Hunt, "Iconic and Aniconic: Unknown Thirteenth and Fourteenth Century Byzantine Icons from Cairo in their Woodwork Settings", in: Lucy-Anne Hunt, *Byzantium, Eastern Christendom and Islam. Art at the Crossroads of the Medieval Mediterranean*, I, London: The Pindar Press 1999, 60-96 (reprint from *Poikila Byzantina* 6 (1987), 31-48).

62 This hybrid structure was used to frame the icon of St Mark now preserved at the Coptic Museum. It is composed with figurative panels, maybe dating back to the late Fatimid or Ayyubid period, and ornamental panels of various dating, from the Mamluk to the Ottoman period. See: Zuzana Skalova, "St. Mark the Evangelist with Severed Head: Unique Iconography in Egypt", *Byzantino-Slavica* 56 (1995), 721-732, on 732.

63 The icon was restored by Zuzana Skalova, who dates it to the thirteenth century. She gives the same dating to the frame, which seems far too early. See: Skalova/Gabra, *Icons*, no. 8. See also: Hunt, "Iconic", 68, 93.

64 Alfred J. Butler, *The Ancient Coptic Churches of Egypt*, II, Oxford, 1884, 65. This lectern has also been recorded by: M. Fowler, *Christian Egypt: Past, Present and Future*, London 1901, 190; Charalambia Coquin, *Les édifices chrétiens du Vieux-Caire*, le Caire 1974.

been dated from the thirteenth century without any convincing argument.[65] Richly adorned with ivory or bone inlaid with precious wood (ebony and palisander), its central star-shaped motif is carved with the popular pattern depicting a lion and its prey. Two points of the star were lost and restored using similar ones taken from another piece. The geometric composition decorating this panel is unusual; we find equivalents on the reverse of a door preserved in the Louvre, dated from the first half of the fourteenth century. Elise Anglade compares this composition to the *minbar* panels of the Mosque of Sitt Ṭaṭar al-Ḥijāziyya (a daughter of Qalāwūn and sister of al-Nāṣir Muḥammad), dating approx. 1360. She also compares it to the illumination of the first page of an Islamic Egyptian manuscript preserved at the Museum of Asian Arts in St Petersburg, dated between 1288 and 1318.[66] Another manuscript displays the same pattern: the frontispiece of an Egyptian Koran from the fourteenth century, preserved in the British Library.[67] Thus, the decagonal grid seems to be rather commonly used for vertical rectangular panels. The panel reused on the lectern of Ḥārat al-Rūm could date from the first half of the fourteenth century, perhaps contemporary with the reign of al-Nāṣir Muḥammad. This panel also bears other noteworthy elements: two small isolated swords, a very rare pattern in Egypt, carved and inlaid in the two rectangular pieces making up the upper and lower registers of the panel's composition.

A still vivid figurative Christian tradition also considered doors, wooden panels and liturgical furniture as a mean of expression. One case already discussed by Lucy-Anne Hunt in several articles consists of ten cedar panels carved with scenes from the New Testament. She identifies them as belonging to a former sanctuary screen, helped in her reconstitution by the description given by Greville Chester in 1872.[68] These panels make up

65 The whole pulpit is dated back to the thirteenth century by Markus Simaika in *A Brief Guide to the Coptic Museum*, Cairo 1938, n° 905. But this dating probably only refers to the main panel, which seems to have been reused on this pulpit, dating probably from the eighteenth or nineteenth century. See also: Carl Johan Lamm, "Fatimid woodwork, its style and chronology", *Bulletin de l'Institut d'Egypte* 18 (1936), 72; Maria Cramer, *Koptische Buchmalerei*, Recklinghausen 1964, 52.

66 Anglade, *Catalogue*, n° 92, 94-95: the Leningrad manuscript is thought to have belonged to Muzaffar al-Dīn Mūsā ibn al-Malik al-Saliḥ ʿAlī ibn Qalāwūn, who reigned from 1288 to 1318. This manuscript recounts the expedition of al-Nāṣir Muḥammad against Qutlusah.

67 Or. 848 fo. 1 v.; reproduced in: Eva Wilson, *Islamic Designs for Artist and Craftspeople*, New York 1988, Fig. 48.

68 Chester mentions that the door had been dismantled, and was at this time preserved in the storage of the church. This seems to indicate strongly that it came from the Church of Al-Muʿallaqa, at least at the time when it was acquired. See: Greville J. Chester, "Notes on the Ancient Christian Churches of Musr El Ateekah, or Old Cairo, and its Neighbourhood", *Archaeological Journal* 29 (1872), 120-134.

the so-called 'door of al-Muᶜallaqa' preserved in the British Museum.[69] The author dates it back to the early fourteenth century on the basis of a documented iconographic analysis in line with Byzantine models, and the depiction of liturgical feasts. Moreover, she uses a historical reference to confirm her analysis. Yet this source cannot be verified: no refurbishing of the Church of al-Muᶜallaqa by the Byzantine power is mentioned in the *Histoire des Sultans Mamelouks* by M. Quatremère.[70] Hunt's hypothetical dating from the early fourteenth century is, so far, only supported by her iconographic analysis. Nothing indicates that this door used to belong to a sanctuary screen. It had already been removed from its original setting when Chester found it in the church's storage room.

We have seen above that Mamluk screens are characterized by their geometrical decoration, doors included. However, a figurative painted curtain could also have been suspended in front of the entrance to the sanctuary, is suggested by the shroud or hanging from Antinoe with the depiction of an archangel. Two other doors with figurative and ornamental patterns exist, but they were also not found in their original context. The first is the lost door of the Greek Church of Mār Jirjis, recorded and photographed by Joseph Strzygowski in 1898, and the second is the so-called 'door of Rashid' (Damietta) which, like the door of al-Muᶜallaqa, is composed of ancient panels reassembled within a new structure.[71] The first door is decorated with biblical scenes and saints, while the second shows only a few figures and many ornamental patterns. Both are characterized by flat carving. Little is known about their original context. Strzygowski mentions that the door of Mar Girgis was said to have formed part of a sanctuary screen, but had already been dismantled when he found it. As for the door of Rashid, nothing more is known about it than that the separate panels were purchased by Markus Simaika for the Coptic Museum in 1938. Both doors are thought to date from the late Fatimid or the Ayyubid period (late twelfth or thirteenth century). This means the Byzantine door of al-Muᶜallaqa would be the only case of a (hypothetical) Mamluk figurative door among a large number

69 Lucy-Anne Hunt, "Al-Muallaqa Doors Reconstructed: An Early Fourteenth-Century Sanctuary Screens from Old Cairo", in: Hunt, *Byzantium,* 282-318 (reprint from Gesta 28,1 (1989), 61-77). See also: H.C. Evans (ed.), *Byzantium, Faith and Power. Catalogue of the Exhibition at the Metropolitan Museum of Art, New-York, March 23-July 4 2004*, New-York, 2004, no. 260.

70 M. Quatremère, *Histoire des Sultans Mamelouks d'Egypte, écrite en arabe par Taki-Eddin-Ahmed-Makrizi*, Tome Second, Paris, 1845, 180: "*Des ambassadeurs, envoyés de Lascaris, empereur des Francs, étant venus solliciter l'ouverture de ces édifices, on rouvrit l'église de Moallakah, située dans la ville de Misr (...)*".

71 Joseph Strzygowski, "Die christlichen Denkmäler Aegyptens", *RQS* 12 (1898), 27-30.

of sanctuary doors decorated with polygonal designs. This does not allow us to confirm the hypothesis that the door used to be inserted in a screen, though this can be considered an option.

The three altar canopies preserved, again, in the Church of al-Muᶜallaqa, about which little can be said for the moment as their restoration is still in progress, are also worthy of note (Pl. 15). The southern sanctuary's canopy has only been described very briefly (as a "charming baldaquin over the altar"), in Dorothy Russell's historical guide to Cairo, written in 1963.[72] The apparently 'Byzantine' iconography of the canopy's painted interior (a central Christ in Glory surrounded by the archangels in the spandrels) and its delicate and pale colours (light pink and grey shades) contrast with the flat aspect of the medieval wall paintings usually encountered in the monasteries of the deserts and within the churches of Cairo. Nevertheless, we should not be mistaken by the cupolas' striking style and ascribe them a too early Byzantine dating. Among Egyptian wall paintings, Sinai icons or Byzantine paintings, for instance, in Cappadocia and Greece, no convincing parallels have been found to be compared to their style. So far, the only clue to the origin of this uncommon style for Egyptian paintings should probably be sought in Cyprus, where some painted cupolas and wall paintings from the fourteenth or fifteenth century could provide a few preliminary parallels.[73] For the moment a late Mamluk dating should be preferred.

A final matter to be mentioned briefly is the possibility of icon production in Egypt during the Mamluk period. Although the bulk of icons in Egypt date from the eighteenth and nineteenth century, several dozen examples of earlier pieces are known, some of which were repainted later on. Many of them display Byzantine influences and therefore may have been painted by Byzantine-trained Copts, or Byzantine artists working in Egypt, or may have been imported from abroad. This is mainly the case when it comes to icons dated from the fourteenth - sixteenth centuries. Awaiting broader studies on this subject, we prefer to keep silent on the matter of a possible icon industry in Cairo during Mamluk rule.[74]

---

[72] Dorothy Russell, *Medieval Cairo and the Monasteries of the Wadi Natrun. A Historical Guide*, London 1963, 88-89.

[73] Adeline Jeudy, "Icônes et ciboria: relations entre les ateliers de peinture d'icônes et l'iconographie du mobilier liturgique en bois", *Eastern Christian Art* 1 (2004), 67-88, on 83-86.

[74] For medieval icon production see: Skalova/Gabra, *"Icons"*, 96-119; for the collection in the Coptic Museum see: P. van Moorsel, M. Immerzeel and L. Langen, *Catalogue général du Musée Copte. The icons*, Cairo 1994.

Conclusion

There is nothing to point to any continuation of Christian art production in Bilād al-Shām after the Mamluk conquest. In several cases, dated murals, historical details, evidently Latin 'fingerprints', and stylistic elements all confirm that these paintings were made before or during the crusader presence in the Levant - even those in territories that were never occupied. Despite the severe damage done to those medieval murals that have survived, there is no evidence for any mutilation inflicted in the Mamluk period. A possible exception to this is the decoration of the Chapel of the Prophet Elijah at Maʿarrat Ṣaydnāyā, but even here, the proof is not conclusive enough to point in the direction of the Mamluks.

The situation in Egypt is somewhat different. However weakened it was, the Coptic community could still afford to provide its churches with richly adorned objects, mostly made of wood. In continuity with the earlier tradition, Coptic churches under the Mamluks were still being furnished with screens and altar cupolas, lecterns and framed icons. The progressive absorption of the Egyptian Christians into the increasingly Muslim society resulted in the adoption of a mixed decorative repertoire featured in the art of both communities. There was little renewal of the existing wall-paintings, but new screens and pieces of liturgical furniture, most of them showing a geometric decoration of inserted inlaid pieces, were commissioned. Since those pieces do not bear any indication of a precise dating, we must rely on stylistic analysis. This means that the most appropriate methodology to date these objects is to compare them with dated Islamic works which show the same patterns as those encountered on the Coptic ecclesiastical furniture. As a result, we can see that the reign of al-Nāṣir Muḥammad Ibn Qalāwūn was characterized by intensive artistic creativity, for the Muslims, as well as for the Copts, thus giving birth to new geometric patterns. Most of the Coptic works of art discussed seem to date from the first half of the fourteenth century.

The reign of al-Nāṣir was marked by persecution that put an end to the Copts' influence on Egyptian society; the last wave of Coptic artistic activity occurred in this period, after a greatly productive period from the middle of the thirteenth to the beginning of the fourteenth century (known as the 'Golden Age of Copt – Arabic thought'). This artistic activity had almost vanished by the end of the fourteenth century. In this way, it is true that we observe a strong decline of Coptic art in the late Mamluk and early Ottoman periods.[75]

75 The authors would like to express their gratitude to Maria Sherwood-Smith and Bas Snelders for their assistance. The research of Mat Immerzeel is funded by the Netherlands Organisation for Scientific Research (NWO).

Figures:

1. Map of Lebanon (by M. Immerzeel)
2. St George; Dayr Ḥammāṭūra (reconstruction M. Immerzeel)

Plates (Photographs by the authors, unless mentioned otherwise):

1. Donor; Church of Mār Tādrus, Biḥdaydāt
2. St Bacchus; Dayr Mār Mūsā
3. St Sergius; Church of St Sergius and St Bacchus, Qārah (B. ter Haar Romeny)
4. Ascension of Elijah; private collection (after Van Rijn, *Icons*, pl. on 80).
5. St George; Dayr Ḥammāṭūra
6. Virgin and Child; Chapel of the Prophet Elijah, Maᶜarrat Ṣaydnāyā (Bas ter Haar Romeny)
7. Bishop on south wall; Chapel of the Prophet Elijah, Maᶜarrat Ṣaydnāyā
8. Wall painting; Dayr Anbā Būlā
9. Detail of the geometric decoration; screen of Abū Sargā
10. Detail of the geometric decoration; screen of Ḥārat Zuwaylah
11. Detail of the door; screen of Ḥārat Zuwaylah
12. Central sanctuary screen of Al-Muᶜallaqa
13. Detail of the geometric decoration; screen of Al-Muᶜallaqa
14. Lectern from the Church of Ḥārat al-Rūm; Coptic Museum, Cairo
15. Central ciborium of Al-Muᶜallaqa

Craftsmen and Upstarts in the Late Mamluk Period

Doris Behrens-Abouseif

It is well-known that Mamluk literary sources have little to say about craftsmen and artists. The considerable biographical literature of the period hardly dedicates any attention to the craftsman's class, although some of the scholars it documents earned their living in various trades and crafts. This general lack of interest in artists and craftsmen not only concerned the low or simple crafts, but the visual arts altogether including the highly prestigious art of calligraphy. Interestingly, however, musicians and singers received more attention. Many of them figure in obituaries as celebrities who enjoyed the patronage of the Mamluk aristocracy.[1] The disregard of the craftsmen is not only symptomatic of Mamluk literature, neither is it an exclusively Islamic phenomenon; but it is rather an aspect of the traditional separation between manual and intellectual activities.

This paper presents some glimpses into the life and career of craftsmen of the late Mamluk period, based on accidental information related to the phenomenon of the craftsman as a social upstart. As the narrative element in Mamluk chronicles increases during the fifteenth century - in itself a revealing phenomenon of socio-historical significance - they provide indirectly, through narrated incidents and current events, information on the lives and status of contemporary craftsmen.

The first sultan of the Circassian period al-Ẓāhir Barqūq (784-91/1382-89) may have inaugurated a new era in the status of the Egyptian medieval craftsman when he married into a family of builders, which was something unheard of in the past. He even married twice into this family, marrying the daughter and the sister of *al-Muᶜallim* Aḥmad al-Ṭūlūnī his master-

[1] ᶜAl-Sayyid Maḥmūd, *al-Jawārī fī-mujtamaᶜ al-qāhira 'l-Mamlūkiyya*, Cairo 1988, pp. 89f.; al-Jawharī al-Ṣayrafi, *Nuzhat al-nufūs waʾl-abdān fī tawārīkh al-zamān*, 4 vols., ed. Ḥasan Ḥabashī, Cairo, 1970, I, p. 169; Ibn Iyās, *Badāʾiᶜ al-zuhūr fī waqāʾiᶜ al-duhūr,* ed. M. Muṣṭafā, Wiesbaden-Cairo, 1961-75, II, p. 346.

builder, who began his career as stone-cutter, mason and carpenter.[2] We may assume that he was already an important contractor when he was appointed chief architect or master builder to the sultan. Aḥmad is described as *muhandis* and as *kabīr al-ṣunnāᶜ*, or *kabīr al-muhandisīn,* which seems to correspond to the post of *shād al-ᶜamāʾir,* or Supervisor of the Royal Constructions that was traditionally held by a Mamluk Amir of Ten. Although Aḥmad was not given this title, his professional and private connections with the sultan opened the door to the Mamluk establishment. He was appointed Amir of Ten and began to dress as a Mamluk. Furthermore, his extraordinary career brought him considerable fame.[3]

Aḥmad is associated with the construction of the funerary *madrasa*-mosque of sultan Barqūq in Cairo[4] and with civil engineering projects in the Holy Cities and on the pilgrimage road. These tasks alone might not have earned him an obituary in the chronicles or an entry in biographical literature, however, the fact that he was a member of the Mamluk establishment and the sultan's brother and father-in-law did.

Ibn Taghrībirdī often emphasized, and deplored, the fact that posts formerly reserved for the Mamluk aristocracy were increasingly taken over by bureaucrats and even tradesmen.[5] One of these posts was that of the *shād al-ᶜamāʾir al-sulṭāniyya*, or supervisor of the royal constructions, which was taken over by a native *muᶜallim al-muᶜallimīn.* Although Aḥmad's descendants turned to the white-collar careers of scholars and bureaucrats, they continued to the end of the Mamluk period to be involved in the administration of the royal constructions as *muᶜallim al- muᶜallimīn.* In Syria the title *muᶜallim al-sulṭān* was carried by a chief master-builder operating in Damascus.

In the Mamluk period the title *muᶜallim* was used by all kinds of craftsmen, who were mostly non-Mamluks, Egyptians, Syrians and others. The Mamluk instructor of equestrian and military training in the barracks was also called *muᶜallim.* sultan Qāʾitbāy in his earlier career had been a

---

2 Al-Sakhāwī, *al-Ḍawʾ al-lāmiᶜ li-ahl al-qarn al-tāsiᶜ*, 12 vols., Cairo 1896 (reprint), I, p. 243.

3 D. Behrens-Abouseif, "*Muhandis, Shād, Muᶜallim* - Note on the Building Craft in the Mamluk Period", *Der Islam* XII/2 (1995), pp. 293-309.

4 D. Behrens-Abouseif, *Islamic Architecture in Cairo, an Introduction,* Leiden 1998, reprints Cairo; Saleh Lamei Mostafa, *Madrasa, Ḫanqāh und Mausoleum des Barqūq in Kairo (Abhandlungen des Deutschen Archäologischen Instituts, Islamische Abteilung Kairo)*, Vol IV, Glückstadt 1982.

5 Ibn Taghrībirdī, *al-Nujūm al-zāhira fi mulūk miṣr wa'l-qāhira*, 16 vols., Cairo 1963-71, XIV, p. 42, XVI, pp. 74f.

muʿallim al-rammāḥa or teacher of the lancers.[6] Signatures on artifacts by Egyptian and Syrian craftsmen often include this title.

In Ibn Taghrībirdī's terminology the term *muʿallim* had rather negative connotations. This historian was the most outspoken critic of what appeared to him an increasing social permeability that enabled craftsmen and other commoners to occupy high positions in the administrative-political establishment. He, himself the son of a Mamluk amir, attributed the decline of this period to this development.[7] To justify his discontent about the rise of riffraff and upstarts (*awbāsh wa aḥdāth*), he tells interesting stories about contemporary individuals. One of the upstarts he mentions is the *muʿallim* Muḥammad al-Bibāwī (d. 868/1463), an Upper Egyptian from a poor family who came to work in Cairo as apprentice in a butcher's shop.[8] He then set out to sell cooked food and to trade in meat and eventually became the chief meat supplier of the Mamluk barracks which made him a rich man. This opened the way for the *muʿallim* to become vizier, "the highest position in Islam after the caliphate." Another contemporary upstart was Ibn Āqbars, the owner of a shop in the amber market, who became the Supervisor of the *awqāf.* [9]

However, it is the coppersmith Abū 'l-Khayr al-Naḥḥās (d. 863/1459) who occupies pride of place in Ibn Taghībirdī's account of contemporary upstarts. Abū 'l-Khayr managed to gain the confidence of sultan Jaqmaq, who first appointed him in 851/1447 as *wakīl bayt al-māl* or secretary of the public treasury, later adding other functions to his portfolio including the supervision of the *awqāf al-ḥaramayn* or the pious endowments of Mecca and Medina, the hospital of Qalāwūn, the *khanqāh* of Saʿīd al-Suʿadāʾ founded by Ṣalāḥ al-Dīn, and of the sultan's Treasury. This of course gave him the opportunity to accumulate wealth and power. Ibn Taghrībirdī dedicates a substantial part of volume 15 of the *Nujūm,* and several passages in the *Ḥawādith,* which read like a thriller, to the extraordinary career of this person, and makes no attempt to disguise the loathing and contempt he feels towards him.[10]

---

6 Ibn Taghrībirdī, *Ḥawādith al-duhūr fī madā 'l- ayyām wa 'l-shuhūr*, ed. W. Popper, II, Berkeley 1931, III, p. 456f.

7 Ibn Taghrībirdī, *Nujūm*, XVI, p. 780ff.

8 Ibn Taghrībirdī, *Ḥawādith,* III, pp. 512f, IV, pp. 771, 780ff. The author also mentions an entry in his *al-Manhal al-Ṣāfī*, which he, however, did not include.

9 Ibn Taghrībirdī, *Nujūm,* XV, pp. 388, 397.

10 Ibn Taghribirdī, *Ḥawādith*, I, pp. 35, 49, 54, 68, 76f, 80f, 84, II, pp. 329, 392, III, pp. 408, 410-23, III, p. 658, *Nujūm*, XV, pp. 375f, 382, 395-401, 418-22, 429, 441, XVI, pp. 131, 132, 133, 210f; al-Sakhāwī, *al-Tibr al-masbūk fī dhayl al-sulūk*, Cairo n.d., pp. 141f; Ibn Iyās, II, pp. 260, 262f, 274f, 278f, 279f, 281, 285, 296, 318, 352.

Abū 'l-Khayr learned the coppersmith's craft from his father, and excelled at it. He owned a shop in the Coppersmith's Market, Sūq al-Naḥḥāsīn in the center of Cairo. However his great opportunity came after he had gone bankrupt and could no longer repay his debts. When his creditor brought his case before the sultan, Abū 'l-Khayr managed to turn the situation to his advantage by discrediting his adversary for having himself usurped funds belonging to one of the amirs. This denunciation earned him Jaqmaq's attention and confidence. He became a regular visitor to the Citadel and was increasingly involved in the sultan's administration. He began to dress like a gentleman and to ride a horse, and thus managed to climb the social ladder until he became the supreme authority (*ṣāra huwa al-ḥall wa 'l-ʿaqd*), so that even the amirs feared him.

Ibn Taghrībirdī is vague about the accusations brought against Abū 'l-Khayr; he mentions abuse, intrigue and arrogance, but it seems that the former coppersmith was caught in the midst of an insurgence of the sultan's Mamluks (*julbān*) against their master's policy, which also victimized the royal majordomus Zayn al-Dīn Yaḥyā. Abū 'l-Khayr was unpopular to the extent of provoking an unusual alliance between Mamluks and populace (*ʿāmma*), who one day rallied in the streets between Bāb Zuwayla and the Citadel Square waiting for him to show up. As he appeared they attacked him, forcing him to escape through the first door he could find which turned out to belong to the residence of Yashbak al-Khāṣikī whom he had previously denounced to the sultan. The chase continued, however, and Abū 'l-Khayr, almost beaten to death, was stripped of his clothes and mounted on a donkey, to the accompaniment of curses from the raging mob, and obliged to seek another hiding place until he could finally reach his house in the dark.

This episode notwithstanding, for a while Abū 'l-Khayr continued to enjoy the favor of the sultan – who following this incident bestowed on him a robe of honor. But the Mamluks would not give in, and plundered and burnt down his house, and demanded that the sultan exile him. Finally Jaqmaq ordered an inventory of Abū 'l-Khayr's estate and an investigation by the Shāfiʿī judge. While the confiscation of his considerable possessions was taking place, the Mamluks along with the mob who had gathered in the streets found another opportunity to catch him and beat him. Eventually he was stripped of all the positions he held and thrown in prison.

In the meantime Jaqmaq transferred his case to the Māliki judge to prosecute him for apostasy, which would have entailed a death sentence. Upon the Shāfiʿī judge's objection, however, he was acquitted of apostasy, but sentenced on other charges. After a period in jail Abū 'l-Khayr was exiled in 854/1450 to Tarsus, but it seems he was released and lived there freely, for the sultan sent orders to have him beaten and his slaves and

Mamluks there confiscated. A year later, he was back in Cairo and went to see the sultan who again sentenced him to be beaten and jailed. Ibn Taghrībirdī comments that the sultan's role in this matter was ambiguous and no one was able to decipher the confusing reports.

Eventually Abū 'l-Khayr was exiled once more, this time to the fort of Ṣubayba in Tripoli, where he was released after a while and allowed to settle in the city. In the meantime Jaqmaq died and was succeeded by sultan Īnāl, who in 863/1459 sent for Abū 'l-Khayr al-Naḥḥās to return to Cairo to be reinstated as Supervisor of the Royal Treasury and Secretary of the Public Treasury (*nāẓir al-dhakhīra 'l-sulṭāniyya* and *wakīl bayt al-māl*). Once more, the Mamluks of the *julbān* royal corps opposed this appointment and went after him to beat him. By then Abū 'l-Khayr's health was severely damaged, and he died shortly afterwards in 864/1460.

Ibn Taghrībirdī writes contemptuously of Abū 'l-Khayr's common looks and behavior: he was typical of his class, and looked like his craft, *kānat ṣifātuhu mushbiha li-ṣanʿatihi;* he was devoid of knowledge, and recited the Koran like a popular performer rather than a professional reader; his ostentatious behavior and his lavish dress contrasted with his speech, which was that of common rabble; and he maintained the appearance that he was practicing his trade in his shop. However, Ibn Iyās' report on Abū 'l-Khayr corresponds to that of Ibn Taghrībirdī, with the difference, that not being contemporary to the events, it is less emotional and lacks the virulent polemic of its predecessor. Ibn Iyās adds, however, that Abū 'l-Khayr was a very unpopular person. He refers to him as *qāḍī* Zayn al-Dīn Abū 'l-Khayr and describes him with the ambivalent words *takhallaqa bi akhlāq al-fuqahāʾ,* which can be interpreted as having adopted the demeanor of scholars. The historian adds that Abū 'l-Khayr belonged to the Koran readers who perform with melody.[11]

Abū 'l-Khayr himself wished to convey the image of being a Shāfiʿī scholar and a Sufi in the service of the sultan. In the domed mausoleum he built for himself in the cemetery he inscribed his name as Abū 'l-Khayr Muḥammad al-Ṣūfī al-Shāfiʿī *wakīl mawalānā al-maqām al-sharīf.* The mausoleum, dated 853/1449[12], was founded before he fell into disgrace under Jaqmaq's rule.

It seems therefore that while being a tradesman, Abū 'l-Khayr was able to acquire, like many other contemporaries, some kind of *madrasa* knowledge that justified his appointment in the higher bureaucracy.

---

11 Ibn Iyās, II, pp. 260, 262, 274f, 278ff, 280f, 285, 296, 318, 352, 354, 357, 379.

12 M. van Berchem, *Matériaux pour un Corpus Inscriptionum Arabicarum. (Mémoires publiés par les Membres de la Mission Archéologique Française au Caire)*, XIX/1-4, Cairo 1894-1903, p. 277f. This mausoleum was pulled down in 1977 for the construction of a new street.

Although not as virulent, Ibn Iyās was likewise displeased by the appointment of craftsmen in important administrative posts[13], as in the case of Abū 'l-Jawd. The owner of a sweetmeat shop and the son of a carpenter called *al-muʿallim* Ḥasan, he became the supervisor of the *awqāf*, a post that gave him authority to extort money from merchants and tradesmen.[14] Another *nāẓir al-awqāf* was Muḥammad Ibn al-ʿAẓama, a fur tailor, who was appointed by Qāʾitbāy to this office in April 1482, only to be dismissed in September 1484, beaten and imprisoned. Qāʾitbāy's son al-Nāṣir Muḥammad reinstated him in his position, but complaints led to his final dismissal and exile to the city of Qūṣ – of course not, before he had been thoroughly beaten up![15] The position of the *nāzir al-awqāf* had become so problematic at that time that al-Nāṣir eventually abolished it in 1496, to general satisfaction.[16]

The emergence of craftsmen and other commoners in the higher bureaucracy indicates that these individuals were at least affluent enough to join the established practice of buying their way into such offices. This may explain a late sixteenth century anonymous document on Egyptian guilds, speaking in strong polemical terms against Ottoman rule, while praising in nostalgic terms the rule of the late Mamluks, which the author viewed as a golden age for craftsmen, who at that time enjoyed great privileges.[17]

The upstarts have been mentioned in the sources as negative examples of the administrative establishment. As mere craftsmen or tradesmen, they would not be recorded even for having produced outstanding works. It is remarkable that the names of no builders or craftsmen are mentioned in connection with the mosque of sultan Ḥasan, although it was, in its own time, acknowledged as being one of the most stunning monuments of the Muslim world. In his *Khiṭaṭ* Maqrīzī mentions only one architect, the *muʿallim* al-Suyūfī, al-Nāṣir Muḥammad's chief master-builder who built the mosques and minarets of the amirs Aqbughā and al-Māridānī.[18]

---

13 Ibn Iyās mentions a villager named Ibn ʿAwaḍ who dressed and spoke like a fellah even after he ascended to a high position in the bureaucracy, which gave him access to sultan al-Ghawrī; IV, pp. 376f.

14 Ibn Iyās, IV, pp. 44f.

15 Ibn Iyās, III, pp. 192, 209, 212, 382, 446.

16 Ibn Iyās, III, p. 336.

17 D. Behrens-Abouseif, "Une Polémique Anti-Ottomane par un Artisan au Caire du XVIIe Siècle" in: *Mélange André Raymond*, IFEAD (Institut Français d'Etudes Arabes à Damas), Damas 2001, pp. 55-64.

18 Al-Maqrīzī, *Kitāb al-mawāʿiẓ wa' l-Iʿtibār bi dhikr al-khiṭaṭ wa'l-āthār,* Bulāq 1306/1889, II, p. 384.

Ibn al-Himṣī's account of the restoration of the Umayyad mosque of Damascus by Qāʾitbāy following the fire of 1479, is in many respects an exceptional case in Mamluk historiography, because of the dramatic and moving description it provides of the catastrophe that shook the entire population of Damascus, who spontaneously rose up to save their mosque. Moreover, the fact that the author mentions the names of the chief craftsmen involved in the restoration work is an unusual feature of this account.[19]

While Mamluk historians were not interested in the craftsmen's careers, they did greatly value their work. Al-Maqrīzī's description of Cairo's markets in the *Khiṭaṭ* praises their trades and crafts before the period of decline. The historians admired the buildings erected by the Mamluk aristocracy, the textiles, weapons and horse trappings displayed by the Mamluks, as well as the trousseaus of Mamluk ladies. They viewed artifacts as symbols of power, prestige and affluence, rather than as creative achievements of individuals or ateliers.

Craftsmen's signatures indicate that names of designers and workshops were significant throughout the entire Mamluk period and that they must have added to the value of the objects.[20] At the same time they demonstrate the craftsmen's pride in their work and their quest for fame, perhaps to make up for their absence among the elite in literary sources. The artist who made the famous basin known as the Baptistère de St Louis, probably in the late thirteenth century, signed his name six times on it.[21] But, unlike the decorative arts, it was not common for architects or builders in Cairo to inscribe their names on Mamluk monuments. One exception is the signature at the portal of the palace of Qawṣūn built in 738/1337;[22] another is the signature of Ibn al-Qazzāz, who built the twin minarets of the Mosque of sultan al-Muʾayyad Shaykh (1418-20) and commemorated his achievement on two cartouches above the minaret entrances.[23] Al-Maqrīzī does

19 D. Behrens-Abouseif, "The Fire of 884/1479 at the Umayyad Mosque of Damascus and an Account of its Restoration", *Mamluk Studies Review* VIII/1(2004), pp. 279-296.

20 L.A. Mayer, *Islamic Metalworkers and their Work*, Geneva 1959.

21 D.S. Rice, *The Baptistère de St Louis*, Paris 1953.

22 Ḥasan ʿAbd al-Wahhāb, "Tawqīʿāt al-ṣunnāʿ ʿalā āthā miṣr al-islāmiyya", *Bulletin de l'Institut d'Egypte* 36 (1953-54), pp. 553-58, p. 555. The craftsman's signature must refer to the remarkable muqarnas vault and not, as assumed by the author, to the rather unexceptional marble frieze above the entrance.

23 Max Van Berchem, *Matériaux pour un Corpus Inscriptionum Arabicarum. (Mémoires publiés par les Membres de la Mission Archéologique Française au Caire)*, XIX/1-4, Caire 1894-1903, p. 339.

not mention the name of Ibn al-Qazzāz although he was an eyewitness of the mosque's construction.

We also witness during the first quarter of the fifteenth century an unprecedented proliferation of craftsmen's signatures on underglaze painted pottery.[24] A few decades later, metalworker's signatures are given a prominence that is hitherto unprecedented. *Al-Muᶜallim* Maḥmūd inscribed his name in the very center of several of his highly refined vessels in the so-called "Veneto-Saracenic" style, made for export to Europe. Furthermore, as his signature he even used the form of epigraphic blazon that was traditionally reserved for the sultan's name. Maḥmūd also seems to be the author of a poem preceding his name on the rim of a bowl in the Khalili Collection.[25]

An extraordinary signature is that of ᶜAbd al-Qādir al-Naqqāsh, inscribed at the very center of the *miḥrāb* of the mosque of Qijmas al-Isḥāqī in Cairo, built in 1479. Not even the Mamluk sultans inscribed their names on *miḥrābs*.[26] Although it may be justified by the novel style of the inlaid marble created by the craftsman, the appearance of his signature here is by all traditional standards striking if not extravagant.

Also, the content of the epigraphy of late Mamluk metalwork suggests an increasing consciousness of the craftsman's value. Poetic inscriptions praising their craftsmanship and beauty are characteristics of metal vessels of this period. This praise is given in the first person. One of the most widespread texts reads: "[He] who contemplates my beauty will find in me leisure for the eye, my looks are full of good meanings". The notion of meanings (*maᶜānī)* reveals a kind of intellectual ambition. Some of these inscriptions seem to have been compiled by the craftsmen themselves.

The diverse features presented here, which still need further investigation and research, suggest that under the rule of the Circassian sultans entry into Mamluk society could be gained more easily by other social groups than had previously been the case.

The late Mamluk period is sometimes indiscriminately characterized by its own historians as one of decline, in which corruption reaches such proportions as to allow unqualified persons to purchase high administrative posts, and to exploit them to the detriment of others. Although the upstarts are always accused by the chroniclers of abusing their position to make a profit at the expense of others, another aspect of this development was

---

24 E. Gibbs, "Mamluk Ceramics 648-923/1250-1517", *Transactions of the Oriental Ceramic Society,* Vol. 63 (1998-1999), pp. 19-44.

25 D. Behrens-Abouseif, "Veneto-Saracenic Metalware, a Mamluk Art", *Mamluk Studies Review* IX/2 (2005), pp. 147-172.

26 D. Behrens-Abouseif, *Introduction*, p. 151.

the creation of unprecedented opportunities for lower social groups to fill gaps which the Mamluk establishment could not. The continuous Mamluk patronage of educational institutions enabled individuals of modest background to join the educated class and hence climb the social ladder, making fortunes and gaining power. Even those who did not join the elite, but were content to remain in the craftsmen's milieu were able to emphasize their own status and prestige.

Writings on the Wall: Mamluk Monuments of Tripoli

HOWAYDA AL-HARITHY

The central role played by Arabic inscriptions employed on monuments and objects of the various historical periods of Muslim rule has long been acknowledged. Numerous volumes have been published documenting and classifying inscriptions. These in turn have paved the way for more analytical and theoretical studies. For a long time, however, the widespread use of Arabic inscriptions on artefacts was addressed as a general phenomenon, for which an equally universal explanation was given. Ettinghausen argued that it is not the reading of the inscriptions that is the essence of their employment on art objects, but their overall presence that endows the item with official and religious status: "Readability was only a secondary concern. The Gestalt of the inscription as a whole and the inclusion of the caliph's name were the essential elements. It was this aspect which made the garment a symbol of the public recognition of the official by the ruler."[1] Dodd argued that due to the ban on figural imagery the word came to replace the image in the symbolism of art of the Muslim world.[2] It is only in more recent studies, such as Bierman's *Writing Signs. Fatimid Public Text*,[3] that the specifics of style

Author's note: This paper was presented at the conference entitled *Towards a Cultural History of Bilād al-Shām in the Mamlūk Era*, organized by the Orient Institute and Balamand University, held in Beirut and Tripoli, May 4-7, 2005. When I was asked to present my research on Mamlūk Tripoli, I modified the earlier text published in *Arabic Calligraphy in Architecture: Islamic Monuments Inscriptions in the City of Tripoli during the Mamluk Period,* ed. Amin el-Bizri (Beirut, 1999): 151-157. This is an illustrated and modified version of the text which expands the classification of inscriptions from five to six categories that now include the more rarely found inscriptions containing royal decrees.

1 R. Ettinghausen, "Arabic Epigraphy: Communication or Symbolic Affirmation," in *Near Eastern Numismatics, Iconography, Epigraphy, and History. Studies in Honor of George C. Miles*, ed. Dickran K. Kouymjian (Beirut, 1974): 304.

2 Dodd, E. C. and Khairallah, S., *The Image of the Word* (Beirut, 1981).

3 Bierman, I. A., *Writing Signs. The Fatimid Public Text* (University of California Press, 1998).

and content of inscriptions are addressed against the particularities of the period to which they belong; thus what makes distinct their nature. It is the intention of this paper to investigate the role served by Arabic inscriptions as employed on the façades of Mamluk buildings in the urban context of Tripoli. In particular, I will focus on their role in projecting the self-image of the patrons and conveying their socio-political messages.

By the time the Mamluks rose to power in 1260, the use of architectural inscriptions had become a traditional form of visual communication. Though the use of inscriptions on buildings dates back to the first monument of Islam, the Dome of the Rock (691), the roots for the Mamluk practice lie in the Fatimid tradition in Cairo[4] and its interpretation by the Ayyubids after them. The Fatimids in Cairo revolutionized the use of inscriptions. They introduced inscriptions on the exterior façade, to which they assign a primary urban role and made public their Ismaʿili religious doctrine and political legitimacy. This is the tradition that the Ayyubids, and the Mamluks after them, had to appropriate and utilize to their advantage as a military-political power that established itself in opposition to the Fatimid caliphate. The façades of major monuments became the context for self-projection. Though they sustained the use of inscriptions as public text with a political agenda they departed from the Fatimid tradition in style and content. They adopted the *naskhi*, as opposed to the Fatimid kufic script, and advertised themselves as defenders of the faith, as opposed to the descendants of the *ahl al-bayt* that the Fatimids were, a point to which I will come back later.

It is against this background that I will investigate the particular case of inscriptions in Mamluk Tripoli. It is the Mamluk interpretation of such a tradition in Cairo that was the source of the practice found in Tripoli. In this paper, I will argue that the inscriptions on Mamluk monuments were neither reduced to a purely visual form of art as Ettinghausen claimed, nor were they simply religious text that replaced figural imagery. Rather, such inscriptions played a dual role: visual and textual, in which multiple systems of signification were in operation. To illustrate this, I will apply Panofsky's iconology or method of investigating meaning. According to Panofsky's model, these monumental inscriptions can be interpreted at several levels. The first is the primary or natural subject matter, which is simply the identification of the pure form and one which he describes as a pre-iconographical description.

At this formal level Mamluk inscriptions are presented either as bands or as panels. The band, referred to as *ṭirāz*,[5] usually runs horizontally the

[4] For the discussion on Fatimid inscriptions see Bierman, I. A., *Writing Signs. The Fatimid Public Text* (University of California Press, 1998).

[5] *Ṭirāz* is a term borrowed from the textile industry.

length of the façade, or part of it. A survey of the monuments in Tripoli indicates that the *ṭirāz* band extensively used in Mamluk buildings in Cairo and Damascus is not as commonly found in Tripoli. The Saqraqiyya Madrasa (1359) renders one such rare example in Tripoli (Figs.1a and b). The *ṭirāz* bands are rather limited to running the sides of the recess of the portal. The text is mostly inscribed on panels, carved on marble and inserted into the wall, or carved directly onto the construction material, which is usually of stone. They are located in the most visually prominent areas. The main façade, especially the portal recess, is the focal point around which the inscriptions are concentrated (Figs. 2a and b).

Mamluk inscriptions are stylistically sober. The *naskhi*, the most commonly used script, is highly legible and hardly ornamented.[6] Examples from the Great Mosque (1294) and the ᶜAjamiyya Madrasa (1365) are testimony (Figs. 3a and b). The aesthetic role of inscriptions was not one that adhered to their decorative visual play, but was rather limited to the *ṭirāz,* or the panel, as an element of architectural composition of the façade. Its width, level and general proportions were in response to the façade, as a composition, and in response to their urban setting. This sobriety and style of script is characteristic of the Mamluk period and not peculiar to architecture. The Mamluks relied heavily on epigraphic designs in their portable arts as well. The evolution in their art indicates a change of taste with a growing preference for epigraphic designs as they gradually dominated figural and vegetal motifs. Under Mamluk patronage calligraphy flourished as it was applied across media, starting with manuscripts to metalwork, textile, and glassware. This was due to the high demand and level of production as the Mamluks sponsored thousands of art objects to be sent as gifts, to decorate buildings or to be used in their elaborate ceremonies. In such production, two monumental scripts, the *thuluth* and *muhaqqaq,* were heavily employed on royal and ceremonial objects, thus reaching a climax during the fourteenth century. While the *muhaqqaq* was used in Qurʾans the *thuluth* was used on buildings, as well as portable objects.

The kufic scripts played a secondary role and one that is mostly decorative. The ornate kufic characteristic of Fatimid inscriptions fell out of favour and was rarely used. One example is found on the tympanum of the inner portal of Jāmiᶜ Ṭaynāl (1336) (Figs. 4a and b). Of the kufic scripts, the square kufic was better favoured during the Mamluk period and was widely used in religious institutions in Cairo. It is one of the types or variations of the geometric kufic, which flourished and spread widely in Iran

6 Perhaps the earliest known monumental use of the cursive script is found at the Great Mosque at Qazwin dating back to the twelfth century.

and Iraq under the Seljuks, beginning in the twelfth century. This type of script was transferred into Egypt during the Mamluk period, i.e., in the second half of the thirteenth century. Its first recorded appearance is in the Mausoleum of Qalāwūn attached to his madrasa complex on al-Muᶜizz Street in Cairo (1284-85). Examples in Tripoli are found in the recess of the portals of Jāmiᶜ Ṭaynāl (1336) and the Madrasa-Mosque of al-Burṭāsī (c. 1324) (Figs. 5a and b). They contained typical religious declarations, such as the *shahāda* or the names of God, Muḥammad or the caliphs. Their use was primarily decorative as they formed part of the visual effect of the polychrome marble panels that featured geometric designs composed to articulate wall surfaces.

The second level is an iconographical one. It is the conventional or secondary subject matter described by Panofsky as the ability to read the conventional references of the art form. The process of signification here is one of denotation. According to the general practice, inscriptions at this level and as a written text, Qurʾanic or otherwise, are simply selected or composed to denote aspects pertaining to the function, the history or the patronage of the building. For example, in the Bīmāristān of Nūr-al-Dīn in Damascus the Qurʾanic verses selected make references to healing, both spiritual and physical. "Who created me, and Himself guides me, and Himself gives me to eat and drink, and, whenever I am sick, heals me."[7]

As for the inscriptions found in Mamluk Tripoli, they can be divided according to their conventional subject matter into the following major categories:

1. Qurʾanic text: It is the most commonly inscribed text. An example is the Qurʾanic verses from Sūrat al-Hijr, 15.45-47, inscribed on the lintel above the entrance to the al-Qarṭāwiyya Madrasa (1316-26) (Figs. 6a and b). It is a verse often employed in religious structures signifying the rewards promised to pious individuals: "The God-fearing shall be amidst gardens and fountains. Enter you thee, in peace and security. We shall strip away all rancour that is in their breast; as brothers they shall be upon couches set face to face."[8] Another verse carrying a similar reward message that quotes from Sūrat al-Dukhkhān 55:51-54 is inscribed above the windows of the ᶜAjamiyya Madrasa: "Surely the God-fearing shall be in a station secure among gardens and fountains, robed in silk and brocade, set face to face. Even so and we shall espouse them to wide-eyed houris."[9]

---

[7] Dodd, E. C. and Khairallah, S., *The Image of the Word* (Beirut, 1981): 39.

[8] Salam-Liebich, H. *The Architecture of the Mamluk City of Tripoli* (Cambridge, MA, 1983): 111.

[9] Ibid.: 143.

2. Legal text of the *waqf:* An example is found in the Khātūniyya Madrasa (1373-74) (Figs. 7a and b). "In the name of God the Merciful, the Compassionate, Glory to Allah, God of the Universe and may God bless our Lord Muḥammad, our master has built this blessed place, the very noble, high Excellency, the master, the well served, the governor ᶜIzz al-Dīn Aydamīr al-Ashrafī, our master king of the princes, may God fortify his victories in concert with his noble wife, the well-guarded Lady Arghūn, may God protect her with His mercy, according to the will previously prepared by her. She has constituted as waqf: the entire qayṣariyyah known as Duhaysha and the establishment of the silk weavers, and the nine shops and stores to the outside of it and known after it- and the store to the outside of the qiblah wall attached to it...."[10]

3. Foundation inscriptions: Generally a text that records the name of the founder, the function of the edifice and the date of construction. The foundation inscription on the portal of the Great Mosque, founded in 1294 by al-Ashraf Khalīl ibn Qalāwūn (Figs. 8a and b), follows a standard formula for foundation inscriptions and reads as follows: "In the name of God the Merciful, the Compassionate, our master the most powerful sultan, lord of Arab and Persian kings, conqueror of the frontiers and exterminator of the infidels, al-Malik al-Ashraf Ṣalāḥ al-Dunyā wa'l-Dīn Khalīl, the associate of the commander of the faithful, son of our master al-Sulṭān al-Malik al-Manṣūr Sayf al-Dunyā wa'l-Dīn Qalāʾūn al-Ṣaliḥī, may God perpetuate his reign, has ordered the construction of this sacred mosque [jamiᶜ], during the governorship of His High Excellency the great Amir al-ᶜIzzī ᶜIzz al-Dīn Aybak al-Khazandār [the treasurer] al-Ashrafī al-Manṣūrī, governor of the sultanate in the conquered lands and protected shores, may God forgive him. In the year six hundred and ninety-three [A.D. 1294]. Glory to the One and Only."[11]

4. Sultanic emblems: An example is found in the al-Nāṣiriyya Madrasa (1354-1360) (Figs. 9a and b) in the medallion above the door of the main portal. "Glory to our Lord Sultan al-Malik al-Nāṣir Ḥasan bin Muḥammad."[12]

5. Signature of artists: A less commonly inscribed text. An early Mamluk example is found in Jāmiᶜ al-ᶜAṭṭār (1350) (Figs. 10a and b) and located on the visually prominent location which normally contains the foundation inscription, the main portal. The inscription mentions the name of the architect responsible for it: "This is the work of Abū Bakr al-Baṣīṣ, may God have mercy on him."[13]

---

10 Ibid.: 147.

11 Ibid.: 18.

12 Ibid.: 132.

13 Ibid.: 71.

6. Royal decrees: These are the rarest of inscriptions. Several examples are, however, found on the façade of the Qarṭāwiyya Madrasa (1316-26), which is adjacent to the Great Mosque and leads to one of its eastern entrance (Figs. 11a and b). One of the royal decrees reads as follows: "Praise be to God on the date of the twentieth of the month of God al-Muharram al-haram the year eight hundred and ninety-eight the honourable decree was declared by his excellency the royal sultan al-mawlawy al-ashrafy al-saify abou al-Nasir Kaitbay praise him God, honour him, and increase his future power, and empower him to cancel the taxes on silk and meat in al-Kahif and al-Kadmous, and the taxes on butchery of all cattle in Kadmous and al-Khawaby due to the honourable decrees released that are usually always subject to change, from the people of al-Kahif, al-Khawaby, and al-Kadmous on the ninth of the glorious month of Ramadan the year eight hundred and eighty-eight."[14]

The third of Panofsky's layers is the intrinsic meaning, or content, the reading of which is meant to reveal references to the ideologies of the people who produced the work of art.[15] The process of signification here is one of connotation. Therefore, the intrinsic meaning of Mamluk inscriptions will be interpreted against the socio-economic and political context of their own time. At this iconographical level, many layers can be found.

As a textual system of signification, the written texts communicate meaning in various ways. They operate both as icons and as narratives, whether by displaying the name of a patron in a medallion or by telling the story of the foundation, in which the name of the patron appears framed by titles, honorific and eulogies. Titles such as the king, the victorious, conqueror of the frontier, and the associate of the commander of the faithful, are all operative references in the projection of a very particular self-image. They make references to the conquest of territories and the victory over enemies such as the Mongols and the Crusades on the one hand, and to the alliance with the Abbasid caliph, whom the Mamluks reinstated in Cairo after the sack of Baghdad, on the other. Therefore, they connote both military power and political legitimacy. Evidence for the significance of displaying the name of a patron in such a context is the practice of replacing the name of one patron with another. For example, the name of al-Nāṣir Muḥammad ibn Qalāwūn replaced that of Kitbughā on a building he erected on al-Muᶜizz Street next to Qalāwūn's complex in Cairo, after

[14] El-Bizri, Amin (ed.) *Arabic Calligraphy in Architecture: Islamic Monuments Inscriptions in the City of Tripoli during the Mamluk Period* (Beirut, 1999): 132, Arabic part.

[15] Panofsky, I. *Meaning in the Visual Arts* (New York, 1974): 28-30.

it was appropriated, completed and came to be known as al-Madrasa al-Nāṣiriyya.[16]

The *waqf* text also contributes significantly to the construction of the self-image projected. While the foundation inscription carries political connotations, the *waqf* text carries economic and religious ones. It makes clear and concrete references to the wealth of the patrons but, more importantly, to their pious intentions and good deeds, and thus the projection of a militarily powerful, politically legitimate and religiously pious image for sultans and amirs. This was an image that was necessary to reiterate on façades especially given the short, and at times unstable, rule of Mamluk commanders, keeping in mind that such text was only a small part of a more elaborate public program advertising and projecting such an image of the patron. This went hand in hand with the oral tradition that also ensured the mention of the patron's name, titles and accomplishments after reciting the Qurʾan, for which they assigned readers in these institutions, after the call to prayers and during public ceremonies.

Inscribing royal decrees on the walls of buildings is of extreme significance. This is official text inscribed on walls of existing buildings. Unlike medallions, foundation inscriptions and *waqf* text, the official text is not directly linked to the building, its patron or endowment. It is applied to existing buildings and not conceived as part of their initial design. The examples found on the Qarṭāwiyya Madrasa (1316-26) were issued by different authors and inscribed on different dates (1423, 1442, 1483 and 1504). These examples are therefore the strongest evidence that inscriptions were meant to be read and to deliver a message.

It must be noted here that this reading of the content of inscriptions applies for the most part to monuments built under the patronage of sultans. The emphasis on the economic, religious or political message shifted according to the status of the patron and the urban context to which the buildings belong. This is particularly clear when comparing monuments built by sultans to those built by members of their family. It is also clear when Mamluk monuments in Tripoli are compared to their counterparts in Cairo. In fact, in Cairo, the capital of the Mamluks, the *waqf* inscriptions take a marginal role and the emphasis is more on the politically charged references, while the opposite is true for the port city, Tripoli.

---

16 This is a practice that goes back to the Abbasid era. The name of the original Umayyad patron of the Dome of the Rock, Caliph ʿAbd al-Malik, was replaced by that of the Abbasid Caliph al-Maʾmūn upon his restoration of the building. See R. Ettinghausen, "Arabic Epigraphy: Communication or Symbolic Affirmation," in *Near Eastern Numismatics, Iconography, Epigraphy, and History. Studies in Honor of George C. Miles*, ed. Dickran K. Kouymjian (Beirut, 1974): 311.

As a visual sign system, the display of the Arabic script is in itself a signifier of utter importance. The Mamluks, having been recruited as young slave soldiers and new converts into Islam, had little ties with the Arabic culture of their subjects, and had little basis for their legitimacy as leaders of the Muslim community. The Arabic text does not only carry religious connotations but deeper cultural ones too. Its employment signifies the Mamluks' commitment to both Islamic religion and Arabic culture, and thus acts as a bridge of alliance with the general public. It might be argued that it is a form of laying claim over a cultural symbol such as the Arabic language that most Mamluks did not speak in order to overcome their alien status. The inscriptions can therefore be read as a system of appropriation of the most distinguished and rich cultural products. Specific to Tripoli, the Arabic script, which came to be associated with Islamic rule, further connotes an identity of Muslim authority over new territory.

To conclude, Mamluk inscriptions as applied to religious monuments were quite distinct when compared to other traditions. Inscriptions were not entered into part of an elaborate decorative program inclusive of geometric and vegetal designs such as those found in Timurid architecture, nor was their content limited to Qur'anic verses with religious connotations such as those found in Abbasid monuments. They are visually prominent, textually legible and stylistically sober. Set within façades articulated to give them a plain surface against which they operate as a means of communication, primarily as text. Mamluk inscriptions were politically charged and were most definitely intended to be read.

Part Three

Fields of Cultural Production: Historical Literature

The Chronicle of Ibn Iyās as a Source for Social and Cultural History from Below[1]

Axel Havemann

In the past fifteen years Mamluk studies have flourished and are now more popular than ever. This is particularly true with regard to politics and political history, as well as to Mamluk historiography and archival sources, scholarship and religion, art and architecture. Issues related to economic development have also been thoroughly investigated, based on a wide range of source material such as endowment deeds, inscriptions and coins.[2]

However, what has been studied to a much lesser extent are sciences, literature (*belles-lettres*), social and cultural history, daily and popular culture. As for the last two subjects it must be noted that despite some basic works on social strata in Mamluk cities[3], on popular preaching and veneration of saints[4], and on the issue of poverty, including banditry and other illegal activities[5], we know little about lower and marginal (or marginal-

1 The following article presents some preliminary results as part of a larger project under preparation: "Marginal Groups in Late Medieval Islam. A History of Daily Life between Social Hierarchy and Mobility".

2 For a survey of the state of the art (until 2002), see Stephan Conermann, "Es boomt! Die Mamlūkenforschung (1992-2002)", in: *Die Mamlūken. Studien zu ihrer Geschichte und Kultur. Zum Gedenken an Ulrich Haarmann (1942-1999)*, eds. Stephan Conermann, Anja Pistor-Hatam, Schenefeld: EB-Verlag 2003, 1-68.

3 Ira M. Lapidus, *Muslim Cities in the Later Middle Ages*, Cambridge (Mass.): Harvard University Press 1967; with a quite different approach: Michael Chamberlain, *Knowledge and Social Practice in Medieval Damascus, 1190-1315*, Cambridge: Cambridge University Press 1992; Jonathan P. Berkey, *The Transmission of Knowledge in Medieval Cairo: A Social History of Islamic Education*, Princeton: Princeton University Press 1992.

4 Jonathan P. Berkey, *Popular Preaching and Religious Authority in the Medieval Islamic Near East*, Seattle: University of Washington Press 2001; Christopher S. Taylor, *In the Vicinity of the Righteous: Ziyāra and the Veneration of Muslim Saints in Late Medieval Egypt*, Leiden: Brill 1999; Th. Emil Homerin, *From Arab Poet to Muslim Saint. Ibn al-Fāriḍ, His Verse, and His Shrine*, Columbia (South Carolina): University of South Carolina Press 1994.

5 Adam Sabra, *Poverty and Charity in Medieval Islam. Mamluk Egypt, 1250-1517*, Cambridge: Cambridge University Press 2000.

ized) groups of urban society, and almost nothing about rural and nomadic life[6]. This lack of knowledge is partly due to the scarcity of informations in primary sources, but also to the simple fact that such subjects have mostly been neglected by research which preferably focuses on 'high culture' (whatever this term may include or exclude[7]). A re-reading of the sources available from Mamluk times utilizing another approach, namely popular history (history from below), may shed some new light on issues which so far are largely unknown.

For this purpose historical works that were so abundantly produced in Mamluk culture can be used as a promising genre of sources. The present article will focus on the chronicle of Ibn Iyās, *Badāʾiʿ al-zuhūr fī waqāʾiʿ al-duhūr*, strictly speaking on those parts of the work dealing with the period of which Ibn Iyās was an eyewitness observer (the years 872-928/1467-1522). The author lived in Cairo during the last decades of Mamluk rule and well into the time of their Ottoman successors (852/1448 to ca. 930/1524).[8] Much like Ibn Taghrī Birdī (ca. 812/1409-10 to 874/1470)[9], his predecessor as Mamluk historian, Ibn Iyās was a member of *awlād al-nās* which was a regiment made up of sons of Mamluk amirs. Because of his lower social standing than Ibn Taghri Birdi and that he had less personal access to court life and high politics, Ibn Iyās is particularly interesting and informative as a mouthpiece of the medium strata of society. However, he also reports many details from the daily lives of the lower classes: amusing events as

---

6 On peasants and nomads in Mamluk times, see J.-C. Garcin, "La 'méditerranéisation' de l'empire mamlouk sous les sultans baḥrides", *Rivista degli studi orientali* 48 (1973-74), 109-16; J.-C. Garcin, "Notes sur les rapports entre bédouins et fallahs à l'époque mamluke", *Annales Islamologiques* 14 (1978), 147-63; Carl F. Petry, "Disruptive 'Others' as Depicted in Chronicles of the Late Mamlūk Period", in: *The Historiography of Islamic Egypt (c. 950-1800)*, ed. Hugh Kennedy, Leiden: Brill 2001, 167-94, here: 170-80.

7 For the contested terms 'high culture' and 'low culture' (popular culture) – and their overlapping or even incompatibility, see Boaz Shoshan, "High Culture and Popular Culture in Medieval Islam", *Studia Islamica* 73 (1991), 67-108; Stefan Leder, "Postklassisch und vormodern: Beobachtungen zum Kulturwandel in der Mamlūkenzeit", in: *Die Mamlūken. Studien zu ihrer Geschichte und Kultur. Zum Gedenken an Ulrich Haarmann (1942-1999)*, eds. Stephan Conermann, Anja Pistor-Hatam, Schenefeld: EB-Verlag 2003, 289-312; with regard to Europe, see Peter Burke, "Popular Culture Reconsidered", in: *Mensch und Objekt im Mittelalter und in der frühen Neuzeit. Leben, Alltag, Kultur*, ed. Gerhard Jaritz, Wien: Österreichische Akademie der Wissenschaften 1990, 181-91.

8 W. M. Brinner, art. "Ibn Iyās", in: *The Encyclopaedia of Islam*, new ed., vol. 3, Leiden: Brill 1971, 812-13.

9 W. Popper, art. "Abu'l-Maḥāsin ... B. Taghrībirdī, in: *The Encyclopaedia of Islam*, new ed., vol. 1, Leiden: Brill 1960, 138.

well as scandals, robberies, and misfortunes.[10] His notes, a kind of journal, are filled with sensations and are mostly narrated in a quite entertaining manner that is often written in non-classical Arabic. They reveal a lot about common people's behaviour and daily life in general. By extracting such information from a work of historiography one may gain some insight into a neglected but fascinating field of research which is part of the cultural and popular history of the medieval Islamic world.

The few examples chosen from Ibn Iyās' daily notes refer to criminal acts committed by civilian people[11] – individuals or groups not belonging to the Mamluk caste (among them the ill-famed *zuʿar/ zuʿʿār*[12] who were somehow connected with the ideology, or more precisely, ideologies of *futuwwa* and *futuwwa* groups[13]). These criminal acts include murders, thefts, and robberies, sexual affairs ranging from adultery to professional prostitution and pederasty, witchcraft and blasphemy. The second component of the account are amusing events, small scandals and sensations from the world of the common people. Some of them are not considered as really criminal though sometimes they are nearly so. Others are simply funny and fantastic. The third aspect consist of stories about beggars with different intentions: be it that they were forced to beg out of misery or because they considered poverty a religious ideal (as holds true for many pious men: *ṣūfīs*). Others may have simply pretended to be poor and weak; in other words, professional beggars who were often associated with violence and combativeness – the able-bodied beggars (*...arāfīsh*) who were sometimes also used as manual labourers or as auxiliary troops.[14]

10 Insofar Ibn Iyās was rather exceptional and quite different from Ibn Taghrī Birdī, let alone al-Maqrīzī (ca. 766/1364-845/1442), who both were only marginally interested in the life of the common people; see Irmeli Perho, "Al-Maqrīzī and Ibn Taghrī Birdī as Historians of Contemporary Egypt", in: *The Historiography of Islamic Egypt (c. 950-1800)*, ed. Hugh Kennedy, Leiden: Brill 2001, 107-20.

11 The following remarks draw partly on Petry, "Disruptive Others", 167-94; for crimes committed by civilians and their punishment through the Mamluk authorities, see also Carl F. Petry, "'Quis Custodiet Custodes?' Revisited: The Prosecution of Crime in the Late Mamluk Sultanate", *Mamlūk Studies Review* 3 (1999), 13-30; M. Espérionner, "La mort violente à l'époque mamlouke: Le crime et le châtiment", *Der Islam* 74 (1997), 137-55.

12 There are also various other forms, such as *dhuʿʿār* (rascal, scoundrel); see Th. Bianquis, art. "zuʿʿār", in: *The Encyclopaedia of Islam*, new ed., vol. 11, Leiden: Brill 2002, 546-47; Lapidus, Muslim Cities, 153-64, 173-77.

13 Axel Havemann, "Männerbünde im islamischen Orient: Soziale Bewegungen in Iran, Irak und Syrien", in: *Geregeltes Ungestüm. Bruderschaften und Jugendbünde bei indogermanischen Völkern*, eds. Rahul Peter Das, Gerhard Meiser, Bremen: Hempen Verlag 2002, 68-90.

14 William M. Brinner, "The Significance of the „arāfīsh" and their 'Sultan'", *Journal of the Economic and Social History of the Orient* 6 (1963), 190-215; see also Lapidus, *Muslim Cities*, 177-83.

During the month of Shawwāl in 879 (February-March 1475), Ibn Iyās describes the execution of a Circassian slave woman in Cairo. She had become pregnant from a Mamluk recruit and then killed her new-born baby for fear of the Sultan's anger. The Sultan (i.e., Qāʾitbāy) ordered her death by hanging and at first also intended to execute the recruit by drowning: "but it was said that he commanded his castration and exile to Syria."[15] Qāʾitbāy regarded himself as a pious defender of morality who strictly enforced penalties for sexual offences. The woman's death was predictable, but the amnesty of the Sultan towards the man revealed the priority enjoyed by males in sexual affairs.

In another case Ibn Iyās describes sexual infidelity committed by slaves and their partners. On Saturday the ninth of Jumādā II, 921 (21 July 1515), the Sultan (i.e., Qānṣūh al-Ghawrī) ordered four persons hanged: a white female slave of Anatolian origin (*rūmiyya*), a female slave from Ethiopia (*ḥabashiyya*), a young son of a notable (from "turbaned people", *nās laffāf*) and a bow maker. The reason for this was that the two men had fornicated with the two slave women and then urged them to assassinate their master, a son of a Mamluk (*min awlād al-nās*). After murdering him and throwing his body into a latrine, the women stole everything in his house. Only five months later their crime was discovered; they were apprehended and, upon interrogation, confessed their acts. After investigating the case and finding the putrid corpse, the Sultan ordered its burial and then sentenced the four perpetrators to be hanged in public. On the day of their execution, all of Cairo witnessed it.[16]

While in both of these incidents the male victims belonged to the Mamluk elite, in several other cases the victims were prominent civilians. It seems, however, that in general the act of murder committed by slaves, especially slave women with the implication of sexual offence against members of upper social strata, clearly outranked the number of cases where no slaves were involved. On the other hand, Ibn Iyās reports several instances of murder within families – even cases of mutilation.[17] Again, all of the female perpetrators were slaves.

Furthermore, it appears that the frequency of theft linked to murder was often of secondary importance. However, there are striking exceptions where thievery went hand in hand with killing and, of course, numerous cases of thefts and robberies without murdering the victims. One intrigu-

15 Ibn Iyās: *Badāʾiʾ al-zuhūr fi waqāʾiʾ al-duhūr*, vol. 3, 104-5 (ed. Muḥammad Muṣṭafā, Kairo: Franz Steiner Wiesbaden 1960ff., 2nd. ed.).

16 Ibid., vol. 4, 461.

17 Ibid., vol. 3, 198; vol. 4, 129, 160.

ing story involves the murder of prostitutes followed by robbing them of their possessions. A certain man described as a peculiar bachelor living in a shabby shack bestowed gifts upon a woman among 'the daughters of sin' and her mother. He provided them with expensive clothes and jewels, supplied them abundantly with wine and incited them to illicit behaviour. Then, he strangled them, stole what they had gained (from their customers) and escaped. After eight days the two murdered women were found naked among wine vessels and rumpled bed sheets. The prefect ordered them buried and investigated the case. It was rumoured some days later that a group selling the victims' stolen effects had been arrested. But nobody cared to track down the man who committed the crimes.[18] Apparently the authorities were indifferent to matters of prostitution which was acknowledged as ubiquitous in society; if its practitioners turned on each other, no threat was posed to the social order.[19]

In general, the authorities prosecuted thievery according to the status of its victims rather than the extent of their losses. They reacted most harshly to their own property losses. Ibn Iyās reports several incidents of theft from the royal treasury.[20] Two other incidents that he refers to are violations of holy shrines. Individuals disguised as mendicant Sufis stole the screens surrounding the tombs of revered Muslim saints at the Qarāfa cemetery of Cairo (872/1468 and 889/1484).[21] In all cases, the thieves were searched for, finally arrested and punished in public: by execution, by flogging or by cutting off their hands.

A full picture is given, both by Ibn Iyās and other chroniclers, to eruptions of mob violence. Riots of street gangs (*zuʿar*) and black slaves (*ʿabīd*) were depicted as paralyzing entire districts of Cairo.[22] In this context the sources sometimes indicate collusions between senior officers and civilian gangs. In his report on two *zuʿar* bands fighting each other during Jumādā II 913 (October-November 1507), Ibn Iyās states that the Sultan refused to intervene because each group claimed protection from high military figures

18 This story is not from Ibn Iyās but reported by his contemporary al-Ṣayrafī; see Petry, "Disruptive Others", 184-85.

19 On prostitution in Mamluk times, see Aḥmad ʿAbd ar-Rāziq: *La femme au temps des Mamlouks en Égypte*, Cairo: Institut français d'archéologie orientale du Caire 1973, 45-48; Robert Irwin, "ʿAlī al-Baghdādī and the Joy of Mamluk Sex", in: *The Historiography of Islamic Egypt (c. 950-1800)*, ed. Hugh Kennedy, Leiden: Brill 2001, 45-57; ibid., *Die Welt von Tausendundeiner Nacht*, Frankfurt: Insel Verlag 1997, 215-16.

20 Ibn Iyās: *Badāʾiʿ al-zuhūr*, vol. 3, 110, 115; vol. 4, 126, 130, 181.

21 Ibid., vol. 3, 17, 205.

22 Ibid., vol. 3, 240, 274; vol. 4, 96, 163.

– powerful adjutants whose support the Sultan could not risk to lose.[23]

We have two reports on pederasty[24] which underline Ibn Iyās' appetite for immoral and scandalous stories. In the first case that occurred in Ṣafar of 879 (June-July 1476), a former official belonging to a Mamluk amir's staff was accused of repeated sexual contact with youthful trainees in the amir's service. He seems to have opted for castration, possibly to escape execution. The operation was performed by a Jewish surgeon famous for his expertise. In fact, the official survived to live a long life, probably relieved of his sexual desires.[25] The second incident, in Rabīᶜ II of 920 (May-June 1514), refers to a tailor who violated (i.e., *raped*) a ten-year old boy. When the latter screamed for help, the tailor strangled him and threw the body into a well. After the boy's mother discovered what had happened to her son, she denounced the tailor before the Sultan. Upon confessing his crime, the tailor was hanged at the place where he had violated the victim. Presumably, the Sultan had ordered his castration in advance.[26] It may be surprising that only two cases of pederasty were reported by Ibn Iyās, and even more surprising that only one of the perpetrators was executed. However, this does not necessarily indicate the rarity of such crimes but instead it illustrates that a death sentence was rarely imposed for committing pederasty.[27] Similar conclusions have been drawn with regard to the study of *ḥanafī* court records in south-eastern Anatolia, namely in the city of ᶜAynṭāb in 1540/41.[28] For Ibn Iyās it was obviously the sensational appeal of the two cases which attracted his attention.

During the month of Shaᶜbān in 911 (December-January 1505/06), our chronicler reported a case of sorcery and blasphemy (or heresy). A dervish from Upper Egypt with the name of Mahdī came to Cairo. Rumours cir-

23 Ibid., vol. 4, 122-23.

24 For this issue, see the recent and well-balanced study by Khaled el-Rouayheb: *Before Homosexuality in the Arab-Islamic World, 1500-1800*, Chicago: The University of Chicago Press 2005. Although this book focuses on the Ottomans' times, many of the points made are also valid for the Arab-Islamic world in earlier (Abbasid and Mamluk) periods. Examples of homoeroticism during Mamluk times in Everett K. Rowson, "Two Homoerotic Narratives from Mamluk literature: al-Ṣafadī's Lawᶜat al-shākī and Ibn Dāniyāl's al-Mutayyam", in: *Homoeroticism in Classical Arabic Literature*, eds. E. K. Rowson, J. W. Wright, New York: Columbia University Press 1997, 157-98.

25 Ibid., vol. 3, 96.

26 Ibid., vol. 4, 378.

27 El-Rouyaheb, *Homosexuality*, 118-28, 136-39.

28 Leslie Peirce, *Morality Tales. Law and Gender in the Ottoman Court of Aintab*, Berkeley: University of California Press 2003, 358-60.

culated that this man used to act in a way that offended the *sharīʿa*. When he was brought to the court of the Sultan, it was established that he was a heretic and a magician. He was accused of performing the ritual ablution for prayer with milk and also, of cleaning his body with milk after relieving himself. Upon investigating these and other accusations, the *mālikī* judge sent for by the Sultan concluded that the defendant was an unbeliever (*kāfir*). Thereafter, he was paraded in the streets of Cairo riding naked on a camel and then executed by cutting off his head.[29]

Apart from narrating such criminal cases Ibn Iyās provides his readers with many amusing events and gossip, which come close to what we find today in the rainbow press. These stories are more or less harmless, they are stories that were meant to entertain and perhaps to distract from the serious realities of life. We learn about strange and funny events. For example, in 913 (1507/08) the Sultan ordered that each of the chief judges of the four schools of law should hold the Friday sermon (*khuṭba*) on a certain Friday. When it was the *mālikī* judge's turn, he ascended the pulpit (*minbar*) of the citadel mosque to preach, but he was so excited and frightened that he spoke incomprehensibly and fell down when descending the pulpit. After this, he became very sick and stayed in bed and died shortly after.[30]

Another story, dated in the next year, 914 (1508/09), runs as follows: since almost fifteen years, balm (*balasān*, *balsam*) was not cultivated any longer. Previously, the balm from Egypt had been famous for its top quality, and European kings had paid high prices for getting balm oil which was needed as ingredient for baptismal waters. The Sultan was distressed about the financial loss and searched tirelessly for a solution until finally he received a balm plant with its soil from the Hijaz. He ordered it to be planted in the same place in Egypt where balm had sprouted earlier so abundantly. Upon irrigation, the new plant prospered and the crop became as profitable as before.[31]

Then, in 915 (1509/10), hemp (*ḥashīsh*) was cultivated for the first time in Egypt, according to Ibn Iyas. The hemp grew very quickly and many people saw it and were impressed by its abundance. The connoisseurs of hemp and the smokers of drugs were filled with enthusiasm. A contemporary poet called the place where the hemp was planted a paradise (*janna*), and he praised the smell disseminating from it.[32]

---

29 Ibn Iyās: *Badāʾiʿ al-zuhūr*, vol. 4, 78.

30 Ibid., vol. 4, 128.

31 Ibid., vol. 4, 149.

32 Ibid., vol. 4, 156. – For drugs in medieval Islam, see Franz Rosenthal, *The Herb. Hashish versus Medieval Muslim Society*, Leiden: Brill 1971; Irwin, *Tausendundeine Nacht*, 188-91 (as per note 19).

The third category of stories, addresses the lives of the lower classes. In particular, Ibn Iyas focuses on stories related to the issue of beggars. This large topic certainly deserves a more thorough discussion than is possible in the scope of this article. Fortunately, we have some basic studies that illustrate the different aspects of begging and mendicancy. First of all the groundbreaking work of Bosworth which is followed by more recent publications such as Sabra's with the focus on Mamluk Egypt.[33] Selections from the chronicle of Ibn Iyās are as follows:

On the day of *ʿĀshūrāʾ* in 912 (1506), the Sultan ordered the poor and the vagabonds (i.e., the professional, able-bodied beggars) (*al-fuqarāʾ wa-l-ḥarāfīsh*) of Cairo to assemble. Then he rode down from the citadel to their assembly place and gave every poor person a gold coin. It was recorded that about 3000 dinars were spent during this one day. However, because of the large crowd of people that caused the death of three people, the Sultan did not repeat this gesture of charity again.[34]

Some months later in the same year, a silk merchant was found dead in his shop together with 4000 dinars and many items of gold and silver which were concealed in small pots below the roof. This man always appeared to be poverty stricken but only pretended to be poor. Similar was the case of a woman who used to beg at the door of the Ibn ³ūlūn Mosque. When she died 700 dinars were found with her, in addition to pots with new coins of copper and about 800 balls of yarn. The people of Cairo were very astonished.[35]

In 913 (1507/08), a woman called Khadīja al-Kulaibāṭiyya passed away. She had always claimed to be very pious and went into the houses of the rich in order to beg. After her death, gold coins with a value of 3000 dinars and furniture worth 500 dinars were found. Ibn Iyās considered this a very strange event, as the woman had always taken alms (*ṣadaqa*) from the people.[36]

In addition to these cases, Ibn Iyās mentioned incidents where poverty and banditry appeared more or less interwoven. For the year of 907 (1501/02), he reports that gangsters and black slaves (*al-zuʿar wa-l-ʿabīd*) in downtown Cairo jointly plundered several carpet shops. Additionally,

---

33 Clifford Edmund Bosworth: *The Mediaeval Islamic Underworld. The Banū Sāsān in Arabic Society and Literature*, 2 vols., Leiden: Brill 1976; Adam Sabra: *Poverty and Charity in Medieval Islam. Mamluk Egypt, 1250-1517*, Cambridge: Cambridge University Press 2000.

34 Ibn Iyās: *Badāʾiʿ al-zuhūr*, vol. 4, 94.

35 Ibid., vol. 4, 108.

36 Ibid., vol. 4, 130.

they stole silk, candles, fruits, sugar and gold and killed the shop owners. The criminal activities went on for a whole day until the prefect intervened, apprehended some of the perpetrators and executed them.[37]

During one particular night in the beginning of the next year (908/1502), a troop of gangsters attacked the inhabitants of one city quarter of Cairo and killed a guardian and destroyed several houses. Pursuing them, the city prefect (*wālī*) and his Mamluk soldiers managed to catch some of the gangsters who were paraded in public before being executed. In this case, it is not clear from the text whether, or how far, the perpetrators were related to poor people.[38] The same holds true for an event in 913 (1507/08) when a group of thieves drove into the gold magazine, killed the guardian and robbed gold and silver worth 10.000 dinars. Ibn Iyās comments that nobody "cared a fig." Then during the night, these thieves broke up four shops in one of the markets. The next night they attacked a rich foreign merchant, killed him and stole all of his possessions. Some of the perpetrators were arrested and executed by the authorities.[39]

As indicated above, the boundaries between poverty, begging, and banditry cannot always be sharply drawn. In many cases it is difficult to clarify what motivated people to live on begging and when or why begging led to violence and criminal behaviour. The *ḥarāfish* and the *zuʿar* appear periodically in Arab sources. They are groups of people who emerged from time to time under different names in Muslim regions - for example, in pre-Mamluk times as *aḥdāth* in Syria and as *ʿayyārūn* in Iraq and Iran.[40] Regarding the *...arāfish* whose leader was called *sulṭān* (since the late 8th/14th century), it is interesting to observe that with time they developed from a profession of beggars ready to use violence to a guild-like organization (*ṭāʾifa*). Guilds, especially those of artisans, were somehow connected to Sufism, and Sufism was in certain cases linked to the social category of *ashrāf*, the so-called descendants of the Prophet. Based on the assumption that Sufism somehow linked the *ashrāf* to artisans, who organized themselves in guilds, it would be challenging to study also the *...arāfish* in relation to the *ashrāf*. All these questions certainly need further research. It has been argued that in early Ottoman Damascus one *ashrāf* family (the ʿAjlānī family) held the title of *shaykh al-mashāyikh*. The family was responsible

---

37 Ibid., vol. 4, 17.

38 Ibid., vol. 4, 39-40.

39 Ibid., vol. 4, 126.

40 Havemann, "Männerbünde im islamischen Orient".

both for the guilds of artisans and for Sufi orders, and their title indicated a clear improvement over the status of *sulṭān al-ḥarāfish*.[41]

In view of these larger contexts and far-reaching questions, the chronicle of Ibn Iyās is a helpful tool to study social and cultural history. As is the case with other chronicles, with tales contained in Mamluk poetry and prose literature,[42] as well as from anonymous 'popular' sources (*siyar shaʿbiyya*)[43], Ibn Iyās can be read as an account of the history of people's mentalities and patterns of behaviour. His chronicle is a valuable source to gain a better insight into the history of late medieval daily life.

At this point, it is important to note that the term 'history of daily life', which has undergone controversial discussions on the part of social and cultural historians, always implies 'history from above' and 'history from below' i.e., the social elite (or elites) as well as the common people.[44] The focus of this article on marginal or marginalized groups does not intend to reduce the scope of history of daily life. Rather it was initiated because relatively little research has so far been done on the lower and lowest social strata. Secondly, it is only through a comprehensive view of a society - of its different groups or elements in daily life that the mutual dependences and interactions between hierarchy, marginality, and

41 Axel Havemann, "Some Reflections on the Problems of Research on Ashrāf: Examples from 10th and 11th Century Syria", *Oriente Moderno* 18, n.s. (1999), 483-90, here: 485-86 (= *The Role of the Sādāt/ Ašrāf in Muslim History and Civilization, Proceedings of the International Colloquium, Roma, 2-4/3/1998*, eds. Biancamaria Scarcia Amoretti, Laura Bottini, Roma 1999).

42 For poetry and prose literature (*adab*), see Thomas Bauer, "Ibrāhīm al-Miʿmār: Ein dichtender Handwerker aus Ägyptens Mamlukenzeit", *Zeitschrift der Deutschen Morgenländischen Gesellschaft* 152 (2002), 63-93; ibid., "Literarische Anthologien der Mamlūkenzeit", in: *Die Mamlūken. Studien zu ihrer Geschichte und Kultur. Zum Gedenken an Ulrich Haarmann (1942-1999)*, 71-122; for works of religious and legal scholars, see Stefan Leder, "Charismatic Scripturalism – The Ḥanbalī Maqdisīs at Damascus", *Der Islam* 74 (1997), 279-304; ibid., "Postklassisch und vormodern" (as per note 7).

43 Thomas Herzog, *Geschichte und Imaginaire. Entstehung, Überlieferung und Bedeutung der Sīrat Baibars in ihrem sozio-politischen Kontext*, Wiesbaden: Otto Harrassowitz 2005; Boaz Shoshan, "Comedy, Pornography, and Social Critique in the Romance of Aḥmad Danif", *Journal of Arabic Literature* 27 (1996), 216-26.

44 P. J. Brüggemeier, Jürgen Kocka, eds., *Geschichte von unten und Geschichte von innen. Kontroversen um die Alltagsgeschichte*, Hagen: Fernuniversität Gesamthochschule Hagen 1985; Hans-Werner Goetz, "Geschichte des mittelalterlichen Alltags. Theorie – Methoden – Bilanz der Forschung", in: *Mensch und Objekt im Mittelalter und in der frühen Neuzeit. Leben, Alltag, Kultur*, ed. Gerhard Jaritz, Wien: Österreichische Akademie der Wissenschaften 1990, 67-101; Eric J. Hobsbawm, "Geschichte von unten", in: Ibid., *Wieviel Geschichte braucht die Zukunft*, München: DTV 2001, 256-74.

mobility within that society are clearly perceived. It is exactly this that occured in the period under discussion. When the political and territorial integrity of the Islamic *umma* finally and irreversibly collapsed after 1258, culture, economy, and society continued to unfold to a considerable extent. Important changes occurred through the spread of educational institutions and endowments, the growing importance of Sufi orders even within the circle of legal scholars, and the increasing diversification of crafts and trade. A new relationship between the different groups of society can be observed. In particular since the 13th century parts of the population began to participate in religious and literary activities. Popular literary genres also increased, and preaching and brotherhoods brought people from different social levels together or linked them to certain concerns. In other words, social hierarchy and marginality became qualified by mobility. Social demarcations went along with social border crossing: not for the first time but certainly more than before.

In any case, the contemporary sources for the 13th, 14th and 15th centuries, mostly historical narratives and collections of popular stories, reveal a distinct interest in daily events especially with regard to the common people. In general, popular culture becomes more important. The weak and the poor are more often subjects of literary discussions, and sometimes, representatives of specific marginal groups constitute the principal or sole actors: (professional) beggars, rascals and tricksters, treacherous sufis and preachers, prostitutes, pederasts and transvestites, street entertainers such as musicians, dancers, clowns, showmen of animals and jugglers, magicians, quacks, sellers of alcoholic drinks and drugs.[45] All of them were part of an 'alternative subculture' rather than of an offensive 'counter-society', not self-contained but many-coloured and non-uniform with its own values and codes of honour. This 'underworld' operated according to its own laws and forms of organization.

In the long run, an approach as the one suggested in this paper may make it possible to write a comprehensive 'history of society', a *Gesell-*

45 Concerning most of these protagonists of marginal groups, very little is known; despite a few important studies on single issues or types of profession, we are lacking a comprehensive and systematic analysis. A very recent tool for future research is Manuela Höglmeier, *Al-Ǧawbarī und sein Kašf al-asrār – ein Sittenbild des Gauners im arabisch-islamischen Mittelalter (7./13. Jahrhundert). Einführung, Edition und Kommentar*, Berlin: Klaus Schwarz Verlag 2006. For medieval Europe similar issues are much better investigated; see, among many others, Wolfgang Seidenspinner, *Mythos Gegengesellschaft. Erkundungen der Subkultur der Jauner*, Münster: Waxmann 1998; Bernd-Ulrich Hergemöller, ed., *Randgruppen der spätmittelalterlichen Gesellschaft*, Warendorf: Fahlbusch Verlag 2001 (new ed.).

schaftsgeschichte, of the Middle East.[46] Of course, the choice of one historical period within one specific region of the Islamic world is just a small step towards this goal and necessitates further work. Beyond this goal, a history of society of the Middle East would also mean a contribution to the current debate on culture/cultures, identity/identities and their borders.

46 For this concept, see Hans-Ulrich Wehler, *Deutsche Gesellschaftsgeschichte*, vol. 1, München: C. H. Beck 1996, 6-30; critical and sceptical of Wehler's opinion: Eric J. Hobsbawm, "Von der Sozialgeschichte zur Gesellschaftsgeschichte", in: Ibid., *Wieviel Geschichte braucht die Zukunft*, 100-27.

PART FOUR

Fields of Cultural Production: Science

"Gathering the Stars": Scientific Activities During Mamluk Times

George Saliba

Introduction

The scientific activities that took place during Mamluk times constitute a crucial and mature stage in the long trajectory of the development of Islamic science that started sometime during the late eighth and early ninth centuries and continued well into the sixteenth and thereafter. One should not have expected otherwise, as it is in the very nature of scientific activities to be accumulative, and for one generation of scientists to build on the results reached by earlier scientists. But the very vitality and vigor of the scientific activities that were conducted during Mamluk times have yet another important significance of their own. Because of their demonstrable creativity, those activities constitute a critical evidence for rebutting the commonly held opinion that Islamic scientific activities began to wane as early as the eleventh century A.D., or even earlier as some would want to put it.[1] As links

[1] This periodization of Islamic intellectual history was best encapsulated by Max Meyerhoff, in his famous article for *The Legacy of Islam*, ed. Sir Thomas Arnold and Alfred Guillaume, London: Oxford 1931, 337, where he titled section 4 of his essay: "Age of Decline from about 1100." G. E. von Grunebaum implicitly adopts a very similar intellectual chronology, especially in his beautifully written but badly conceived essay "The Profile of Muslim Civilization", first published as "Islam in a Humanistic Education," *Journal of General Education*, 4 (1949) 12-31, and reprinted in G. E. von Grunebaum, *Islam: Essays in the Nature and Growth of a Cultural Tradition*, Westport – Connecticut: Greenwood Press 1981, 1-30. The very concept of decline itself is formally treated in a brief essay by Robert Brunschvig, in "Problème de la décadence" in *Classicisme et Déclin Culturel dans l'Histoire de l'Islam* (Actes du symposium international d'histoire de la civilization musulmane organisé à Bordeaux du 25 au 29 juin 1956 par R. Brunschvig et G. E. Grunebaum) Paris: Maisonneuve 1956, 29-51, reprinted in Robert Brunschvig, *Études d'Islamologie*, avant-propos et bibliographie de l'auteur par Abdel Magid Turki, tome I, Paris: Maisonneuve et Larose 1976, 21-38. A similar conclusion is reached in several essays in the collection *Classicisme et Déclin* just cited. See for example the essay of Hellmut Ritter, "L'Orthodoxie a-t-elle une part dans la décadence?" *ibid*, 167-181, and where he says while talking of al-Ghazālī (d. 1111) "ainsi finit non seulement la vie personelle de Ghazālī, mais aussi

in a chain, those activities become coherent for a modern researcher only when the whole chain is considered together and when one tries to explain the novelty that those activities brought about against a much more detailed background, and when one also considers the foundations they laid for later results to be achieved.

I will take the Mamluk times to fall roughly between the middle of the thirteenth century and the middle of the sixteenth. Thus I will restrict my remarks to scientific activities that were produced during that period. I will also lay a greater emphasis on the field of astronomy and on planetary theories in particular, not only because I have some competence in that field but because of the mathematical nature of those disciplines which makes it easier to demonstrate the connectivity between what was happening then with what happened before and what happened thereafter.

The paper will conclude by characterizing those activities as generalizing theoretical activities that made use of the basic scientific foundations that were laid between the ninth and the eleventh centuries. It will also demonstrate that the mature activities that were brought about by the Mamluk astronomers also had a lasting effect on all major astronomers that followed up to and including the astronomers of the European Renaissance.

Background of Mamluk Astronomical Sciences

The most significant aspect of Arabic/Islamic astronomy is that it was at once a continuation of the Greek astronomical tradition and at the same time one of the most sophisticated critics of that tradition. As Greek astronomical texts became first known in the Islamic tradition, when they were first translated into Arabic, the official and intellectual language of the Islamic empire from the time of the Umayyad caliph ʿAbd al-Malik b. Marwān (685-705) onward, it was noticed early on that those texts contained concepts and

l'histoire spirituelle de l'Islam au Moyen âge en général," 168, and Willy Hartner's essay "Quand et comment s'est arrêté l'essor de la culture scientifique dans l'Islam," *ibid*, 319-337, where he also says: "en effet, je viens de le faire en constatant que la haute floraison de la science arabe se termina vers la fin du XIIIe siècle et que c'est tout au plus deux cents ans plus tard que s'évanouirent les dernières traces d'une activité scientifique, quelque peu notable qu'elle fût," 322, or slightly more generously when he says: "... le dernier véritable essor qu'avait pris la science musulmane sous le règne de Hülägü, venait de s'arrêter après la mort du grand Naṣīr al-dīn (1274)," 320. After that, Hartner argues "... nous rencontrons encore de savants compilateurs et commentateurs auxquels on ne saurait même contester un certain degré d'originalité," 320. More recent literature still reflects that periodization as can be seen in a recent article by Tzvi Langermann, "The Book of Bodies and Distances of Ḥabash al-Ḥāsib," *Centaurus* 28 (1985) 108-128, especially 108, where he says "the most productive period of Arabic astronomy (roughly the ninth to the thirteenth centuries)."

numerical values that did not correspond to what one saw with his own eyes at this later time when the translations were taking place.

On the level of concepts, those texts contained, for example, units of measure that made no sense in an Islamic environment that used completely different units. A Greek *stadion (stade)* meant very little to a practicing astronomer or a mathematical geographer in early ninth-century Baghdad.[2] And thus when the measure of one degree on the meridian was first encountered in the Greek sources, originally on the authority of Eratosthenes (d.c. 195 B.C.), as being 500 stades[3], that presented a real problem for the astronomers of the caliph al-Maʾmūn (rl. 813-833). The only way the measure could make sense was to have it expressed in a unit they were familiar with. And in order to do that, they had to initiate a geodetic project and re-measure that same meridian degree in the then current *sawād* (black) or *sharʿī* (legal) cubits, and Arab miles. That measurement allowed them to establish at once a new value for the meridian degree, and thus the circumference of the earth, and to equate the stade of the Greek sources to the Arabic cubits and miles that were in use at their time.

Other concepts were simply required by the new Islamic civilization and had no equivalents in the earlier cultures from which they could be sought. For example, the idea of praying in the direction of the cubic building (*kaʿba*) in the city of Mecca, i.e. facing the *qibla*, was a particular Islamic religious demand, and had no Greek or other previous equivalents. The demand itself gave rise to a technical mathematical problem that could not be readily solved simply by resorting to a ready-made solution in the ancient scientific

2 This predicament was already reported in the contemporary ninth-century sources themselves. See, for example, the text of Ḥabash al-Ḥāsib *Book of Bodies and Distances*, which was published by Tzvi Langermann "The Book of Bodies", and republished by David King in his "Too Many Cooks... A New Account of the Earliest Muslim Geodetic Measurement," *Suhayl* 1 (2000), 207- 241". This and other reports were repeated in the eleventh century by Bīrūnī, especially in his *The Determination of the Coordinates of Cities*, tr. Jamil Ali, Beirut: American University of Beirut 1967, 178-179, where he also reports the difficulties involved in building observational instruments and in determining the value of the meridian degree along the surface of the earth.

3 There is much literature on the history of the measurement of the meridian degree. For a more detailed discussion of it, see Paul Tannery, Recherche sur l'histoire de l'astronomie ancienne, Paris: Gauthier-Villars 1893, 103-121; Otto Neugebauer, *A History of Ancient Gauthier-Villars Mathematical Astronomy*, Berlin, Heidelberg, New York: Springer 1975, 652f; and more recently F. J. Ragep, *Naṣīr al-Dīn al-Ṭūsī's Memoir on Astronomy*, New York: Springer 1993, 506f, where the results should have been corrected as indicated in the present author's review of Ragep's work in George Saliba, "Writing the History of Arabic Astronomy: Problems and Differing Perspectives," *Journal of the American Oriental Society* 116 (1996), 711f, but were unfortunately ignored in David King, "Too Many Cooks ....

texts.[4] Mathematicians of early Islam had to solve that problem anew, even if they did have to use helping tools from the earlier cultures. But as a result of that effort one can argue that the field of spherical trigonometry developed to where it developed in early Islam, at the hands of such distinguished astronomers and mathematicians as Ḥabash al-Ḥāsib (d.c. 870)[5], simply because of the urgency that such problems created.

Other problems like observing the new crescent, with all the more sophisticated complications involved, also had a real interest only for a civilization like the Islamic civilization, whose calendar was punctuated by such sightings. Very sophisticated mathematical tables for the computations involved in the lunar crescent sightings were also developed from the earliest times of Islamic science, and specifically to attend to this problem.[6]

On the level of numerical observational values, usually called "parameters", several encounters with the original Greek texts that were being translated into Arabic at the time also demonstrated very clearly, at least to the translators who had to render the intent of those texts into Arabic, that they harbored what looked like mistakes that could not be tolerated by the translators. One such instance was encountered by the translator al-Ḥajjāj b. Maṭar (fl. C. 830)[7] from whose pen we still have two consecutive translations of Euclid's *Elements* and Ptolemy's *Almagest*. They were both completed during the caliphates of Hārūn al-Rashīd (786-809) and his son al-Maʾmūn (813-833) and both of them survive in several complete and fragmented manuscripts. While translating the *Almagest*, al-Ḥajjāj apparently noticed that the numbers given by Ptolemy (in *Almagest* IV, 2) for the derivation of the length of the lunar month did not actually yield the results Ptolemy said they would yield if the arithmetical division is carried out "properly."[8] In other

---

4 In fact the discussion of the *qibla* determination was at times brought about in the same context as the determination of the meridian degree as was elegantly demonstrated by David King and others. See now the well documented account in David King's, "Too Many Cooks…".

5 For more information on this brilliant astronomer, see *Dictionary of Scientific Biography*, ed. Charles Guillispie, New York: Scribner's Sons 1970-1980, vol. 5, 612-620.

6 See, for example, the very interesting and hard to find study of such new demands of the Islamic civilization by David King in his *Al-Khwārizmī and New Trends in Mathematical Astronomy in the Ninth Century*, Occasional Papers on the Near East, No. 2, Near Eastern Studies, New York: New York University 1983.

7 On this translator, see, Heinrich Suter, *Die Mathematiker und Astronomen der Araber und Ihre Werke, Abhandlungen zur Geschichte der Mathematischen Wissenschaften*, X. Heft, Leipzig: Teubner 1900, reprinted New York and London: Johnson Reprint Corporation 1972, 9.

8 In fact this apparent "mistake" in the Ptolemaic text was the subject of an article by Asger Aaboe, "On the Babylonian Origin of Some Hipparchian Parameters," *Centaurus* 4 (1955), 122-125.

words, if one divided the number of 126007 days and 1 hour separating two lunar eclipses by the number of 4267 lunar months that separated the eclipses apart, one would get the length of a lunar month of 29;31,50,8,20 days.[9] But if one took those numbers, just in the order given by Ptolemy, and carried out the said division one would get as a result a lunar month of 29;31,50,8,9,20 days, a number clearly at variance with the one given by Ptolemy from the fourth sexagessimal fraction onward.

The surviving copies of al-Ḥajjāj’s translation of the *Almagest*, e. g. British Library Add. 7474, fol. 75r, indeed record the “correct” value and not the value that appeared in the original Greek text.

The problem, however, was not as simple as that. In fact, it was much more involved than it appears at first sight. The result of the division that was reported by Ptolemy was already the canonical Babylonian value for the length of the lunar month, a value that was reached by a different circuitous route and not the one described by Ptolemy as a straightforward division of two numbers.[10] But it also meant that Ptolemy himself was accepting, as did Hipparchus some two centuries and half before him, a much older Babylonian value rather than re-determining it for himself by using his own observations.

For the translator al-Ḥajjāj, the adoption of the new “corrected” value can only mean that al-Ḥajjāj was indeed double checking the original text before he translated it. Or more accurately, he was apparently competent enough to check such a complicated text as he was translating it. This will not be surprising only when looked at in light of the social and intellectual conditions that must have prevailed at the time, and which I have already described at great length somewhere else.[11] Those conditions dictated that no translator or scientist could afford to overlook what seemed like mistakes in the original texts that were being sought for translation. The suspicion with which the new incoming tradition was being received did not leave room for mistakes to be incorporated simply because those mistakes appeared in the original texts. There were competent people who could double-check those values, and who

---

9 We follow here the system of notation that was developed by Neugebauer to designate sexagessimal numbers and fractions by using the semi-colon “;” in an analogous fashion to the decimal point “.”. Thus the number given here means 29 days, and 31/60 of a day, and $50/60^2$ of a day, etc., just as 9.87 in the decimal system would mean 9 and 8/10 and $7/10^2$ (=100).

10 For a discussion of the problem see G. Toomer, *Ptolemy’s Almagest*, New York: Springer 1984, 176, note 10, and Aaboe, “Babylonian Origin.”

11 See George Saliba, *Al-Fikr al-ʿilmī al-ʿarabī: Nashʾatuhu wa-taṭawwuruhu*, Balamand: Center for Christian Islamic Studies 1998, 23-72.

were competent enough to offer better solutions even at this very early stage. The likes of al-Ḥajjāj could not make a living against those competent people if they did not prove that they were equally competent themselves.

And once the texts themselves were perceived to contain or lack of, such blatant mistakes, or such alien concepts that in itself necessitated new initiatives, as the one taken by al-Ḥajjāj, and new observations, as in the case of the Maʾmūn astronomers re-measuring the length of a meridian degree or solving the more involved problem of the *qibla* as we have seen. Those same astronomers and translators had to be constantly alert in screening the incoming texts for all such blemishes. And there were many more such blemishes to be found, some easily determinable, while others were slightly more involved.

Of the easily determinable aberrations was the precession value that was adopted by Ptolemy in all of his astronomical works, namely the rate at which the point of the vernal equinox seemed to be regressing backward with respect to the fixed stars, thus giving rise in our modern times to the famous song "This Is the Age of Aquarius". The song means that the vernal equinox has now slid back to the zodiacal sign of Aquarius instead of Aries where it used to be. The rate of this back-sliding was given by Ptolemy as 1 degree for every 100 years. Now, if this value were true, then all the fixed stars would appear to have changed with respect to the ecliptic by as much as some seven degrees as a result of the seven centuries that separated Ptolemy's times (c. 150) from mid-ninth century Baghdad. There are stars in the sky that are very close to the ecliptic, such as the famous royal star Regulus which is also known as the "heart of the lion" in the Leo constellation. Any casual observer in ninth century Baghdad, even with crude instruments, could easily determine that this star had changed its position by about 10 to 11 degrees in 700 years rather than only 7 as would have been anticipated by Ptolemy. In fact, a century later, the famous text of ʿAbd al-Raḥmān al-Ṣūfī on the description of the star constellations, called *Ṣuwar al-Kawākib*, which was completed in 965 AD used a value of 12 degrees and 42 minutes to mark the change of position for the stars that were recorded by Ptolemy in about 150 AD instead of the expected change of position of some 8 degrees as would have been anticipated by Ptolemy. Ṣūfī stated explicitly that he did that because he adopted the more accurate value of precession of 1 degree in every 66 years or so, which was determined by the astronomers working during the caliphate of al-Maʾmūn, instead of using the value of 1 degree for every 100 years that he found in the Ptolemaic text.[12]

Other equally easily determinable values were such values as the inclination of the ecliptic, the position of the solar apogee, the eccentricity

12 See ʿAbd al-Raḥmān al-Ṣūfī, *Ṣuwaru'l-Kawākib (Or Uronometry)*, Hyderabad: Osmania 1953, 25.

of the solar orbit and the value of the maximum solar equation. Each and every one of those values was re-determined in ninth-century Baghdad, and some of the results, like the inclination of the ecliptic, are still with us today. When children are taught nowadays that the seasons' changes are caused by the 23½ degrees inclination of the earth's axis (which is the same as the inclination of the ecliptic)[13] this teaching is the result of what was established in ninth-century Baghdad.

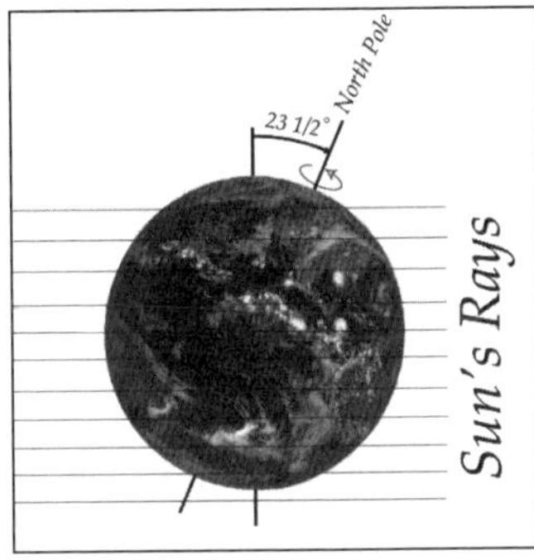

Figure 1. The inclination of the ecliptic as reflected as a tilt of the earth axis of 23 ½ degrees as determined in ninth-century Baghdad. The old Greek value for the same parameter was 23;51,20 degrees and the Indian value was 24 degrees.

13 On the determination of an "erroneous" value of this parameter by Ptolemy, see G. Toomer, *Almagest*, 61f and the reference to John P. Britton, "Ptolemy's Determination of the Obliquity of the Ecliptic," *Centaurus* 14 (1969), 29-41. On the long history of this value and the various Islamic and pre-Islamic sources that quote the "erroneous" ancient values as well as the "corrected" value of about 23 ½ established in Islamic times, see the interesting letter on the subject that was sent by Edward Bernard (d. 1697), the Savillian Professor of Astronomy at Oxford from 1673 to 1691 to the famous Royal astronomer John Flamsteed (d. 1719) that was first published in the *Philosophical Transactions of the Royal Society of London* 14 (1684), 721-725, and reprinted together with other articles in F. Sezgin, *Islamic Mathematics and Astronomy*, Frankfurt: Institute for the History of Arabic-Islamic Science 1998, 1-5. For the actual records of the results established during Islamic times see, for example, Edward S. Kennedy, "A Survey of Islamic Astronomical Tables", *Transactions of the American Philosophical Society*, New Series, 46 (1956), 123-177, esp. 145 where the value that was established during the time of al-Maʾmūn is given as 23;33 degrees, and 151, where the same value is also quoted from another astronomical table from the same period, as well as the value 23;35 from yet another source, and other values in other sources from the same period all close to the "correct" value of 23 ½ degrees. For a description of the manner in which the observation was made and the result of the inclination was deduced, we are lucky to have had a couple of contemporary sources in which those observations were carried out. See, for example, the interesting treatise of the tenth-century astronomer and mathematician Abū Maḥmūd Ḥāmid b. al-Khuḍr al-Khujandī (d. 992), "On the Inclination [of the ecliptic] and the Geographical Latitude," which describes the observational process as well as the instruments that were set up for the purpose in Louis Cheikho S.J., *al-Machriq*, 11 (1908), 60-69.

Other parameters such as the position of the solar apogee, as well as the eccentricity of the solar sphere and the value of the maximum solar equation could all be determined by a single observational process as was done by a ninth-century astronomer in a treatise ascribed to the mathematician Thābit b. Qurrā (d. 901) but may have come from the circle of Banū Mūsā, especially the oldest among them Muḥammad b. Mūsā b. Shākir.[14] In it, the author does not only question the values for these parameters that have come down to him from the Greek sources, but goes a step further to question the reasons that gave rise to those erroneous values. In doing so, he concluded that the old Greek method of observation followed by Ptolemy, namely, the method of observing the change in the solar declination at the cardinal points of equinoxes and solstices, was itself the culprit, for it is very difficult to determine with acute precision the times when the sun crosses the solstices, as the declination at those times are extremely small. In layman's terms, the sun seems to rise and set on the same points on the horizon for several days when it gets close to the summer solstice around June 21 and the winter solstice around December 21. During this period it would be very difficult to determine the exact date when the sun crossed the solstitial points.

The ninth-century astronomer who noted that difficulty, proposed an ingenious solution, which kept all the derivative methods of Ptolemy intact, while he shifted the observation times from the cardinal points to the mid seasons, that is when the sun reached the middle of Taurus, middle of Leo, middle of Scorpio and middle of Aquarius. He reasoned that at those points the solar declination would be large enough to make more accurate determination of the required values. In fact the new method, which was called the *fuṣūl* (seasons) method on account of the timing of the observations in the middle of the seasons, was so successful that it determined in one full swoop new values for the solar eccentricity, and thus the maximum solar equation, and determined a new position for the solar apogee, which proved observationally that the solar apogee did indeed move along with the other planetary apogees, and did not remain fixed at Gemini 5 ½ degrees as was reported by Ptolemy.

---

14 The treatise was translated into Latin during medieval times and is now translated into English and commented upon by Otto Neugebauer, in "Thabit ben Qurra 'On the Solar Year' and 'On the Motion of the Eighth Sphere,'" *Proceedings of the American Philosophical Society* 106 (1962), 264-299. For a more detailed historical study of this treatise, its authenticity and its attribution to Thābit b. Qurra as well as a full edition of the Arabic text with French translation and commentary, see the more recent work of Régis Morelon, *Thābit Ibn Qurra: Oeuvres d'Astronomie*, Paris: Belles Lettres 1987, xlvi – lxxv.

The new observational results that marked this radical departure from the values reported in the Greek sources, and the ability to explore the causes that gave rise to the mistakes, must have impressed the early astronomers of Islamic civilization, or at least impressed them enough to wonder why the ingenious Greek astronomers could not reach the same results. Excuses for those errors, some even resting on fictitious phenomena, were definitely put forth by the astronomers of the period, for no one could honestly belittle the achievements of Ptolemy, the greatest astronomer of all times. But the more realistic ones raised such questions as human error, stability of instruments, observational strategies and the like. Those questions in turn must have given rise to various attempts to revamp the Greek foundational astronomical system. Treatises, such as that of Khujandī just mentioned, and the ninth-century astronomer who attacked the Greek observational methodology, must have become wide spread and must have engaged larger and larger segments of the society. In one instance we have reports of observations that were conducted by Abū Sahl al-Kūhī (c. 988) which were public events *par excellence*, so much so that a report about the observations was signed by a judge, fellow astronomers, instrument makers, and social dignitaries and the like.[15] A similar situation apparently took place at the time of Khujandī according to the statement that was also made in his aforementioned treatise. In it he says that other people were also present at the time of the observation and that they too have signed the report (*wa-dhālika bi-mashhad jamāʿa min al-mahara bi-hādhā al-ʿilm al-muthbata asmāʾuhum fī thubut al-irtifāʿāt (*sic*) fa-qad amḍū khuṭūtahum bi-dhālika fīhi*."[16]

These reports, coming from as late a period as towards the end of the tenth century, clearly indicate the social acceptability of such sophisticated scientific practices, that their procedures were regularized, if not "legalized" since the witnesses involved a judge, and seem to indicate an awareness of the necessity for public scrutiny of scientific processes. That must also mean that the groundwork for solid scientific research, in the sense that scientific research was open to public scrutiny, was already well developed during the first two centuries of Islamic civilization. It also seems to have covered a very wide range of activities as we have just seen. As a consequence, it would be hard to find an astronomer who lived, say after the eleventh century, who would still accept the

---

15 See the account of the observations including the names of the people involved as witnesses in Jamāl al-Dīn al-Qifṭī (d. 1248), *Taʾrīkh al-Ḥukamāʾ*, ed. Julius Lippert, Leipzig: Dieterich'sche Verlagsbuchhandlung 1903, 351-354.

16 Khujandī, "On the Inclination," 62.

Greek fundamental astronomical values as valid. The greatest majority of the scientific sources from the later periods clearly testify to the widespread acceptability of the new results that were established after the ninth century.

The very success of the early scientists in unearthing the main faults of Greek scientific doctrines, and their ability to create alternative foundational values in such sophisticated fields as astronomy, gave rise to a more interesting phenomenon. Theorists who were witnessing the dismantling of the foundational aspects of Greek science by their empirically-oriented colleagues began to be emboldened themselves and began to raise theoretical questions of their own touching upon the very theoretical foundations of Greek science. It is then that new genres of writings began to appear, such as the treatise of Muḥammad b. Mūsā b. Shākir (d. 873) in which he questioned the absurd notion of Ptolemy who stipulated that the ninth sphere, which was responsible for the daily motion of the whole universe, was itself made of the simple Aristotelian element ether, and was at the same time concentric with the equally simple eighth sphere that carried the fixed stars and moved them by the other motion of precession.[17] How could a celestial sphere made of the eternal element ether, as Aristotle and Ptolemy after him would put it that did not have the sublunar physical properties of friction move another celestial sphere that was concentric with it? Something was wrong with the theoretical cosmological foundations of Greek astronomy that stipulates the existence of such spheres, and Ptolemy had affirmed that they indeed existed.

The centuries that followed witnessed an intensification of this line of questioning and yet another new genre of writing also began to appear. New treatises began to be devoted to the exposition of the theoretical absurdities, such as the ones we have seen, that were embedded in the Greek scientific tradition. Scientists began to go way beyond the mere act of conducting new experiments and new observations to correct this or that parameter. They became fully emboldened to question such authorities as the Greek physician Galen or the Greek astronomer Ptolemy on issues relating to the very theoretical foundation of Greek science. Some of those scientists included such famous names as Abū Zakarīya al-Rāzī (Latin Rhazes d. 924) who wrote a critical work against Galen, called *al-Shukūk ʿalā Jālīnus* (Doubts Against Galen), and Ibn al-Haytham a century later who produced a similar work against Ptolemy called

---

17 For the text with translation and commentary of this treatise see George Saliba, "Early Arabic Critique of Ptolemaic Cosmology: A Ninth-Century Text on the Motion of the Celestial Spheres," *Journal for the History of Astronomy* 25 (1994), 115-141.

al-Shukūk ʿalā Baṭlamyūs (*Dubitationes in Ptolemaeum*), and the anonymous eleventh-century Andalusian astronomer who wrote a similar work called *al-Istidrāk ʿalā Baṭlamyūs* (Recapitulation against Ptolemy).[18] It is unfortunate that the last work does not seem to have survived like the other two, but we have enough information about it to conclude that it was of the same genre.

By the end of the eleventh century this wave of criticism began to produce serious responses all signaling the end of the supremacy that was enjoyed by the incoming Greek scientific tradition, and that the status quo could not continue as it was then. There was a wide-spread social realization that new theories not sharing the faulty assumptions of the Greek scientific tradition had to be created. Few scientists began to take up the challenge of producing such theories. The earliest attempt at an alternative construction of new theoretical mathematical foundations, which we know of, and which was hopefully meant to replace the old Greek mathematical model came from the philosopher Abū ʿUbayd al-Jūzjānī (d. c. 1070) the student of the famous ʿAlī b. Sīnā (Latin Avicenna).[19] But like all beginnings, this hesitant, shy attempt did not meet with much success, most probably because it came from a philosopher who was not mathematically well equipped. But like all beginnings it was also a harbinger of things to come.

Mamluk Science

If the discipline of astronomy is any indication we can conclude that by the middle of the thirteenth century, that is by the beginning of the Mamluk era, Islamic science had by then come of age and began to leave its mark on future developments. There was no doubt by then, that things had to change, and more importantly that there was no place else to go. No other tradition could solve the problems that were encountered in the Greek tradition; nor

---

18 For the text of Rāzī, see Mahdī Muḥaqqeq (ed.), *Kitāb al-Shukūk ʿalā Jālīnus li-Muḥammad b. Zakarīya al-Rāzī*, Tehran: Muʾassasah-i Muṭālʿāt Islāmī 1993. Although Rāzī's text on Smallpox can be construed as a partial apology for Galen, it is nevertheless one of the most constructive criticisms of the latter. A useful translation of this work and extensive commentaries can be found in William Alexander Greenhill, *A Treatise on the Small-Pox and Measles by Abú Becr Mohammed Ibn Zacaríyá ar-Rází (commonly called Rhazes),* London: Sydenham Society 1848. Ibn al-Haitham (d. 1049), *al-Shukūk ʿalā Baṭlamyūs (Dubitationes in Ptolemaeum)*, ed. A. Sabra and N. Shehaby, Cairo: Dār al-Kutub 1971. George Saliba,"Critiques of Ptolemaic Astronomy in Islamic Spain," *al-Qanṭara*, 22 (1999), 3-25.

19 See George Saliba, "Ibn Sīnā and Abū ʿUbayd al-Jūzjānī: The Problem of the Ptolemaic Equant," *Journal for the History of Arabic Science*, 4 (1980), 376 - 403.

was there any ancient tradition that could solve the new problems posed by the introduction of Islam into the picture. One had to rely on oneself alone, and begin the reconstruction of science on new foundations, such foundations that would not harbor the problems of the Greek tradition, but at the same time would not necessarily cast away all that was good and valid in that tradition. One can certainly use the metaphor of maturity to describe the status of science at that time. Things looked promising, and challenges abounded in almost every discipline. Scientists who had learned from their predecessors about the faults in the Greek tradition, and had started to see the benefits of the new observations, the new instruments, and the new strategies of observations, and had already studied the detailed rebuttals that were expressed in terms of *shukūk* in the previous centuries, did indeed rise up to those challenges and began to plough new grounds that were not contemplated before.

If one were to characterize the scientific environment during the Mamluk period, one could do well by emphasizing the new approach that was adopted then and which seems to have led to the pursuit of scientific activities to their logical conclusions. In the previous centuries, there were people who were mostly solving individual problems whenever and wherever those problems could be identified. But by Mamluk times there came to be a new tendency to solve all problems, for all times, even for hypothetical times and places, and to create answers that would be applicable at all times and in all places. No discipline could illustrate this tendency better than the discipline of astronomy with its sub-branches of scientific instruments and timekeeping. When we consider the galaxies of brilliant scientists who ploughed their trade in Egypt and Syria during the fourteenth century, for example, one is amazed at the extent to which this universalizing tendency was prevalent.

Taken together, and when one considers the most important names of instrument makers, observers, calculators, mathematicians and planetary theorists, one cannot but be impressed by the level of sophistication those scientists had achieved during this period. We shall soon discuss the remarkable results that were reached in the more advanced theoretical cosmological discipline of planetary motions, but before we do that some illustrative examples of the universalizing tendency that was truly the hallmark of Mamluk science could help us appreciate its nature and extent.

In the case of instrument making we find astrolabists such as Ibn al-Sarrāj (d.c. 1349) producing universal astrolabes that were inspired by the earlier developments that took place in eleventh-century Andalus, if not rediscovered afresh, and were crafted in such a way that they could be used for any locality of the inhabited world.[20] Earlier astrolabes, more or less, solved the same problems. But in order to do so, they had to make room for individual plates that had to be used for individual cities if they were to be used properly. With Ibn al-Sarrāj, who was apparently driven by this universalizing tendency, a single plate was crafted that could replace all the earlier plates, and yet it could still perform all the functions all the others once performed. In the words of David King this astrolabe of Ibn al-Sarrāj is "the most sophisticated astronomical instrument from the entire medieval and Renaissance periods."[21]

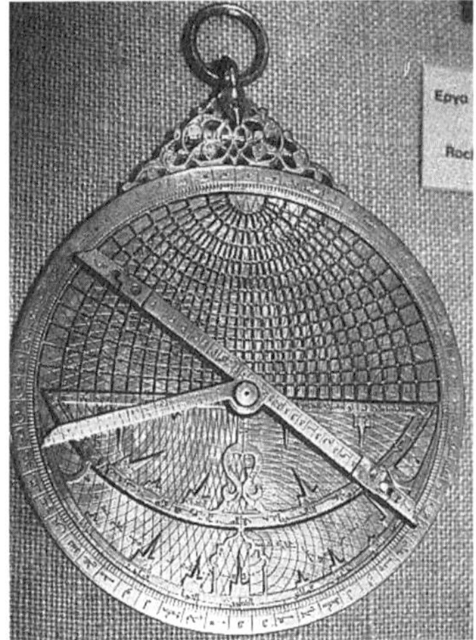

Figure 2. Universal astrolabe of Ibn al-Sarrāj. Courtesy Benaki Museum. Photo by George Saliba.

20 Much work has already been done on Ibn al-Sarrāj, but most extensively by François Charette, *Mathematical Instrumentation in Fourteenth-Century Egypt and Syria: The Illustrated Treatise of Najm al-Dīn al-Maṣrī*, Leiden: Brill 2003, 14-17, *et passim*, and David King in *In Synchrony With The Heavens: Volume One, The Call of the Muezzin*, Leiden: Brill 2004, 724f, David King in "The Astronomical Instruments of Ibn al-Sarrāj: A Brief Survey," printed as section IX in David King, *Islamic Astronomical Instruments*, London: Variorum 1987, David King, "Universal Solutions to Problems of Spherical astronomy from Mamluk Egypt and Syria," in *A Way Prepared: Essays on Islamic Culture in Honor of Richard Bayly Winder*, eds. F. Kazemi and R.D. McChesney, New York: NY Press 1988, 153-184, especially 160-163, reprinted as section VII in David King, *Astronomy in the Service of Islam*, London: Variorum 1993, David King, "The Astronomy of the Mamluks," *Isis* 74 (1983), 531-555, especially 544-545, reprinted as section III in David King, *Islamic Mathematical Astronomy*, London: Variorum 1986.

21 David King, "Astronomical Instrumentation in the Medieval Near East," printed as section I in David King, *Islamic Astronomical Instruments*, 1-21, esp. 7, correctly quoted by Charette, *Mathematical Instrumentation*, p. 16, but mistakenly referenced in note 71.

Similarly, the timekeeper of the Umayyad mosque of Damascus, and a contemporary of Ibn al-Sarrāj, Shams al-Dīn al-Khalīlī (d.c.1360), also inherited a long tradition of mathematical computations that could solve the rather sophisticated problem of determining the *qibla* direction for a specific locality. But he also carried the art of problem solving to another extreme when he produced tables of some 40,000 entries, all yielding the more precise *qibla* computations for every degree of longitude and latitude of the inhabited world, even in places he had never visited or even heard of Muslims there requiring a solution for their *qibla* problem.[22] It is this kind of generalities and of universal solutions that seem to have motivated those astronomers. And with it, they moved science from attending to particular problems into the realm of more theoretical discussions where general scientific strategies were devised, and new theories were developed. It is this kind of "unparalleled[23]" scientific maturity that was reached during Mamluk times, and which began to delve into the realm of theorization, that became the hallmark of scientific progress and modern science during the latter part of the seventeenth century.

One could go on listing one instrument maker after the other, and one timekeeper after the other all illustrating this tendency of universalization that characterized the scientific activities of Mamluk times, but the lack of space forces me to only mention one more early Mamluk encyclopedist by the name of Sharaf al-Dīn al-Ḥasan b. ᶜAlī al-Marrakushī (d. bet. 1282 and 1324) who produced a monumental *summa* called *Jāmiᶜ al-mabādiʾ wa-l-ghāyāt fī ᶜilm al-mīqāt* (Summa of Principles and Final Quests in the Science of Timekeeping) that did for the field of timekeeping and instrument making something similar to what Ibn Sīnā's *Qānūn* did for medicine.[24] There, in one voluminous work, an early Mamluk timekeeper, muezzin or instrument maker could find all the results of the previous generations, thus preparing the grounds for the next steps of the likes of Ibn al-Sarrāj and al-Khalīlī that followed in the next century.

22 Like Ibn al-Sarrāj, al-Khalīlī was also extensively studied by David King, especially in his "Al-Khalīlī's Auxiliary Tables for Solving Problems of Spherical Astronomy," *Journal for the History of Astronomy* 4 (1973), 99-110, and David King, "Al-Khalīlī's *Qibla* Table," *Journal of Near Eastern Studies* 34 (1975), 81-122, both reprinted as sections XI and XIII respectively in David King, *Islamic Mathematical Astronomy*, London: Variorum 1986.

23 A term used by Charette in *Mathematical Instrumentation*, 22, summarizing many of the works of King before him.

24 This analogy was first drawn by Charette, *Mathematical Instrumentation*, 11-12.

Planetary Theories

But nowhere else is this theoretically generalizing tendency more obvious than in the field of planetary theories. And again because of the lack of space, I will once more illustrate this discipline with reference to the works of two[25] distinguished theorists from this period, one from the very beginning of Mamluk times by the name of Muʾayyad al-Dīn al-ʿUrḍī (d. 1266)[26] of Damascus and the other from the midst of the Mamluk era and a contemporary and colleague of both Ibn al-Sarrāj and al-Khalīlī by the name of ʿAlī b. Ibrāhīm Ibn al-Shāṭir (d. 1375)[27] who was also a timekeeper at the same Umayyad mosque where his colleague al-Khalīlī worked.

No one that we know of before ʿUrḍī had ever attempted to overhaul the whole of Greek astronomy. Some had tried to summarize that astronomy in smaller more accessible renditions, at times even modifying it a little to include the new findings that were established in Islamic times, from as early as the ninth century. People like Ibn Kathīr al-Farghāni (d. c. 850)[28] and Qusṭā b. Lūqā (d. c. 860)[29], did just that. Others, like Kharaqī[30] and Naṣīr

---

25 The reader should be advised that the period produced some 75 distinguished astronomers whose works cannot possibly even be sampled here. For a full list of their names see David King, "Astronomy of the Mamluks," 109-111.

26 The interest in ʿUrḍī's works on observational instruments dates back to the beginning of the nineteenth century if not before, as noted in Amable Jourdain, "Mémoire sur les instruments employés à l'observatoire de Maragha," *Magasin encyclopédique ou journal des sciences, des letters et des arts* 6 (1809), 43. See also the translation of the same work of ʿUrḍī by H. Seeman "Die Instrumente der Sternwarte zu Maragha nach den Mitteilungen von al-ʿUrdi," *Sitzungsberichte der Physikalisch- Medicinischen Societät,* Erlangen 1928.

27 Much of what is known about Ibn al-Shāṭir, together with a sample of the modern literature on his theoretical work, had already been gathered together by E. S. Kennedy and Imad Ghanem in *The Life and Work of Ibn al-Shāṭir: An Arab Astronomer of the Fourteenth Century*, Aleppo: Institute for the History of Arabic Science 1976. Add to that George Saliba, "Theory and Observation in Islamic Astronomy: The Work of Ibn al-Shāṭir of Damascus," *Journal for the History of Astronomy* 18 (1987), 35-43, reprinted in George Saliba, *A History of Arabic Astronomy: Planetary Theories During the Golden Age of Islam*, New York: NYU Press 1994, 233-41.

28 See *Elementa astronomica*, tr. by J. Golius, Amsterdam 1669, reprinted by F. Sezgin as Golius, Jacob [Ed., Transl.]: *Muhammedis Fil. Ketiri Ferganensis, qui vulgo Alfraganus dicitur, Elementa Astronomica, Arabice et Latine. [al-Farghânî (c. 850): Jawâmi' 'ilm al-nujûm wa-usûl al-harakât al-samâwîya.]* Amsterdam 1669. Repr. 1997 (Islamic Mathematics and Astronomy. 9-10, Publications of the Institut für Geschichte der Arabisch-Islamischen Wissenschaften)

29 Qusṭā b. Lūqā's *Kitāb al-hayʾa* is still in manuscript form kept at Oxford, Bodleian Library, Seld3144/2. The present author, together with Dr. Régis Morelon, are preparing an edition of it.

30 For more information on this astronomer, see Suter, *Die Mathematiker*, 116.

al-Dīn al-Ṭūsī (d. 1274) abridged that astronomy and, in the case of the second, first produced an abridged account of it in Persian and then later added an appendix, in Persian as well, in which he objected to specific issues in that astronomy and tried to remedy them.[31] In the period in between the abridgement and the appendix, Ṭūsī produced a new updated version of the Arabic translations of the *Almagest*, and in it he signaled specific points in the text that he found particularly troublesome.[32] Still, a few years later still he wrote another full abridgement of that astronomy, in Arabic this time, which he called *al-Tadhkira fī ʿilm al-hayʾa* (Memento in Astronomy), and in it he devoted a chapter to what he called problematic issues in Greek astronomy.[33] In that chapter he tried, as much as he could, to solve all those problems.

In the process of criticizing the Greek astronomical tradition in that single chapter of his *Tadhkira*, which Ṭūsī tellingly titled "*fī al-ishārat ilā ḥall mā yanḥal min al-ishkālāt al-wārida ʿalā ḥarakāt al-kawākib al-latī subaqat al-ishāra ilayhā*" (An Indication of the Solution – of That Which is Amenable to Solution – of the Difficulties Referred to Previously That Arise from the Aforementioned Motions of the Planets)[34], a prototype of which was already produced a few years earlier in the Persian appendix-type text that he called *Ḥall-i mushkilāt-i muʿīnīya* (Solution of the Difficulties of the Muʿīnīya)[35] which he in turn wanted it to be read with his still earlier Persian rendition of Greek astronomy, Ṭūsī had by then accumulated a chain of solutions of specific problems in that astronomy. His attempts at solving those specific problems, whether in the Persian *Ḥall*, or in the individual chapter in the later *Tadhkira*, were both based on a significant insight into the solution of one of the critical problems of Greek astronomy. We know that he had arrived at this insight in his famous *taḥrīr al-majisṭī* (Redaction of the Almagest)[36] which he tells us was completed in the year 1247.

---

[31] Much is written about Ṭūsī's astronomy. One could begin with the article in the *Dictionary of Scientific Biography*, ed. Gullipsie, New York: Scribner's Sons 1970-1980, for the recent literature. But for a much more exhaustive study of Ṭūsī's Arabic works on astronomy, see F.J. Ragep, *Naṣīr al-Dīn al-Ṭūsī's Memoir on Astronomy (al-Tadhkira fī ʿilm al-hayʾa)*, New York: Springer 1993.

[32] See George Saliba, "The Role of the *Almagest* Commentaries in Medieval Arabic Astronomy: A Preliminary Survey of Ṭūsī's Redaction of Ptolemy's *Almagest*," in *Archives Internationales d'Histoire des Sciences* 37 (1987), 3-20.

[33] See Ragep, *Ṭūsī*, 195-222.

[34] *Ibid*, 194.

[35] Naṣīr al-Dīn al-Ṭūsī, *Ḥall-i Mushkilāt-i Muʿīnīya*, published in facsimile with introduction by Muḥammad Taqī Dānish-Pīzush, Tehran: Intishārāt Dānishgāh Tehrān 1956.

[36] See George Saliba, "Role of commentaries".

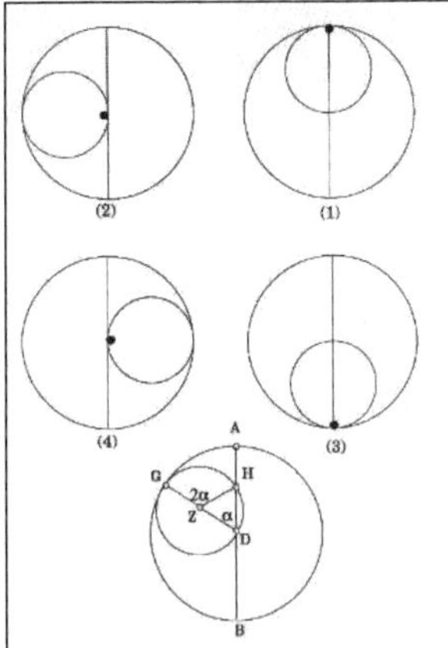

Figure 3. The Ṭūsī Couple as presented in the *Tadhkira*. In essence it says that if two spheres such as *AGB* and *GHD* touch internally at point *A*, and if *AGB*'s diameter is twice as long as that of *GHD*, and if the larger sphere moves uniformly in the direction indicated and the smaller sphere moves in the opposite direction at twice the speed of the first, then point *A* will oscillate up and down along the diameter of the large sphere *AB*.

In the context of the proposed solution for one of the problems of Greek astronomy, Ṭūsī followed his insight, which as we already noted was first articulated in 1247, and introduced a new mathematical theorem, now called the Ṭūsī Couple. He used that theorem to solve the problem, for which it was first developed, namely, that of the latitudinal motion of the planets, but later on used it to solve more complicated issues such as the motion of the moon and the upper planets. When it came to the motions of the planet Mercury, Ṭūsī clearly confessed that he had not yet figured that out, and in his own words said that "if God Most High should enable me to accomplish this, I will append it / to that place, / God willing."[37]

As far as we can tell, Ṭūsī seems to have left his last work, as a work-in-progress so to speak, and was apparently waiting for further inspiration. What he had achieved though, in the twelve years that separated his first articulation of his Couple in 1247 and its final formal statement and incorporation in a much more elaborate mathematical system in his last work in 1259 was indeed of tremendous importance. As it turned out, the Ṭūsī Couple was not a mean achievement. In one full swoop it could be used to solve difficulties in the planetary motions in latitude as he attempted to do in his *Redaction of the Almagest*[38], the complicated motions of the moon, and more interestingly the same theorem could also solve a crucial problem in the motions of the upper planets Saturn, Jupiter, Mars and Venus. At the same time, and because of the ingenious properties of the theorem, the Ṭūsī Couple also managed to destroy the separation between the Aristotelian divisions of the universe that were stipulated by Aristotle on the basis of the motions that were appropriate

37 Ragep, *Ṭūsī*, 208.

38 See George Saliba, "Role of Commentaries".

to the various parts of the universe. As the Ṭūsī Couple could demonstrate, with mathematical rigor, that circular motion could produce linear motion, then the division between the celestial regions of the Aristotelian universe whose nature of motion was circular and the sublunar region whose motion was linear was no longer tenable. Ṭūsī did not derive that conclusion explicitly, but his commentators were very quick to notice it.[39]

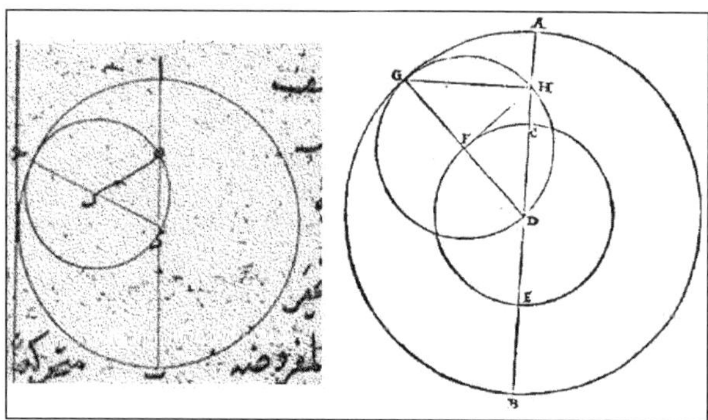

Figure 4. The proof of the Ṭūsī Couple in Ṭūsī's Tadhkira on the left written in 1259, and in the De Revolutionibus of Copernicus, written in 1543, on the right. The late Willy Hartner had noticed that the lettering of the diagram in the two cases was the same, i.e. where Ṭūsī used the Arabic letter "*alef*" Copernicus used the Latin equivalent "*A*", where Ṭūsī used "*Bāʾ*", Copernicus used "*B*", etc.

The mathematical value of the Ṭūsī Couple, once it was clearly demonstrated by Ṭūsī himself in his formal proof in the *Tadhkira*, was widely appreciated by almost every astronomer that followed him including Copernicus himself, the father of Renaissance astronomy. But in the context of the developments within the history of Arabic astronomy it remained to be an ingenious solution for some particular problems of Greek astronomy. The rest of that astronomy was cosmologically either the same or fraught with problems that Ṭūsī could not solve, as he explicitly said.

What ʿUrḍī did was slightly different. In his final version of his fundamental astronomical work, called simply *kitāb al-Hayʾa*[40], he waited till he

---

39 See George Saliba and E. S. Kennedy, "The Spherical Case of the Ṭūsī Couple" in *Arabic Sciences and Philosophy* 1 (1991), 285-291, reprinted with minor mistakes in *Naṣīr al-Dīn al-Ṭūsī: Philosophe et savant du xiiie siècle*, ed. N. Pourjavadi et Z. Vesel, Teheran: Institut Français de Recherche en Iran et Presses Universitaires d'Iran 2000, 105-111.

40 See George Saliba, *The Astronomical Work of Muʾayyad al-Dīn al-ʿUrḍī (d.1266): A Thirteenth Century Reform of Ptolemaic Astronomy,* critical edition with English introduction of 'Urḍī's *Kitāb al-Hayʾa*, based on all extant manuscripts, Beirut: Markaz Dirāsāt al-Waḥda al-ʿArabīya 1990, 1995, 2nd edition 2001.

finished the recasting of the whole of Greek astronomy in his own words and introduced all the corrections that he could bring to it as well as the corrections that were already well established during Islamic times. He then published his work as a complete alternative to Greek astronomy. In the process, he also had to introduce a new theorem in order to solve the problem of the upper planet's motion. And his theorem, which I have dubbed the ʿUrḍī Lemma[41], was also incorporated in the Copernican astronomy and was the subject of a specific detailed correspondence between Kepler and his teacher Maestlin.[42] He also had his own impact on later astronomers as can be easily demonstrated by anyone reading their works. But what he accomplished was the unifying vision of a complete astronomy free of problems.

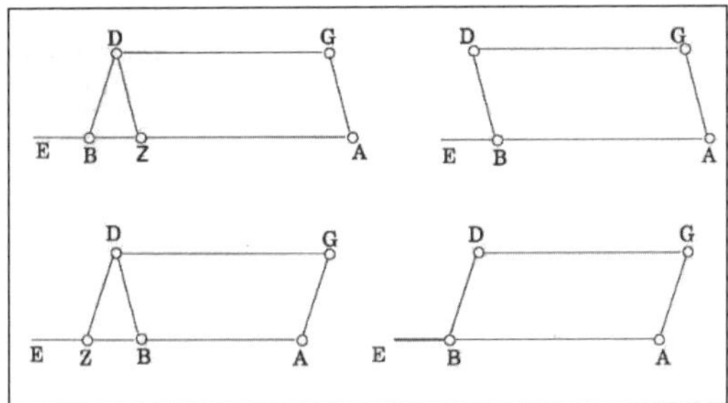

Figure 5. ʿUrḍī's Lemma. Stated briefly it says that if two equal lines *AG*, *BD* form equal angles with line *AB*, either internally or externally, then the line *DG* joining their extremities will be parallel to *AB*.

Furthermore, in ʿUrḍī's work astronomy was no longer Greek in the strict sense of the word. It became a new astronomy, free from the problems that had bedeviled its Greek counterpart. Moreover, ʿUrḍī's successful attempt challenged others to produce alternatives of their own. As a result a series of astronomers, each of them trying to outsmart his predecessors, continued to take up the challenge throughout the Mamluk period. And when we remember that the astronomy of the European Renaissance, which was inaugurated by Copernicus in the first half of the sixteenth century, was itself a form of an alternative to Greek astronomy, one can then see a continuity between the scientific activities that took place during Mamluk times and those that took place during the European Renaissance. If nothing else, they were at least both motivated by the same desire to cleanse Greek astronomy of the cosmo-

41 George Saliba, *A History*, 12, 239, 241, *et passim*.

42 See Anthony Grafton, "Michael Maestlin's Account of Copernican Planetary Theory", *Proceedings of the American Philosophical Society* 117 (1973), 523-552.

logical problems that had been widely debated and hotly condemned in the Islamic world for a few centuries, as we have already seen.

By the following century, Ibn al-Shāṭir also responded to the challenge, but from a much more purist position. While ʿUrḍī had managed on one hand to solve the major sticking problems of Greek astronomy, he remained on the other hand silent on a relatively minor infraction. In its final formulation, ʿUrḍī's astronomy, much like Ptolemy's, made use of eccentric spheres which did indeed violate a cardinal Aristotelian cosmological principle. Aristotle had already argued – against common sense observations it seems – that all the planets and the stars revolved around a center of heaviness that was located at the center of the earth, which was in turn placed at the immovable mathematical center of the sphere of the universe. He would almost say that if we did not happen to have a stable heavy earth at the center of the universe, we should invent one and place it there.[43] In this respect, eccentric spheres would then be a form of infraction of that principle, for they would imply that there is a center of heaviness other than the earth.

Ptolemy was apparently aware of the problem, although he did not mention it explicitly. But in a round about way, he confronted it by resorting to an old theorem of Apollonius of Perga (c. 200 BC) which allowed him to replace the eccentric sphere of the sun with a concentric one that carried a smaller epicycle at its periphery.[44] In layman's terms an epicycle is a small sphere stuck within the surface of the larger sphere that carries it in such a way that its outer surface would be tangent to the inner surface of the outer sphere, just like sticking a ping pong ball inside the periphery of a tennis ball. For its effects, though, the Apollonian theorem offered a general solution that one could use at anytime one wanted to remain strictly within the Aristotelian requirements and avoid using eccentric spheres. Although ʿUrḍī did not explicitly mention this ready-made escape either, he too used the same Apollonian theorem for the motion of the sun and one could assume that he would always use it to replace all the eccentrics that he had deployed in his own astronomy if he was pressed to do so.[45]

However, Ibn al-Shāṭir's purist attitude, would not tolerate that. Instead, he took it upon himself to produce a full-scale alternative astronomy that did not deploy any eccentric spheres whatsoever. And once he set his

---

43 In Aristotle, *On the Heavens*, tr. W.K.C. Guthrie, Cambridge: Harvard Press 1939, Book II, chap. 3, he says: "It follows that there must be earth, it is that which remains at rest in the middle," 151. For more of the same arguments see also Book II, chap. 14.

44 Ptolemy discussed this equation in *Almagest*, III, 3. In particular see Toomer, *Almagest*, 144.

45 For ʿUrḍī's use of the Apollonian theorem, in essence repeating the same Ptolemaic use of it, see George Saliba, *ʿUrḍī*, 69.

mind to it, he accomplished the task brilliantly, and produced a complete set of mathematical models for all the planetary motions without ever using a single eccentric sphere. However, this success came at a high price.

In the same Apollonian theorem that allowed the equation between eccentric constructions and epicyclic ones, there was implied another violation of another Aristotelian principle, namely that of the introduction of the concept of an epicycle. As we have just said, a sphere by its very Aristotelian nature must have a center at rest when it moves. And if an epicycle had to carry any planet by its own motion, it must have its own immovable center. And that would mean that there would be another immovable center or a center of heaviness besides the earth. Ibn al-Shāṭir used epicycles upon epicycles in his own astronomical constructions. At first sight one could conclude that he was in dire contradiction of one Aristotelian principle when he was puritanically avoiding the other. Generations of astronomers had already argued the inadmissibility of epicycles just on that Aristotelian ground.[46] So what was Ibn al-Shāṭir, and after him Copernicus, doing by mounting all those epicycles on top of each other as they both did?

Ibn al-Shāṭir knew that very well, and had obviously thought about the problem before he ventured into the formation of his alternative astronomy. His solution was to attack the Aristotelian principle itself rather than comply with it when he could demonstrate that it did not make much sense. In his own questioning of Aristotle, he would argue that what gave rise to the problem was the faulty Aristotelian assumption that all the celestial bodies were made of the same simple element Ether, an element that did not partake of the qualities of heaviness and lightness as the other elements of Earth, Air, Fire and Water did. For Ibn al-Shāṭir, if the sphere that carried the stars was made of the same element as the stars themselves, as Aristotle would argue, then there is an essential contradiction in the fact that the stars emit light, and the sphere does not. Ibn al-Shāṭir would then suggest that Aristotle must admit, by his own cosmological logic, that there was some form of composition (*tarkīb*[un] *mā*) in the celestial world, and that it was not as simple as he said it was. And if some composition is allowed, then Ibn al-Shāṭir's epicycles would be of the same composite nature.

In that manner, Ibn al-Shāṭir managed to remain philosophically consistent, a feature that was definitely violated by Ptolemy before and by all the astronomers who had followed him. But on the mathematical level, there remained the task of devising mathematical predictive models that would foretell the positions of the planets at all times and at all places. And that challenge was also met by Ibn al-Shāṭir.

46 For a quick reference to the debates and to other literature on the subject, see George Saliba, *A History*, 24.

By carrying out a full program of observations, modifying and correcting the earlier observational results whenever it was needed,[47] and by committing himself to a purist Aristotelian cosmology, Ibn al-Shāṭir finally managed to produce an alternative astronomy that met the two essential requirements any scientific theory must meet, namely, to account for the observed reality and to offer a predictive model for the planetary conditions at all times by the use of mathematical models that were themselves consistent with the conditions of that reality. For example, one could not devise a predictive model for the behavior of a flying saucer by assuming a mathematical representation of a rolling sphere. Ibn al-Shāṭir was consistent on both counts. And thus, on the technical level, his newly devised mathematical models, that described the behavior of planetary motions, turned out to be very useful for later astronomers and particularly to Copernicus himself when he came to devise his own alternative astronomy some one hundred and fifty years later.

I should digress at this point to emphasize that Ibn al-Shāṭir remained faithful to the Aristotelian geocentric cosmology, of course in the manner he understood it as we just mentioned, and would have never contemplated a universe that revolved around the sun as Copernicus was to do later. In fact, a great debate should be raised as to the consistency of Copernicus himself who objected to Greek astronomy for exactly the same reasons that earlier astronomers from the Islamic civilization had objected to, and yet at the end devised an astronomy of his own that violated the same cosmological principles the older Greek astronomy had violated. That is, before the adoption of the scientific universal law of gravitation, a universe revolving around the sun could not have made much cosmological sense. And that universal law of gravitation was not conceived until a hundred years or so after Copernicus. No wonder then that Copernican astronomy did not meet with an immediate success and had to be debated for almost a century before it became validated by the law of universal gravitation.

As far as the technical constructions of mathematical predictive models that would describe the motions of the planets are concerned, it does not make much difference whether one assumed the center of the universe to be at the center of the earth or at the center of the sun. After all, it all comes down to the choice of the reference point to which one wishes to relate all the motions of the celestial bodies. For a mathematical model it would simply imply reversing the single vector that connected the earth to the sun – if we were to use the modern terminology of vectors. In fact, Copernicus did just that, conceived the

---

47 He did that in a work that he called *Taʿlīq al-Arṣād* (Accounts of Observations), which seems to be lost now, and to which he refers in his other works.

models as geocentric and then reversed the connection between the earth and the sun to achieve heliocentrism. With that understanding, it remains therefore perfectly legitimate to compare the kind of predictive models that were devised by Ibn al-Shāṭir with those that were later devised by Copernicus.

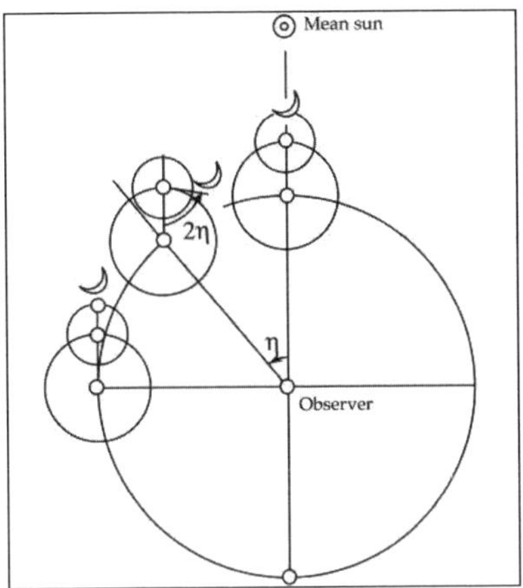

Figure 6. The lunar model used by both Ibn al-Shāṭir (d. 1375) and Copernicus (d. 1543)

When that is done, some remarkable results begin to appear. First, it turns out that the mathematical model that was devised afresh by Ibn al-Shāṭir for the motion of the moon was in every respect identical to the one devised by Copernicus. For those who still think that heliocentrism made a difference, they should be reminded that the moon is a geocentric body in both systems, and thus the comparison becomes quite significant in terms of possible transmission of ideas from the Mamluk world to Renaissance Europe. For the model of the upper planets, i.e. for Saturn, Jupiter, Mars and Venus, Ibn al-Shāṭir simply modified the earlier model of ʿUrḍī by replacing its eccentric sphere with a concentric-epicyclic one. The rest he kept exactly the same. And that too turned out to be the same model that was also adopted by Copernicus if one adjusts for the last vector shift between the earth and the sun as we just said. Finally, regarding the last model for the planet Mercury – a very difficult planet to observe and whose position it is difficult to predict with accuracy – Ibn al-Shāṭir found himself in need of creating a linear motion out of two circular motions as was done earlier by Naṣīr al-Dīn al-Ṭūsī in the case of the moon and the upper planets. By taking over the Ṭūsī Couple, and embedding it within a model to which Ṭūsī himself had never dreamt of applying, Ibn al-Shāṭir managed to describe the motions of the planet Mercury with a remarkable accuracy, or at least with as much accuracy as the Ptolemaic or later the Copernican models could predict. And there too,

Copernicus came to use the same Ṭūsī Couple that was used by Ibn al-Shāṭir for exactly the same purpose, and at exactly the same juncture in his predictive model for the planet Mercury. Taken all together, and suppressing the problematic question of heliocentrism for a moment, one could see the works of Copernicus as incorporating all the ingenious mathematical constructions of Ibn al-Shāṭir, and that he only modified them by re-orienting the last vector that connected the earth to the sun.

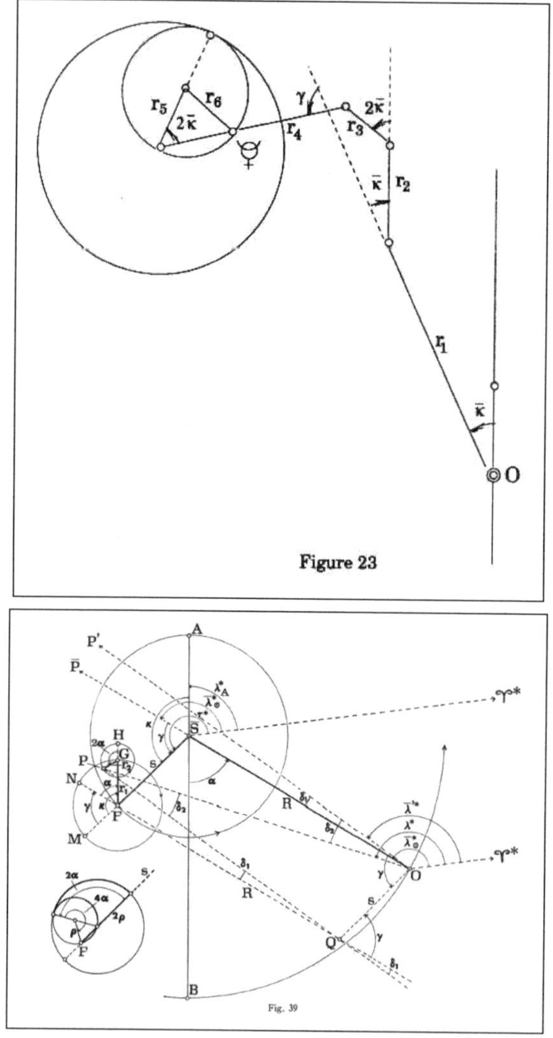

Figure 7. The model for the motion of Mercury as conceived by Ibn al-Shāṭir on the left, and Copernicus on the right. Note that they both use a version of the Ṭūsī Couple to allow the planet to oscillate back and forth in linear motion along the last connection.

Conclusion

With Ibn al-Shāṭir, one could easily say that Mamluk science reached the same maturity that was only reached in European science during the Renaissance. And by connecting Mamluk science to the preceding period, as we have done, one can also see the context in which both Mamluk and Renaissance astronomy grew, and in a more concrete sense appreciate the manner in which Copernican astronomy in particular was itself deeply grounded within the earlier Mamluk works. One should not be surprised at that. After all, that is the natural progress of scientific ideas, and scientists then, as their modern counterparts continue to do, built their theories on each others' works and refined their observations in order to produce a more coherent explanation of the world around them. Many of the problems that continued to motivate earlier scientists, such as problems of consistency and the like, and many of the results that were already reached by meticulously detailed, scientific, observational work, such as the results that were already achieved in ninth century Baghdad and thereafter, continue to be part and parcel of our modern understanding of the basic construction of the world. With every solstice and every equinox, we should continue to remember the exact measure of the inclination of the earth's axis that was already reached by the scientists of early Islamic times. And whenever the linear up-and-down motion of a piston translates into circular motion to run our cars, we should remember that ingenious discovery of the Ṭūsī Couple that demonstrated feasibility of this translation.

La codification du savoir médical dans la tradition dite «prophétique» à l'époque mamelouke

FLORÉAL SANAGUSTIN

> Car la tradition n'est pas que routine et refus de l'invention,
> elle est aussi [...] épreuve d'efficacité, mise au jour
> de conséquences d'abord latentes, bref, expérience d'usage.
>
> G. CANGUILHEM

Introduction

Depuis quelques décennies, on constate, dans le monde arabo-musulman, un regain d'intérêt pour la médecine prophétique (*al-ṭibb al-nabawī*). Cette tendance se manifeste notamment par l'organisation de nombreux colloques sur la médecine islamique et par la publication d'une multitude d'articles et d'ouvrages qui mettent en évidence l'apport de l'islam, tout au long de son histoire, au développement des sciences médicales. Toutefois l'appellation de «médecine islamique», souvent confondue avec «médecine prophétique», est relativement galvaudée et justifie la formulation d'une définition à même d'enlever certaines ambiguïtés.

La constitution de ce courant nous semble intéressante du point de vue épistémologique car il s'agit, à l'évidence, d'une réalité ancrée dans une relecture mythique de l'histoire des idées et fondée sur un processus original de structuration d'un savoir à partir de données relevant d'une part du sacré et d'autre part de la rationalité. Il faudrait d'ailleurs parler de reconstruction, car ce savoir s'est effectivement constitué en un système général à l'époque mamelouke, à savoir entre les VIème / XIIIème et IXème / XVème siècles. Cette entreprise, menée essentiellement par des théologiens, visait à intégrer ce savoir – qui dans la tradition gréco-arabe relevait des sciences rationnelles (*ʿulūm ʿaqliyya*) – aux sciences traditionnelles (*ʿulūm naqliyya)* fondées, dans la civilisation arabo-musulmane, sur le donné révélé.

Ainsi, la médecine prophétique s'est nourrie de trois sources majeures: la tradition empirique pré-islamique; le Coran et le *Ḥadīth*; la médecine arabe (i.e. d'expression arabe) rationnelle ou, autrement dit, savante.

1. L'état de la médecine pré-islamique

On sait qu'en Arabie ancienne, certaines maladies étaient endémiques bien avant l'avènement de l'islam. C'est le cas par exemple de la tuberculose, de la malaria, du trachome, de la dysenterie amibienne ou de la lèpre. De même, certaines affections causées par des parasites étaient communes: vers de Médine (*ʿirq madanī*) ou vers intestinaux. Certains mots arabes anciens dénommaient ces maladies comme *ramad* ou *qamaʿ* pour les ophtalmies; *sill* ou *sulāl* pour la phtisie ou la consomption; *baraṣ, judhām* ou *wadah* pour les affections de la peau.

Les connaissances médicales dont disposaient les Arabes pour lutter contre ces maux relevaient de la tradition populaire et avaient souvent un rapport étroit avec la magie; on croyait que les djinns étaient à l'origine de l'épilepsie et des épidémies de peste. Les principaux organes (foie, cœur, estomac) étaient connus et cités dans la poésie archaïque; les poètes situaient le siège des sentiments et des passions dans le cœur[1]. De même, les principaux vaisseaux sanguins avaient été observés comme *al-abḥār* (veine médiane du bras[2]) ou *al-akhdaʿān* (artères carotides)[3]. Il en est de même pour les membranes enveloppant le cerveau que l'on désignait par: *umm al-dimāgh* ou de *umm al-raʾs*[4]. D'autre part, les Arabes maîtrisaient les techniques de la petite chirurgie telles que la cautérisation, la scarification et la phlébotomie[5]. La cautérisation sera d'ailleurs proscrite par un *ḥadīth*

---

1 On songera ici au *habl al-warīd* du Coran (S. 50, v. 16) et au *matlaʿ* de la *Burda* de Kaʿb b. Zuhayr: «*Bānat Suʿādu fa-qalbī l-yawma matbūlū * mutayyamun ithrahā, lam yujza, makbūlū* (Suʿad s'en est allée et, aujourd'hui, mon cœur s'alanguit * eslave d'elle, insatisfait, enchaîné) ». Cf. Abū Saʿīd al-Sukkarī, *Sharh diwān Kaʿb ibn Zuhayr*, Dār al-Qāmūs al-Jadīd, Beyrouth, 1968, p. 12. La *Muʿallaqa* d'Imru' al-Qays fait aussi référence au cœur comme siège du sentiment amoureux: «*Tasallat ʿamāyātu al-rijāli ʿan al-sibā * wa laysa fuʾādī ʿan hawāki bi-munsalī*». Cf. al-Zawzanî, *Sharh al-Muʿallaqāt al-sabʿ*, Dār Ihyāʾ al-ʿUlūm, Beyrouth, 1990, p. 31. Nous inspirant de la traduction donnée récemment par P. Larcher, nous proposons la version suivante de ce vers: «Avec jeunesse passe l'aveuglement de l'homme: de sa passion pour toi oncques mon cœur ne se passa». Cf. «La *Muʿallaqa* d'Imruʾ al-Qays, introduction, traduction et notes», in *Arabica*, t. 45, 1998, p. 253. La lèpre était une maladie connue puisque l'un des poètes de l'anté-islam, al-Hārith ibn Hilizza, était - dit-on - lépreux; on pensera aussi, étant donné la signification de son *nasab*, à ʿUbayd ibn al-Abras, auteur d'une *Muʿallaqa*. Cf. al-Zawzanī, *Sharh al-Muʿallaqāt al-sabʿ, op. cit.*, p. 154, 191; al-Jāhiz, *Kitāb al-bursān wal-ʿurjān wal-ʿumyān wal-hūlān,* éd. ʿAbd al-Salām Hārūn, Dār al-Jīl, Beyrouth, 1990, p. 52-170.

2 Le *Lisān al-ʿArab,* cite le *ḥadīth* «*inna Saʿdan rumiya fī akhalihi*» (Saʿd fut blessé à la veine médiane du bras), éd. Dār Sādir, Beyrouth, s. d., t. 2, p. 586.

3 On retrouve, dans le *hadīth* : «*innahu uhtujima ʿalā al-akhdaʿayni*» (On lui appliqua des ventouses aux carotides), la mention de ce vaisseau. *Ibid.*, t. 8, p. 66.

4 *Ibid.*, t. 12, p. 32. Sur cette question voir M. Ullmann, *Islamic Medicine*, Edinburgh University Press, 1978, p. 1-6.

5 Sur la phlébotomie, voir le vers de Zuhayr ibn Abī Sulmā: «*Yunajjimuha qawmun li-qawmin gharāmatan * wa lam yuhrīqū baynahum milʾa mihjamī*» (Les uns payèrent leurs dettes aux autres * et il ne fut versé entre eux que de quoi remplir le bol d'un phlébotomiste). Cf. al-Zawzanī, *Sharh al-Muʿallaqāt al-sabʿ, op. cit.*, p. 83. La traduction que donna J. Berque de ce vers est en partie erronée car le premier hémistiche s'y trouve tronqué: «Il n'y a entre eux de versé que de quoi remplir le bol d'un phlébotomiste». Cf. J. Berque, *Les dix grandes odes de l'Anté-islam*, Sindbad, Paris, 1979, p. 101.

célèbre: «Je défends à mon peuple la cautérisation»; elle se maintiendra cependant, malgré cette interdiction, jusqu'à nos jours.

Sur le plan de la thérapeutique, la poésie atteste l'usage de l'urine de chameau, notamment dans une pièce de Labîd. Le lait de chamelle était aussi utilisé ; quant au traitement des ulcérations de la peau, on avait recours au henné. D'autres remèdes courants étaient le miel et la nigelle (*habbat sawdāʾ*). On pourra noter enfin, et cela atteste une pratique médicale courante en Arabie, que les praticiens portaient divers noms en arabe ancien: *ṭabīb*, qui s'imposera par la suite, mais aussi *ʿāsī* et *nitāsī* qui tomberont en désuétude[6].

2. *Le corpus coranique et le* ***ḥadīth***

Bien que le Coran ne fasse pas directement référence à l'art médical, la notion de guérison (*shifāʾ*) y est attestée six fois. C'est le cas dans les deux versets suivants: «De leurs entrailles sort un breuvage bigarré qui est un remède pour les hommes» (S. 16, v. 69); «Nous révélons aux hommes, dans le Coran, la guérison et la grâce divine» (S. 17, v. 82). Ainsi, dans la tradition musulmane, l'idée selon laquelle le Coran est le meilleur des remèdes pour l'homme s'établira définitivement parmi les croyants, comme le confirme ʿAbd al-Laṭīf al-Baghdādī: «*khayr al-dawāʾ al-Qur'ān*». Le Coran affirme aussi la nécessité pour l'homme de respecter une hygiène alimentaire stricte, source d'équilibre et de vie harmonieuse et condition d'un rapport idéal au monde environnant.

Le verset: «Mangez et buvez mais sans excès, car Dieu n'aime point ceux qui commettent des excès» (S. 7, v. 31) résume parfaitement la condition nécessaire de la maîtrise de soi pour vivre sa foi dans la plénitude et ne pas sombrer dans la passion (*hawā*), source de maux extrêmes, tant physiques que psychiques. La foi elle-même apparaît comme le remède souverain face aux assauts des maladies avec l'idée sous-jacente – qui connaîtra une grande fortune au sein des confréries soufies à partir des VIIème /XIIIème siècles – que Dieu protège les vrais croyants des grandes manifestations morbides.

Un nombre considérable de *ḥadīth* se rapporte à des principes d'hygiène, de prophylaxie et de traitement, le Prophète les ayant formulés devant ses

---

6 *Nitāsī* ou *natāsī* vient d'une racine désignant un homme savant et, par extension, habile dans l'art médical. Cf. *Lisān al-ʿArab*, *op. cit.*, t. 6, p. 232; *ʾāsī* est tiré d'une racine désignant la médication. *Ibid.*, t. 14, p. 34. La cautérisation est mentionnée dans un *ḥadīth* célèbre: «La guérison dépend de trois choses: les ventouses scarifiées, l'absorption de miel et la cautérisation par le feu, mais j'interdis à ma communauté la pratique de la cautérisation». Cf. A. al-Baghdādī, *al-Ṭibb min al-Kitāb wal-Sunna*, Dār al-Maʿrifa, Beyrouth, 1988, p. 210.

épouses ou ses Compagnons en des occasions diverses. Par le respect de ces règles, les musulmans cherchent à imiter Muḥammad dans son rapport à la maladie, à l'hygiène et à la médecine de façon générale. Les grands traditionnistes rassemblèrent, dès les IIIème / IXème siècles, un corpus de *ḥadīth* à caractère médical, dont certains paraissent cependant douteux. Ils eurent, et ont toujours, sur l'inconscient collectif musulman une influence déterminante ce qui explique le recours fréquent en médecine traditionnelle, à des simples dont la charge symbolique demeure intacte. Le henné, le *miswāk* (racine de l'*ārāk*, *Salvadora persica*), le miel sont au nombre de ceux-là. Nous citerons, parmi les *ḥadīth*, trois des plus connus: «*ʿAlaykum bi-shifāʾayn: al-ʿasal wal-Qurʾān* (Suivez deux cures: le miel et le Coran)»; «*Inna Allāh anzala al-dāʾ wa jaʿala li-kull dāʾ dawāʾ* (Dieu a créé les maladies et leur remède et il a affecté à chaque maladie son remède)», ce qui est une invitation à faire usage de la raison; «*Al-maʿida bayt al-dāʾ wal-himya raʾs kull dawāʾ* (L'estomac est le siège des maladies et la diète le premier des traitements)»[7].

On sent affleurer, dans ce corpus, un savoir empirique issu de la tradition orale et de pratiques ancestrales dont nous percevons encore de nos jours les réminiscences dans la médecine populaire des pays musulmans. Ce savoir sait aussi tirer des enseignements de l'observation - en reconnaissant le caractère contagieux d'une maladie - comme le démontre la recommandation prophétique fort connue invitant les musulmans à respecter certains principes sanitaires en cas d'épidémie de peste: «*fa-idhā samiʿtum bihi bi-ʾard, fa-lā tadkhulū ʿalayhi; wa-ʾidhā waqaʾa bi-ʾard wa-antum bihā, fa-lā takhrujū, minhā firāran minhā*»[8].

3. *La médecine arabe rationnelle*

La médecine arabe (i. e. d'expression arabe) représente un système médico-philosophique qui se constitua, à partir des IIème / VIIIème siècles, sur un substrat gréco-sémitique, persan et indien. Puis, après une période d'assimilation, grâce notamment aux traductions effectuées à *Bayt al-ḥikma* de Bagdad et à un mouvement de création terminologique unique

[7] Voir, sur le rapport des *ḥadīth* à la médecine, S. Ammar, *Médecins et médecine de l'islam*, éd. Tougui, Paris, p. 15-39, 86-94.

[8] «Si vous apprenez qu'une épidémie [de peste] s'est déclarée dans une contrée, n'y allez pas; et si elle se déclare dans un lieu où vous vous trouvez, ne vous enfuyez pas pour y échapper». Cf. Ibn Qayyim al-Jawziyya, *al-Ṭibb al-nabawī*, Dār al-Waʿy, Alep, 1983, p. 145. Voir aussi J. Bellakhdar, *Médecine traditionnelle et toxicologie ouest saharienne*, Editions techniques nord-africaines, Rabat, 1978, p. 103-144; *La pharmacologie marocaine traditionnelle*, Ibis Press, Paris, 1997, p. 77-88.

en son genre, cela donna lieu à une production scientifique originale[9]. Ce système cohérent forme ce qu'il est convenu d'appeler, avec T. Kuhn, un paradigme, c'est-à-dire un cadre conceptuel rationnel dans lequel se reconnaissent, pour un temps donné, des savants ou encore des intellectuels.

Ceux-ci sont en mesure d'en décoder les significations profondes et la portée dans le cadre d'une théorie générale de la connaissance. Les œuvres médicales d'Abū Bakr al-Rāzī et d'Ibn Sīnā, par exemple, s'inscrivaient dans ce paradigme et les concepts qu'ils produisirent furent opératoires tant qu'il dura, c'est-à-dire jusqu'à la grande rupture épistémologique que représentèrent les découvertes anatomiques et physiologiques de M. Servet et W. Harwey. Les médecins arabes (souvent également philosophes) vont s'efforcer d'accéder à la vérité par la mise en œuvre de critères de vérification fondés sur la logique; ils construiront ainsi, aux alentours de l'an mil, une pensée répondant aux nécessités de l'enseignement, suffisamment abstraite pour se démarquer de l'empirisme et de la superstition.

Cette pensée appartient à la culture urbaine et demeure, de ce fait, l'apanage d'une aristocratie d'intellectuels capables d'en faire une lecture profonde. Du statut d'art (*ṣināʿa*), la médecine accède à celui de science (*ʿilm*). Ce savoir s'appuie sur l'usage de la raison, rejette le mythe, les croyances, la superstition et met l'accent sur la nécessité de la transmission. Il est, de ce fait, fondé sur une tradition exclusivement scripturaire, en rupture avec la tradition orale ou empirique, même si dans le domaine de la chirurgie, il doit beaucoup à cette dernière[10]. La médecine rationnelle développa des théories bien connues, telles que celles des humeurs, des éléments, de l'équilibre (*crasis*, dyscrasie), de l'obstruction, de la pléthore etc., théories qui déterminèrent l'ensemble de la thérapeutique arabe médiévale.

---

[9] Cf. D. Gutas, *Greek Thought, Arabic Culture. The Greco-Arabic Translation Movement in Baghdad and Early ʿAbbāsid Society (2nd - 4th/8th - 10th centuries),* Routledge, Londres, 1998; G. Troupeau, «Le rôle des Syriaques dans la transmission et l'exploitation du patrimoine philosophique et scientifique grec», in Arabica, t. 38, 1991, p. 1-10; «Du syriaque au latin par l'intermédiaire de l'arabe: le *Kunnāsh* de Yuhannā ibn Sarābiyūn», in *Arabic Science and Philosophy*, vol. 4, 1994, p. 267-277; I. Ben Mrad, *al-Muṣallaḥ al-aʿjamī fī kutub al-ṭibb wa-l-ṣaydala al-ʿarabiyya,* 2 vol., Dār al-Gharb al-Islāmī, Beyrouth, 1985; *Buhūth fī taʾrīkh al-ṭibb wal-ṣaydala ʿinda al-ʾArab*, Dār al-Gharb al-Islāmī, Beyrouth, 1991; G. Endress, "The circle of al-Kindī: Early Arabic translations from Greek and the rise of Islamic philosophy", in *The Ancient Tradition in Christian and Islamic Hellenism*, G. Endress-R. Kruk éds., Research School CNWS, School of Asian, African and Amerindian Studies, Leiden, 1997, p. 43-76.

[10] Cf. Ibn Sīnā, *Kitāb al-qānūn fī-l-ṭibb,* éd. Bûlâq, Le Caire, 1877, t. 1, p. 204-213; t. 2, p. 18, 115-119, 162; t. 3, p. 136-137; Abū Sahl al-Masīḥī, *Kitāb al-miʾa fī-l-ṭibb*, éd. F. Sanagustin, IFEAD, Damas, 2000 (voir notamment vol. 1, chapitre introductif); F. Sanagustin, "La chirurgie dans le *Canon de la médecine* d'Ibn Sīnā", in *Arabica*, t. 33, 1986, p. 84-122.

4. La codification de la médecine prophétique

La médecine prophétique qui ne constituait pas à l'origine un ensemble structuré, mais plutôt une série de recommandations d'ordre médical inspirées du Coran et de la Sunna et n'était, en aucune manière, une tentative de conceptualisation, peut être assimilée à une forme de lecture mythique du passé glorieux dans lequel le Prophète s'identifie à l'archétype de l'homme parfait, modèle de tous les musulmans. À une époque relativement tardive – à partir des VIIème/XIIIème siècles, en pleine époque mamelouke – ce savoir va être codifié grâce à un processus de réappropriation du cadre conceptuel propre à la médecine rationnelle gréco-arabe. Ce processus, très intéressant sur le plan épistémologique, s'accompagna d'une islamisation en profondeur d'un savoir d'inspiration non-islamique puisque fondé sur le seul usage de la raison: on ramenait pourtant la médecine dans le giron des sciences traditionnelles (*ʿulūm naqliyya*).

Il s'agissait, à l'évidence, dans un contexte général de reprise en mains par les théologiens sunnites de la science rationnelle (philosophie et médecine surtout), de contrer le courant médical rationaliste suspect, à leurs yeux, d'être allogène et incompatible avec l'esprit arabo-musulman. On remarque d'ailleurs que la plupart des auteurs de traités de médecine prophétique sont des théologiens ou des juristes et non pas des médecins de formation. De même, la pharmacologie arabe sera islamisée c'est-à-dire que l'usage des simples et leur efficacité seront corroborés par des *ḥadīth* ou par l'exemple comportemental du Prophète. Nous citerons, à l'appui de notre hypothèse, le polygraphe et juriste al-Suyūṭī:

«Henné: [...] A quiconque avait une plaie ou une épine [fichée dans les chairs], le Prophète faisait appliquer un topique à base de henné. Jamais personne ne se plaignait [...] de douleurs au pied que le Prophète ne lui dit: Teins-les au henné ! Le henné est l'arbre le plus chéri de Dieu. Les juifs et les chrétiens ne se teignent jamais avec le henné, faites l'inverse»[11].

On verra donc fleurir, à compter des VIIème/XIIème siècles, un genre nouveau de textes médicaux, intitulés le plus souvent *Kitāb al-ṭibb al-nabawī*. Le premier auteur attesté, antérieur à cette époque, est Abū Bakr b. al-Sunnī (m.436/1044), mais la plupart sont plus tardifs: ʿAbd al-Laṭīf al-Baghdādī (m.629/1231) auteur du *al-Ṭibb min al-Kitāb wal-Sunna*[12]; Ibn al-Jawzī (m.596/1200) auteur du *al-Ṭibb al-rūhānī*[13]; Ibn Qayyim al-Jaw-

[11] Cf. al-Suyūtī, *La médecine du Prophète*, trad. A. Perron, rééd. Al-Bustane, Paris, 1997, p. 97-98.

[12] Ed. Dār al-Maʿrifa, Beyrouth, 1998.

[13] Ed. Dār al-Anwār, Damas, 1993.

ziyya (m.751/1350) auteur de *al-Ṭibb al-nabawī*[14]; Jalāl al-Dīn al-Suyūṭī (m.911/1505) auteur de *al-Manhaj al-sāwī wa-l-manhal al-rāwī fī-ṭibb al-nabawī*[15] et du *al-Raḥma fī-l-ṭibb wa-l-ḥikma*[16].

Ces ouvrages ont contribué à la constitution d'un cadre paradigmatique propre à la médecine prophétique, cadre qui favorisera son adoption dans l'ensemble du monde musulman, et ce jusqu'à nos jours. L'établissement de ce paradigme scientifique appelle cependant un certain nombre de remarques. Tout d'abord, on notera que les traités de *ṭibb nabawī* posent la science médicale comme un enseignement divin et qu'ils établissent définitivement son rapport au sacré et à la révélation; elle s'inscrit, par conséquent, en rupture avec le courant rationalisant puisque l'accession à la vérité scientifique ne passe plus par les seuls schémas logiques, mais bien par l'adhésion à un donné révélé. ᶜAbd al-Laṭīf al-Baghdādī écrira à ce sujet: «*Innahu [i.e. al-ṭibb] min taᶜlīm Allāh taᶜālā wa-ilhāmih wa huwa al-ḥaqq, thumma udīfat ilayhi al-tajārib wal-qiyās*»[17]. Dans la continuité de ce savant, les auteurs des éditions récentes affirment, sans ambages, le caractère islamique de l'ensemble de la médecine médiévale. Ainsi, dans sa préface au *K. al-ṭibb al-nabawī* d'Ibn Qayyim al-Jawziyya, ᶜAbd al-Mutīᶜ al-Qalᶜajī écrit: «La médecine est née en islam et a atteint son apogée à l'ombre de cette religion»[18]. Dans une telle perspective, le Prophète apparaît bien comme le détenteur d'un savoir médical d'essence supérieure.

Mais alors que l'on pouvait s'attendre à ce que ces deux systèmes antinomiques demeurent étrangers l'un à l'autre, on constate au contraire un processus d'appropriation et de réinterprétation par la médecine prophétique de la plupart des doctrines fondatrices du courant rationaliste d'inspiration philosophique que représentèrent ᶜAlī b. Rabbān al-Ṭabarī, Abū Bakr al-Rāzī, Ibn Sīnā ou Ibn Zuhr. Alors que, dans ce courant, les principes fondamentaux de la médecine (éléments, qualité, humeurs, tempéraments etc.) sont interprétés comme des objets naturels – relevant donc de l'action de la

---

14 Ed. Dār al-Waᶜy, Alep, 1983.

15 Ed. Bûlâq, La Caire, 1870.

16 Ed. Dār al-Qalam, Beyrouth, s. d. Sur la médecine prophétique en général, voir A. Muhammad Matlûᶜ, *Mudkhal ilā al-ṭibb al-islāmī*, Le Caire, 1985; A. Muʾnis, *ᶜAlā hāmish al-ṭibb al-nabawī*, Le Caire, 1986.

17 «La médecine est un enseignement et une inspiration d'essence divine; elle est pourtant la science vraie; puis on [i.e. les hommes] lui associa l'empirisme et le raisonnement». Cf. ᶜAbd al-Laṭīf al-Baghdādī, *al-Ṭibb min al-Kitāb wa-l-Sunna*, *op. cit.*, p. 187. On remarquera l'ordre dans lequel l'auteur cite les trois fondements de la médecine en mettant au dernier rang le *qiyās* qui, dans le système médico-philosophique arabe, se situe au contraire au premier rang.

18 *K. al-Ṭibb al-nabawī*, *op. cit.*, p. 10.

Nature – ils deviennent dans la médecine prophétique, effets de la seule volonté divine[19]. De ce fait, le rôle des médecins anciens se trouve idéalisé à l'instar d'Hippocrate par exemple qui, reconnu pour sa sagesse, sa science et sa rigueur déontologique, est perçu à travers le prisme de l'hagiographie, comme le serait un saint musulman. En outre, la guérison ne se trouve plus uniquement subordonnée à la simple action des remèdes, mais elle dépend aussi, en grande part, de l'intervention de Dieu[20]. Il semblerait que ce courant ait pris de l'ampleur même avant le développement des confréries mystiques puisque plusieurs auteurs en font état et notamment Abū Sahl al-Masīḥī (IVème/Xème siècles) qui se plaignait d'un «groupe» qui remettait en cause le bien-fondé de l'art médical. Ibn Qayyim al-Jawziyya évoque également «ceux qui s'opposent au traitement ou à la médication (*tadāwī*)»[21] .

Un autre trait spécifique de la médecine prophétique est l'intrusion de la croyance et de la superstition dans les pratiques de santé. Cela se manifeste de deux manières: d'une part, grâce à la justification médicale de certaines pratiques cultuelles telles que le jeûne et, d'autre part, par l'utilisation de talismans et de formules cabalistiques destinées à hâter la guérison. En effet, les traités de médecine prophétique établissent un lien direct entre le respect du culte, dans tous ses aspects, et le maintien de la santé; c'est ainsi que les médecins mettent en évidence les bienfaits du jeûne de ramadan sur le système digestif et au-delà, sur l'ensemble du corps, car il opère à la manière d'une purge ou d'un sédatif permettant d'éliminer les humeurs peccantes de l'organisme. De la même manière, la prière a un aspect salutaire pour l'équilibre psychologique de l'homme dans la mesure où elle lui permet de vivre en harmonie au sein de sa société et de maîtriser ses passions. Il ne s'agit pas ici d'expliquer le réel, mais de le justifier et surtout de le codifier comme le fait l'éditeur de ᶜAbd al-Laṭīf al-Baghdādī lorsqu'il condamne l'adultère comme source majeure des maladies vénériennes[22].

En ce qui concerne la superstition, elle se manifeste dans la médecine prophétique par l'usage des talismans et de ce qu'al-Suyūṭī appelle *al-ʿilāj bi-l-kitāba*, appellation qui couvre toutes les pratiques faisant appel à ces

---

19 Cf. al-Suyūṭī, *al-Raḥma fī-l-ṭibb wa-l-ḥikma*, *op. cit.*, p. 3-4.

20 «Dieu a créé la chaleur, puis le froid, puis les hommes» écrit al-Suyūṭī, *Ibid.*, p. 3. Dans ce même ouvrage, l'auteur répète, après chaque recette médicinale, la formule suivante: «Le malade guérira s'il plaît à Dieu» (*ibraʾu bi-idhni Allāh*). *Ibid.*, p. 108-109. Ibn Qayyim al-Jawziyya présente, pour sa part, la médecine comme un enseignement venant de Muḥammad, chaque recommandation ou prescription symbolisant la voie tracée par lui (*hadyuhu*). Cf. *al-Ṭibb al-nabawī*, *op. cit.*, p. 130-144.

21 *Ibid.*, p. 99.

22 *Ibid.*, p. 51, 53.

formules cabalistiques auxquelles Ibn Qayyim al-Jawziyya consacre une partie de son livre[23]. Dans la médecine arabe tardive, après les VIIIème/XVème siècles, les pratiques divinatoires relevant de la superstition pénètreront en force dans les traités de médecine arabe, comme on peut le constater dans la *Tadhkira ʾūlī al-albāb* de Dāwūd al-Antākī[2] où les références à la magie ne sont pas rares[24].

On peut expliquer la permanence dans la médecine de ces pratiques liées à la superstition, par l'existence d'une vieille tradition orientale pré-islamique qui ne fut jamais éradiquée - malgré les efforts de savants tels qu'al-Rāzī et les vives condamnations qu'il adressa aux charlatans - mais aussi par le fait, qu'à l'origine, ces pratiques s'appliquaient essentiellement aux cas d'empoisonnement. Or, la toxicologie, partie importante de la pharmacologie, s'est toujours située à la frontière entre médecine, alchimie et magie, et entre connaissance savante et savoir occulte. Il suffit, pour s'en convaincre, de feuilleter la *Filāḥa nabaṭiyya* d'Ibn Waḥshiyya, livre qui se veut la synthèse de la science des ancêtres mésopotamiens de cet auteur (IVème/Xème siècles) et dont les pages fourmillent d'allusions aux croyances populaires et à la superstition[25].

Sous l'influence des théologiens, la médecine prophétique introduisit, d'autre part, la distinction entre médecine du corps et médecine de l'âme en accordant à cette dernière une importance primordiale. Outre l'idée que la santé du corps et celle de l'esprit sont intimement liées, des auteurs comme Ibn al-Jawzī considèreront qu'il existe une véritable hygiène spirituelle – que les médecins rationalistes ont trop longtemps négligée selon lui - seule garante d'une pratique orthodoxe de la foi. Dans les deux livres qu'il a écrits sur cette question, *dhamm al-hawā* et *al-ṭibb al-rūhānī*, Ibn al-Jawzī démontre la nécessité d'un bon usage de la raison et d'une parfaite maîtrise de soi pour éviter les errements de la passion (*hawā*) et leurs conséquences fâcheuses pour l'harmonie collective de la cité musulmane. Le terme *ʿaql* n'est pas à prendre ici au sens strictement philosophique cher aux rationalistes arabes, mais au sens de discernement, de disposition

---

23 *Ibid.*, p. 328, 529. Cet auteur consacre même un passage à la conservation de la santé par l'usage des parfums dont le Prophète était friand: *ḥifẓ al-siḥḥa bi-l-ṭibb. Ibid.*, p. 417; ʿAbd al-Laṭīf al-Baghdādī, *al-Ṭibb min al-Kitāb wa-l-Sunna*, *op. cit.*, p. 5, 13; Ibn Qayyim al-Jawziyya, *al-Ṭibb al-nabawī, op. cit.*, p. 55; al-Suyūṭī, *al-Raḥma*, *op. cit.*, p. 132-158, 190.

24 Cf. Dāwūd al-Antākī, *Tadhkira ʾūlī al-albāb*, Le Caire, 1864, rééd. Beyrouth, s. d., p. 154-163; E. Dermenghem, *Le culte des saints dans l'islam maghrébin*, Gallimard, Coll. «Tel», Paris, 1954, p. 126-134.

25 Cf. Ibn Waḥshiyya, *Kitāb al-filāḥa al-nabaṭiyya*, éd. T. Fahd, IFEAD, Damas, 2 vol., 1993-1995; T. Fahd, *La divination arabe*, Sindbad, Paris, 1987.

intellectuelle de l'homme lui permettant d'envisager les conséquences de ses actes, qu'elles soient conformes ou non à l'éthique. Ibn al-Jawzī précise cela en ces termes: «Quant à la raison (*ʿaql*), elle envisage les conséquences et examine attentivement la validité des actes humains»[26].

Compte tenu du caractère islamique, maintes fois affirmé, de cette médecine prophétique, ces savants lui dénient toute dimension universelle et, qui plus est, en réservent la pratique aux seuls médecins musulmans; les autres communautés vivant dans le *dār al-islām* ne sont pas concernées et doivent donc recourir à des médecins issus de leurs rangs. Ces auteurs se situent donc dans une perspective diamétralement opposée à celle de la médecine arabe «rationnelle» qui, résultant de lois générales, a l'ambition d'être un système universel dénué de tout rapport particulier à une communauté. Poussant leur logique à l'extrême, aucun de leurs traités n'aborde la question de savoir si un non-musulman (*dhimmī)* peut exercer l'art médical et si un patient musulman pourrait alors le consulter légalement[27].

L'enjeu est donc de savoir si la vérité scientifique fondée sur l'usage de la raison représente toute la vérité ou non; et s'il y a place pour l'affirmation d'une vérité scientifique liée au sacré, c'est-à-dire fondée sur un donné révélé et sur le modèle archétypique d'une tradition prophétique. Il s'agit là d'un vieux débat entre discours mythique et discours conceptuel, entre *muthos* (récit-fable) et *logos* (langage-raison) si l'on veut. La médecine prophétique serait alors une recherche de sens, la relecture d'un passé mythique idéalisé. De ce fait, elle est porteuse de représentations sur un fait religieux, une pratique et elle a pour fonction d'alimenter une mémoire collective chargée d'assurer la transmission de comportements et de savoirs constitutifs de la culture islamique.

L'hypothèse que nous avançons est que la médecine prophétique, est avant tout, une forme de récit sur les origines. Pour reprendre Mircea Eliade, nous dirons que le mythe a ici une fonction d'instauration d'un savoir lié à une révélation. Ce savoir introduit également la dimension particulière du merveilleux qui s'explique probablement par son caractère hagiographique et son appartenance à la tradition orale. Dans ce sens, des anthropologues, comme J. Goody, ont montré que la mémoire active d'une société possède un rythme et qu'elle réorganise régulièrement les informations qu'elle est chargée de transmettre[28]. L'antinomie du *muthos* et du *logos*, que nous

---

26 Cf. Ibn al-Jawzī, *al-Ṭibb al-rūḥānī*, *op. cit.*, p. 30; *Dhamm al-hawā*, Dār al-Bāz li-l-Nashr wal-Tawzīʿ, La Mekke, 1987, p. 13-17 (*fī dhikr al-ʿaql*), 473-497 (*fī muʿālajat al-zāhir; fī muʿālajat al-bāṭin*).

27 Cf. ʿAbd al-Laṭīf al-Baghdādī, *al-Ṭibb min al-Kitāb wa-l-Sunna*, *op. cit.*, p. 184.

28 Cf. J. Goody, *La raison graphique*, Les Editions de Minuit, Paris, 1979, p. 85-107.

croyons être au cœur du débat, est signalée dans la *Muqaddima* d'Ibn Khaldūn. Il écrit, dans le chapitre consacré aux parties du savoir, à propos des sciences rationnelles dont fait partie la médecine:

«Quant aux sciences rationnelles, elles sont naturelles pour l'homme en tant qu'être doué de raison; au surplus, elles ne sont pas l'apanage d'une communauté [au détriment d'une autre]. »[29]

Il atteste donc clairement l'universalité de l'usage de la raison par rapport aux traditions issues de la révélation comme cela est le cas de la médecine prophétique. Plus loin, à propos de la médecine, il signale l'existence, à côté de la médecine rationnelle dont l'émergence est liée à la fondation de la cité, d'une médecine bédouine empirique transmise de génération en génération et, par conséquent, uniquement orale. Il y associe la médecine véhiculée par la *sunna* en lui déniant toute valeur islamique:

«Le Prophète - que la paix et le salut soient sur lui - nous a été envoyé pour nous enseigner une loi (*sharīʿa*) et non pour nous apprendre la médecine ou quelque autre science antique»[30].

Il est donc clair que, pour Ibn Khaldūn, la médecine comme science est le produit de la seule raison, idée qui induit cependant l'existence d'autres formes de savoir médical de type empirique à l'instar de la médecine prophétique. Cette dernière correspond à une fonction subjective d'accession au savoir dans lequel interviennent le merveilleux et la croyance. Ainsi donc était brossé à grands traits, l'état du savoir médical à l'époque mamelouke, période de transition entre une tradition médico-philosophique et une lecture idéologisée de la connaissance scientifique.

---

29 Ibn Khaldūn, *al-Muqaddima*, Dār al-Kitāb al-Lubnānī, Beyrouth, 1967, p. 888.

30 *Ibid.*, p. 918-919.

Part Five

Cultural Contexts of Political Practice and Social Relations

Legends against Arbitrary Abuse: The Relationship between the Mamluk Military Elite and their Arab Subjects.[1]

ALBRECHT FUESS

There are some fine bath houses in Tripoli, (...) one which is called after Sandamūr, who was a former governor of this city. Many stories are told of his severity towards evil-doers. Here is one of them: A woman complained to him that one of the Mamluks of his personal staff had seized some milk that she was selling and had drunk it. She had no evidence, but Sandamūr sent for the man. He had him cut into two halves and the milk came out of his intestines.[2]

The famous Arab traveller Ibn Baṭṭūṭa heard this legend about the strict but just governor Sandamūr when he passed through Tripoli in the summer of 1326. Sandamūr's behaviour was noteworthy indeed if we compare it to the usual relationship between Mamluk amirs and their Arab subjects at that time. In most cases it was quite difficult for the ordinary Arab to press charges against representatives of the Mamluk military elite. Therefore, Arab people remembered a just governor for a long time and attributed all kinds of legends to him, as happened in this case, turning Sandamūr from a real historical person into a legend.

The Amir Sayf al-Dīn Asnadamur al-Kurjī[3] became the so-called governor of the coasts and the conquests in 1301.[4] In the following period As-

---

1 This text is a revised and extended version of a paper which was first presented under the title "Legends against Injustice" at the 37th Annual Meeting of the Middle East Studies Association (MESA) in November 2003 in Anchorage, Alaska.

2 Ibn Baṭṭūṭa (d. after 1368): *Riḥlat Ibn Baṭṭūṭa*, Beirut 1980, 65; Ibn Baṭṭūṭa: *Travels in Asia and Africa 1325-1354*, translated and selected by H. A. R. Gibb, London [5]1963, 60.

3 al-Kurjī, i.e. the Georgian, see: Abu'l Fidāʾ (d. 1331): *The Memoirs of a Syrian Prince*, translated by Peter M. Holt, Wiesbaden 1983, 39.

4 Abu'l Fidāʾ (d. 1331): *The Memoirs of a Syrian Prince*, 39, 53. The governorship was alternatively also called "governorship of the fortresses and the coast". The term "governor of Tripoli" was apparently not used for the head of the province of Tripoli prior to 1333, see: al-Qaṭṭār, Alyās: *Niyābat Ṭarābulus fī ʿahd al-mamālīk* (688-922 h./ 1289-1516), Beirut 1998, 79.

nadamur conquered with his troops the island of Arwād, the last stronghold of the crusaders on the Syrian coast, opposite the town of Ṭarṭūs in 1302[5], fought successfully against the Mongols in Syria in 1303[6], and two years later he participated in a large military expedition against the local population of the region of Kisrawān, north of Beirut, who were apparently Shiites.[7] He was a powerful local governor and his term of office lasted until 1310.[8] It might have been his long governorship of almost ten years that made him so remarkable and unforgettable in the memory of the local people, but there seems to have been something special about his personality as well. According to the biographical dictionary of aṣ-Ṣafadī governor Sayf al-Dīn Asnadamur was a man of excellence and taste. He enjoyed the solving of riddles (*ghawāmiḍ*). At one time he asked several religious scholars, including a certain Ibn Taymiyya (d. 1328), to explain to him who was better in the following two cases: "Either the Saint or the Martyr or the Angel or the Prophet." Asnadamur was also very much known for his brutality. He brought law and order to Tripoli by shedding a lot of blood in order to achieve this goal. This rigorous enforcement of the law and the restoration of regional security earned him the reputation of a just governor. Only his excessive appetite is mentioned by aṣ-Ṣafadī as one of his few weaknesses. Every evening he used to eat an entire young sheep and loads of sweets.[9]

From another source we learn more of the unorthodox behaviour of Sayf al-Dīn Asnadamur. Apparently he allowed his Jewish secretary to ride on a horse, a privilege that was normally reserved for members of the Mamluk military elite. When upset Mamluk soldiers attacked the Jewish secretary and almost beat him to death, Asnadamur decided to throw the leader of the Mamluk soldiers who had led the assault into prison. In the meantime the story of the incident with the "infidel" Jewish secretary had reached Damascus. The Māliki Qadi of Damascus ordered the execution of the Jew and the release from jail of the Mamluk.[10]

---

5 Ibn Kathīr, ʿImād al-Dīn (d. 1373): *al-Bidāya wa'l-nihāya fī tārīkh*, ed. by Aḥmad Abī Mulḥim, vol. 7/14, Beirut ³1987, 23.

6 Abu'l Fidāʾ (d. 1331): *The Memoirs of a Syrian Prince*, 41.

7 Ṣāliḥ ibn Yaḥyā ibn Buḥtur (d. after 1436): *Tārīkh Bayrūt. Akhbār al-salaf min dhurrīyat Buḥtur ibn ʿAlī amīr al-Gharb bi-Bayrūt*, ed. by Francis Hours and Kamal Salibi, Beirut 1969, 28, 96.

8 Abu'l Fidāʾ (d. 1331): *The Memoirs of a Syrian Prince*, 39, 51-52.

9 al-Ṣafadī, Ṣalāḥ al-Dīn Khalīl ibn Aybak (d. 1363): *Al-Wāfī bi'l-wafayāt*, vol. 9, ed. by Josef van Ess, Wiesbaden 1974, 248-249.

10 al-Maqrīzī (d. 1442): *Kitāb al-Sulūk li-maʿrifat duwal al-mulūk*, ed. by M. Ziyāda, vol. 2 part 1, Cairo 1941, 3, 4, 14; Tadmurī, ʿUmar ʿAbd al-Salām: *Tārīkh Ṭarābulus al-siyāsī wa'l-ḥaḍārī ʿabr al-ʿuṣūr*, vol. 2, Beirut 1981, 197-199.

This example suggests that Asnadamur was a rather unusual and unorthodox governor, but finally he could not overrule higher Mamluk authorities. In any case, he was still a member of the Mamluk military elite. In 1310, Asnadamur was appointed governor of Ḥamāh. In September 1310, Sultan al-Nāṣir Muḥammad wanted to send Asnadamur back to Tripoli, which he refused. Asnadamur only left Ḥamāh some weeks later, after he became governor of Aleppo. After this episode the sultan doubted Asnadamur's loyalty and sent troops to capture him in the palace of Aleppo on May 1st, 1311. Asnadamur was taken in chains first to Cairo and later to al-Karak, where he died. The sultan confiscated his huge property.[11] In that manner an unusual Mamluk governor ended his life in the usual Mamluk way. The numerous privileges a member of the Mamluk upper class enjoyed was compensated by the fact that Mamluk amirs were also running the risk of falling into disgrace with the ruling sultan.

Asnadamur was no exception. Still, his rulings and his way of governance in Tripoli apparently earned him the respect of his Arab subjects who commemorated his government with legendary stories, which still circulated sixteen years later when Ibn Baṭṭūṭa visited the region.

Mamluks as "Outlaws"

Instead of laudatory legends, stories of Mamluks arbitrarily abusing Arabs abound. Ibn Iyās recounts an event of the year 1507:

> "A Mamluk went to the slave market, to buy or exchange a slave. Then he started a quarrel with the trader. Finally the Mamluk hit the trader on the head with his wooden shoe *(qabqāb)* – and this in open public among all these people. The man was taken home and died after one month and nobody cared"[12].

Even in the eye of contemporary historians like Ibn Iyās this represented a clear transgression, but Mamluks were usually not punished for their deeds against ordinary subjects. Another example for such "outlaw" behaviour is given for Atabeg Qayt al-Rajabī, who lived at the beginning of the 16th century and had an evil and brutal reputation. Among his minor misdeeds was that he never paid for services of Arab craftsmen. Finally he was arrested. However, according to a contemporary source his abuse of the local population was only used as a pretext, the real reason being that Sultan Qānṣawh al-Ghawrī (1501-1516) had feared that Qayt intended to overthrow him as

11 Abu'l Fidā' (d. 1331): *The Memoirs of a Syrian Prince*, 39, 52-56.

12 Ibn Iyās (d. around 1524): *Badā'iᶜ al-zuhūr fī waqā'iᶜ al-duhūr*, ed. by Mohamed Mostafa, Kairo – Wiesbaden² 1960, vol. 4, 115; Ibn Iyās (d. around 1524): *Alltagsnotizen eines ägyptischen Bürgers*, translated by Annemarie Schimmel, Stuttgart 1985, 87.

sultan.[13] It may therefore not have been the misbehaviour towards ordinary people that caused the arrest of a Mamluk, but his ambitions towards the job of his boss. Nevertheless, even if the charges were entirely fabricated against Qayt, they imply a minimum level of expected good governorship even among the ruling stratum. Anyhow, the mistreatment of the local population was not limited to individual Mamluks. Sometimes larger groups of Mamluks looted towns and raped women even in their own territory during military expeditions as in the case of the Aleppo campaign in 1515.[14] In the rare instance when a Mamluk soldier was imprisoned after having killed a peasant, because he wanted to get hold of the peasant's donkey and a sack of grain, his Mamluk comrades could free him without repercussion as happened in June 1516. Fearing a mutiny among the soldiers, the officials dropped the charge of homicide and tensions subsided.[15]

Interpreting the Mamluk actions of ignoring the law when they dealt with their subjects Petry concludes: "Yet the impression one takes away from their choice of crimes and perpetrators is of vulnerability by the civilian majority compelled to abide the indiscipline of those who sapped their assets."[16] Moreover, he observes that Mamluk authorities reacted only in criminal matters against other Mamluks when the hegemony of the state was at risk or the honour of the leading representatives was severely sullied.[17]

Ideally though, a Mamluk sultan should be just towards his people as it is stipulated by a memorandum of Sultan Qalāwūn (1279-1290) for his son al-Malik al-Ṣāliḥ ʿAlī (d. 1288) on how to govern Egypt during the absence of his father. In this memorandum is stated:

> "The Prince knows that justice is the profitable capital of the kings and an act that brings them success. (…) So the Prince acts justly towards His subjects: those who are close and distant, present and absent. (…) And if the case be of religious nature, he sends it back to the qadis and judges whom we have appointed to separate between the lawful and the forbidden. If the case concerns maliciousness, the Prince himself exacts punishment, for He is a man of pertinent thought and clever mind."[18]

---

13 Ibn Iyās (d. around 1524): *Badāʾiʿ al-zuhūr*, vol. 4, 73; Ibn Iyās (d. around 1524): *Alltagsnotizen eines ägyptischen Bürgers*, 71.

14 Ibid., 195.

15 Ibid., 50.

16 Petry, Carl F.: "Quis Custodiet Custodes?" Revisited: The Prosecution of Crime in the Late Mamluk sultanate", in: *Mamluk Studies Review*, 3 (1999), 30.

17 Ibid.

18 Lewicka, Paulina: "What a King Should Care About. Two Memoranda of the Mamluk Sultan on Running the State's Affairs", in: *Studia Arabistyczne I Islamistyczne*, 6 (1998), 13.

As we understand from this memorandum the Mamluks reserved jurisdiction in criminal matters or in cases of public affairs for themselves. Only cases of religious nature were given to the qadis. Ashtor argues that in doing so, "l'aristocratie militaire turque, qui se réservait la juridiction en matière criminelle, laissait aux juges indigènes la liberté de persécuter leurs ennemies, qui étaient aussi les leurs".[19] Therefore, the Mamluks gained the support of the Arab scholars in the Islamic religious sciences, the *ʿulamāʾ*. The *ʿulamāʾ* were dependent on the Mamluk elite in terms of being granted jobs in the legal administration and in education. On the other hand the *ʿulamāʾ* legitimized the rule of the Mamluks, although they had been brought into the Empire as military slaves and unbelievers. Therefore it might have been a problem for the well-trained scholars to follow the policies and decisions of an academically ignorant sultan, but they had to comply with it as the sultan rule was supreme. Anyhow, the *ʿulamāʾ* found a way to explain that the Mamluks would not be able to maintain their power without the help of the *ʿulamāʾ*. The Scholar Abū Ḥāmid al-Qudsī (al-Maqdisī) (d. 1483) explains that these Mamluk heroes of Islam, victors against Crusaders and Mongols, would have never attained their dominant position and remained totally uncivilized unless the local Arab *ʿulamāʾ* had taught them the basic knowledge of Islam and the 'two phrases of the Muslim creed'.[20] This self-serving argumentation is highly questionable and overestimates the actual role of the *ʿulamāʾ*. Fernandes claims regarding this matter the sultan "listened to whoever was providing him with the opinion he wanted to hear. In other words, the Mamluk sultan listened to himself."[21]

Nevertheless, the Mamluks concluded something of an alliance with the religious establishment against the common people, whereby the status of the Mamluks as occasional "outlaws" above the Islamic law was in practice justified and tolerated by the *ʿulamāʾ*. Therefore most legal complaints against Mamluks were ignored by both Mamluk rulers and religious scholars. At the beginning of the 15th century Ibn Khaldūn (d. 1406) noted that the legal system was corrupt. Judges openly favoured military men in order to profit from

---

19 Ashtor, Eliyahu: « L'inquisition dans l'état mamlouk », in: *Revista degli studi orientale*, 25 (1950), 14, 15.

20 Haarmann, Ulrich: "Mongols and Mamluks. Forgotten Villains and Heroes of Arab History", in: Neuwirth, Angelika and Pflitsch, Andreas (eds.): *Crisis and Memory in Islamic Societies*, Beirut 2001, 174.

21 Fernandes, Leonor: "Between Qadis and Muftis: To whom Does the Mamluk Sultan Listen?", in: *Mamluk Studies Review*, 6 (2002), 108.

the system.[22] Complaints were apparently only effectively pursued when the sultan himself had serious doubts about the accused officials.[23]

It seems therefore that Mamluks were "more equal" than their Arab subjects in the eyes of the jurisdiction. Petry summarizes this as follows.

> "The behaviour (of the Mamluk caste) was determined by moral standards that differed from concepts of right or wrong as perceived by civilians who wielded no military power. Mamluk trainees matured in a milieu that actively encouraged conspiracy as a normative form of competition. Their code of responsibility subordinated them to the wishes of their superiors but not to the sensibilities of their civilian subjects. The chroniclers repeatedly condemned their riots as criminal. But unless their acts adversely affected a senior member of their caste, the legal authorities rarely held them to account."[24]

Mixed Emotions of Arab Subjects towards their Mamluk Masters

Understandably enough, the locals must have felt helpless towards the "system", consisting of the Mamluk military and their *ʿulamāʾ* collaborators. This led to occasional outbursts of "rituals of hate" against dead Mamluks or high dignitaries of the Mamluk state.[25] For example, the Cairenes loathed the corpse of Amir Sanjar al-Shujāʿī, who had conquered Beirut from the crusaders in 1291.[26] A Mamluk source informs us that,

> "after he had been murdered by a (Mamluk) rival in 1294, his head was stuck on a javelin and carried all over Cairo. The people paid the javelin bearers so that they could have the head, which they stuck with shoes. (...) There were (also) claims that they urinated on the victim's head. In a matter of three days, the officials, complying with popular demand, were able to earn a large sum of money."[27]

---

22 Meloy, John L.: "The Privatization of Protection: Extortion and the State in the Circassian Mamluk Period", in: *Journal of the Economic and Social History of the Orient*, 47/2 (2004), 209; Kosei, Morimoto: "What Ibn Khaldun Saw: The Judiciary of Mamluk Egypt", in: *Mamluk Studies Review*, 6 (2002), 131.

23 Nielsen, Jorgen S.: "Maẓālim and Dār al-ʿAdl under the Early Mamluks", in: *The Muslim World*, 66 (1976), 125-126.

24 Petry, Carl F.: "Disruptive "Others" as Depicted in Chronicles of the Late Mamluk Period", in: Kennedy, Hugh (ed.): *The Historiography of Islamic Egypt (c. 950-1800)*, Leiden 2001, 180.

25 Shoshan, Boaz: *Popular Culture in Medieval Cairo*, Cambridge 1993, 57.

26 Ṣāliḥ ibn Yaḥyā ibn Buḥtur (d. after 1436): *Tārīkh Bayrūt*, 23, 24.

27 Ibn Iyās (d. around 1524): *Badāʾiʿ al-zuhūr*, vol. 1, 383-384; Shoshan, Boaz: *Popular Culture*, 57.

Another case was that of the hated high Mamluk official al-Nashw. When in 1339 rumours about his arrest spread, merchants stopped their business and whole families gathered below the citadel and celebrated by raising Qurʾans and waving banners. Celebrations, which included music performances, lasted for a week. Poetry was written for this event. Sweets representing the punishment of Amir Nashw were sold. Then a crowd attempted to lynch the former official.[28]

One might conclude that it was the custom of high Mamluk dignitaries to allow and encourage this public outcry against a former Mamluk official from time to time in order to give the population the possibility to express their anger. In permitting a safety valve through providing scapegoats to the public, they avoided that the system was questioned as a whole or that the popular wrath turned against them too. Nevertheless, if the Mamluks would have treated their subjects more humanely, they would not have needed to resort to these extreme practices.

Examining the issue of the relationship of the common Arabs towards their Mamluk Masters, one is surprised to discover a lack of large scale uprisings of the population. Maybe there were also advantages for ordinary people in this system. Or in other words, how did it come about that people were ready to cope with such kind of behaviour that was even considered by contemporary authors as clear crimes against humanity. The answer seems to be twofold. One argument is that the common people lacked any military infrastructure. The Mamluk monopoly on military training, arms, etc., deprived the Arabs of the means to sustain an uprising. However, in times of instability of the regime, which prevailed during large parts of the 15th century they might have struck, even if it would have been very difficult.

Nevertheless, it seems that these incidents of Mamluk misbehaviour were perceived as a common nuisance, but the fact that the Mamluk government provided outer security and a certain inner stability seems to have outweighed the occasional abuses of the Mamluk military class. We should not overestimate the number of these crimes. They were common but did not happen on a day-to-day basis. From time to time, Mamluk officials even tried to tame their soldiers by circumscribing their movements. For example at the end of 920/1514 the Mamluk *dawādār* (the bearer of the

---

28 al-Maqrīzī (d. 1442): *Kitāb al-Sulūk*, vol. 2, part 2, Kairo 1942, 479-482; Kortantamer, Samira: *Ägypten und Syrien zwischen 1317 und 1341 in der Chronik des Mufaḍḍal b. Abī l-Faḍāʾil*, Freiburg 1973, 78 (Arabic Text), 210 (German Translation); Shoshan, Boaz: *Popular Culture in Medieval Cairo*, 57, 121 n. 33; Levanoni, Amalia: "The al-Nashw Episode: A Case Study of "Moral Economy", in: Mamluk Studies Review 9/1 (2005), 207.

sultan's inkwell, i.e. the head of the royal chancery), Ṭūmān Bāy, forbade all the Mamluks to be on the road with weapons after the evening prayer and no Mamluk was allowed to cover his face when going to the market. The punishment for doing so would be hanging. Once the order came out the people blessed Ṭūmān Bāy and cried out loud to praise him.[29]

It is no contradiction to the story of occasional abuse that the Mamluks stood in high regard among their Arab subjects. They were respected for their military skills during their great military successes at the beginning of their reign in the mid 13th century, when they fought victoriously against the Crusaders and the Mongols. For example, the victory of the mostly Turkish born Mamluks against their Central Asian Mongol "cousins", led Abū Shāma (d. 1268) to say in the midthirteenth century that against any (evil) thing "there is a cure from its own kind" (*Wa-li-kulli shayʾin āfatun min jinsihi*)[30].

And even more than hundred years later, the Muslim philosopher Ibn Khaldūn (d. 1406) said regarding the Mamluk victory over the Mongols that their slavery was a manifestation of God's grace for the Muslims of Egypt.[31]

The Arabs were even in their own eyes not capable to uphold the banner of Islam as powerful as the Turks did. It was the military conquests of the Turks that made them stand out above others. The Arabs could only base their reputation as chosen people in religious matters on the authority of the Arab prophet Muḥammad as seen in the following episode: After the Mamluk Sultan al-Ashraf Khalīl had conquered the capital of the crusaders Acre in 1291 he was praised in panegyric: "Praise be to God, the nation of the cross has fallen; through the Turks the religion of the Arabs triumphed."[32]

So far the theory, but the Mamluk blessing lost its magic touch somehow during the 250 years of their rule in Egypt and Syria. Mamluk historians complained openly about the misbehaviour of Mamluk dignitaries and invoked memories of better times. Ibn Taghrībirdī (d. 1470) formulated it in the mid-fifteenth century as follows:

---

29 Ibn Iyās (d. around 1524): *Badāʾiʿ al-zuhūr*, vol. 4, 415; Ibn Iyās (d. around 1524): *Alltagsnotizen eines ägyptischen Bürgers*, 192.

30 Abū Shāma (d. 1268): *al-Dhayl ʿalā ʾl-rawḍatayn. Tarājim rijāl al-qarnayn al-sādis wal-sābiʿ*, ed. by Z. al-Kawtharī, Beirut [2]1947, 208.

31 Ibn Khaldūn (d. 1406): *Kitāb al-ʿibar*, Beirut 1284/1867 (rpr. 1392/1971), vol. 5, 371.

32 Ibn al-Furāt (d. 1405): *Tārīkh ibn al-Furāt*, ed. by Qusṭanṭīn Zurayq and Najla ʿIzz al-Dīn, vol. 8, Beirut 1939, 115; Here cited after: Haarmann, Ulrich: "Ideology and History, Identity and Alterity: The Arab Image of the Turk from the ʿAbbasids to Modern Egypt", in: *International Journal of Middle East Studies*, 20 (1988), 182.

> "How excellent was their behaviour; how brilliant the way they raised the young and honoured the elderly. Therefore they reigned over the country and the people were satisfied. They won the hearts of their subjects. (…) However, in our times they became the opposite of all this. The commanders are ignorant and the young Mamluks are mean."[33]

The same reasoning can be found by al-Maqrīzī (d. 1442). He argues that the Mamluks of the sultan were the meanest and most horrible people under the sun. In contrast to them the first Mamluk sultans had been real role models.[34]

And some Mamluk authors even criticized in a humorous way the language problems of the Turks and therefore their inability to communicate on a personal level with Arabs as is shown in a love poem of al-Ṣafadī (d. 1363) about a Turkish man: "I love his Turkish look which raises my excitement, he is to be blamed if he separates from me for too long, but how could he ever be capable of true love, if his tongue can't even pronounce the Fāʾ."[35]

Despite these criticisms of Mamluk behaviour, they failed to call for a general abolition of the institution of military slavery. The Arab population was already too used to the rule of the Turkish military upper class. Their rule was seen as god given and was internally never threatened by large uprisings. Moreover, there was the age-old prejudice expressed from authors like Abū Ḥāmid al-Qudsī (d. 1483) at the end of the fifteenth century. He stated that Egyptians were un-martial people and not able to protect themselves. Therefore the Turks would cheerfully shoulder the burden of the Holy War and devote their lives to the defence of the community of believers.[36] That is why the Turks should rule and the

33 Ibn Taghrībirdī (d. 1470): *al-Nujūm al-zāhira fī mulūk Miṣr wa'l-Qāhira*, 16 vol., Kairo 1929-1972, vol. 8, 228; Peter Thorau: "Einige kritische Bemerkungen zum sogenannten 'mamluk phenomenon'", in: Conermann, Stephan and Pistor-Hatam, Anja (eds.): *Die Mamluken. Studien zu ihrer Geschichte und Kultur. Zum Gedenken an Ulrich Haarmann (1942-1999)*, Hamburg 2003, 368.

34 al-Maqrīzī (d. 1442): *Kitāb al-mawāʿiẓ wa'l-iʿtibār fī dhikr al-khiṭaṭ wal-āthār*, vol. 2, Cairo 1987, 214; Peter Thorau: „Einige kritische Bemerkungen", 368.

35 Here we find a play on words between the word true love (*wafāʾ*) and the Arabic letter Fāʾ, see: al-Ṣafadī, Ṣalāḥ al-Dīn Khalīl ibn Aybak (d. 1363): *al-Ḥusn al-ṣarīḥ fī miʾat malīḥ*, ed. by Aḥmad Fawzī al-Hayyab, Damaskus 2003, 41.

36 Abū Ḥāmid al-Qudsī (d. 1483): *Kitāb duwal al-islām al-sharīfa al-bahīya*, ed. by Subhi Labib and Ulrich Haarman, (German Subtitle: *Traktat über die Segnungen, die die Türken dem Lande Ägypten gebracht haben*), Beirut 1997, 119; Haarmann, Ulrich: „Rather the Injustice of the Turks than the Righteousness of the Arabs. Changing ʿUlamāʾ attitudes towards Mamluk rule in the Late Fifteenth Century", in: *Studia Islamica*, 68 (1988), 70.

population should have to cope with their crimes. Abū Ḥāmid al-Qudsī says that he would prefer a tyrannical and unjust Turkish Mamluk to even the noblest Arab.[37]

If we consider these justifications of Mamluk rule, then one understands the sense of superiority the Mamluk caste displayed towards the Arabs, a notion stressed even further by the fact that Mamluks were the only ones allowed to ride on horses and to wear weapons. And when on some occasions common people challenged the power of the Mamluks, the rulers responded with an excessive show of force. In 1281 Sultan Qalāwūn suppressed a demonstration in Cairo, resulting in three days of violence and was stopped only after the *ʿulamāʾ* intervened.[38]

The Arab population possessed very little military power to overthrow their rulers and so the critique had to be phrased in religious and moral terms, and preferably not in the presence of any Mamluk. The Venetian merchant Emmanuel Piloti (b. 1371) heard from a Bedouin that the Bedouins should rule over the Mamluks as even the Prophet Muḥammad was originally a Bedouin. And he continued his complaints by saying that after all, the Mamluks enjoyed their status only because they had been bought initially with the money of the Arab-Egyptian taxpayers.[39] Apparently for him this represented a waste of money.

Conclusion

To conclude, even if Berkey has recently argued that it would be misleading to overemphasize the Mamluks' alienation from native Egyptian society, because of numerous links which bound them together to Islamic culture[40], at least in the field of criminal justice, it seems that there were great differences between Mamluks and their Arab subjects.

Therefore a just Mamluk like the Mamluk governor Sayf al-Dīn Asnadamur of Tripoli, who cared about the rights of the common peo-

---

37 Abū Ḥāmid al-Qudsī (d. 1483): *Kitāb duwal al-islām*, 109; Haarmann, Ulrich: "Rather the Injustice", 71.

38 Amalia Levanoni: *A Turning Point in Mamluk History. The Third Reign of al-Nāṣir Muḥammad Ibn Qalāwūn (1310-1341)*, Leiden 1995, 109.

39 Emmanuel Piloti (b. 1371): *L'Égypte au commencement du Quinzième siècle d'après le traité d'Emmanuel Piloti de Crète (incipit 1420)*, ed. by P.-H. Dopp, Cairo 1950, 11, 19; Haarmann, Ulrich: "The Mamluk System of Rule in the Eyes of Western Travellers", in: *Mamluk Studies Review*, 5 (2001), 5.

40 Jonathan P. Berkey: "Culture and Society during the late Middle Ages", in: The Cambridge History of Egypt, vol. 1, ed. by Carl F. Petry, Cambridge 1998, 392.

ple even when adverse Mamluk interests were involved, seemed to have been the great exception. No wonder that legends emerged about him, recounting that he listened to the complaints of the ordinary people and went as far as cutting a Mamluk in half in quest of stolen milk. Therefore the telling of these stories might have given the people the courage to endure the usual misbehaviour of the Mamluk military elite or perhaps was meant as a lesson for other Mamluks as to how they were supposed to behave. On the other hand, it is an indication of how helpless the Arab subjects were towards their Mamluk masters when they had to resort to legends or in other cases, even to mockery, to express their discontent with the present situation. When the Mamluk amirs started to wear greater horns on their typical hats (sg. *takhfīfa*)[41] at the beginning of the 16th century, a voice from the common people commented upon this as follows: "Every ram is wearing wool and also horns, and what for horns! And I am happy to be in peace, without wool, without horns."[42]

41 *Takhfīfa*, "the lighter one", was originally a cap with a light cloth around it, but it grew bigger and bigger until the amirs started to put horns on it. The so-called "great *takhfīfa*", or *nāʿūra* (Waterweel) was worn by the sultan instead of a crown, see: Ibn Iyās (d. around 1524): *Alltagsnotizen eines ägyptischen Bürgers*, 22 (Introduction by Annemarie Schimmel).

42 Ibn Iyās (d. around 1524): *Badāʾiʿ al-Zuhūr*, Bd. 4, 138; Ibn Iyās (d. around 1524): *Alltagsnotizen eines ägyptischen Bürgers*, 99. (*Qad labasa aṣ-ṣūfa kullu kabaʾin/ qurūnuhu yā lahā qurūnu/ faraḥtu min d̲āk mustarīhān/ lā ṣūfun ʿindī wa-lā qurūnu).*

Figure: Jean Thenaud: *Le voyage d'outremer (Égypte, Mont Sinay, Palestine) de Jean Thenaud Gardien du couvent des Cordeliers d'Angoulême: suivi de la relation de l'Ambassade de Domenico Trevisan auprès du Soudan d'Égypte 1512*, ed. by Ch. Schefer, (Repr. of the edition Paris 1884), Frankfurt 1995, 91.

Marriage and Mental Illness in the Mamluk Period

ALIYA SAIDI

While doing research on marriage patterns among urban women of the Mamluk period, I came across numerous references to mental illness. The appearance of mental illness in a number of women seemed to be directly linked to their problematic marriages. The examples I will look at are taken from a centennial biographical dictionary of the late Mamluk period. *Al-Ḍawʾ al-Lāmiʿ li Ahl al-Qarn al-Tāsiʿ* was written by Sakhāwī, a historian of the fifteenth century in Cairo. In *al-Ḍawʾ al-Lāmiʿ*, Sakhāwī compiled the biographies of about 13,000 of his contemporaries, roughly 12,000 men and just over 1,000 women. All the people he included were notables who lived during the fifteenth century in the urban centres of Egypt, Syria and the Hijāz.

In general, Mamluk biographical dictionaries are exceptional sources of information for the social history of the Mamluk period. However, some of the most vivid details about Mamluk society come to us specifically from Sakhāwī's *Al-Ḍawʾ al-Lāmiʿ*. In many ways, *Al-Ḍawʾ al-Lāmiʿ* is unique among Islamic biographical dictionaries, specifically in the material it provides about women. First, the sample Sakhāwī included of over 1,000 women is much larger than that cited in any other biographical dictionaries. Second, in almost every one of these women's biographies, Sakhāwī included an account of some aspect of their private lives. He provided anecdotes about their various ailments, physical descriptions, observations on their character, moral standing and intelligence, comments on their travels, education and teaching, and so on. But the richest and most numerous anecdotes by far are those which concern their marriages. Sakhāwī mentioned the marital status of nearly 660 of these women. Among these, 590 were married. In the biographies of married women, he often included intimate and graphic details about their marriages. He listed each woman's marriages and usually provided the names of her husbands. He pointed out how marriages ended, whether in divorce or in the death of one of the spouses. He also gave clues as to whether each marriage was happy or not and sometimes provided the reasons why a divorce took place. Therefore, *al-Ḍawʾ al-Lāmiʿ* reads almost like a gossip column of Mamluk society.[1]

In line with his habit of including personal anecdotes about the women he cited, Sakhāwī also pointed out that a number of them had experienced some form of mental illness. In several cases, these women appear to have become mentally ill due to some kind of marriage-related problem, most notably, polygamy. Sakhāwī's accounts of polygamous marriages are the most vivid examples of the links between mental illness and problematic marriages. Polygamy in Mamluk society was extremely rare. Sakhāwī mentioned only fifteen cases out of more than 1,000 women.[2] Polygamy appears to have carried a strong social stigma, because the attitude of Sakhāwī and his contemporaries towards it was so negative. Sakhāwī provided nearly every polygamous marriage he cited with an explicit account of the problems that were caused by such marriages. In some cases he cited, a man's first wife would strongly oppose the introduction of a second wife. The result was either that the first wife compelled her husband to divorce his second wife, or that she obliged her husband to grant her a divorce if he refused to give up his new marriage. However, some women, unable to resolve the situation to their advantage, became mentally ill. Therefore, despite the fact that polygamy was highly uncommon, there is substantial evidence that wives felt seriously threatened by the thought of a co-wife encroaching on their marriages.

In sharp contrast to the stigma associated with polygamous marriages, Sakhāwī and his contemporaries viewed divorce and remarriage with remarkable tolerance. Far more divorces took place than polygamous marriages, even though both divorce and polygamy are sanctioned by Islamic law. Sakhāwī cited numerous cases of repeated remarriage, both after a divorce or the death of a spouse. Nearly 30% of the women included in *al-Ḍawʾ al-Lāmiʿ* were married more than once, which shows that there was no stigma attached to marrying a woman who had been previously married. The great majority of Sakhāwī's descriptions of divorce and serial monogamy reflect how socially acceptable these two practices were, as opposed to the problems connected with polygamy.

The best example of a woman who simply refused to submit to her husband's new marriage is that of Ḥabībat Allāh.[3] Her husband con-

---

1 Carl Petry, *Protectors or Praetorians? The Mamluk sultans and Egypt's waning as great power*, Albany 1994.

2 1.74% of marriages were polygamous.

3 Shams ad-Dīn Muḥammad b. ʿAbd al-Raḥmān al- Sakhāwī, *Al-Ḍawʾ al-Lāmiʿ li Ahl al-Qarn al-Tāsiʿ*, vols. 1-12, Cairo: Maktabat al-Qudsī 1353 AH, vol. 12, p. 19, no. 102.

tracted a marriage with another woman secretly while he was still married to Ḥabībat Allāh. However, as soon as Ḥabībat Allāh found out, her husband was quickly forced to divorce his new wife, because he was afraid of Ḥabībat Allāh's anger. As Sakhāwī puts it, *khawfan min sakhtihā*.

Nevertheless, not all women were able to control their husbands. For instance, a woman called Kamaliyya[4] also refused to accept her situation as a co-wife. However, she was not able to coerce her husband into divorcing his new wife. Instead, she had to settle for getting a divorce herself. As Sakhāwī says, *faraqahā ...li ʿadam riḍahā ḥīna tazawwaja ʿalayhā*.

For some women, however, the strain of being involved in a polygamous marriage was so distressing that they eventually became mentally ill. One example is that of a woman from Cairo identified only as the wife of ʿAbd al-Raḥīm al-Abnāsī .[5] Apparently, the mere suspicion that her husband had taken a second wife behind her back drove her to become mentally ill. Sakhāwī tells us that ʿAbd al-Raḥīm and his wife had a stable and uneventful marriage for many years, during which she was a patient and obedient wife. However, at some point, she began to imagine and to have delusions (*tatakhayyal wa tatawahham*) that he had married another woman without her knowledge. Sakhāwī expressed his own conviction that ʿAbd al-Raḥīm was innocent of his wife's accusations. But because she had become delusional, she was unable to believe ʿAbd al-Raḥīm's innocence. As a result of her fears, her behaviour towards ʿAbd al-Raḥīm changed completely. Her conduct became extremely vulgar, something which caused ʿAbd al-Raḥīm a lot of harm. As a result, the rest of their married life was full of turmoil. Because ʿAbd al-Raḥīm was apparently unable to put his wife's suspicions to rest, the couple divorced and remarried each other several times. This pattern of divorce and remarriage continued until her death. In this case, Sakhāwī sounds more sympathetic towards the husband than the wife. But this is due to his belief that ʿAbd al-Raḥīm had <u>not</u> contracted a polygamous marriage, and that his wife's suspicions were unfounded. Generally, Sakhāwī exhibits his aversion as well as society's aversion towards polygamous marriages.

Umm al-Ḥusayn[6] was a woman from Mecca who married several times. Apparently, while she was married to her last husband, she became mentally deranged. In order to provide a reason for Umm al-Ḥusayn's mental

4 *Ibid.*, vol. 12, p. 119, no. 726.

5 *Ibid.*, vol. 4, pp. 164-166, no. 437.

6 *Ibid.*, vol. 12, pp. 140-141, no. 866.

breakdown, Sakhāwī offered a piece of gossip which was apparently making the rounds in Meccan circles at the time: it was said that she became deranged because her husband had taken another wife. Therefore, Sakhāwī wrote: (*ḥaṣala fi ʿaqlihā ikhtilāl, yuqāl bi sabab tazawwujihi ʿalayhā*).

A similar example is Umm Kulthūm[7], another Meccan woman. Her first husband had died, and she remarried twice after his death. Her problems began with her third husband, who took a second wife, called Umm al-Ḥasan[8], while he was still married to Umm Kulthūm. As Sakhāwī puts it, (*jamaʾa baynahā wa bayna Umm al-Ḥasan*). Umm Kulthūm was unable to tolerate her husband's introduction of a co-wife into their marriage. As a result, Sakhāwī says, Umm Kulthūm went insane (*junnat*).

In these examples, it was the first wife who suffered distress at the introduction of a new wife into her marriage. As might be expected, first wives were far more disturbed by the fact of being involved in a polygamous marriage than second wives. Sakhāwī provided only one example of a second wife who became mentally ill, that of ʿĀʾisha[9], a woman from Cairo. ʿĀʾisha's fourth husband, Muḥammad, already had a wife when she married him. The marriage of Muḥammad and ʿĀʾisha, which lasted only for a few days, took place in Cairo while Muḥammad's other wife was away travelling in the Hijāz. Muḥammad must have taken advantage of his other wife's absence in order to secretly contract his marriage to ʿĀʾisha. But ʿĀʾisha was unable to cope with her secret polygamous marriage. After her brief marriage to Muḥammad ended, presumably in divorce, ʿĀʾisha remained unmarried. But eventually, she became melancholic, and as a result, she was placed in a mental hospital for a few days. Therefore, Sakhāwī wrote: *ḥaṣala lahā makhūliyya uwdiʿat bi sababihā al-bimāristān ayyāman.* Whether she felt guilty about marrying Muḥammad behind his wife's back, or she had hoped her marriage to Muḥammad would last longer, or even she had expected that Muḥammad would divorce his other wife for her sake is not clear. In any case, the circumstances of ʿĀʾisha's marriage to Muḥammad and their subsequent divorce seem to have sent her into a deep depression. After her stay in hospital was over, ʿĀʾisha returned to her family: her maternal aunt took her home, where she died shortly afterwards. The example of ʿĀʾisha is the only one available in which we have a glimpse of the hospitalization of mentally ill women in Mamluk society.

Polygamous marriages stand out as unusual in *al-Ḍawʾ al-Lāmiʿ*. There are no examples of any other marital problem which caused women so

---

7 *Ibid.*, vol. 12, p. 149, no. 923.

8 *Ibid.*, vol. 12, p. 135, no. 831.

9 Ibid., vol. 12, p. 80, no. 492.

much distress. This stands in contrast to the tolerance towards divorce and serial monogamy. Divorce and polygamy are equally legal according to Islamic law. However, divorce was seen as a normal practice, whereas polygamy was not. The fact that Sakhāwī clearly linked mental illness with polygamy shows that polygamy was considered scandalous. Women therefore did their best to ensure that their husbands remained monogamous. However, when their efforts failed, some of them suffered from a mental breakdown as a result.

INDEX

المعهد الألماني للأبحاث الشرقية

ORIENT-INSTITUT BEIRUT

BEIRUTER TEXTE UND STUDIEN

1. MICHEL JIHA: Der arabische Dialekt von Bišmizzīn. Volkstümliche Texte aus einem libanesischen Dorf mit Grundzügen der Laut- und Formenlehre, Beirut 1964, XVII, 185 S.
2. BERNHARD LEWIN: Arabische Texte im Dialekt von Hama. Mit Einleitung und Glossar, Beirut 1966, *48*, 230 S.
3. THOMAS PHILIPP: Ǧurǧī Zaidān. His Life and Thought, Beirut 1979, 249 S.
4. ʿABD AL-ĠANĪ AN-NĀBULUSĪ: At-tuḥfa an-nābulusīya fī r-riḥla aṭ-ṭarābulusīya. Hrsg. u. eingel. von Heribert Busse, Beirut 1971, unveränd. Nachdr. Beirut 2003, XXIV, 10 S. dt., 133 S. arab. Text.
5. BABER JOHANSEN: Muḥammad Ḥusain Haikal. Europa und der Orient im Weltbild eines ägyptischen Liberalen, Beirut 1967, XIX, 259 S.
6. HERIBERT BUSSE: Chalif und Großkönig. Die Buyiden im Iraq (945–1055), Beirut 1969, unveränd. Nachdr. 2004, XIV, 610 S., 6 Taf., 2 Karten.
7. JOSEF VAN ESS: Traditionistische Polemik gegen ʿAmr b. ʿUbaid. Zu einem Text des ʿAlī b. ʿUmar ad-Dāraquṭnī, Beirut 1967, mit Korrekturen versehener Nachdruck 2004, 74 S. dt., 16 S. arab. Text, 2 Taf.
8. WOLFHART HEINRICHS: Arabische Dichtung und griechische Poetik. Ḥāzim al-Qarṭāǧannīs Grundlegung der Poetik mit Hilfe aristotelischer Begriffe, Beirut 1969, 289 S.
9. STEFAN WILD: Libanesische Ortsnamen. Typologie und Deutung, Beirut 1973, unveränd. Nachdr. Beirut 2008, XII, 391 S.
10. GERHARD ENDRESS: Proclus Arabus. Zwanzig Abschnitte aus der Institutio Theologica in arabischer Übersetzung, Beirut 1973, XVIII, 348 S. dt., 90 S. arab. Text.
11. JOSEF VAN ESS: Frühe muʿtazilitische Häresiographie. Zwei Werke des Nāšiʾ al-Akbar (gest. 293 H.), Beirut 1971, unveränd. Nachdr. Beirut 2003, XII, 185 S. dt., 134 S. arab. Text.
12. DOROTHEA DUDA: Innenarchitektur syrischer Stadthäuser des 16.–18. Jahrhunderts. Die Sammlung Henri Pharaon in Beirut, Beirut 1971, VI, 176 S., 88 Taf., 6 Farbtaf., 2 Faltpläne.
13. WERNER DIEM: Skizzen jemenitischer Dialekte, Beirut 1973, XII, 166 S.
14. JOSEF VAN ESS: Anfänge muslimischer Theologie. Zwei antiqadaritische Traktate aus dem ersten Jahrhundert der Hiǧra, Beirut 1977, XII, 280 S. dt., 57 S. arab. Text.
15. GREGOR SCHOELER: Arabische Naturdichtung. Die zahrīyāt, rabīʿīyāt und rauḍīyāt von ihren Anfängen bis aṣ-Ṣanaubarī, Beirut 1974, XII, 371 S.
16. HEINZ GAUBE: Ein arabischer Palast in Südsyrien. Ḫirbet el-Baiḍa, Beirut 1974, XIII, 156 S., 14 Taf., 3 Faltpläne, 12 Textabb.
17. HEINZ GAUBE: Arabische Inschriften aus Syrien, Beirut 1978, XXII, 201 S., 19 Taf.
18. GERNOT ROTTER: Muslimische Inseln vor Ostafrika. Eine arabische Komoren-Chronik des 19. Jahrhunderts, Beirut 1976, XII, 106 S. dt., 116 S. arab. Text, 2 Taf., 2 Karten.
19. HANS DAIBER: Das theologisch-philosophische System des Muʿammar Ibn ʿAbbād as-Sulamī (gest. 830 n. Chr.), Beirut 1975, XII, 604 S.
20. WERNER ENDE: Arabische Nation und islamische Geschichte. Die Umayyaden im Urteil arabischer Autoren des 20. Jahrhunderts, Beirut 1977, XIII, 309 S.
21. ṢALĀḤADDĪN AL-MUNAǦǦID, STEFAN WILD, eds.: Zwei Beschreibungen des Libanon. ʿAbdalġanī an-Nābulusīs Reise durch die Biqāʿ und al-ʿUṭaifīs Reise nach Tripolis, Beirut 1979, XVII u. XXVII, 144 S. arab. Text, 1 Karte, 2 Faltkarten.

22. ULRICH HAARMANN, PETER BACHMANN, eds.: Die islamische Welt zwischen Mittelalter und Neuzeit. Festschrift für Hans Robert Roemer zum 65. Geburtstag, Beirut 1979, XVI, 702 S., 11 Taf.
23. ROTRAUD WIELANDT: Das Bild der Europäer in der modernen arabischen Erzähl- und Theaterliteratur, Beirut 1980, XVII, 652 S.
24. REINHARD WEIPERT, ed.: Der Dīwān des Rāʿī an-Numairī, Beirut 1980, IV dt., 363 S. arab. Text.
25. ASʿAD E. KHAIRALLAH: Love, Madness and Poetry. An Interpretation of the Maǧnūn Legend, Beirut 1980, 163 S.
26. ROTRAUD WIELANDT: Das erzählerische Frühwerk Maḥmūd Taymūrs, Beirut 1983, XII, 434 S.
27. ANTON HEINEN: Islamic Cosmology. A study of as-Suyūṭī's al-Hayʾa as-sanīya fī l-hayʾa as-sunnīya with critical edition, translation, and commentary, Beirut 1982, VIII, 289 S. engl., 78 S. arab. Text.
28. WILFERD MADELUNG: Arabic Texts concerning the history of the Zaydī Imāms of Ṭabaristān, Daylamān and Gīlān, Beirut 1987, 23 S. engl., 377 S. arab. Text.
29. DONALD P. LITTLE: A Catalogue of the Islamic Documents from al-Ḥaram aš-Šarīf in Jerusalem, Beirut 1984, XIII, 480 S. engl., 6 S. arab. Text, 17 Taf.
30. KATALOG DER ARABISCHEN HANDSCHRIFTEN IN MAURETANIEN. Bearb. von Ulrich Rebstock, Rainer Osswald und A. Wuld ʿAbdalqādir, Beirut 1988, XII, 164 S.
31. ULRICH MARZOLPH: Typologie des persischen Volksmärchens, Beirut 1984, XIII, 312 S., 5 Tab., 3 Karten.
32. STEFAN LEDER: Ibn al-Ǧauzī und seine Kompilation wider die Leidenschaft, Beirut 1984, XIV, 328 S. dt., 7 S. arab. Text, 1 Falttaf.
33. RAINER OSSWALD: Das Sokoto-Kalifat und seine ethnischen Grundlagen, Beirut 1986, VIII, 177 S.
34. ZUHAIR FATḤALLĀH, ed.: Der Diwān des ʿAbd al-Laṭīf Fatḥallāh, 2 Bde., Beirut 1984, 1196 S. arab. Text.
35. IRENE FELLMANN: Das Aqrābāḏīn al-Qalānisī. Quellenkritische und begriffsanalytische Untersuchungen zur arabisch-pharmazeutischen Literatur, Beirut 1986, VI, 304 S.
36. HÉLÈNE SADER: Les États Araméens de Syrie depuis leur Fondation jusqu'à leur Transformation en Provinces Assyriennes, Beirut 1987, XIII, 306 S. franz. Text.
37. BERND RADTKE: Adab al-Mulūk, Beirut 1991, XII, 34 S. dt., 145 S. arab. Text.
38. ULRICH HAARMANN: Das Pyramidenbuch des Abū Ǧaʿfar al-Idrīsī (gest. 649/1251), Beirut 1991, XI u. VI, 94 S. dt., 283 S. arab. Text.
39. TILMAN NAGEL, ed.: Göttinger Vorträge – Asien blickt auf Europa. Begegnungen und Irritationen, Beirut 1990, 192 S.
40. HANS R. ROEMER: Persien auf dem Weg in die Neuzeit. Iranische Geschichte von 1350–1750, Beirut 1989, unveränd. Nachdr. Beirut 2003, X, 525 S.
41. BIRGITTA RYBERG: Yūsuf Idrīs (1927–1991). Identitätskrise und gesellschaftlicher Umbruch, Beirut 1992, 226 S.
42. HARTMUT BOBZIN: Der Koran im Zeitalter der Reformation. Studien zur Frühgeschichte der Arabistik und Islamkunde in Europa, Beirut 1995, unveränd. Nachdr. Beirut 2008, XIV, 590 S.
43. BEATRIX OSSENDORF-CONRAD: Das „K. al-Wāḍiḥa" des ʿAbd al-Malik b. Ḥabīb. Edition und Kommentar zu Ms. Qarawiyyīn 809/49 (Abwāb aṭ-ṭahāra), Beirut 1994, 574 S., davon 71 S. arab. Text, 45 S. Faks.
44. MATHIAS VON BREDOW: Der Heilige Krieg (ǧihād) aus der Sicht der malikitischen Rechtsschule, Beirut 1994, 547 S. arab., 197 S. dt. Text, Indices.
45. OTFRIED WEINTRITT: Formen spätmittelalterlicher islamischer Geschichtsdarstellung. Untersuchungen zu an-Nuwairī al-Iskandarānīs Kitāb al-Ilmām und verwandten zeitgenössischen Texten, Beirut 1992, X, 226 S.
46. GERHARD CONRAD: Die quḍāt Dimašq und der maḏhab al-Auzāʿī. Materialien zur syrischen Rechtsgeschichte, Beirut 1994, XVIII, 828 S.

47. MICHAEL GLÜNZ: Die panegyrische qaṣīda bei Kamāl ud-dīn Ismāʿīl aus Isfahan. Eine Studie zur persischen Lobdichtung um den Beginn des 7./13. Jahrhunderts, Beirut 1993, 290 S.

48. AYMAN FUʾĀD SAYYID: La Capitale de l'Égypte jusqu'à l'Époque Fatimide – Al-Qāhira et Al-Fusṭāṭ – Essai de Reconstitution Topographique, Beirut 1998, XL, 754 S. franz., 26 S. arab. Text, 109 Abb.

49. JEAN MAURICE FIEY: Pour un Oriens Christianus Novus, Beirut 1993, 286 S. franz. Text.

50. IRMGARD FARAH: Die deutsche Pressepolitik und Propagandatätigkeit im Osmanischen Reich von 1908–1918 unter besonderer Berücksichtigung des „Osmanischen Lloyd", Beirut 1993, 347 S.

51. BERND RADTKE: Weltgeschichte und Weltbeschreibung im mittelalterlichen Islam, Beirut 1992, XII, 544 S.

52. LUTZ RICHTER-BERNBURG: Der Syrische Blitz – Saladins Sekretär zwischen Selbstdarstellung und Geschichtsschreibung, Beirut 1998, 452 S. dt., 99 S. arab. Text.

53. FRITZ MEIER: Bausteine I-III. Ausgewählte Aufsätze zur Islamwissenschaft. Hrsg. von Erika Glassen und Gudrun Schubert, Beirut 1992, I und II 1195 S., III (Indices) 166 S.

54. FESTSCHRIFT EWALD WAGNER ZUM 65. GEBURTSTAG: Hrsg. von Wolfhart Heinrichs und Gregor Schoeler, 2 Bde., Beirut 1994, Bd. 1: Semitische Studien unter besonderer Berücksichtigung der Südsemitistik, XV, 284 S.; Bd. 2: Studien zur arabischen Dichtung, XVII, 641 S.

55. SUSANNE ENDERWITZ: Liebe als Beruf. Al-ʿAbbās Ibn al-Aḥnaf und das Ġazal, Beirut 1995, IX, 246 S.

56. ESTHER PESKES: Muḥammad b. ʿAbdalwahhāb (1703–1792) im Widerstreit. Untersuchungen zur Rekonstruktion der Frühgeschichte der Wahhābīya, Beirut 1993, VII, 384 S.

57. FLORIAN SOBIEROJ: Ibn Ḫafīf aš-Šīrāzī und seine Schrift zur Novizenerziehung, Beirut 1998, IX, 442 S. dt., 48 S. arab. Text.

58. FRITZ MEIER: Zwei Abhandlungen über die Naqšbandiyya. I. Die Herzensbindung an den Meister. II. Kraftakt und Faustrecht des Heiligen, Beirut 1994, 366 S.

59. JÜRGEN PAUL: Herrscher, Gemeinwesen, Vermittler: Ostiran und Transoxanien in vormongolischer Zeit, Beirut 1996, VIII, 310 S.

60. JOHANN CHRISTOPH BÜRGEL, STEPHAN GUTH, eds.: Gesellschaftlicher Umbruch und Historie im zeitgenössischen Drama der islamischen Welt, Beirut 1995, XII, 295 S.

61. BARBARA FINSTER, CHRISTA FRAGNER, HERTA HAFENRICHTER, eds.: Rezeption in der islamischen Kunst, Beirut 1999, 332 S. dt. Text, Abb.

62. ROBERT B. CAMPBELL, ed.: Aʿlām al-adab al-ʿarabī al-muʿāṣir. Siyar wa-siyar ḏātiyya. (Contemporary Arab Writers. Biographies and Autobiographies), 2 Bde., Beirut 1996, 1380 S. arab. Text.

63. MONA TAKIEDDINE AMYUNI: La ville source d'inspiration. Le Caire, Khartoum, Beyrouth, Paola Scala chez quelques écrivains arabes contemporains, Beirut 1998, 230 S. franz. Text.

64. ANGELIKA NEUWIRTH, SEBASTIAN GÜNTHER, BIRGIT EMBALÓ, MAHER JARRAR, eds.: Myths, Historical Archetypes and Symbolic Figures in Arabic Literature. Proceedings of the Symposium held at the Orient-Institut Beirut, June 25th – June 30th, 1996, Beirut 1999, 640 S. engl. Text.

65. Türkische Welten 1. KLAUS KREISER, CHRISTOPH K. NEUMANN, eds.: Das Osmanische Reich in seinen Archivalien und Chroniken. Nejat Göyünç zu Ehren, Istanbul 1997, XXIII, 328 S.

66. Türkische Welten 2. CABBAR, SETTAR: Kurtuluş Yolunda: a work on Central Asian literature in a Turkish-Uzbek mixed language. Ed., transl. and linguistically revisited by A. Sumru Özsoy, Claus Schöning, Esra Karabacak, with contribution from Ingeborg Baldauf, Istanbul 2000, 335 S.

67. Türkische Welten 3. GÜNTER SEUFERT: Politischer Islam in der Türkei. Islamismus als symbolische Repräsentation einer sich modernisierenden muslimischen Gesellschaft, Istanbul 1997, 600 S.

68. EDWARD BADEEN: Zwei mystische Schriften des ʿAmmār al-Bidlīsī, Beirut 1999, VI S., 142 S. dt., 122 arab. Text.

69. THOMAS SCHEFFLER, HÉLÈNE SADER, ANGELIKA NEUWIRTH, eds.: Baalbek: Image and Monument, 1898–1998, Beirut 1998, XIV, 348 S. engl., franz. Text.

70. AMIDU SANNI: The Arabic Theory of Prosification and Versification. On ḥall and naẓm in Arabic Theoretical Discourse, Beirut 1988, XIII, 186 S.

71. ANGELIKA NEUWIRTH, BIRGIT EMBALÓ, FRIEDERIKE PANNEWICK: Kulturelle Selbstbehauptung der Palästinenser: Survey der modernen palästinensischen Dichtung, Beirut 2001, XV, 549 S.

72. STEPHAN GUTH, PRISKA FURRER, J. CHRISTOPH BÜRGEL, eds.: Conscious Voices. Concepts of Writing in the Middle East, Beirut 1999, XXI, 332 S. dt., engl., franz. Text.

73. Türkische Welten 4. SURAYA FAROQHI, CHRISTOPH K. NEUMANN, eds.: The Illuminated Table, the Prosperous House. Food and Shelter in Ottoman Material Culture, Beirut 2003, 352 S., 25 Abb.

74. BERNARD HEYBERGER, CARSTEN WALBINER, eds.: Les Européens vus par les Libanais à l'époque ottomane, Beirut 2002, VIII, 244 S.

75. Türkische Welten 5. TOBIAS HEINZELMANN: Die Balkankrise in der osmanischen Karikatur. Die Satirezeitschriften Karagöz, Kalem und Cem 1908–1914, Beirut 1999, 290 S. Text, 77 Abb., 1 Karte.

76. THOMAS SCHEFFLER, ed.: Religion between Violence and Reconciliation, Beirut 2002, XIV, 578 S. engl., franz. Text.

77. ANGELIKA NEUWIRTH, ANDREAS PFLITSCH, eds.: Crisis and Memory in Islamic Societies, Beirut 2001, XII, 540 S.

78. FRITZ STEPPAT: Islam als Partner. Islamkundliche Aufsätze 1944–1996, Beirut 2001, XXX, 424 S., 8 Abb.

79. PATRICK FRANKE: Begegnung mit Khidr. Quellenstudien zum Imaginären im traditionellen Islam, Beirut 2000, XV, 620 S., 23 Abb.

80. LESLIE A. TRAMONTINI: „East is East and West is West"? Talks on Dialogue in Beirut, Beirut 2006, 222 S.

81. THOMAS SCHEFFLER: Der gespaltene Orient: Orientbilder und Orientpolitik der deutschen Sozialdemokratie von 1850 bis 1950. In Vorbereitung.

82. Türkische Welten 6. GÜNTER SEUFERT, JACQUES WAARDENBURG, eds.: Türkischer Islam und Europa, Istanbul 1999, 352 S. dt., engl. Text.

83. JEAN-MAURICE FIEY: Al-Qiddīsūn as-Suryān, Beirut 2005, 358 S., 5 Karten.

84. Istanbuler Texte und Studien 4. ANGELIKA NEUWIRTH, JUDITH PFEIFFER, BÖRTE SAGASTER, eds.: Ghazal as World Literature II: From a Literary Genre to a Great Tradition. The Ottoman Gazel in Context, Istanbul 2006, XLIX, 340 S. engl., dt. Text.

85. Türkische Welten 8. BARBARA PUSCH, ed.: Die neue muslimische Frau: Standpunkte & Analysen, Beirut 2001, 326 S.

86. Türkische Welten 9. ANKE VON KÜGELGEN: Die Legitimierung der mittelasiatischen Mangitendynastie in den Werken ihrer Historiker (18.-19. Jahrhundert), Beirut 2002, XII, 518 S.

87. OLAF FARSCHID: Islamische Ökonomik und Zakat. In Vorbereitung.

88. JENS HANSSEN, THOMAS PHILIPP, STEFAN WEBER, eds.: The Empire in the City: Arab Provincial Capitals in the Late Ottoman Empire, Beirut 2002, X, 375 S., 71 Abb.

89. THOMAS BAUER, ANGELIKA NEUWIRTH, eds.: Ghazal as World Literature I: Transformations of a Literary Genre, Beirut 2005, 447 S. engl. Text.

90. AXEL HAVEMANN: Geschichte und Geschichtsschreibung im Libanon des 19. und 20. Jahrhunderts: Formen und Funktionen des historischen Selbstverständnisses, Beirut 2002, XIV, 341 S.

91. HANNE SCHÖNIG: Schminken, Düfte und Räucherwerk der Jemenitinnen: Lexikon der Substanzen, Utensilien und Techniken, Beirut 2002, XI, 415 S., 130 Abb., 1 Karte.

92. BIRGIT SCHÄBLER: Intifāḍāt Ǧabal ad-durūz-Ḥaurān min al-ʿahd al-ʿUṯmānī ilā daulat al-istiqlāl, 1850-1949, Beirut 2004, 315 S. arab. Text, 2 Karten.

93. AS-SAYYID KĀẒIM B. QĀSIM AL-ḤUSAINĪ AR-RAŠTĪ: Risālat as-sulūk fī l-aḫlāq wa-l-aʿmāl. Hrsg. von Waḥīd Bihmardī, Beirut 2004, 7 S. engl., 120 S. arab. Text.

94. JACQUES AMATEIS SDB: Yūsuf al-Ḫāl wa-Maǧallatuhu „Šiʿr". In Zusammenarbeit mit Dār al-Nahār, Beirut 2004, 313 S. arab. Text.

95. SUSANNE BRÄCKELMANN: „Wir sind die Hälfte der Welt!“ Zaynab Fawwāz (1860-1914) und Malak Ḥifnī Nāṣif (1886-1918) – zwei Publizistinnen der frühen ägyptischen Frauenbewegung, Beirut 2004, 295 S. dt., 16 S. arab., 4 S. engl. Text.

96. THOMAS PHILIPP, CHRISTOPH SCHUMANN, eds.: From the Syrian Land to the State of Syria and Lebanon, Beirut 2004, 366 S. engl. Text.

97. HISTORY, SPACE AND SOCIAL CONFLICT IN BEIRUT: THE QUARTER OF ZOKAK EL-BLAT, Beirut 2005, XIV, 348 S. engl. Text, 80 S. farb. Abb., 5 Karten.

98. ABDALLAH KAHIL: The Sultan Ḥasan Complex in Cairo 1357-1364. A Case Study in the Formation of Mamluk Style, Beirut 2008, 398 S., 158 Farbtaf.

99. OLAF FARSCHID, MANFRED KROPP, STEPHAN DÄHNE, eds.: World War One as remembered in the countries of the Eastern Mediterranean, Würzburg 2006, XIII, 452 S. engl. Text, 17 Abb.

100. MANFRED S. KROPP, ed.: Results of contemporary research on the Qurʾān. The question of a historio-critical text of the Qurʾān, Beirut 2007, 198 S. engl., franz. Text.

101. JOHN DONOHUE SJ, LESLIE TRAMONTINI, eds.: Crosshatching in Global Culture: A Dictionary of Modern Arab Writers. An Updated English Version of R. B. Campbell's “Contemporary Arab Writers”, 2 Bde., Beirut 2004, XXIV, 1215 S. engl. Text.

102. MAURICE CERASI et alii, eds.: Multicultural Urban Fabric and Types in the South and Eastern Mediterranean, Beirut 2007, 269 S. engl., franz. Text, zahlr. Abb., Karten.

103. MOHAMMED MARAQTEN: Altsüdarabische Texte auf Holzstäbchen. In Vorbereitung.

104. AXEL HAVEMANN: Geschichte und Geschichtsschreibung (BTS 90). Arab. Übersetzung. Im Druck.

105. SUSANNE BRÄCKELMANN: „Wir sind die Hälfte der Welt“ (BTS 95). Arab. Übersetzung. In Vorbereitung.

106. MATTHIAS VOGT: Figures de califes entre histoire et fiction – al-Walīd b. Yazīd et al-Amīn dans la représentation de l'historiographie arabe de l'époque abbaside, Beirut 2006, 362 S.

107. HUBERT KAUFHOLD, ed.: Georg Graf: Christlicher Orient und schwäbische Heimat. Kleine Schriften, 2 Bde., Beirut 2005, XLVIII, 823 S.

108. LESLIE TRAMONTINI, CHIBLI MALLAT, eds.: From Baghdad to Beirut... Arab and Islamic Studies in honor of John J. Donohue s.j., Beirut 2007, 502 S. engl., franz., arab. Text.

109. RICHARD BLACKBURN: Journey to the Sublime Porte. The Arabic Memoir of a Sharifian Agent's Diplomatic Mission to the Ottoman Imperial Court in the era of Suleyman the Magnificent, Beirut 2005, 366 S.

110. STEFAN REICHMUTH, FLORIAN SCHWARZ, eds.: Zwischen Alltag und Schriftkultur. Horizonte des Individuellen in der arabischen Literatur des 17. und 18. Jahrhunderts, Beirut 2008, 204 S., Abb.

111. JUDITH PFEIFFER, MANFRED KROPP, eds.: Theoretical Approaches to the Transmission and Edition of Oriental Manuscripts, Würzburg 2006, 335 S., 43 Abb.

112. LALE BEHZADI, VAHID BEHMARDI, eds.: The Weaving of Words. Approaches to Classical Arabic Prose, Beirut 2009, 217 S.

113. SOUAD SLIM: The Greek Orthodox Waqf in Lebanon during the Ottoman Period, Beirut 2007, 265 S., Abb., Karten.

114. HELEN SADER, MANFRED KROPP, MOHAMMED MARAQTEN, eds.: Proceedings of the Conference on Economic and Social History of Pre-Islamic Arabia. In Vorbereitung.

115. DENIS HERMANN, SABRINA MERVIN, eds.: Shi'i Trends and Dynamics in Modern Time. Courants et dynamiques chiites à l'époque moderne. Im Druck.

116. LUTZ GREISIGER, CLAUDIA RAMMELT, JÜRGEN TUBACH, eds.: Edessa in hellenistisch-römischer Zeit: Religion, Kultur und Politik zwischen Ost und West, Beirut 2009, 375 S., Abb., Karte.

117. MARTIN TAMCKE, ed.: Christians and Muslims in Dialogue in the Islamic Orient of the Middle Ages, Beirut 2007, 210 S. dt., engl. Text.

118. MAHMOUD HADDAD et alii, eds.: Towards a Cultural History of the Mamluk Era. Im Druck.

119. TARIF KHALIDI et alii, eds.: Al-Jāḥiẓ: A Muslim Humanist for our Time, Beirut 2009, IX, 295 S.

120. FĀRŪQ ḤUBLUṢ: Abḥāṯ fī tārīḫ wilāyat Ṭarābulus ibbān al-ḥukm al-ʿUṯmānī, Beirut 2007, 252 S.

121. STEFAN KNOST: Die Organisation des religiösen Raums in Aleppo. Die Rolle der islamischen religiösen Stiftungen (*auqāf*) in der Gesellschaft einer Provinzhauptstadt des Osmanischen Reiches an der Wende zum 19. Jahrhundert, Beirut 2009, 350 S., 8 Abb., 3 Karten.

122. RALPH BODENSTEIN, STEFAN WEBER: Ottoman Sidon. The Changing Fate of a Mediterranean Port City. In Vorbereitung.

123. JOHN DONOHUE: Robert Campbell's Aʿlām al-adab al-ʿarabī (Arbeitstitel). In Vorbereitung.

124. ANNE MOLLENHAUER: Mittelhallenhäuser im Bilād aš-Šām des 19. Jahrhunderts (Arbeitstitel). In Vorbereitung.

125. RALF ELGER: Glaube, Skepsis, Poesie. Arabische Istanbul-Reisende im 16. und 17. Jahrhundert. In Vorbereitung.

126. MARTIN TAMCKE, ed.: Christliche Gotteslehre im Orient seit dem Aufkommen des Islams bis zur Gegenwart, Beirut 2008, 224 S. dt., engl. Text.

127. KIRILL DMITRIEV, ANDREAS PFLITSCH, transl.: Ana A. Dolinina: Ignaz Kratschkowskij. Ein russischer Arabist in seiner Zeit. In Vorbereitung.

128. KRISTIAAN AERCKE, VAHID BEHMARDI, RAY MOUAWAD, eds.: Discrimination and Tolerance in the Middle East. In Vorbereitung.

129. ANDREAS GOERKE, KONRAD HIRSCHLER, eds.: Manuscript Notes as Documentary Sources. In Vorbereitung.

130. MIKHAIL RODIONOV, HANNE SCHÖNIG: The Hadramawt Documents, 1904-51. Family Life and Social Customs Under the Last Sultans. In Vorbereitung.

131. SARA BINAY, STEFAN LEDER, eds.: Linguistic and Cultural Aspects of Arabic Bible Translation (Arbeitstitel). In Vorbereitung.

132. STEFAN LEDER, SYRINX VON HEES, eds.: Educational Systems in the Eastern Mediterranean: From Mamluk to Ottoman Rule (Arbeitstitel). In Vorbereitung.

133. MAFALDA ADE WINTER: Picknick mit den Paschas. Aleppo und die levantinische Handelsfirma Fratelli Poche (1853-80) (Arbeitstitel). In Vorbereitung.

Die Unterreihe „Türkische Welten" ist in die unabhängige Publikationsreihe „Istanbuler Texte und Studien" des Orient-Instituts Istanbul übergegangen.

Orient-Institut Beirut
Rue Hussein Beyhum, Zokak el-Blat,
P.O.B. 11-2988, Beirut - Lebanon
Tel.: +961 (0)1 359 423-427, Fax: +961 (0)1 359 176
http://www.orient-institut.org

Vertrieb in Deutschland:
Ergon-Verlag GmbH
Keesburgstr. 11
D-97074 Würzburg
Tel: +49 (0) 931 280084
Fax: +49 (0)931 282872
http://www.ergon-verlag.de

Vertrieb im Libanon:
al-Furat
Hamra Street
Rasamny Building
P.O.Box: 113-6435 Beirut
Tel: +961 (0)1 750054, Fax: +961 (0)1 750053
e-mail: info@alfurat.com

Stand: August 2010

نحو تاريخ ثقافي للمرحلة المملوكية

نُصوصٌ وَدِرَاسَات بَـيرُوتيـَّة

سِلْسِلة يُصْدرُها
المعهَد الألمانيّ للأبحاث الشرقيّة في بَيروت

١١٨

نحو تاريخ ثقافي للمرحلة المملوكية

هيئة التحرير
محمود حداد، أرنيم هاينمان،
جون ميلوي وسعاد سليم

بيروت ٢٠١٠
يطلب من دار النشر «إرغون فرلاغ» فورتسبورغ

تصميم الغلاف:
Taline Yozgatian

صورة الغلاف:
Screen of Abū Sargā, Cairo, detail of the geometric decoration.
Photography by Adeline Jeudy.

الطبعة الأولى

٢٠١٠

طُبع على نفقة وزارة الثقافة والأبحاث العلميّة
التابعة لجمهوريّة ألمانيا الاتّحاديّة
وجامعة البلمند
بإشراف المعهد الألماني للأبحاث الشرقيّة في بيروت
في مطبعة درغام، بيروت – لبنان

المحتويات

المحور الرابع:

مجالات الإنتاج الثقافيّ: العلوم

المحور الخامس:

الدولة والإدارة والعلاقة بالمجتمع

المقدّمة

إشكاليّة الدراسة

تفصح الأبحاث التاريخيّة المرتبطة بعصر المماليك عن تغيّر جذريّ في مقاربة المرحلة المملوكيّة. إذ طالما اعتبرت هذه المرحلة حقبة تراجع وانحطاطٍ بالنسبة إلى العالمين العربيّ والإسلاميّ، اللذين تعرّضا خلالها لحملات الفرنجة على شاطئ البحر الأبيض المتوسّط ولغزوات المغول. والحقّ أنّ التراجع السياسيّ-العسكريّ لم يكن فقط وليد التهديد الخارجيّ، بل ثمّة عوامل داخليّة أيضًا ساهمت في تقهقر الأوضاع الاقتصاديّة والاجتماعيّة. وقد أوجدت الأوضاع العسكريّة خصوصًا حاجات دفاعيّة اقتضت تحويل المجتمع إلى كيانات إقطاعيّة. غير أنّ التراجع السياسيّ-العسكريّ لم يشمل كلّ قطاعات الحياة. فالدراسات الحديثة تظهر أنّ الحقبة المملوكيّة شهدت ازدهارًا ملحوظًا في المجالين الاقتصاديّ والاجتماعيّ وفي الحياة الفكريّة. من هنا ضرورة عقد مؤتمر يسلّط الضوء على هذا «التغيّر في النموذج» البحثيّ عبر مجموعة من المساهمات العلميّة المتخصّصة التي يشترك فيها باحثون محلّيّون وأجانب.

إنّ هذا الكتاب هو نتيجة للمؤتمر الذي نظمه كلّ من «معهد التاريخ والآثار والتراث المشرقيّ» في جامعة البلمند و«المعهد الألمانيّ للأبحاث الشرقيّة» بين الخامس والسابع من شهر أيّار ٢٠٠٥. وينطوي المؤتمر على المحاور التاليّة:

المحور الأوّل: الجماعات الدينيّة والتفاعل بينها

اعتبر الباحثون في مجال الدراسات الديموغرافيّة أنّ المرحلة المملوكيّة عرفت تراجعًا حادًّا في عدد المسيحيّين، إذ كثرت القرارات المسيئة إليهم. غير أنّ البعض يعتبر أنّ تعدّد هذه «القرارات الرسميّة» لهو خير دليل على عدم تطبيقها. ويطرح السؤال عن

مدى تراجع دور المسيحيّين خلال الحقبة المملوكيّة في الوظائف الرسميّة وفي بعض المهن التي كانت شبة مقتصرة عليهم.

ويظهر أنّ المسيحيّين الذين لم يتعاطفوا مع الفرنجة تحمّلوا نتائج اندحار هؤلاء من الشرق، فيما دفع المسيحيّون الذين أيّدوا المغول ثمن هزيمتهم. من جهة أخرى كثيرًا ما يشار إلى دور المسيحيّين خلال هذه الحقبة في جباية الضرائب ومرافقة الحكّام كمسؤولين عن الجهاز الإداريّ أو كأطبّاء.

من جهة أخرى، كانت الحقبة المملوكيّة منطلقًا لتمركز سكانيّ جديد في جبل لبنان بخاصّة والساحل المتوسّطيّ بعامّة. وقد عاشت الطوائف الدينيّة المعروفة حاليًّا في لبنان بوصفها أقلّيّات، كالدروز والموارنة والشيعة، في الزمن المملوكيّ مفصلاً مهمًّا من تاريخها ومساريها الدينيّ والاجتماعيّ.

المحور الثاني: مجالات الإنتاج الثقافيّ – الفنّ

عمل فنّانو الحقبة المملوكيّة على تطوير التعبير الفنيّ وربط التشكيلات الفنّيّة بالطقوس الدينيّة والاجتماعيّة. في هذا الصدد، تشكّل جدرانيّات كنائس سورية ولبنان أثرًا فنّيًّا فريدًا في الشرق. ويمتدّ هذا النشاط في المنمنمات وعلى صفحات المخطوطات حيث نرى الأساليب الفنّيّة المحلّيّة تختلط وتمتزج. علاوةً على ذلك، سجّل فنّ العمارة المملوكيّ نهضة أتت بتقنيّات وعناصر جديدة كالمقرنص وتداخل الحجرين الأسود والأبيض.

تميّز عصر المماليك بازدهار التأريخ (ابن إيّاس، المقريزيّ، القلقشنديّ...). ومن البديهيّ طرح السؤال عن مدى شموليّة هذه الكتابات التاريخيّة أو تخصّصها، إخلاصها للتقليد أو سيرها في ركاب التجديد.

المحور الثالث: مجالات الإنتاج الثقافيّ – الأدب والتأريخ

شهدت المرحلة المملوكيّة تواصلاً للحياة الثقافيّة بين المشرق والمغرب عبر الفلسفة والأدب، فضلاً عن تكاثر المصنّفات التاريخيّة. ويعتبر بعض الدارسين المعاصرين، مثلاً، أنّ بعض أساليب فنّ الرواية الحديث نشأ في الأدب الشعبيّ المملوكيّ.

المحور الرابع: مجالات الإنتاج الثقافيّ – العلوم

يعتبر بعض المؤرّخين أنّ المرحلة المملوكيّة كانت غنيّة بالدراسات العلميّة، ولا سيّما في الطبّ والفلك والرياضيّات. ولعلّ أبرز مثل عن حضور العلم في ذلك الزمن، هو انتقال ابن خلدون من مصر إلى أسوار دمشق، بغية إقناع الفاتح تيمورلنك بدخول المدينة سلمًا حفاظًا على تراثها الفكريّ وثروة مكتباتها. والملاحظ، في هذا الصدد، أنّ الحملات المغوليّة حملت الحضارة العربيّة-الإسلاميّة إلى الهند ووسط آسية، وذلك على يد العمّال والحرفيّين الذين نقلهم الفاتح من ديار العرب إلى هناك. أمّا في ما يختص بالمسيحيّين فيتّهمهم الجاحظ بالاستئثار بمهنة الطبّ.

المحور الخامس: الدولة والإدارة والعلاقة بالمجتمع

غالبًا ما شدّدت الدراسات على طابع الحقبة المملوكيّة الإقطاعيّ العسكريّ، ولا سيّما على تمكّن المماليك من صدّ هجمات الفرنجة والمغول عن مصر وسورية. لكنّ الملاحظ أيضًا أنّ هذه المرحلة شهدت تنظيمات إداريّة وعسكريّة جديدة استمرّت لمرحلة طويلة بعد سقوط الدولة المملوكيّة. فتنظيم الدواوين، مثلاً، في الولايات المملوكيّة أثّر على نحو حاسم في توحيد القرار وفاعليّته، رغم أنّ إيجابيّات هذا التنظيم كثيرًا ما كانت تذهب سدىً بسبب خلافات الفرق المملوكيَّة المتصارعة.

المحور الأوّل

الجماعات الدينيّة والتفاعل بينها

الموارنة واليعاقبة والشيعة والدروز في الجبل اللبنانيّ في العهد المملوكيّ: جدليّة الاضطهاد والتسامح

إلياس القطّار
الجامعة اللبنانية

أوّلاً – السكّان المحلّيّون في لبنان في نهاية حكم الفرنج

المصادر المعروفة لا تفصّل أنواع السكّان وهويّاتهم الدينيّة والمذهبيّة، لكنّ الاجتهاد يفصح عن أنّ هؤلاء كانوا خليطًا و«موزاييك» من الديانات، وفي داخل كلّ منها طوائف متنوّعة.

بشكل عامّ، في مملكة القدس اللاتينيّة، في الأرياف، كانت الأكثريّة من المسلمين، مع وجود تجمّعات مسيحيّة مهمّة في بعض المناطق. وفي المدن كان العنصر الإسلاميّ، رغم الإبقاء عليه في بعض المدن، التي حافظ فيها الصليبيّون على تعهّداتهم، ضعيفًا بعد المجازر التي تعرّض لها إبّان الفتح.

١. المسلمون

بما أنّ المسلمين في صور، لم يلقوا المصير الذي لقيه هؤلاء في المدن الأخرى التي فتحها الصليبيّون، كان يوجد عدد لا يستهان به منهم داخل المدينة ولهم مساجد عدّة، ولهم «ريسّ» منهم[١].

---

١ ابن جبير، رحلة ابن جبير، دار صادر، بيروت ١٩٨٠، ص ٢٧٧–٢٨٣.
Rohricht, *Regesta Regni Hierosolomytani*, Oeiniponti 1893, p. 39.

في ظلّ الاحتلال الصليبيّ، غدت طرابلس مركزًا علميًا مرموقًا يفد إليه طلاب العلم من أوروبا، لأخذه على علمائها المسلمين والنصارى البلديّين[٢]. فقد أجاز رجال الدين المسيحيّون للمسلمين أن يؤمّوا المساجد التي كانت ما تزال في طرابلس وأنطاكية[٣].

وإثر فتح صلاح الدين مناطق من لبنان، وصلت قوّاته إلى القلمون حيث استقرّت جماعة من المسلمين[٤].

ومن الطريف والغريب، بالقياس على المعلومات التقليديّة عن لبنان، وجود مسلمين سنّة في جبّة بشراي، إذ يذكر الذهبيّ بهذا الخصوص، في معرض كلامه عن الإمام ابو محمد الجبّائيّ الطرابلسيّ الشاميّ، أنّه: « من قرية الجبّة من عمل طرابلس بجبل لبنان.[٥]».

الإسماعيليّة كانوا يعيشون في كونتيّة طرابلس، وجزء منهم داخل لبنان في الجبال الكسروانيّة كما ستظهر ذلك الحملات المملوكيّة التأديبيّة على لبنان.

ويشير ابن ميسّر، إلى وجودهم في جبل عاملة على أنّهم من جماعة الصبّاح النزاريّة[٦]، كما يشير ابن الأثير ومن بعده النويريّ وابن خلدون، إلى وجودهم في وادي التيم إلى جانب الدروز والنصيريّة والمجوس[٧].

النصيريّة كانوا في القرن الحادي عشر بين عكّار وصافيتا، حيث ما نزال نجدهم اليوم. ويبدو أنّهم، استنادًا إلى حملات المماليك على كسروان، كانوا موجودين في الجبال الكسروانيّة.

الموحّدون – الدروز تدّعي مصادرهم انتشارهم في بيروت وفي الساحل اللبنانيّ إبّان الحملة الصليبيّة الأولى، مع أنّ المصادر الإسلاميّة والمسيحيّة لا تؤكّد ذلك. وما يمكن قوله هو أنّ الدروز كانوا موجودين شرق «سنيوريات» بيروت وصيدا، وبكثافة

---

٢ جواد بولس، تاريخ لبنان، بيروت ١٩٧٢، ص٢٨٣. ولا ندري مصدر معلوماته.
H. Lammens, La Syrie, précis historique, 2 vol., Beyrouth 1921, p. 246.

٣ ول ديورانت، قصّة الحضارة، ترجمة محمد بدران، القاهرة ١٩٥٧، ج٣/١٥
Lammens, Syrie, p. 246.

٤ عمر تدمريّ، تاريخ طرابلس السياسيّ والحضاريّ، عصر الصراع العربيّ – البيزنطيّ والحروب الصليبيّة، مؤسّسة الرسالة، بيروت ط.٢ ١٩٨٤، نقلا عن روايات محلّيّة من القلمون، ص ٥٤٥–٥٣٦.

٥ شمس الدين الذهبيّ، تاريخ الإسلام، تحقيق عمر تدمريّ، ٣٠ج، دار الكتاب العربيّ، بيروت ١٩٨٧–١٩٩٣، حوادث ٦٠١–٦١٠، ص ١١٥.

٦ ابن ميسّر، **أخبار مصر**، نشر هنري ماسيه، المعهد العلميّ الفرنسيّ، القاهرة ١٩١٩، ص٦٨.

٧ شهاب الدين النويريّ، **نهاية الأرب**، ٣١ج، مصر ١٩٥٤–١٩٩٢، ج٧٩/٢٧. ابن خلدون، **العبر**، دار الكتب العلميّة، بيروت ١٩٩٢، م١٨٤/٥.

في منطقة وادي التيم قرب قلاع شقيف «بوفور» وبانياس. وقد ذكرنا ذلك أعلاه. وأوّل وصف لهؤلاء الدروز نجده في رحلة اليهوديّ بنيامين التطيلي الذي يجعل المنطقة التي ينتشر فيها الدروز ممتدّة من شرق صيدا إلى جبل حرمون. ...»[٨]. ولهم دور متقدّم في «جبل بيروت» بخاصّة في ما يعرف بالغرب حيث كان الأمراء من آل عبدالله في «الغرب» المتحدّرين من التنوخيّين. وقد عرفوا في ما بعد ب «بني بحتر[٩]».

الشيعة الإماميّة بالكاد نعرف شيئًا عن أوضاعهم في جبل عامل. وأبرز نصّ يصف واقعهم هو نصّ ابن جبير.

وتخبر المصادر الإسلاميّة أنّهم كانوا على علاقة وطيدة بالفرنج ومضافين إليهم ما حمل المسلمين على إلحاق الضرر بهم في غزواتهم لمواقع هؤلاء[١٠].

٢. اليهود

كانوا موجودين في المدن الفرنجيّة كافّة[١١].

٣. المسيحيّون

غالبيّة المسيحيّين المنتشرين في مملكة القدس كانت من الملكيّين ومن اليعاقبة(السريان)، وقد عمّمت تسمية السريان على كلّ المسيحيّين المشرقيّين، ويجتهد «براور» بأنّ الملكيّين كانوا أكثريّة في المدن، واليعاقبة في القرى. والأمر الأكيد هو فقط في كونتيّة أنطاكية، حيث كان الملكيّون هم الأكثريّة [١٢]. ولربّما، كان الوضع كذلك في كونتيّة طرابلس.

---

٨ Benjamin de Tudèle, voir la traduction dans E. Rey, *Les Colonies franques de Syrie aux XIIme et XIIIme siècles*, Paris 1883, p. 98. et dans J. Prawer, *Histoire du Royaume Latin de Jérusalem*, 2 t., Paris 1975, I, p. 511.

٩ صالح بن يحيى، **تاريخ بيروت**، تحقيق كمال الصليبي وفرنسيس هورس وغيرهما، دار المشرق، بيروت ١٩٦٩، ص ٣٩–٤٢. راجع كمال الصليبي، منطلق تاريخ لبنان، ط. كارفان، نيويورك ١٩٧٩، ص ٩٧.

١٠ ابن القلانسيّ، ذيل تاريخ دمشق، نشر آمدروز، ليدن ١٩٠٨، ط. سهيل زكّار، دار حسّان ١٩٨٣، ص ٥١٧، ٥١٩–٥٢٠. أبو شامة، شهاب الدين، كتاب الروضتين في أخبار الدولتين النوريّة والصلاحيّة، ٤ أجزاء، مؤسّسة الرسالة، بيروت ١٩٩٧، تحقيق إبراهيم الزيبق، ٢٦٩/١، ٣٤٠. دار الكتب العلميّة، ج١/ ٣١١. ابن العديم، كمال الدين، زبدة الحلب في تاريخ حلب، تحقيق سامي الدهّان، منشورات المعهد العلميّ الفرنسيّ، ٣ أجزاء، دمشق ١٩٦٨، ج٢/٣٠٨.

١١ **رحلة بنيامين التطيليّ**، ترجمة عزرا حداد، بغداد ١٩٤٥، ص ٨٧–٨٨. ابن العبريّ، **تاريخ مختصر الدول**، المطبعة الكاثوليكيّة، بيروت ١٩٨٥، ص ٢٣٩.

Rey, Colonies franques, p. 102.

١٢ Prawer, Royaume, I, p. 513.

كان المسيحيّون يسكنون في المدن، كما في الأرياف. ولذلك نجد جالية مسيحيّة شرقيّة في صور[١٣]. ولم تكن العلاقات حسنة بين المسيحيّين الشرقيّين والفرنج، بسبب محاولة الأخيرين فرض التراتبيّة الدينيّة اللاتينيّة عليهم، وبسبب معاملتهم معاملة دنيا وعدم إعطائهم وضعيّة مميّزة عن المسلمين[١٤].

النساطرة كانوا موجودين في طرابلس وجبيل وبيروت وعكّا[١٥]. ولا نعرف مقدار حجمهم وما إذا كان وجودهم رمزيًّا.

كان بطرابلس عدد كبير من الاطبّاء اليعاقبة والملكانيّين والمسلمين[١٦]. كان اليعاقبة موجودين في جبل لبنان[١٧]. والإدريسي(+ ١١٦٤–١١٦٥) يذكر وجودهم في جونية[١٨].

الموارنة كان لهم موقع خاصّ في مملكة القدس(في سنيوريات صيدا وبيروت) وفي كونتيّة طرابلس. وقد اشتهروا بأنّهم من الرماة الماهرين ومن العسكر الجيّدين، والوحيدين الذين تقرّبوا من كنيسة الفرنج. وقد قدّر غليوم الصوري عددهم بأربعين ألف نسمة ونيّف، وبأنّهم ينتشرون في نواحي أسقفيّة جبيل والبترون وطرابلس عند سفوح جبال لبنان[١٩].

وقد انتقل البطاركة الموارنة، بسبب صراعهم مع فرنج جبيل، من يانوح قرب العاقورا إلى إيليج قرب ميفوق، التي ستعتمد مركزًا بطريركيًّا جديدًا في١٢٧٨[٢٠].

ورغم ما آلت إليه حالة الفرنج لم تكن العلاقات بين رؤساء طرابلس والموارنة على ما يرام[٢١].

---

١٣ ibid, I, p. 516.

١٤ ibid, I, pp. 516–518.

١٥ Rey, Colonies Franques, p. 82.

١٦ Lammens, Syrie, p. 246.

١٧ الدويهيّ، **تاريخ الازمنة**، ط. توتل، المطبعة الكاثوليكيّة، بيروت **١٩٥١**، ص **١٥**.

١٨ الإدريسيّ، **كتاب نزهة المشتاق في إختراق الآفاق**، عالم الكتب، بيروت **١٩٨٩**، ص **٣٧٢**.

١٩ Guillaume de Tyr, *Le Royaume de Jérusalem*, éd. L'Orient, 3t. Beyrouth 1992, t.III, pp. 390–392.

٢٠ الدويهيّ، الأزمنة، ط. توتل، ص **١٤١**. الصليبي، منطلق، ص **٨٩**.

٢١ الدبس، **من تاريخ سوريا الدنيويّ والدينيّ**، بيروت ١٨٩٩، ج٦/٢٩٧–٢٩٨.

ثانيًا – الحملات المملوكيّة على كسروان وعلى الموارنة في مطلع عهد المماليك وأثرها على جغرافيّة وجود الطوائف

كانت كسروان في القرون الوسطى تشمل ما يعرف حاليًّا بالمتن وكسروان، وماتزال منطقة من كسروان الحاليّ تعرف باسم فتوح كسروان نسبة إلى هذه الفتوحات المملوكيّة التي طالت هذه المنطقة ومناطق أخرى كان يوجد فيها موارنة.

فعشيّة ترحيل الصليبيّين، خضعت مناطق جبليّة من لبنان، قبيل فتح السواحل وبعيده لسلسلة من الحملات العسكريّة، كانت الغاية منها، كما سنرى، تأديب الطوائف المناهضة للمماليك السنّة، أي الموارنة «وغلاة» الشيعة والشيعة بعامّة، الذين كانوا بشكل أساس عرضة لقمع المسلمين السنّة بشكل دائم منذ عهد الزنكيّين. وقد ألهبت هذه الحملات، الأقلام سابقًا ولاحقًا، وكانت مدار تحليلات وتأويلات، ترتكز في غالبيتها على منطلقات طائفيّة – سياسيّة[٢٢].

١. مصادر المعلومات

المؤرّخون، سواء أكانوا من المصادر الإسلاميّة القديمة أم من المحدثين (مستشرقين ولبنانيّين وغيرهم)، مختلفون في عدد هذه الحملات وفي تواريخها[٢٣]. والموضوع مايزال حتّى اليوم يثير فضول المؤرّخين الذين يختلفون حول هويّة الذين كانوا هدفًا للحملات. هذا الغموض، في صورة الحملات المملوكيّة، مردّه إلى نوعيّة المصادر التي استقى منها الباحثون معلوماتهم. في طليعة هذه المصادر المعاصرة والمشاركة في هذه الحملات، نجد فتاوى ورسائل، شيخ الإسلام الحنبليّ، الإمام أحمد ابن تيميّة (+١٣٢٨م) الذي أطلق فتوى تدعو للفتك بالنصيريّة والدروز لأنّ قتالهم أولى من قتال الأرمن: «لأنّهم عدوّ في دار الإسلام وشرّ بقائهم أضرّ» على حدّ قول القلقشنديّ نقلا عن ابن تيميّة[٢٤].

وكان ابن تيميّة قد بعث رسائل عدّة توضح موقفه من الحملات، أكثرها إفصاحًا عن أسباب الحملات رسالتان إلى السلطان المملوكيّ الناصر محمّد بن قلاوون (٦٩٣–٦٩٤هـ، ٦٩٨–٧٠٨هـ، ٧٠٩–٧٤١هـ/١٢٩٣–١٢٩٤م، ١٢٩٩–١٣٠٩م، ١٣١٠–١٣٤١م). وهاتان

---

٢٢ حاول من مدّة وجيزة، د. أحمد بيضون، مقاربتها بنقد للتاريخ الطائفيّ الإيديولوجيّ عند المؤرّخين المعاصرين من دون الاستناد إلى نصوص هذه الحملات كافّة، مركّزًا فقط على ثلاثة منها.

٢٣ وقد أثار هذا الموضوع لأوّل مرّة المستشرق «هنري لاوست» في العام ١٩٤٢.

٢٤ القلقشنديّ، **صبح الأعشى**، القاهرة ١٩١٣–١٩١٨، ج١٣/٣٤٨–٣٤٩.

الرسالتان تطالان الإسماعيليّة والنصيريّة والباطنيّة المنتشرين بأعمال دمشق، وصفد، وطرابلس، وحماة، وحمص وحلب، وأهل الجبل والجرد والكسروان وأهل جزّين وما حواليها، وجبل عامل ونواحيه.

وقيمة كتابات ابن تيميّة وفتاواه ترجع إلى أنّه ذهب إلى حدّ المشاركة فيها شخصيًّا كما يشير إلى ذلك بنفسه ويؤكّده ابن كثير.

ومن المصادر المهمّة التي أغفلها الذين درسوا هذه الحملات ومنهم «هنري لاوست» رغم أنّها معاصرة لها: اليونينيّ وابن أيبك الدواداريّ والمؤرّخ المجهول والذهبيّ والنويريّ والجزريّ وابن الفرات وابن قاضي شهبة والعينيّ وغيرهم.

والنصوص التي تعوّد أن يشتغل المؤرّخون عليها كانت تلك العائدة إلى كلّ من ابن تيميّة وأبو الفداء وابن الورديّ وابن الأثير وابن كثير والمقريزيّ وصالح بن يحيى وابن سباط وتادرس المارونيّ وابن القلاعيّ ومن المصادر المتأخّرة في الزمن البطريرك اسطفان الدويهيّ.[٢٥].

٢. سير الحملات

أ) الحملات على الموارنة

مهّد المماليك لحملاتهم على المعاقل الجبليّة المتنوّعة الطوائف بسلسلة حملات على مناطق الموارنة الذين، على ما يبدو تعرّضوا، من قبل المماليك، لحملتين:

الحملة الأولى: كانت في العام **١٢٦٨م**، عندما قامت قوّات السلطان الملك الظاهر بيبرس، إبّان حملتها الثانية على طرابلس، بالهجوم على قرية الحدث في جبّة بشراي.

الحملة الثانية جرت في العام **١٢٨٣م** [٢٦]. وقد جاءت كمحاولة تمهيديّة من قبل قلاوون للسيطرة على المناطق الجبليّة المحيطة بطرابلس. وانتهت بالقضاء على بطريرك للموارنة كان منشقًّا عن الموارنة الموالين لروما، وأخذ المغاور العاصية وقطع الأشجار وخرّب الكنائس[٢٧]، وتفاصيل هذا الخبر نجدها عند الدويهيّ في معرض كلامه على

---

٢٥ لقطع دابر الاجتهادات المتناقضة، عمدنا، في كتابنا: **نيابة طرابلس في عهد المماليك** إلى نشر نصوص هؤلاء، المعروفة وتلك التي اكتشفناها، بتمامها وكمالها فلتراجع هناك إلياس القطّار، نيابة طرابلس في عهد المماليك، منشورات الجامعة اللبنانيّة، بيروت **١٩٩٨**.

٢٦ الدويهيّ، أزمنة، ط. توتل، ص **١٤٦**، **١٦٠**، **١٦٣**.

٢٧ ابن عبد الظاهر، **تشريف الأيّام والعصور في سيرة الملك المنصور**، حقّقه د. مراد كامل، وزارة الثقافة والإرشاد القوميّ، القاهرة، **١٩٦١**، ص٤٧. المقريزيّ، **السلوك لمعرفة دول الملوك**، **٤** أجزاء في **١٢** قسمًا، دار الكتب المصريّة، بدءًا **١٩٣٦**، **٥٦٦/١**.

الحملة على بلاد بشراي وإهدن والحدث في العام ١٢٨٣[٢٨]. وبسقوط الحدث، الجيب العسكريّ المسيحيّ في خاصرة المماليك، انطلق هؤلاء لمتابعة الفتح.

هاتان الحملتان وسقوط طرابلس وباقي مدن الساحل بيد المماليك أجبرتا الموارنة على الخلود إلى السكينة من جهة، في الوقت الذي أخضعوا فيه لمراقبة مشدّدة.

كانت للمماليك شكوك وظنون بحقّ الموارنة، ويبدو أنّها كانت محقّة. ففي الواقع كان الصليبيّون يضعون التصاميم لاحتمال استعادة الأراضي المقدّسة، وقد خصّصوا للموارنة مركزًا أساسيًّا لأنّهم كانوا يشكّلون موطىء قدم يمكنهم الاستفادة منه في أيّة عودة محتملة إلى المشرق.

ب) الحملات على كسروان

يمكن الكلام على ثلاث حملات:

الحملة الأولى في «١٢٩٢/٦٩١»، وكانت قد تقرّرت في «١٢٨٨/٦٨٧»[٢٩].

ويبدو أنّ هذه الحملة كانت موجّهة لربما ضدّ الموارنة تمامًا كما كانت موجهة ضدّ «غلاة» الشيعة. ويضعها ابن القلاعيّ في إطار كلامه على انتصار ملحميّ للمقدّمين الموارنة على المسلمين. ويحصرها بالموارنة فقط. وقد استنتج كمال الصليبي عبر نقده نصّ ابن القلاعي أنّ الحملة في ١٢٩٢ م لم تكن محصورة بكسروان فقط وبأنّها تجاوزت ذلك إلى بلاد جبيل [٣٠].

الحملة الثانية جرت في العام ١٣٠٠ م للثأر من الانكسار في العام١٣٠٠. جرت بعد رحيل المغول وانحسار خطرهم. وصالح بن يحيى يؤكّد، بعد ابن كثير، حصول هذه الحملة فيسمّيها «نوبة»، ويحدّدها بالنوبة الثانية خلال فترة حكم الملك الناصر محمد بن قلاوون [٣١] ويرى الصليبي أنّها «موجّهة ضدّ الموارنة بقدر ما كانت موجّهة ضدّ «غلاة الشيعة»» [٣٢]، وقد قادها جمال الدين آقوش الأفرم، نائب دمشق، بصحبة ابن تيميّة. وقد فضّل الكسروانيّون الإذعان للسلام فأعلنوا الخضوع مرحليًّا للمماليك[٣٣].

---

[٢٨] الدويهيّ، أزمنة، ص٢٦١.

[٢٩] صالح بن يحيى، تاريخ بيروت، ص٢٤–٢٥، ٥٣.

[٣٠] Salibi, Maronite historians of mediaeval Lebanon, Beirut 1959, pp. 69–73.

[٣١] صالح بن يحيى، تاريخ بيروت، ص ٢٧.

[٣٢] Salibi, Maronite historians, p. 72.

الصليبي، منطلق، ص ١٣٤–١٣٥.

[٣٣] H. Laoust, Remarques sur les expéditions de Kisrawan sous les premiers mamelouks, Bulletin du musée de Beyrouth, IV (1942), pp. 101–103.

وإضافة إلى الكسروانيّين، يذكر اليونينيّ وابن أيبك أنّ الحملة كانت موجّهة ضدّ الدرزيّة أيضًا.

الحملة الثالثة والحاسمة كانت في العام **١٣٠٥** م. ويؤكّد صالح بن يحيى، كما ابن كثير، أنّ مفاوضات بين ابن تيميّة وسكّان هذه المناطق العاصية كانت قد سبقتها، على أمل إعادتهم إلى حظيرة الإيمان الإسلاميّ السنيّ. ولكن بفشل ابن تيميّة في تحقيق مسعاه، أعطي الأمر بإنهاء هذه الثورة الخطرة. ولذلك، وفي **٢** محرم **٧٠٥ / ٢٥** تموز**١٣٠٥**، توجّه الجيش إلى كسروان والجرد بقيادة أقوش وبمشاركة ابن تيميّة[٣٤].

كلّ ممالك الشام شاركت في الهجوم، وعلى رأس كلّ جيش منها نائب السلطنة عليها، وكان من بينهم نائب طرابلس ونائب صفد. وبالنتيجة، وبعدما صعدوا إلى جبال كسروان والجرد من أصعب مسالكها وأطبقوا عليها من كلّ الجهات، تملّكوها ووطئوا أرضًا كان أهلها لا يظنّون أنّ بمقدور أحد أن يطأها[٣٥].

المصدر المارونيّ، الدويهيّ، يضع المعركة الفاصلة في العام **١٣٠٧** م. وهو يستوحي رواية ابن اسباط الذي وضعها في العام**١٣٠٥**م. ويظهر أنّ الدويهيّ يحاول وضع رواية وسطى بين الروايات المختلفة. ولكنّ الشيء الجديد الذي يقدّمه لنا هو بجعله المعركة الفاصلة في عين صوفر[٣٦]، من دون أن ندري السبب في ذلك.

٣. هويّة الطوائف المهاجمة

الحملات الأولى على الجبّة كانت موجّهة ضدّ الموارنة. ولكنّ المشكلة تكمن في تحديد هويّة سكّان كسروان (كسروان الحاليّ والمتن). وتحديد أيضًا موضع الجرد. والجواب على ذلك عند الذهبيّ الذي يذكر أنّ قرية حراجل من جبل الجرد[٣٧].

أصاب المماليك عصافير عدّة بحجر واحد في هجومهم على كسروان: فمن جهة اقتصّوا من المسيحيّين ومن جهة أخرى من الشيعة، بخاصّة «المتطرّفين». والاثنان متّهمان بالتآمر مع الصليبيّين ثمّ مع المغول، ولربّما طالت الحملات الموارنة لجهة بلاد جبيل، وبعض الجيوب من «الرافضة» لجهة بلاد الشوف. وبهذا الخصوص يؤكّد

---

٣٤ صالح بن يحيى، تاريخ بيروت، ص٢٧.
Laoust, Remarques, pp. 103–106.

٣٥ صالح بن يحيى، تاريخ بيروت، ص ٢٧–٢٨.

٣٦ ابن اسباط، **تاريخ ابن اسباط او كتاب صدق الأخبار**، المكتبة الوطنيّة في باريس مخطوط رقم١٨٢١، ص **١١٥**. الدويهيّ، أزمنة، ط. توتل، ص**١٦٣**.

٣٧ الذهبيّ، تاريخ الإسلام، حوادث ٦٧١–٦٨٠، ص ١٦٥.

ابن تيميّة أنّ الحملات كانت موجّهة ضدّ « الجبل»، الجرد وكسروان[٣٨]. الدروز أيضًا كانوا هدفًا للحملة. فابن كثير يسمّيهم «التيامنة» نسبة إلى وادي التيم [٣٩] كما أنّ أبا الفداء واليونينيّ وابن أيبك والقلقشنديّ وابن اسباط يؤكّدون صحّة هذا الزعم[٤٠]. وقد شارك الأمراء البحتريّون الدروز في المعركة[٤١].

معركة العام **١٣٠٥** م أصابت أيضًا الموارنة بقدر إصابتها الشيعة. فالمصدر المارونيّ المعاصر لهذه الأحداث، أي المطران تادرس المارونيّ، يروى، ويأخذ عنه لربّما ابن القلاعيّ، أنّه لم ينج لهم من التدمير أي دير أو كنيسة أو حصن ما عدا كنيسة مار شليطا. ويخبر تادرس، أيضًا، أنّ زعماء الثوّار كانوا من عائلة بوللمع، العائلة الدرزيّة الشهيرة[٤٢]. ولم ينج من هذه المجزرة سوى سكّان جونية الذين لاذوا بالفرار في مراكبهم. ثمّ عاد الموارنة بعد وقت قليل، قدّر بعشرات السنوات، للسكن في كسروان، رغم وجود التركمان، المكلّفين من قبل المماليك[٤٣] مراقبة المنطقة وحمايتها.

واذا ذهبنا في العمق، لوجدنا أنّ المشكلة هي في تحديد هويّة الشيعة الذين تصدّوا للحملات. فهل هم من الشيعة الاثني عشريّة؟ أم من النصيريّة أو الرافضة الإسماعيليّة أو الجميع معًا؟

هناك في الواقع آراء عدّة واجتهادات حول الموضوع[٤٤]. وبالعودة إلى النصوص القديمة والأساسيّة، يمكن الوصول إلى تحديد هويّة الشيعة الذين طالتهم الحملات.

في فتاوى ابن تيميّة، هذه الحملات توجّهت ضدّ «الرافضة» أي النصيريّة والإسماعيليّة والقرامطة وأنواع الباطنيّة كافّة حسبما يفسّر هو، شخصيًّا، مفهوم الرافضة. وفي عرف ابن تيميّة، يمكن توسيع مفهوم الرافضة وتطبيقه على كلّ الذين يرفضون

---

٣٨ ابن تيميّة، تقي الدين، **مجموع فتاوى شيخ الاسلام أحمد ابن تيميّة**، ٣٧ج، الرياض **١٩٦١**، ج**٤٠٢/٢٨**.

٣٩ ابن كثير، الحافظ، **البداية والنهاية**، **١٤** ج، مطبعة السعادة، القاهرة **١٣٥٨**هـ، ج**٣٢٨/١٣** ج**١٢/١٤**، **٣٥**.

٤٠ أبو الفداء، **جغرافية أبو الفداء**، باريس **١٨٤٠**، ص **٢٢٩**. القلقشندي، صبح، ج**٢٤٨/١٣**. ابن سباط، المخطوط، ص **١١٥–١١٦**.

٤١ صالح بن يحيى، تاريخ بيروت، ص **٩٥–٩٦**.

٤٢ راجع حول هذه العائلة، **قواعد الاداب حفظ الانساب**، تحقيق الياس القطّار، منشورات الجامعة اللبنانية، بيروت **١٩٨٦**، ص **٣١**، **٤٣**.

Salibi, Maronite historians, pp. 72–75.

٤٣ قرألي، بولس، **حروب المقدّمين**، بيت شباب **١٩٣٧**، ص **٨٥–٨٦**.

٤٤ محمّد علي مكيّ، **لبنان من الفتح العربيّ إلى الفتح العثمانيّ**، دار النهار، بيروت **١٩٧**، ص **٢٢٨–٢٢٩**، **٢٣٢**.

الجهاد ضدّ الكفّار، وإجبار أهل الكتاب على دفع الجزية، وذلك يشمل حتّى الشيعة الإماميّة الاثني عشريّة [٤٥].

بالنسبة إلى صالح بن يحيى، الطوائف موضوع الحملات هي الباطنيّة[٤٦]. والباطنيّة، عادة، هي الشيع التي تميّز في الدين بين الظاهر والباطن وتؤول الآيات القرآنيّة، ومنها الإسماعيليّة والدرزيّة والنصيريّة. وبالنسبة إلى ابن الورديّ، فهذه الطوائف هي من الظنّيّين والنصيريّة[٤٧]. فإذا أخذنا في الاعتبار أنّ النصيريّة هم حسب رواية ابن الورديّ غير الظنّيّين يبقى لنا أن نجتهد في أنّ الظنّيّين هم الإسماعيليّة والدروز، أي: الباطنيّون الآخرون.

بالنسبة إلى المقريزيّ هم من الدروز. ويردّ الصليبي على ذلك بأنّه خطأ واضح يعود إلى قلّة معرفة المؤرّخين المصريّين (ولو كان بعلبكيّ الأصل) في ذلك الوقت بشؤون الشام الداخليّة. هذا مع العلم أنّ بعض الدروز كانوا مقيمين آنذاك في قرى من «الخارجة» (أي كسروان)[٤٨].

بالنسبة إلى النصوص كلّ من اليونينيّ والنويريّ وابن أيبك وابن الفرات وابن قاضي شهبة والعينيّ والجزريّ توجّهت الحملات إلى كسروان، وإضافة إلى كسروان إلى الجرديّين أيضًا عند اليونينيّ والنويريّ والعينيّ والجزريّ. لكنّ اليونينيّ يضيف أنّها قد توجّهت إلى كسروان والدرزيّة وكذلك ابن أيبك. ويصنّفهم النويريّ بالباطنيّة والذهبيّ بالرافضة والعينيّ بأعظم غلاة الرافضة والزنادقة.

٤. أسباب الحملات

الحملات الأولى ضدّ الموارنة في العامين ١٢٦٨و١٢٨٩م، كانت لها أسباب عسكريّة. فالمماليك كانوا يرغبون في قطع الطريق على أيّة مساعدة للفرنج في طرابلس، لأنّ ذلك سيؤدّي حتمًا إلى إطالة عمر الحصار وتاليًا عدم سقوطها بسرعة بأيديهم. فالمماليك كانوا على بيّنة من القيمة الإستراتيجيّة للموارنة في الجبال المحيطة بطرابلس. حتّى إذا ما انكسر الموارنة سهل على الدولة الإسلاميّة الناشئة القضاء على آخر معاقلهم المشتّتة في الجبال الحصينة.

المماليك، كانوا مقتنعين بأنّ من أسباب انهيار قوّة المسلمين أمام الصليبيّين انقسام الأمّة الإسلاميّة إلى ملل ونحل... وكان أكثر المقتنعين بذلك العالم الشيخ أحمد ابن

---

٤٥ ابن تيميّة، فتاوى، ج٢٨/٤٠١-٤٠٢، ٤٠٨، ٥٢٨، ٥٤٥.

٤٦ صالح بن يحيى، تاريخ بيروت، ص ٢٨.

٤٧ ابن الورديّ، زين الدين، **تاريخ ابن الورديّ**، جزءان، القاهرة ١٨٦٨، ج٢/٢٥٤.

٤٨ المقريزيّ، السلوك، ٩٠٢/١-٩٠٣. الصليبي، منطلق، ص ١٣٥.

تيميّة، الذي كان يقرع دائمًا ناقوس خطر احتمال عودة المسيحيّين إلى احتلال الأراضي المقدّسة، طالما بقيت الأمّة الإسلاميّة مشتّتة ومنقسمة على ذاتها. وكان يعتقد، أنّ الإمساك برؤوس الشيعة الذين يضلّلونهم يزيل الشرّ، ويلزم هؤلاء بشرائع الإسلام. وبقطع النظر عمّا يعتقده فيهم من ممارستهم وعقيدتهم وتكفيرهم فهو يتّهمهم بتقديم الفرنج والتتار على المسلمين.

امّا حملة العام ١٢٩٢ م، فكان الدافع إليها الرغبة بالاقتصاص من أهل كسروان لمساندتهم الفرنج. وكان السلطان قلاوون، قد عزم على إنهاء هذا الخطر منذ العام ١٢٨٦م، ولكن تكملة الحرب ضدّ الفرنج وصعوبة اجتياز الجبال، حالت دون تنفيذ هذا المشروع العسكريّ الضخم [٤٩].

أسباب حملة العام ١٣٠٠ م كانت مماثلة للسابقة. زيادة على ذلك، كانت السلطات المملوكيّة غاضبة من تصرّف أهل الجبل والجرد وكسروان لأنّهم نهبوا وباعوا المسلمين الهاربين من وجه المغول للصليبيّين، كما باعوا خيلهم وسلاحهم إلى قبرص الفرنجيّة، وفرح أهل جزّين وجبل عامل بما جرى. وهذا ما أشار إليه ابن تيميّة، وأشار أيضًا إليه صالح بن يحيى، جاعلاً منه السبب الأساس للحملة الحاسمة في العام ١٣٠٥ م. وفي عرض صالح بن يحيى لهذه الأسباب، يحاول، من جهة إبعاد أيّ ظنّ أو شبهة عن عائلته، مدّعيًا أنّ أحد زعمائها الأمير ناهض الدين بحتر، كان يضيف الهاربين من وجه جيش قلاوون بن قازان زعيم التتار، ويقدّم لهم كلّ أنواع المساعدة، منحيًا باللائمة على أهل كسروان وأهل جزّين وغيرهم من الفاسدين، بخاصّة الكسروانيّين [٥٠]، لأنّ فيهم غلاة الشيعة، بينما أهالي جزّين، آنذاك، كانوا من الإماميّة الاثني عشريّة.

إذًا، أسباب حملتي، ١٣٠٠و ١٣٠٥ م كانت متشابهة. أبعد من ذلك، يوضح لنا صالح بن يحيى، أنّ من بين الأسباب أيضًا: تخوّف المماليك من ازدياد عدد الشيعة في تلك الجيوب الثائرة، وتجاوزهم الحدّ المعقول وازدياد سلطتهم. وهذا ما كان وراء هجومهم على الجيش المملوكيّ المكسور، وأدّت استفادتهم من غزو جيش المماليك المهزوم إلى تقلّص مراقبة المماليك لهم من جهة، وإلى استفحال تعدّياتهم على المسلمين من جهة أخرى. فازدادت وقاحتهم ورفضوا الانصياع للسلطان محتمين بجبالهم المنيعة وخلف أعدادهم الغفيرة التي يصعب الوصول إليها وتجاوزها [٥١].

---

٤٩ Laoust, Remarques, pp. 100–101.

٥٠ صالح بن يحيى، تاريخ بيروت، ص ٧٧–٧٨.

٥١ المصدر ذاته، ص٢٧.

ويجمع اليونينيّ والنويريّ وابن أيبك والمؤرّخ المجهول والذهبيّ وابن قاضي شهبة والعينيّ على أنّ أهل الجرد وكسروان آذوا عسكر المسلمين أثناء هربه من أمام عسكر قازان، إضافة إلى أسباب أخرى تنظر في النصوص.

٥. نتائج الحملات

النتيجة الأولى كانت تدمير البلاد وقطع الأشجار وهدم المنازل، وهو أكبر قصاص يمكن أن يلحق بالمزارع الفلاح. ولمّا كانت الجبال مغطّاة بالغابات، ولأسباب استراتيجيّة، تقرّر قطع أشجارها لكشفها وللتمكّن من ملاحقة الهاربين، ولمنع الغابات من التحوّل مجدّدًا معقلاً لثوّار جدد[٥٢]. وكان الدمار كاملاً بحيث تحوّلت البلاد إلى مراع خصبة لقطعان التركمان الذين كلّفوا السكن فيها والسهر على مراقبتها وحراستها.

النتيجة الثانية كانت على الصعيد البشريّ. طبعًا، صالح بن يحيى، كان المصدر الوحيد الذي عني بتلمّس نتائج الحملات، بينما المصادر الإسلاميّة اكتفت بعامّة بالإشارة إلى حدوث الحملة فقط. ولذلك فإنّ صالح يخبر، بأنّ المهاجمين لم يكتفوا بتدمير الحجر والشجر، بل عملوا على تصفية العديد من السكّان، وتشريد الآخرين في البلاد. وقد عمل نائب طرابلس على تشغيل بعضهم في الوظائف المدنيّة. واختفى الباقون في البلاد وامّحى ذكرهم. ثمّ أخضعت الجبال لمراقبة مشدّدة من قبل قراقوش، الذي اشتهر بحكمه القاسيّ الذي أصبح مضرب مثل. فعمد الأخير إلى إجلاء من تبقّى من الأهالي وقتل بعضهم، بخاصّة أعيانهم، ثمّ أعطى الأمان، للبعض، ولمن مكث خارج كسروان ولجأ إلى جزّين وبلادها وبلاد بعلبك[٥٣]..

النتيجة الثالثة كانت تحويل كسروان إلى إقطاع أعطي بادىء الأمر لبعض القادة العسكريّين. لكن الدولة المملوكيّة عادت في العام **١٣٠٦** م إلى إلغاء إقطاع هؤلاء وتحويله إلى عشائر التركمان، مشترطة عليهم تقديم خدمة عسكريّة من **٣٠٠** خيّال، لتأمين الدرك لمرفأ بيروت وللطرق المؤدّية إليه حتّى عمل طرابلس[٥٤]. لذلك أمّن التركمان أعمال الحراسة «البوليسيّة» من إنطلياس إلى مغارة الأسد، عند حدود معاملة طرابلس. وكان عليهم منع أيّ كان من اجتياز «دربند» نهر الكلب، إذا لم يكن مصحوبًا بإجازة مرور صادرة عن متولّي ولاية بيروت، أو من الأمراء البحتريّين حكّام منطقة الغرب[٥٥].

---

٥٢ ابن تيميّة، فتاوى، ج ٤٠٤/٢٨. صالح بن يحيى، تاريخ بيروت، ص٢٨–٢٩.

٥٣ صالح بن يحيى، تاريخ بيروت، ص ٢٨، ٩٦.

٥٤ المصدر ذاته، ص ٢٨–٢٩.

٥٥ المصدر ذاته، ص ٣٧.

وهكذا تكون حملات كسروان قد أدخلت الإقطاع إلى الجبل كما ساهمت في انتشاره في طرابلس، أيضًا، وأدّت إلى تبديل في جغرافيّة وجود الطوائف الدينيّة في الجبل طيلة العهد المملوكيّ.

وبالخلاصة، أدّت هذه الحملات على المناطق الجبليّة إلى إجبار الطوائف الثلاث المارونيّة والدرزيّة والشيعيّة على الخضوع لإحدى التقسيمات الإداريّة المملوكيّة الأساسيّة: طرابلس ودمشق وصفد. وكان نصيب الموارنة وغلاة الشيعة الخضوع لحكم نائب طرابلس، النيابة أو التقسيم الإداريّ الجديد الذي نشأ زمن الفرنج، واعتمد مجدّدًا ليحتضن الطوائف المشاغبة، ومنها: الموارنة والنصيريّة والإسماعيليّة.

ثالثًا – إعادة توزّع الخريطة السكّانيّة بعد ١٣٠٥ وأثر ذلك على انكماش الطوائف الجبليّة على ذاتها وصياغتها كياناتها الداخليّة اجتماعيًّا ودينيًّا

المنطقة الجبليّة في لبنان، كانت، ملجأ للأقلّيّات الدينيّة والمذهبيّة والعرقيّة، والعهد المملوكيّ هو خير شاهد على ذلك. وما الحملات المملوكيّة التي استهدفت سكّان الجبال في النيابة إلاّ دليل على ذلك. ويؤكّد واقع الحال هذا كلام صالح بن يحيى الذي يذكر أنّ سكّان كسروان، كانوا مقتنعين كلّ الاقتناع، في رفضهم الانصياع للمماليك، أنّ جبالهم لا تؤخذ [٥٦].

أ) على صعيد الشيعة

الحملات لم تتّخذ الموقف ذاته من كلّ شيع الشيعة. لذلك كان للدولة المملوكيّة ثلاثة مواقف مختلفة منهم:

أ) العديد منهم قضي عليه أو اختفى في جهات غير محدّدة.

ب) قسم من الناجين أسكن في طرابلس وعملوا في جهات طرابلس في وظائف الدولة وتقاضوا «جامكية وجرابة». وكانوا يحصلون على معاش من الديوان. كما أنّ بعضهم حصلوا على إقطاع من حلقة طرابلس. والبعض اختفوا في البلاد بحيث إنّ ذكراهم انطفأت واختفت أمورهم[٥٧]. ولكن ما هويّة هؤلاء: إسماعيليّة، نصيريّة أم إماميّة؟ لا نظنّ أنّهم من الإسماعيليّة، لأنّ المصادر اللاحقة، وواقع الحال، لا تشير

٥٦ المصدر ذاته، ص ٢٨.

٥٧ المصدر ذاته، ص ٢٨.

إطلاقًا إلى بقاء عناصر إسماعيليّة في لبنان الحاليّ. فلربّما، هم من الإماميّة أو النصيريّة. ويرجّح هنري لاوست أن يكونوا من النصيريّة[٥٨].والوقائع التاريخيّة تؤكّد ذلك، بسبب استمرار وجود فقط النصيريّة في شمال لبنان منذ ذلك التاريخ، وما تسمية الضنيّة إلّا بالنسبة إليهم. أمّا الإماميّة فلا ذكر لهم خارج جنوب لبنان وفي البقاع. وقد تكون الدولة قد سعت لاستيعابهم، وتاليًا تحويلهم إلى السنّة أو أنّهم قد مارسوا التقيّة التي اشتهروا بها. وما تزال بعض الأقلّيّات الشيعيّة الإماميّة موجودة في البترون وجبيل، ولا نعرف ما إذا كانت تعود إلى هذا الزمن أو إلى القرن السادس عشر. وبالرجوع إلى نصّ صالح بن يحيى، الذي كتب مؤلّفه عن تاريخ بيروت وتاريخ عائلته في القرن الخامس عشر، نرى أنّ ذكرى هؤلاء الشيعة، استمرت حتّى ذلك القرن.

ج) قسم من الشيعة لجأ إلى جزّين والبقاع وبعلبك[٥٩]. و لمّا كان سكّان هذه المناطق من الشيعة الإماميّة الاثني عشريّة منذ ذلك التاريخ وحتّى يومنا هذا، يمكننا الاستنتاج أنّ من لجأ إلى هذه المناطق هم من كانوا على هذا المذهب أو من غلاة الشيعة الذين فضّلوا تغيير مذهبهم والانتقال إلى التشيّع العاديّ الذي يجدون فيه جذورهم، من أن يجبروا على اعتناق السنّة لحماية حياتهم. ويمكننا الاجتهاد في القول ممّا آلت إليه النتائج على صعيد الشيعة، أنّ الحملات كانت موجّهة أساسًا ضدّ غلاة الشيعة، وبدرجات متفاوتة، يأتي في طليعتها الإسماعيليّة والرافضة عمومًا، ثمّ النصيريّة، و في درجة أخيرة الاثني عشريّة. لكن لمّا كانت غالبيّة الشيعة على اختلاف مللها ونحلها متّهمة بالتعامل مع الصليبيّين، أعداء الأمّة الإسلاميّة، لذلك اضطرّوا جميعًا إلى حمل السلاح في وجه مصير واحد ينتظرهم وللدفاع عن المجموعة الشيعيّة التي تشعر بقربى إلى بعضها البعض منها إلى الإسلام السنّيّ. ورغم أنّ ابن تيميّة كان قد اتّهم شيعة جزّين وجبل عامل كما الكسروانيّين بالتنكر للقضيّة الإسلاميّة لمصلحة الكفّار أعدائها من الفرنج والتتار[٦٠]، فلم توجّه الحملات، بالدرجة الأولى، سهامها إلاّ إلى كسروان. ما يؤكد أنّ الإسلام السنّيّ كانت له مواقف متدرّجة تجاه الجماعات الشيعيّة المختلفة.

وبعد الحملات بقيت للشيعة جزر صغيرة في بيروت والشوف، وبجوار بلاد الموارنة في المنيطره وبشناتا[٦١].

---

٥٨ Laoust, Remarques, p. 93–115.

٥٩ صالح بن يحيى، تاريخ بيروت، ص ٩٦.

٦٠ ابن تيميّة، فتاوى، ج٢٨/٤٠٠.

٦١ الدويهيّ، أزمنة، ط. توتل، ص٢١٧.

ومع الزمن، تحوّل قسم من الشيعة إلى السنّة بسبب ممارستهم التقيّة على المذهب الشافعيّ. وهذه كانت حال شيعة البقاع الأوسط ووادي التيم وإقليم الخروب والضنّيّة وعكّار[٦٢].

كان الشيعة الإماميّة في برج الوقف في ضواحي بيروت وهم في الأساس كما يذكر كتاب «قواعد الاداب» من الروافض[٦٣]. وبما أنّ المؤلّف كان درزيًّا فهو ينظر إليهم نظرة دونيّة، ويعتبر أنّ شيعة جبل عامل من الروافض أيضًا. كما يذكر هذا المصدر أنّهم كانوا في جبل يبوس وقيتوليه ومزبود في إقليم الخروب[٦٤]. ويذكر أيضًا أنّ قرى سبلين والوردانيّة والجيّه وشحيم ومزبود وعانوت وجوارها والناعمه هم في الأصل من كسروان وسنة[٦٥]. ولعلّهم أصبحوا سنّة بعد تهجيرهم، وإلاّ فلا مبرّر أن يأتوا من كسروان، وكان من الأفضل بقاؤهم فيه إلى جانب من استقدم المماليك من عناصر سنّيّة. والمؤرّخ الدرزيّ، ابن سباط، يشير إلى وجود الشيعة في برج الوقف، ويعيد ذكر القرى المذكورة أعلاه ويضيف إليها بحمدون ومجدل المعوش التي كانت سنّيّة[٦٦]، ونحن نرجح ما ذكرناه عنها.

في القرن الرابع عشر نمت في جزّين مدرسة فقهيّة شيعيّة على يد الشهيد الأوّل الإمام شمس الدين محمد بن مكيّ. ولكنّ نشاطه أثار حفيظة المماليك فألقي القبض عليه وقتل في **١٣٨٤**[٦٧].

هذا الانتقام من الشيعة جعل عددهم يتقلّص في جزّين كما تبرز ذلك الإحصاءات العثمانيّة[٦٨].

في القرن الخامس عشر كانت صور كما لاحظ الرحالة «دو لا برونكيار» مأهولة بالشيعة[٦٩].

ومن العائلات التي اشتهرت في قيادة جبل عامل عائلة ابن بشاره[٧٠].

---

٦٢ J. Goudard, *La Sainte Vierge au Liban*, Paris 1908, p. 333.

٦٣ قواعد الاداب، ص ٤٦–٤٨.

٦٤ المصدر ذاته، ص ٤٧.

٦٥ المصدر ذاته، ص ٤٧–٤٨.

٦٦ ابن سباط، تاريخ، ص ٤٨–٥٠.

٦٧ محمد جابر آل صفا، **تاريخ جبل عامل**، دار النهار، بيروت ١٩٨١، ص ١٨، ٢٣١–٢٣٢، ٢٣٥. **مجلة أوراق لبنانيّة**، بيروت ١٩٩٥، ص ٥٧٦.

٦٨ راجع هذه الاحصاءات في كتابنا: **بتدين اللقش قرية من الجبل اللبنانيّ**، بيروت ٢٠٠٠.

٦٩ De la Bronquière, *Le voyage d'outre mer*, éd. Ch. Scheffer, Paris 1892, pp. 28–29.

٧٠ ابن تغري بردي، **النجوم الزاهرة، في ملوك مصر والقاهرة**، ج١٢، القاهرة ١٩٢٩، ص ٣٠٧. ابن سباط، تاريخ، ص ٢١٦. الدويهيّ، أزمنة، ط. تزتل، ص ٢٢٦.

في العام ١٣٦٤/٧٦٥ أطلق نائب دمشق الحرم بحقّ الشيعة بتوقيع صادر في ٢٥ جمادى الثاني ٣٠ آذار، بعدما علم أنّ معتقد الشيعة بدأ بالانتشار بين سكّان بيروت وصيدا وجوارهما[٧١].

وفي العام ٧٧١ /١٣٦٩، تحرّك الشيعة في بيروت وأظهروا السنّة، لكنّهم كانوا في الباطن يمارسون عقائدهم الشيعيّة[٧٢].

كان النصيريّون أكثريّة سكّانيّة في عكّار والضنّيّة، ومع الوقت تكاثر السنّة هناك. فكيف جرى ذلك؟ يرجّح الدكتور كمال الصليبي أنّهم مارسوا التقيّة لدرء خطر المماليك فنسوا أصولهم النصيريّة وتحوّلوا إلى السنّة. وكان ذلك نتيجة السياسة المملوكيّة التي، عملاً في إحكام السيطرة على عكّار والضنّيّة، ولكبح جماح أيّة ثورة جديدة، عمدت إلى تسليم أمر رقابة المنطقة إلى الأكراد السنّة. فبفضل التقيّة، وبفضل تكاثر الأكراد وغيرهم، تغيّرت هويّة المنطقة[٧٣].

ب) على صعيد الدروز

حصد الدروز خسارة فادحة في الجرد تحت قيادة مقدّميهم من عائلة بوللمع الذين كانوا إلى جانب الثوّار الكسروانيّين[٧٤]. لكن بما أنّ الأمراء البحتريّين التنوخيّين كانوا إلى جانب المماليك، وحتّى إنّهم ذهبوا إلى حدّ مقاتلة شركائهم في الدين، كما في معركة نابيه[٧٥]، تمكّن هؤلاء من تخفيف وطأة القمع المملوكيّ عن الطائفة الدرزيّة. كما تمكّنوا من الحفاظ على مواقعهم التقليديّة في الجرد والغرب والشوف. كما أنّهم بفضل أمرائهم البحتريّين استقرّوا في بيروت كما تركّزوا في الشويفات ووادي التيم[٧٦].

عاش الدروز منكفئين على الذات، ورغم هذه العزلة والانعزال، سعى الدروز، عبر إصلاحات الأمير السيّد عبدالله التنوخيّ، في القرن الخامس عشر، إلى التصالح مع الإسلام السنّيّ، عبر بناء بعض الجوامع في عرامون ودير القمر[٧٧]. الأعيان الدروز كانوا

---

٧١ القلقشنديّ، صبح ج١٧/٨. صالح بن يحيى، تاريخ بيروت، ٣٧.

٧٢ صالح بن يحيى، تاريخ بيروت، ص ٣٧.

٧٣ الصليبي، لبنان الحديث، ص ١٨.

٧٤ تادرس مطران حماه، «نكبة كسروان ودير مار شليطا مقبس في غوسطا» نشر بولس قرألي في كتاب **حروب المقدّمين**، بيت شباب ١٩٣٧، ص ٨٥-٨٦.

٧٥ صالح بن يحيى، تاريخ بيروت، ص ٩٥-٩٦.

٧٦ هذا ما يؤكّده صالح بن يحيى.

٧٧ Toufic Touma, *Paysans et institutions féodales chez les Druses et les Maronites du Liban du XVII à 1914*, Pub. Unv. Libanaise, Beyrouth 1971–1972, p. 474–475.

في صراع مع عائلات أعيان أخرى درزيّة كعائلة الحمرا وعائلات شيعيّة ومع تركمان كسروان كما يستدّل من كتاب صالح بن يحيى. والسبب الرئيس لهذا الصراع اقتصاديّ نتيجة التنافس على الإقطاعات[٧٨].

ج) على صعيد اليعاقبة والأحباش

كان اليعاقبة متغلغلين في جسم المناطق المارونيّة. فالبطريرك الدويهيّ يذكر أنّ هؤلاء استمالوا بعض كبار رجال الدين إلى معتقدهم[٧٩].

وفي النصف الثاني من القرن الخامس عشر نزحت عائلات يعقوبيّة وحبشيّة إلى قرى مارونيّة وبنت أديرة لها فيها[٨٠].

هذه الإشارات من قبل الدويهيّ ترسم واقعًا جديدًا في مناطق الموارنة، فهي تؤشر لهجرة يعقوبيّة إلى تلك المناطق لظروف نجهلها.

ولكن لم يطل عمر اليعاقبة في المناطق المارونيّة، إذ سرعان ما طردوا من دير الأحباش في إهدن فلجأوا إلى وادي حدشيت في ١٤٨٨[٨١].

كان سكن الأحباش اليعاقبة في إهدن وحدشيت كما ذكرنا وفي دير الفراديس ومار آسيا. وقد اكتشفت كتابات حبشيّة وتصاوير في مغارة مار آسيا[٨٢].

وكان استقرار اليعاقبة والأحباش قد حصل زمن مقدّم بشراي عبد المنعم أيّوب. ونجحوا في استمالة المقدّم إلى اليعقوبيّة بعدما أغروه بالمال، وإقدامه على بناء كنيسة على اسم مار برصوما قرب قصره وتسهيل إقامتهم في الجبّة، وفي جعل نوح البقوفانيّ بطريركًا في ١٤٩٣ على اليعاقبة. وبعدما طردوا من إهدن عاد الموارنة فطردوهم من حدشيت ومن كامل الجبّة على يد سكّان إهدن، وانتهى أمرهم بالكامل بعد موت مقدّم بشراي، عبد المنعم[٨٣].

---

٧٨ صالح بن يحيى، ٤١ تاريخ بيروت، ص ٦٣–٦٧، ٧١–٧٢، ٨٠، ٨٥، ٨٩–٩٤، ١٠٦، ١٧٨، ١٨٠، ١٩٨، ٢١٢، ٢١٥. ابن سباط، تاريخ، ١٥٣–١٥٤، ١٦٠، ١٦١. قواعد الآداب، ص ٥٣.

٧٩ الدويهيّ، أزمنة، ط. فهد، ص ٣٢٩.

٨٠ الدويهيّ، أزمنة، توتل، ص٢١٤، ٢١٨.

٨١ الدويهيّ، أزمنة، توتل، ص ٢١٨.

٨٢ Revue Liban souterrain IV(1993) pp. 2–12; Revue Speleorient, I (1996), pp. 27–39.

٨٣ الدويهيّ، أزمنة، ط. توتل، ص ٢١٤، ٢١٦–٢١٩. الصليبي، منطلق، ص ١٦٥–١٦٦.

د) على صعيد الموارنة

انكفأ الموارنة على ذاتهم في القسم الشماليّ الشرقيّ من الجبل اللبنانيّ الواقع ضمن نيابة طرابلس في جبّة بشراي والزاوية وفي سفوح وأعالي البترون وجبيل.

فصائل صغيرة منهم جاءت لتسكن كسروان بعد مدّة حسب رواية الأسقف تادرس المارونيّ، الذي يذكر أنّ دير مار شليطا مقبس قرب بلدة غوسطا في كسروان، نجا من التدمير[٨٤]. وهذه المعلومة التي بنيت عليها نظريّات عن استمراريّة الوجود المارونيّ والمسيحيّ في كسروان تتناقض مع الإحصاءات العثمانيّة بعد قرنين ونصف من الزمن. وعمّا يذكره الدويهيّ عن وصول العائلات مارونيّة إلى كسروان في منتصف القرن السادس عشر[٨٥].

وقد لاحظ الرحالة «بولونير» وجود الموارنة في مدينة طرابلس بالذات في العام ١٤٢٢م[٨٦].

وكان المركز البطريركيّ المارونيّ في تلك الفترة في إيليج قرب ميفوق، ثمّ بسبب الاضطهاد الذي فرض على الموارنة ومهاجمة الدير من قبل عساكر المماليك ألزم البطاركة السكنى في قنّوبين في ١٤٤٠[٨٧].

الطوائف المسيحيّة، ومن بينها الموارنة، كانت تنعم بتسامح الإسلام بوجودها ضمن إطار نظام الذمّة. ولكن لا تلحظ المصادر الإسلاميّة وجود هؤلاء، كما لا يلحظ القلقشنديّ وجود أيّ زعيم أو أمين لأهل الذمّة في نيابة طرابلس تقوم مراسلة بينه وبين الدولة المملوكيّة[٨٨].

الوجود المارونيّ في جبال صعبة المسالك، قليلة الأهمّيّة، اقتصاديًّا وبشريًّا، وعلى طرف الأرياف الشاميّة، ونظرًا إلى أنّ في أحيان لا يستهان بها، يجعل نظام الذمّة نظامًا قيميًّا يصوّر الأوضاع، كما ينبغي أن تكون، لا كما هي في الواقع، ويجعلنا نتساءل في أيّة ظروف طبّق هذا النظام الذميّ؟ على صعيد الحياة الشخصيّة ومسائل الزواج والإرث وعلى صعيد الإرث والحقّ الشخصيّ (وقف، تملّك، بناء).

---

٨٤ تادرس مطران حماه، نكبة كسروان ١٩٣٧.

٨٥ الدويهيّ، ط. توتل، ٢٣٦، ٢٣٨–٢٣٩، ٢٥٧.

٨٦ Lammens, Syrie, vol. II, p. 38.

٨٧ الدويهيّ، أزمنة، ط. توتل، ص ٢٠٦.

٨٨ القلقشنديّ، صبح، ج٤/١٩٤–٢٣٦.
M. Gaudefroy-Demombynes, *La Syrie à l'époque des Mamelouks*, Paris 1923, p. 225.

ومن المصادر المهمّة التي تعطي فكرة عن الوجود المارونيّ وانتشاره وعن علاقات الموارنة بالكرسيّ الرسوليّ وعن أوقاف الكرسيّ البطريركيّ في قنّوبين، وعن مستوى الكتابة عند الموارنة وعن اللغات وأنواع الكتابات التي كانوا يستخدمونها وعن الفقر الماديّ الذي كان يرزح تحته الموارنة: إنجيل «ربولا»، وكلّ هذه المعلومات قد درست بإسهاب في كتابنا المذكور عن نيابة طرابلس.

كان الموارنة يمارسون بحرّيّة نسبيّة، أكثر من غيرهم من المسيحيّين، شعائرهم الدينيّة، متحصّنين في جبالهم بعيدًا عن الرقابة الإسلاميّة المباشرة، وهذا يشكّل اختراقا لنظام الذمّة. ويتساءل الباحث عمّا إذا كانت أمكنة العبادة المارونيّة قد خضعت لمضايقات الأئمّة المسلمين الذين كانوا يمنعون بناء كنائس جديدة في المدن وفي التجمّعات الإسلاميّة المهمّة وقرب المدن. يبدو أنّ الموارنة، كانوا بمنأى عن هذه الشرائع، وذلك لسببين جوهريّين: فمن جهة كانوا يعيشون خارج التجمّع المدنيّ، في حياة ريفيّة على بعد أميال عدّة من مدينة طرابلس، أقرب تجمّع سكنيّ إليهم، ومن جهة ثانية، بعيدًا عن الرقابة المملوكيّة المباشرة.

نتيجة لذلك، أفاد الموارنة من المناسبة المتاحة لهم وعمدوا إلى بناء العديد من الأديار والكنائس في شمال لبنان الحاليّ. غالبيّة هذه الكنائس كانت فقيرة بسيطة، على اسم العذراء مريم، التي كان لها تكريم خاصّ، وغريب من نوعه، عند الموارنة، بخاصّة زمن الخطوب والحروب والأوبئة والفتن.

استعمال اللغة السريانيّة والحرف السريانيّ في قراءة عربيّة (الكرشونيّ) ساهم في حرّيّة العبادة. ومن المعروف أنّه في القرن الخامس عشر، عند زيارة الأخ غريفون، المرسل البابويّ، جبل لبنان، اضطرّ إلى تعلّم السريانيّة للتمكّن من مخاطبة الموارنة[٨٩]. وهذا لا يعنيّ أنّ الموارنة كانوا يجهلون اللغة العربيّة.

على الصعيد الاقتصاديّ، الشرع الإسلاميّ يحمي حقّ الملكيّة للذميّين وحرّيّة العقود والتجارة والصناعة والزراعة. وبالنسبة إلى الملكيّة عند الموارنة، لاحظ المؤرّخون أنّه في العهد العباسيّ الأوّل، كانت لدى الموارنة ملكيّات فلاّحيّة، استمرّت لاحقًا، كما يقول PERROY وCAHEN، وإن يكن بصعوبة، حيث كان نظام الشراكة قائمًا في الملكيّات المجزّأة، المكلّفة، القليلة[٩٠]. ولا ندري ما إذا كانت الملكيّة الخاصّة قد

---

٨٩ فيليب حتّي، **لبنان في التاريخ**، دار الثقافة بيروت ١٩٥٩، ص ٩٧.
Lammens, Syrie. vol. II, p. 39.

٩٠ E. Perroy et Cl. Cahen, *Histoire générale des civilisations*, Le Moyen-Age, Paris 1957, p. 164.

استمرّت لاحقًا عند الموارنة في العهد المملوكيّ، لأنّ لا وثائق لدينا. ولكن بطريقة غير مباشرة، يمكن الاستدلال عليها عبر وجود وقفيّات الأراضيّ الوارد نصّها في إنجيل «ربولا»، إذ لا يمكن وقف الأرض إذا لم تكن مملوكة ملكيّة خاصّة. وكان الموارنة يعانون طبعًا على الصعيد الاقتصاديّ، من الضريبة المفروضة على الذميّين، أي الجزية، ومن الخراج. ويمكن أخذ فكرة معيّنة عن ذلك عبر نصّ من العام ١٤٧٥ م[٩١].

فرضت الشروط العمريّة على الذمّيّين بعامّة لخلق نوع من التمييز بينهم وبين المسلمين. وطاول ذلك مسائل اللباس وآداب الحياة اليوميّة. ولمّا كان الموارنة يعيشون في جبالهم فكانوا لا يتأثّرون بهذه الشروط، ولكن عند دخولهم إلى طرابلس، كانوا، حكمًا، عرضة لتطبيقها.

منذ بدء الطائفة المارونيّة، ارتبطت السلطة الزمنيّة ارتباطًا وثيقًا بالسلطة الروحيّة. لكن في العهد المملوكيّ وفي أواخر القرن الرابع عشر، أقام السلطان برقوق الشدياق يعقوب ابن أيّوب مقدّمًا، وكتب له بذلك صفيحة من نحاس، ثمّ نزل إلى دير قنّوبين وكتب للرهبان، أيضًا، صفيحة من نحاس على أن يكونوا معافين ويكون ديرهم له الرئاسة على ديورة تلك الجهات [٩٢]. وهنا، نجد اعترافًا ورسمًا وتولية للمقدّم على يد السلطان الإسلاميّ لا على يد البطريرك. كما لا نجد أيّ ربط بين سلطة المقدّم والسلطة الدينيّة. إنّما نلاحظ، أنّ الحاكم الذي أقامه السلطان برقوق كان من الرتبة الكهنوتيّة الدنيا، أي شدياقًا.

كان عند الموارنة مقدّمون[٩٣] عدّة. وكثرتهم تقودنا إلى الاعتقاد بأنّه في فترة من الفترات كان لكلّ بلدة مارونيّة أو قرية كبيرة أو تجمّع قرى، زعيم، تطلق عليه تسمية مقدّم. كانوا رؤساء إقطاعيّين ضمن التراتبيّة الإداريّة الصليبيّة. ومن ثمّ، في العهد المملوكيّ، أصبحوا جميعًا خاضعين لحكم مقدّم واحد، أو على الأقلّ، أصبحوا ممثّلين بمقدّم واحد هو مقدّم بشراي الذي توسّعت رقعة صلاحيّاته لتشمل منطقة مارونيّة بكاملها، هي منطقة الجبّة، التي أصبحت مرتبطة بها المقدّميّات الأخرى الأصغر منها، والأقلّ أهمّيّة. هذا، ولربّما، قد أعطى مقدّميّة جبّة بشراي هذه الأهمّيّة، لكون بشراي عنصرًا أساسيًّا في التقسيمات الإداريّة للجبل اللبنانيّ التابع لنيابة طرابلس. فلقد كانت تلك المناطق موزعة بين ولايات عدّة هي: «بلاد الضنّيّين « (أي الضنّيّة)، «بشريه « أي

---

٩١ M. Civezza, Relation de Fr. Ariosti, in: *Histoire Universelle des Missions Franciscaines*, tr. par V. Bernardin de Rouen, Paris, 3 vol. 1898, vol. III, p. 215.

٩٢ الدويهيّ، أزمنة، ص ٣٢٨.

٩٣ المصدر ذاته، ص ٢٠٧، ٢٢٥، ٣٢٨، ٣٦٤، ٣٧٦–٣٧٨، ٤٠٢، ٤٢. انطونيوس العينطوريني، **مختصر تاريخ جبل لبنان**، تحقيق، الياس القطّار، دار لحد خاطر، بيروت ١٩٨٣، ص ٩١–٩٢، ١٢٤–١٢٥.

جبّة بشراي، وأنفه (أي ساحل طرابلس وما يليه من الكوره)، وجبيل، وجبّة المنيطره[٩٤]. ولفظة مقدّم من فعل تقدّم أي كان في مقدّمة الناس في الحرب كما في السلم، وهي تدلّ على رتبة عسكريّة في الدولة المملوكيّة. إضافة إلى ذلك، كانت صلة الوصل بين الطائفة كجماعة وبين السلطة الإسلاميّة. لذلك أطلقت تسمية الكاشف على مقدّمي الموارنة، ولمّا كانت لفظة الكاشف ترمز إلى جباية الضرائب في الدولة المملوكيّة، عرفنا الوجه الأوّل لوظيفة المقدّم عند الموارنة[٩٥].

إضافة إلى ذلك، كان المقدّم رقيبًا، وذلك يعني، لربّما، أنّه كان مفروضًا عليه القيام بالمراقبة والرقابة على جماعته وتأمين الأمن في منطقة حكمه. وظيفة المقدّم، كانت ممّا يمكن استخلاصه عن سيرة المقدّمين الواردّة في التواريخ المارونيّة، وراثيّة ولمدى الحياة طيلة الفترة المملوكيّة وفي مطلع العهد العثمانيّ، لكنّها ستصبح عرضة للمزايدة وتغيير القائمين بها ابتداء من القرن الثامن عشر. وهذا الواقع ليس بالأمر العاديّ، في تاريخ المنطقة، حيث كان الحكّام المحلّيّون عرضة للتقلّب وللتبديل، ولم يكن حكمهم مستقرًّا في منطقة محدّدة، ولم يكن وراثيًّا ولمدى الحياة. وما لاحظناه عن مؤسّسة المقدّميّة عند الموارنة نجده في مؤسّسة أو نظام الإقطاع الذي كان قائمًا عند الدروز بخاصّة. وبهذا يمكن الكلام على تمتّع الجبل اللبنانيّ بخصوصيّة الاستقرار في المؤسّسات والنظم دون غيره من المناطق في بلاد الشام[٩٦]. طبعًا، لا يعني ذلك استقلاليّة تامّة عن السلطة الإسلاميّة، إذ إنّ استلام مقاليد السلطة المحلّيّة كان خاضعًا لاعتراف السلطات الإسلاميّة بذلك. ويلاحظ الباحث، مع البطريرك الدويهيّ، أنّ البطاركة الموارنة منذ القرن الخامس عشر انتقلوا من بلاد جبيل والبترون للسكن في قنّوبين[٩٧]. الدافع إلى ذلك كان، حكمًا، ما تتمتّع به جبّة بشراي من استقرار نسبيّ تحت حكم المقدّم يعقوب وخلفائه.

عيش الموارنة في ريف جبليّ قاس حتّم عليهم العمل في الزراعة وفي الرعي. وهذا ما قاد إلى جملة صراعات على المراعي مع جماعات من طوائف أخرى، ما أدّى إلى جعل النزاعات تتّخذ طابعًا طائفيًا–دينيًّا. ومن هذه الصراعات ما جرى مع أهل المنيطرة في ١٤٨٢ وإقدام أمير شيعيّ على نهب بشراي[٩٨].

---

٩٤ القلقشنديّ، صبح، ج٤/١٤٧–١٤٨.

٩٥ الدويهيّ، **الشرح المختصر في أصل الموارنة...**، نشر بطرس فهد، لبنان ١٩٧٤، ص٢٤٩. الصليبي، منطلق، ص١٣٢.

٩٦ راجع كتابنا عن نيابة طرابلس، ص ٢٧٩.

٩٧ الدويهيّ، أزمنة، ص ٣٤٩–٣٥٠.

٩٨ المصدر ذاته، ص ٢١٧.

رغم هذا التميّيز الدينيّ، الذي قاد إلى جملة اضطهادات، وإلى انطواء على الذات، قامت هذه الطوائف، بمحاولات للانسجام مع محيطها، وتجاوز الانعزال المفروض عليها من المماليك.

رابعًا – الانطواء على الذات ومحاولات الانسجام والخروج من العزلة.

عاشت الأقلّيّات الدينيّة في مناخ من الضغوط النفسيّة والمادّيّة، ما ولّد عندها، وبدرجات متفاوتة، حالات قلق نفسيّ مزمن، وانطواء على الذات، وكان بمقدور الشيعة حلّ المشكلة جزئيًّا باعتماد سلاح التقيّة، أمّا ذلك فكان صعبًا عند الموارنة، وإن يكن، كما ذكرنا، قد اعتمدوها في أسمائهم.

الانطواء على الذات كان مزدوجًا: انطواء تجاه السلطة الإسلاميّة–السنّيّة. وانطواء للطوائف في ما بينها.

كان انطواء الموارنة وليد تاريخ من التشدّد المسيحيّ والإسلاميّ تجاههم ولممارسة المسلمين عليهم شروطًا تشعرهم بالدونيّة، ولم يكن ذلك شيئًا مخلوقًا في ذواتهم، بقدر ما هو حالة ولّدها الجو السياسيّ والدينيّ والاجتماعيّ العامّ.

اعتماد نظام الذمّة، كانت له حسناته وسيّئاته عند الموارنة، فهو نظّم علاقتهم بالمسلمين من جهة، ولكن نمّى عندهم التعصّب الدينيّ والشعور بالمفارقة وبالاستقلاليّة، يدفعهم إلى ذلك كون هويّة الفرد تحدّد بالانتماء الدينيّ. وقد تعرّض الموارنة والنصيريّون لاضطهادات عدّة[٩٩].

ولاحظ «دنديني» أنّ الموارنة يتظاهرون في القرن السادس عشر مثلاً، بلبس ثياب رثّة واقتناء منازل لا قيمة لها لدرء انتباه وجشع السلطات الإسلاميّة[١٠٠]. كانت الإجراءات العامّة التي يطبّقها المماليك بحقّ أهل الذمّة في مصر والشام تطال أيضًا نصارى لبنان الحاليّ، حكمًا. وأهمّ هذه الإجراءات هي التي جرت في **١٢٩٠**، **١٢٩٧**، **١٣٠٠**، **١٣٠٩**، **١٣٢١**، **١٣٣٩**، **١٣٤١**، **١٣٥٣**، **١٣٥٤**، **١٣٦٣**، **١٣٦٥**، وطالت العمل في الإدارة واللباس والقصاص والجزية والحياة الاجتماعيّة والمركوب[١٠١].

---

٩٩ M. Sobernheim, *Corpus inscriptionum arabicarum*, Inst. Fr. du Caire, 1909, p. 125–126.

١٠٠ Dandini, *Voyage du Mont Liban*, Paris 1675, p. 89.

١٠١ ابن كثير، البداية، ج١٤/٥٥، ١٨٦، ١٩٨، ٢٤٩، ٢٥٠، ٣٠٥–٣٠٦، ٣٠٨، ٣١٧، ٣١٩. ابن الفرات، ناصر الدين، **تاريخ ابن الفرات**، تحقيق قسطنطين زريق، بيروت ١٩٤٢، ج٨/٩٣. ابن تغري بردّي، النجوم، ج٨/١٣٣–١٣٥. القلقشنديّ، صبح، ج١٣/٢٠. المقريزيّ، السلوك، ج٢/٩٥٩–٩٦٢.

هذه عيّنات واضحة عمّا كان يعانيه أهل الذمّة من إجراءات تضطهدهم من جهة، وتلجم حريّتهم من جهة أخرى. فخلال خمسين سنة تقريبًا، تعرّض هؤلاء لتسعة إجراءات تعسّفيّة، وقس على ذلك في المراحل الأخرى من التاريخ المملوكيّ. وفي كتب الحسبة إشارة واضحة إلى التمييز الدينيّ العنصريّ الواجب فرضه على أهل الذمّة. ففي كتاب «معالم القربة في أحكام الحسبة»، الباب الرابع، تحت عنوان في «الحسبة على أهل الذمّة» مطالعة قانونيّة فقهيّة لتاريخ هذا التمييز ولما هو واجب تطبيقه من إجراءات، من باب أنّ «التساهل مع أهل الذمّة في أمور الدين خطر عظيم[١٠٢]».

وقد قاد الاضطهاد كلا من الموارنة والشيعة إلى النزوع إلى نوع من الاستقلاليّة الداخليّة ظهرت عند الموارنة بترتيب سلطاتهم الدينيّة (البطريركيّة) والزمنيّة (المقدّمين) وحرّيّة انفتاح ثقافيّ على الغرب بدأت بذوره مع ابن القلاعيّ، واعتماد اللغة السريانيّة والحرف السريانيّ كوسيلة للتخاطب.

أمّا انطواء هذه الطوائف على بعضها البعض فأمر معروف. ورغم حالة الاضطهاد القائمة، ورغم الرقابة المتشدّدة التي مارسها المماليك على هذه الطوائف، لتشكيكهم فيهم وفي ولائهم للسلطة المملوكيّة السنّيّة، فإنّ هذه الطوائف، وبدرجات متفاوتة، حاولت تجاوز العزلة والانعزال في مواضع شتى وعلى مستويات متعدّدة، والانفتاح على الآخرين. طبعًا، الموارنة كانوا أكثر الطوائف الشرقيّة التي حاولت تجاوز الشرنقة التي فرضت عليها. ولئن كان الانفتاح المارونيّ على الغرب المسيحيّ كبيرًا، فهو لم يكن معدومًا باتجاه العرب المسلمين.

وبواسطة ابن القلاعيّ، الأسقف المارونيّ، بدأت أولى خطوات الموارنة الثقافيّة باتجاه الثقافة الغربيّة، وعلى قدر أقلّ باتجاه الثقافة العربيّة–الإسلاميّة، فبدأ يستقي من الأولى بعض مضامينها ومن الثانية وسائل تعبيرها. كتابات ابن القلاعيّ، كانت، على حدّ رأي د. كمال الصليبيّ، تعبيرًا عن شعور بالكرامة، ضمن محيط معاد، وبالفخر نتيجة محافظتهم على شخصيّتهم رغم كلّ الخطوب التي تعرّضوا لها في القرون الوسطى[١٠٣].

أمّا على صعيد الإسماعيليّين والنصيريّة، فالنصوص لا تسجّل محاولات ثقافيّة للانخراط في العالم الشرقيّ أو الغربيّ، اللهمّ، إلاّ باعتماد التقيّة الدينيّة، كوسيلة رضوخ للسلطة الحاكمة، بحيث يلتوون على أنفسهم من دون أن ينكسروا نهائيًّا في حلبة

---

١٠٢ ابن الإخوة، محمد، **معالم القربة في أحكام الحسبة**، القاهرة ١٩٧٦، ص ٩٢–١٠٠.

١٠٣ K. Salibi, Maronite historians, pp. 15–35.

الصراع الدينيّ. على كلّ حال، موضوع الاضطهاد الدينيّ في القرون الوسطى، يتطلّب المزيد من البحث الدقيق والمعمّق، بعيدًا عن المواقف المبدئيّة. فلو توقّفنا عندما ورد عند المؤرخ عزّ الدين بن شدّاد، لوجدنا أنّ الأمر نسبيّ، وأنّ المسألة قابلة للبحث. فهو، في سيرة السلطان بيبرس يقول: «ومن عدله أنّ في أيّامه لم تتمكّن أكابر الأمراء من التعدّي على أقلّ العوام بل على أدنى اليهود والنصارى، ومتى رفع إليه يهوديّ أو نصرانيّ أو أقلّ العوام ظلامة على أحد من أعيان دولته أنصفه منه وكفّه عنه...»[١٠٤]. فهذا الكلام، يتناقض كلّيًّا مع ما نعرفه عن بيبرس من بطش ومجازر بحقّ النصارى في أماكن عدّة، وهو قد يكون من باب تقرّب المؤرّخ من السلطان، لكن على كلّ حال فهو يفتح الباب أمام النقاش حول هذا الموضوع.

مسألة التمييز الدينيّ، كانت قضيّة شديدة الحساسيّة في مجتمع متصلّب دينيًّا، قادت إلى فتن اجتماعيّة. وأثارت الإجراءات ضدّ النصارى، جدلاً دائمًا، بين المؤرّخين، لا يخفي أحيانًا، الموقع الدينيّ أو «الأيديولوجيّ» الذي ينتمي إليه الكاتب. وبينما يرى فيها البعض حالة إسلاميّة عامّة، يرى فيها آخرون ممارسة من المسلمين لضرورات سياسيّة ظرفيّة وآنيّة. واختلفت الرؤية لها بين غربيّين وشرقيّين، ومسلمين ومسيحيّين ويهود.

المفكّر الفرنسيّ «بواسار» يؤكّد في كتابه «الأنسنة في الإسلام»، على تسامح الإسلام على الصعيد الدينيّ[١٠٥].

هذا الموقف المتوازن من مسألة العلاقة بين الإسلام والمسلمين من جهة وأهل الذمّة من جهة أخرى، قد يجد نقيضًا له عند الكتّاب والمفكّرين الإسرائيليّين الذين لهم مواقف «راديكاليّة» من الموضوع، ظهرت في كتب متعدّدة، بعضها يرى أنّ العامّة، بتحريض من العلماء، كانت تطالب بطرد الذمّيّين. وكان الأمراء يحاولون بعض الأحيان حمايتهم ويخيّرونهم بين الاستقالة واعتناق الإسلام، وكان الكثيرون يشهرون إسلامهم للحفاظ على وظائفهم[١٠٦]. ويتّهم الإسلام بعدم التسامح والاضطهاد، وباستغلال اليهود، بإعطائهم موقعًا معقولاً بين السلطة الإسلاميّة «المضطهدة» والعامّة المسيحيّة الخاضعة لها[١٠٧].

---

١٠٤ عزّ الدين ابن شدّاد، **تاريخ الملك الظاهر**، تحقيق أحمد حطيط، فسبادن **١٩٨٣**، ص ٢٨١–٢٨٢.

١٠٥ M. Boisard, *L'humanisme de l'Islam*, Albin Michel, Paris 1979, pp. 190, 197–198.

١٠٦ Bat Ye'or, *Le Dhimmi*: Profil de l'opprimé en Orient et en Afrique du Nord depuis la conquête arabe, éd. Anthropos, Paris 1980, p. 33, 67–68.

١٠٧ Ibid, pp. 67–68.

وفي مواجهة هذا الموقف، نجد موقفًا آخر يميل إلى حدّ كبير إلى الالتزام بالرصانة والموضوعيّة في تحليله مسألة وضعيّة أهل الذمّة، هو موقف المستشرق «كلود كاهين». فالمؤرّخ المذكور، يقارن بين حالة الذمّيّين في النصف الأوّل من القرون الوسطى بالقرون الأربعة الأخيرة منها، أي العهد الصليبيّ فالمملوكيّ، ليلاحظ تصلبًا ظهر في علاقة المسلمين مع الذمّيّين. وهذا التصلّب عائد إلى المناخ الاقتصاديّ السائد الذي كان يثير الشعب، وإلى الاعتبارات السياسيّة أكثر من الاعتبارات الدينيّة. الغزوات المغوليّة، أكثر من الحروب الصليبيّة، أضرّت بالمسيحيّين في المشرق. وفي الدولة المملوكيّة، أصيب المسيحيّون الأصليّون، الموارنة أكثر من الأقباط، من نتائج الغزوات المغوليّة ومن استمرار حالة الحرب مع الفرنج على شواطىء المتوسّط، ومن هيمنة التجّار الغربيّين على التجّار الشرقيّين[١٠٨].

وبالنهاية، يمكن القول إن ما مورس في العهد المملوكيّ من تصرّفات فظّة وضغوط على الذمّيّين، هو حالة فريدة في التاريخ الإسلاميّ في القرون الوسطى، وكانت لذلك أسبابه الاقتصاديّة والاجتماعيّة والسياسيّة والنفسيّة، في جو كان مشحونًا ضدّ الغرباء واحتمالات تعاون الذمّيّين من السكّان المحلّيّين معهم. ولئن لم يكن ذلك سياسة وضع خطوطها السلاطين المماليك، فقد جاء تعبيرًا عن واقع اجتماعيّ وذهنيّة شعبيّة، تحرّكهما غريزة الدفاع عن النفس.

---

١٠٨ Cl. Cahen, art "Dhimma", *E.I.2*, t.II, pp. 234–238.

الأقباط والإدارة المملوكيّة
في عهد الناصر محمد بن قلاوون،
شرف الدين النشو نموذجًا

أحمد حطيط
الجامعة اللبنانيّة

مدخل

ثمّة ملاحظة منهجيّة أودّ أن أعرض لها في مستهلّ مداخلتي، مفادها أنّ حضور «الشائع» أو «المألوف» في ميدان العلوم الإنسانيّة، يضمن نوعًا من الراحة و الترف الفكريّ لكثير من الباحثين عمومًا، و لكتبة التاريخ خصوصًا، لاسيّما إذا كان هذا «المألوف» خطابًا مؤدلجًا يتوسّل البتر والتبسيط حينًا واللبس والمغالطة أحيانًا، بحيث تضحى مراجعته ليست بالشيء اليسير، و لو أنّها ليست بالأمر المستحيل.

ولعلّ أقرب السبل إلى مواجهة هذه المعضلة الشائكة أن نعمل على تجميع البقايا كلّها أو جلّها، فنقرأ ونعيد القراءة بأسلوب علميّ ممنهج ورؤية موضوعيّة حذرة، كي تفضي الملامسة الأولى إلى ارتسام ملامح أخرى غير ملامح «المألوف» وأكثر مصداقيّة منها.

فالمألوف على هالته، ليس إلا نتاجًا ظرفيًّا أريد له أن يخلد من طريق الإلحاح المتحكّم، ثمّ التواتر والاجترار. لذا فإنّ «استدعاءه» بجانب «المنسي» أو «المغيب» مدعاة في حدّ ذاته إلى تعرية الواقع المقنّع واستجلاء المطموس، وتاليًا، فإنّ هذا «الاستدعاء» هو أول الطريق لمن ابتغى أن يدفع الإبهام أو ينصّب بعض النقط على الحروف.

وتحديدًا للمنحى الذي اخترناه لهذه المداخلة، ربّما كان من الأنسب أن نذكّر بظاهرة تاريخيّة تتلخّص في ما نلمسه في العصور الوسطى التي تميّزت بسيادة المفاهيم

الدينيّة، في الشرق كما في الغرب، من تشويش ملحّ قائم بين النصّ وأداء المؤسّسة الحاكمة في النسق الإسلاميّ في التعامل مع مسألة الأقلّيّات الدينيّة بوجه عامّ. وإذا كان لهذه الظاهرة ما يماثلها بالطبع في الأنساق الحضاريّة الأخرى، إلا أنّ من أهم ما يميزّها أنّها استأثرت، في الغالب بتلاوين التطوّر التاريخيّ ووجّهته توجيهًا حاسمًا تصعب مراقبته في الكثير من الأحيان، ما أسهم في جعل العلاقة بين النصّ والممارسة محكومة بنوع من الضبابيّة المشوبة بشيء غير قليل من التعتيم المتواتر و«المكتسب».

ولا جدال في أنّ موضوع الأقلّيّات الدينيّة في التاريخ الإسلاميّ شائق وشائك في آن. فهو شائق من حيث إنّه ينطوي على كثير من العناصر المثيرة لاهتمام الباحث، وشائك من حيث إنّه يمسّ أمورًا فائقة الحساسيّة، تفترض البحث العلميّ الجاد، ونوعًا من الموضوعيّة الخالصة، فضلاً عن التنبّه واليقظة في استخدام المصطلحات (أهل الكتاب أم أهل الذمّة في المصطلح الإسلاميّ مثلا) حتّى لا ينزلق الباحث في منزلق الانسياق عن قصد أو من دون قصد وراء الأهواء والميول.

في ضوء ما تقدّم، فإنّ مداخلتنا حول ملابسات الدور الذي قام به الأقباط في الإدارة المملوكيّة، تندرج في مجال نقد الشائع في العلاقة بين الإسلام السياسيّ وأهل الكتاب في المجتمع الإسلاميّ.

فإذا كان صحيحًا أنّ سياسة الجهاد التي أطلقها السلطان الظاهر بيبرس البندقداري (+١٢٧٨/٦٧٦)، واعتمدها كأحد دعائم تركيز السلطنة المملوكيّة وتعبئة الطاقات الإسلاميّة لمواجهة المغول والفرنج، أدّت في بدء القرن الثامن الهجريّ/الرابع عشر الميلاديّ إلى اتخاذ تدابير قاسية بحقّ أهل الكتاب عمومًا والمسيحيّين على وجه الخصوص، وإلى سوء معاملتهم، فأبعدوا عن وظائف الدولة، وأعمالها وشدّد عليهم في تنفيذ ما سمّي «بالشروط العمريّة» بمنعهم ممّا كان مشروعًا لهم من ركوب الدواب، وهدم ما شيّد من صوامع اليهود وبيع النصارى التي أجازها الإسلام، وحرص على احترامها وصونها منذ ظهوره، كما فرض على أهل الكتاب لباسًا معيّنًا لتمييزهم عن المسلمين، وتجسّد كلّ هذا في مرسوم سلطانيّ نشر في أصقاع السلطنة المملوكيّة من الفرات إلى النوبة، فإنّ هذا المرسوم كغيره من المراسيم المماثلة، لم يلبث في الواقع، أن صار في زوايا الإهمال تدريجًا، وإن ظلّت فرص إعادة تطبيقه خطرًا يتهدّد أهل الكتاب من حين إلى حين[1].

[1] المفضل بن أبي الفضائل، النهج السديد والدر الفريد فيما بعد تاريخ ابن العميد، نشر بلوشية، ج ٢٠، ص ٣٨–٤٠ المقريزيّ، السلوك لمعرفة دول الملوك، ١، ق ٣، تحقيق محمّد مصطفى زيادة، القاهرة، ١٩٣٤، ص ٩٠٩/٩١٣.

ومع ذلك، فإنّنا نقع في المصادر المعاصرة، على معلومات تشيّ بأنّ العنصر القبطيّ احتلّ مكانة مرموقة في دولة المماليك على غرار ما كان شائعًا في زمن الفاطميّين والأيّوبيّين[٢]. فإنّ كثيرًا من الأسر القبطيّة اعتنقت الإسلام، بالإضافة إلى أسر يهوديّة، وعرف هؤلاء بالمسالمة، أو الأسالمة ومفردها «أسلميّ»، و«مسلمانيّ»[٣]، تمييّزًا لهم عن أهل الكتاب الباقين على دينهم من جهة، وعن المسلمين من جهة أخرى.

ولعلّ الدافع إلى هذا ما كان يحوط بأولئك المسلمين الجدد من شكوك ساورت المسلمين المعاصرين حول مدى إخلاصهم للإسلام[٤]. فكان من الأسالمة نوابغ بلغوا المراتب العليا في الدولة، فأسندت إليهم وظائف الدولة الماليّة والإداريّة، فجمعوا إلى جانب خبراتهم وتمرّسهم في الشؤون الإداريّة والماليّة شرط الإسلام. ومن ثمّ، لم تعد الدولة المملوكيّة تشعر بالحرج الناشئ عن وجود أهل الكتاب من اليهود والنصارى في وظائف الدولة. كما بقي في الدواوين المملوكيّة عدد كبير من الأقباط الذين استمرّوا على ديانتهم، ما أثار حفيظة بعض العلماء المسلمين، وبلغ ببعضهم الأمر أن تجرّأ على السلطان في مجلسه، آخذًا عليه تماديه بتولية النصارى في الدواوين. من ذلك ما ذكره المقريزيّ[٥] عن الشيخ نور الدين علي بن عبد الوارث البكريّ الذي أشار إلى السلطان الناصر محمّد بن قلاوون بكلام فيه جفاء و غلظة، معترضًا على توليته في مناصب الدولة، وقال له: «أنت ولّيت الأقباط المسالمة، وحكّمتهم في دولتك و في المسلمين!». ولعلّ السبب في ذلك أنّ دولاب العمل في الإدارة المملوكيّة لم يكن يستطيع أن يستغني عن كفاءة الأقباط، حتّى إنّ الناصر محمّدًا قد أغضبته ثورة المسلمين ضدّ استخدام النصارى وجبه اعتراضهم بالشدّة والقسوة فصلب منهم أي صلب من المسلمين جماعة وقطع أيدي بعضهم[٦].

كانت الدواوين في عصر المماليك تغصّ بالموظّفين من ذوي الخبرة والتمرّس ما مكّن الكثيرين من تحقيق النفوذ والثروة. فكان ذلك من جملة الأسباب المؤدّية إلى قيام سلسلة من المشاغبات والفتن بين المسلمين والأقباط ولاسيّما في القرنين الثامن والتاسع الهجريّين/الرابع عشر والخامس عشر الميلاديّين، والراجح أنّ المسلمين

---

٢ ابن ميسر، تاريخ مصر، تحقيق ماسيه، القاهرة، ١٩٥٩، ص ٢، عبد المنعم ماجد، نظم الفاطميّين ورسومهم، القاهرة، ج١، ص ٩٧–٩٨.

٣ أسلمي، أو مسلمانيّ، لفظ كان يطلق على كلّ من اعتنق الإسلام حديثًا من المسيحيّين أو اليهود، كما أطلق في بعض الأحيان لقب «المشرف بالإسلام» على من يعتنق الإسلام من أهل الكتاب.

٤ راجع: وثائق دير سانت كاترين، رقم ٢٦٦ ورقم ٢٦٥ ورقم ٢٦٨.

٥ المقريزيّ، السلوك ١/٢، ص ١٣٥.

٦ المصدر ذاته، ١/٣، ص ٢٢٤–٢٢٥.

كانوا يهدفون بها إلى إخراج الأقباط من الدواوين، كردّ فعل لاستفزازهم وتماديهم في التباهي والتظاهر بنفوذهم وثرواتهم التي استحصلوا عليها من وظائف الإدارة الماليّة التي تولّوها، في ما كان عامّة المسلمين وبعض نخبهم العلميّة يعانون، من جرّاء وطأة الحاجة والجوع وثقل الضرائب المتنوّعة التي فرضها المماليك على عموم الرعيّة، عدا أنّ الأقباط وغيرهم من أهل الكتاب العاملين في الإدارة كانوا يشكّلون الأداة التي استخدمها سلاطين المماليك لتحصيل الرسوم و الضرائب من المكلّفين، من مسلمين وأهل كتاب[٧]، ما يعني أنّ الحقد على الموظّفين الأقباط لم يكن له علاقة بدين هؤلاء على الإطلاق.

تقدّم لنا المصادر لائحة كبيرة تحتوي على أسماء طائفة كبيرة من الأقباط ممّن تولّوا المناصب العليا في الدولة، نذكر منهم على سبيل المثال لا الحصر، في زمن الناصر محمّد:

(راجع الجدول)

العلم	الوظيفة
إبراهيم بن إسحاق بن عبد الكريم بن القماط	نظر الدولة
إبراهيم بن سعيد الدولة، تاج الدين	الوزارة
إبراهيم بن عبدالله المعروف بالقاضي جمال الكفاة	نظر الجيش و نظر الخاصّ
إسحاق عبد الكريم،بن القماط، تاج الدين	نظر الخاصّ
عبد الكريم بن عبد الرزاق بن مكانس، فخر الدين	الوزارة
عبد الكريم بن عبد الرزاق بن مكانس، كريم الدين	الوزارة
عبد الكريم بن هبة الله بن السديد، المعروف بالقاضي كريم الدين الكبير	نظر الخاصّ
عبدالله بن تاج الرئاسة بن الغنام المعروف بالصاحب أمين الدين أمين الملك	الوزارة

٧ المقريزيّ، المواعظ والاعتبار في ذكر الخطط والآثار المعروف بـ«الخطط المقريزيّة»، بولاق، ١٢٧٠، ج٢، ص ٤٩٧–٥٠٠، ٥١٢–٥١٧.

العلم	الوظيفة
عبد الله بن الصنيعة بن أبي السرور، المعروف بالصاحب غبريال	نظر الشام
عبد الوهاب بن فضل الله، المعروف بالقاضي شرف الدين النشو	نظر الخاصّ
المخلص بن فضل الله (أخو النشو)	كشف الجهات بالديار المصريّة
موسى بن إسحاق بن عبد الكريم بن القماط هبة الله بن إبراهيم بن سعيد الدولة، موفق الدين	نظر الجيش ونظر الخاصّ الوزارة

والجدير ذكره أنّ أولئك الأقباط من «المسالمة» كانوا أداة في يد السلطان، يستخدمهم في ابتزاز أموال الرعيّة من المسلمين وأهل الكتاب على السواء. كما تشهد المصادر التاريخيّة للناصر محمّد أنّه أحسن معاملة كتّاب دواوينه من المسيحيّين ليس لمهارتهم الفنّيّة وولائهم له فحسب، بل لثقته بإنّه لن يكون منهم من يناهضه في السلطة، أو يثير شكوكه أو يحول بينه وبين أطماعه في جمع المال لإنفاقه على هواه وفي غير صعيد.

ومع ذلك، فقد كان كبار الموظّفين الأقباط من جملة المصادرين من السلطان، الذي ما تردّد في إيجاد الذرائع والمبرّرات للإيقاع بهم، باتّهامهم بالفساد، أو بأخذ البلاد بالقسوة والشدّة، أو، في ما يقال، لجمعهم القناطير المقنطرة من الذهب والفضّة، فيأمر السلطان حين ذاك بمعاقبتهم مع أفراد أسرهم، والتنكيل بهم حينًا، وسجنهم أو قتلهم أحيانًا، لاستخراج مقتنياتهم وثرواتهم، وإن كانت تلك الثروات في الغالب قد جمعت بوسائل غير مشروعة.

من ذلك: ما حدث لأولاد التاج إسحاق بن عبد الكريم القماط القبطيّ الثلاثة: علم الدين إبراهيم ناظر الدولة، وشمس الدين موسى ناظر الجيش وناظر الخاصّ، وماجد، في عهد الناصر محمّد من إلقاء القبض عليهم ومعاقبتهم وسجنهم، ومصادرة ممتلكاتهم[٨]،

٨ اليوسفيّ، نزهة الناظر في سيرة الملك الناصر، تحقيق أحمد حطيط، عالم الكتب، بيروت، ١٩٨٦، ص ١١٩–١٢١–١٨٠، ١٩٠، ٢٤٢، ٢٥٨.

وكذلك أمين الدين أمين الملك عبد الله بن الغنّام القبطيّ[٩]، وزير الديار المصريّة في أيّام السلطان ناصر، حيث انتهى أمره بالقبض عليه ومصادرة ثروته، وعبدالله بن الصنيعة المعروف بالصاحب شمس الدين غبريال النصرانيّ[١٠]، ناظر الدواوين بدمشق في نيابة الأمير سيف الدين تنكز[١١]، أمّا عبد الكريم بن عبدالله بن السديد المصريّ، النصرانيّ الأصل، المعروف بالكبير[١٢]، وكيل الناصر محمّد و ناظر خاصّه و مدبّر دولته، فقد قبض عليه في ١٤ ربيع الآخر العام ٧٢٣/ ١٣٢٣ وصودرت أمواله، ومات منفيًا في أسوان العام ٧٢٤/ ١٣٢٤.

ونظرًا إلى كثافة المساحة التي شغلها الأقباط في إدارة دولة المماليك، ومراعاة للوقت المخصّص لمداخلتنا سوف نحصر اهتمامنا بالحديث عن الوزير شرف الدين النشو أو نشيء الدولة قبل إسلامه[١٣]، أحد الكتّاب الأقباط المسالمة في زمن الناصر محمّد. فقصّة النشو ليست إلا سلسلة من الفظائع المثيرة في دولة المماليك. فلو صحّ بعض ما قيل في هذا الرجل وعنه خلال تولّيه الإدارة الماليّة للسلطان الناصر، من ارتكابه الفظائع، في ما اعتمده من فنون وسائط التعذيب ومكائده المتنوّعة لتحصيل الأموال السلطانيّة، لكان ذلك دليلاً قاطعًا على استفحال الفساد وحالات الابتزاز والنهب والاحتكار في عهد الناصر محمّد، حتّى شاع أنّ السلطان نفسه قد انتابته الدهشة عندما اطّلع على قساوة ما كان يقترفه النشو من مظالم لتبرير صدق دعواه[١٤].

---

٩ الصفديّ، الوافي بالوفيّات، ج ١٧ باعتناء دوروتيا كرافولسكي، فاينز شتاينر، فيسبادن، ١٩٦٢، ص ٨٨–٩٨، ابن حبيب، تذكرة النبيه في أيّام المنصور وبنيه، تحقيق محمّد محمّد نبيه، القاهرة، ١٩٨٢، ج٢، ص ٣٢٣–٢، ٣٢٤.

١٠ الجزريّ، حوادث الزمان وأبناؤها ووفيّات الأعيان من أبنائها، مخطوط كوبرلي، رقم ١٠٣٧، ص ٣٤٧–٣٦٦، ابن حبيب، المصدر ذاته ٢١٩–٢٢٠.

١١ الأمير سيف الدين تنكز بن عبدالله الحسامي الناصري، نائب الشام. ولي نيابة دمشق في عهد الناصر محمّد بن قلاوون السنة ٧١٢ هجري. واستمرّ بها حتّى أواخر ١٣٤٠/٧٤٠، ولم يتفق لأحد من نواب سلاطنة المماليك ذلك. راجع ترجمته في: ابن الورديّ، تتمّة المختصر في أخبار البشر، النجف، ١٩٦٩، ج٢، ص ٤٦٦–٤٦٧: ابن كثير، البداية والنهاية في التاريخ، بيروت، ١٩٦٦، ج ١٤، ص ١٨٧، ٢١١، ابن حبيب، المصدر ذاته، ج ٢، ص ٢٢١–٢٢٢.

١٢ ابن أيبك الدواداريّ، كنز الدرر وجامع الغرر، ج٩ (الدرّ الفاخر في سيرة الملك الناصر) تحقيق ٥.ر ريمر، القاهرة، ١٩٦٠ ص ٣١٠، ٣١٥٠، ابن الورديّ، تتمة المختصر، ج٢، ٣٩١–٣٩٢، المقريزيّ، السلوك، ج٢، ق٢، ص ٣٤٣–٣٤٤.

١٣ الصفديّ، الوافي، ج١٩، تحقيق رضوان السيد، دار فرانز شتاينر، شتوتغارت، ١٩٩٣، ص ٣٢٧.

١٤ موير، تاريخ دولة المماليك في مصر، ترجمة محمود عابدين وسليم حسن، مكتبة مدبولي، القاهرة، ١٩٩٥، ص ٩٥.

فمن هو النشو وما الدور الذي قام به في الإدارة المملوكيّة في عهد الناصر محمّد بن قلاوون؟

يُستفاد من كتب التراجم والتاريخ العائدة إلى عصر المماليك، أنّ عبد الوهاب بن فضل الله المعروف بشرف الدين النشو، كان هو ووالده وأخوته يعملون في خدمة الأمير سيف الدين بكتمر الحاجب، ثمّ انفصلوا عنه وأقاموا بطّالين في بيتهم مدّة، ثمّ استخدم النشو المذكور عند الأمير علاء الدين أيدغمش أمير آخور، واستمرّ في خدمته حوالى ستّة أشهر. ويبدو أنّ باب السعادة فتح أمام النشو حينما استدعاه السلطان محمّد كتّاب الأمراء، فلفت نظره شاب طويل نصرانيّ يقف وراء زملائه فاستدعاه و قال له: ايش اسمك؟

قال: النشو. فأجابه السلطان أنا أجعلك (نشوي)، ثمّ رتّبه مستوفيًا في الجيزة، اختبارًا له، فأثبت كفاءة عالية في أداء المهمّة الموكولة إليه ما أثار إعجاب السلطان، فنقله إلى وظيفة استيفاء الدولة مدّة سنة، ثمّ ما لبث أن تدرّج في مسالك الوظائف الكبيرة، بعدما أظهر الإسلام، وتسمّى بعبد الوهاب، وتلقّب بشرف الدين، لتسند إليه على الأثر، إدارة ديوان الأمير ناصر الدين ابن الناصر[١٥] ثمّ أضيف إليه بعد أشهر قليلة من السنة عينها، نظر ديوان الخاصّ السلطانيّ، وبذلك، أصبح النشو الموظّف الأساس في الإدارة المالية بعامّة، وفي إدارة المال السلطانيّ بخاصّة، فبلغ ما لم يبلغه أحد من الأقباط في دولة المماليك، وأطلقت يده في ماليّة البلاد من دون حسيب أو رقيب، ما دام يحظى بثقة السلطان[١٦].

ويبدو أنّ شرف الدين النشو الذي كرهته العامّة والخاصّة في مصر والشام، قد حاز اهتمام المؤرّخين المعاصرين له والمتأخّرين عنه، فشغلت أخباره وسيرته معظم صفحات من أرّخ منهم لدولة المماليك عمومًا ولعهد الناصر محمّد بخاصّة. ويستفاد ممّا جاء في المصادر أنّ هذا الموظف القاسي القلب كانت له دالة على السلطان، واستطاع بذلك أن يواجه المكائد التي نصبها له خصومه ومنابذوه للإيقاع به، حيث كان ينتصر له السلطان ويدافع عنه، حتّى نقل عنه عندما حاول بعض نساء السلطان وحريمه تحريضه على النشو، كي يقصيه عن وظيفته ومعاقبته، أنّه نهر نساءه وحريمه وشتمهنّ وقال لهنّ: «مسكين النشو، ما وجدت أحدًا يحبّه كونه ينصحني ويحصّل أموالي»[١٧].

---

١٥ الصفديّ، الوافي بالوفيّات، ج١٩، ص ٣٢٤–٣٢٥، المقريزيّ، السلوك، ٢/٢، ٣٤٣–٣٤٨، يرجع نشوء ديوان الخاصّ إلى العهد الفاطمي، ثمّ ألغيّ بعد حين، ليعاد أحياؤه بأمر من الناصر محمّد بن قلاوون في ولايته الثانية، حين أبطل الوزارة ونيابة السلطنة. ومهمّة هذه الوظيفة الإشراف على أموال السلطان وأملاكه. القلقشندي، صبح الأعشى في صناعة الإنشا، ج١١، القاهرة، ١٩٢٢، ص ٣١٦–٣١٩.

١٦ المقريزيّ، المصدر ذاته، ص ٥٠٥–٥٠٦.

١٧ اليوسفيّ، المصدر ذاته، ص ٣٥٣.

فهل كان النشو الناظر الخاصّ يملك دائمًا الحجّة الدامغة لإقناع السلطان بصوابيّة تدابيره والفوز بثقته، لاسيّما وأنّ الناصر محمّد شاع أنّه كان شديد الحذر لا يثق بالأخرين، وعرف بالمكر والخداع وكثرة الحيل، فلا يقف عند قول ولا يفي بعهد، حتّى قال معاصره اليوسفيّ[١٨]، إنّ السلطان الناصر: «كان فيه من المكر والدهاء ما لا يقدر عليه ملك غيره»؟.

كان النشو يحظى بثقة السلطان ومؤازرته بقدر ما كان المعبّر الأمين عن مصالحه ورغباته، مع الاعتراف له بحيّز بسيط يحقّق عبره بعض المكاسب الماديّة منها والمعنويّة.

وبالفعل، فإنّ النشو كان يدرك تمامًا شغف السلطان بجمع المال، فحرص على أن يقنع السلطان بأنّه الخادم الأمين لمصالحه، وأنّه يريد أن يملأ خزائنه بالذخائر والأموال والغلال، وأنّ هذا الأمر لن يحصل إلا بوضع حدّ لنفوذ الأمراء في الإدارة الماليّة: «فإن مكّنتني منهم حصّلت لك الأموال»، وصدقه القول والفعل «واتفق معه على خراب البيوت العامرة وهتك الحريم وتحصيل الأموال». فاطمأنّ السلطان إلى النشو وقربّه منه، وأطلق يده في شؤون الدولة كافّة[١٩] وسخر من شكاوى الأمراء وتحريضهم على النشو، ودفعهم بأن قال لهم: «وأنتم تكذبّوا النشو في جميع ما يقوله، وقصدكم أن لا تدعوا أحدًا يخدمني وينصحني»[٢٠]. وقد علّق اليوسفيّ على حظوة النشو لدى السلطان بقوله: «بسبب أنّه لا يقول له شيئًا إلا وهو صحيح»[٢١].

لذا، لم يجد النشو غضاضة، أحيانًا، من تجاهل بعض المراسيم السلطانيّة في ما عرف بالمسامحات، أو الإعفاءات، التي كانت تفيد منها المحاصيل الزراعيّة الحيويّة، مثل القند، الذي يستخرج منه عسل السكر. ففي العام **١٣٣٣/٧٣٣**، حضر النشو إلى دار القند بالفسطاط، وتحقّق من وزن سائر قنود الأمراء، وطالب أصحابها بدفع ما يترتّب عليها من حقوق للسلطان، ولم يمتثل إلى ما في المراسيم السلطانيّة من مسامحتهم، وقال لهم: «أنا هذا الشيء أعرفه، والسلطان يطالبني بماله وأنا ما أخليه!»، ثمّ دخل على السلطان، وأقنعه بصوابيّة ما أقدم عليه، حفظًا لمال السلطان[٢٢].

---

[١٨] اليوسفيّ، المصدر ذاته، ص ١٣٧.

[١٩] اليوسفيّ، نزهة، ص ١٧٦–١٧٩.

[٢٠] اليوسفيّ، المصدر ذاته، ص **٢٧٩**.

[٢١] اليوسفيّ، المصدر ذاته، ص ١٣٧.

[٢٢] اليوسفيّ، المصدر ذاته، ١٢٧، المقريزيّ، السلوك ٢/٢، ص ٣٦٠، العيني، عقد الجمان في تاريخ أهل الزمان، مخطوطة أحمد الثالث، اسطنبول، رقم ١٧/٢٩١١، ٧٤.

وإرضاء لشهيّة السلطان في تحصيل الأموال، ابتدع النشو سابقة مستهجنة في الشأن الماليّ والنقديّ، تمثّلت بإلزام أهل الصاغة ودار الضرب ألا يبيع أحد منهم شيئًا من الذهب، بل يحمل الذهب جميعه إلى دار الضرب ليصكّ بصكّة السلطان، ويضرب دنانير هرجة[٢٣]، تُصرف بالدراهم.

ولكي يطمئنّ النشو إلى نفاذ قراره، تتبّع الذهب المضروب، فأخذ ما كان للتجّار والعامّة، وعوّضهم عنها بضائع أو أوراق ضمان، فجمع بذلك كمّيّات كبيرة من الذهب، وحملها للسلطان، فتوقّفت أحوال الصيارفة، وامتنعوا عن ممارسة أعمالهم احتجاجًا، ثمّ اضطروا إلى معاودة أعمالهم وفقًا لما أمر به النشو[٢٤].

ويبدو أنّ التدابير، الآنفة الذكر، لم تشبع نهم السلطان في الحصول على المال، حتّى إنّه عندما أظهر النشو عجزًا عن تأمين مبالغ جديدة طلبها السلطان، نهره الأخير وهدّده، فلم يجد النشو حرجًا من قصد أمين الحكم وألزمه بكتابة ما تحت يده من مال الأيتام، وأخذ منه قرضًا بعشرة آلاف دينار[٢٥]، ثمّ استولى على مبلغ آخر للأيتام، وعوّضهم عنها بضائع[٢٦]، كما أنّ السلطان لم يتورّع عن دعم موقف ناظر خاصّة ضدّ قرار قاضي القضاة المالكيّ بتحريم مصادرة أموال عائدة لأيتام أحد الأمراء الذين كانوا تحت حجره[٢٧].

وتزدحم الأخبار في المصادر عن شغف الناصر في جمع الأموال المتأتّية من مصادرة ثروات الأمراء والولاة، ورمي البضائع على التجّار والعامّة بأضعاف مضاعفة. وكانت العادة أن يلجأ النشو إلى فتح باب المصادرة و الظلم لتحصيل الأموال، حيث كان يسلم «المذنب» إلى مشدّ الدواوين أو إلى والي القاهرة، الذي يعرّضه لشتّى أنواع العقاب من ضرب بالمقارع والتوسيط، ووضع القصب في الأظافر والخطافات وغيرها من وسائل التعذيب حتّى يعترف باختلاسه الأموال. وممّن تعرّضوا للعقاب بأمر من النشو: ابن هلال الدولة مشدّ الدواوين، وأرباب الوظائف الكبرى في نيابة حلب، وبلاد الصعيد، بالإضافة إلى مصادرة أموال كبار موظّفي الدولة المتوفّين،

---

٢٣ الهرجة: دنانير تستعمل خاصّة في صناعة الحلى، كالأساور والعقود وغيرها، بأن يصاغ في أطرافها، حلقات صغيرة أو يجعل في جوانبها ثقوب.

De Sacy, Traité des monnaies musulmanes, traduit de l'arabe de Makrizi. Bibliothèque des Arabisants Français, Tome 1, Le Caire, 1905, p. 40.n.3.

٢٤ اليوسفيّ، ص **٢٩٢**، المقريزيّ، السلوك **٢/٢**، ص **٣٩٣**.

٢٥ اليوسفيّ، المصدر ذاته، ص **٢٩٧**.

٢٦ المقريزيّ، المصدر السابق، ص **٢٩٣**.

٢٧ اليوسفيّ، المصدر السابق، ص **٢٩٣–٢٩٤**.

ومنهم: الصاحب غبريال ناظر الشام، والأمير علم الدين سنجر الخازن والي القاهرة[٢٨].

وتفنّن النشو في مصادرة التجّار والتعرّض لأموالهم حينًا، وابتزازهم أحيانًا، بفتح مخازنهم ومتاجرهم ونهب محتوياتها بأمر من السلطان. من ذلك، نزول النشو ومعاونيه إلى الأسواق ليلاً، بأمر من السلطان بسبب شكوى المماليك السلطانيّة من تأخّر كسوتهم لعدم توفّر المال لشرائها، ففتح المتاجر والدكاكين، في غياب أصحابها، وصادر محتوياتها، وبخاصّة تلك التي تبيع الملبوسات وما يحتاجه المماليك من كساء ومؤنة من دون أن يكترث لردّ فعل أصحاب هذه المتاجر. فهؤلاء، حين أفاقوا في صباح اليوم التالي، صدمتهم رؤية متاجرهم مفتوحة ومفرغة من محتوياتها، فضجّت الأسواق بأصحابها، وساد فيها حزن عميق «ولم يبق إلاّ باكٍ أو شاكٍ أو صائح أو نائح، كلّ على قدر مصيبته،» حسب تعبير اليوسفيّ[٢٩]. ومن ذلك أيضًا تهديد بعض التجّار بالتشهير بهم كي يتنازلوا عمّا يتوجّب لهم من حقوق لدى الدولة. من ذلك: تواطؤ النشو مع ناصر الدين محمّد بن المحسني، والي القاهرة، لابتزاز أحد كبار التجّار كانت له وديعة في خزانة السلطان، ولمّا ألح على ناظر الخاصّ بطلبها، أمر النشو والي القاهرة وضع التاجر تحت المراقبة، إلى أن ضبطه في الطريق وهو في حالة السكر الشديد، فشهّر به بين الناس، وأشهد عليه بعضهم، وأودعه دار الولاية، ولم يفرج عنه إلا بعد أن كتب عليه حجة إبراء لخزانة السلطان بجميع ما له فيها[٣٠].

ولكي ينهض النشو بمهمّته، ويحاذر السقوط في شرك أعدائه الكثر، تتبّع أخبار هؤلاء كي يسهل عليه النيل منهم. وفي سبيل ذلك، جنّد النشو أشخاصًا من موظّفي الدواوين، ومن العامّة، كي يكونوا له عيونًا على كبار الأمراء والتجّار، حتّى إذا ما انعدمت معه الحيل، والمراقبة، قام بدسّ العجائز من النساء في بيت الأمراء والكتّاب للتجسّس عليهم، ونقل أخبارهم إليه من نسائهم، للإيقاع بهم. وقد اتّبع النشو هذه الطريقة في مصادرة أولاد ابن الجيعان[٣١]، والأمير علاء الدين علي بن هلال الدولة مشدّ الدواوين[٣٢]، وأبي شاكر ابن سعيد الدولة ناظر البيوت[٣٣].

---

٢٨ اليوسفيّ، المصدر ذاته، ص ١٧٧–١٧٨، ١٨٢–١٨٩–٢٧٦، ٢٦٣، ٢٧٧، ٢٧٩، ٣٤٣، ٣٤٤.

٢٩ اليوسفيّ، نزهة، ص٣٥٠–٣٥٨.

٣٠ اليوسفيّ، المصدر السابق، ص ١٩٦–١٩٧، السلوك ٢/٢، ص ٣٧٣.

٣١ ، المصدر ذاته، ٢٦٢–٢٦٤، المقريزي، المصدر، ص ٣٨٥.

٣٢ اليوسفيّ المصدر ذاته، ص ١٨٢–٢٤٢، ١٨٣ وما بعدها.

٣٣ اليوسفيّ، المصدر ذاته، ص ٣٠٨–٣١٠، ابن ثغري بردي، النجوم الزاهرة في ملوك مصر والقاهرة، ج ٩، ص ١١٥.

ورغم المكانة التي احتلّها النشو لدى السلطان، فقد كان يشعر بقلق شديد إزاء محاولات أعدائه الكثر للنيل منه، وهم ما انفكّوا يدبّرون المكائد ضدّه، ولم يعدموا وسيلة للتخلّص منه إلا اعتمدوها. حتّى إنّهم حاولوا قتله، لكنّه نجا من هذه المحاولة بأعجوبة بعد أن أصيب بجراح بالغة وبات لا يخرج من داره أو يعود إليها إلا برفقة حرسه الخاصّ[٣٤]، كما أنّه كان على علم بتحريض كبار الأمراء السلطان عليه للتخلّص منه. ويضاف إلى ما تقدّم، أنّ النشو كان يعرف أخلاق السلطان وسرعة تغيّره، وأنّه كثير الشكّ حتّى بأعوانه المقرّبين، ما جعل الرجل أسير مشاعر الخوف من انقلاب السلطان عليه.

ولئن نجح النشو في التفلّت من المكائد، الآنفة الذكر، بما امتلكه من حنكة وحكمةٍ في مواجهة الصعاب التي اعترضت سبيله، إلا أنّه ما لبث أن وقع ضحيّة ما اقترفته يداه من ظلم وتنكيل ومصادرة وتعذيب وقتل عدد وافر من الولاة والكتّاب، استجابة لإلحاح السلطان في طلب المال. ففي العام ٧٤٠/ ١٣٣٩، تمكّن أعداؤه من تحريض السلطان عليه، فأمر بالقبض على النشو، وعلى أمّه عقيبة، وأخويه المخلص وشرف الدين رزق الله، وصهره ولي الدولة ابن الخطير، بذريعة اختلاسهم المال السلطانيّ وعوقبوا حتّى الموت، باستثناء رزق الله الذي فضل الانتحار على مواجهة مصيره المحتوم بالعقاب[٣٥]. وبذلك أسدل الستار على النشو وعلى أسرته، بعد أن أمضى في نظر الخاصّ سبع سنين وسبعة أشهر.

وفي ما يقال، فإنّ السبب في تغيّر السلطان على النشو، أنّه خشي أن ينعكس تنامي كره الناس، بعامّتهم وخاصّتهم للنشو وحقدهم عليه سلبًا على دولته، ولا سيّما بعد أن بلغ السلطان من أمراء المشورة نقمة مماليكه عليه، وكذلك أصحاب الرواتب والصدقات، بسبب النشو، فوجد من مصلحته أن يتخلّص منه، وهكذا كان وأحلّ مكانه في وظيفة الخاصّ قبطيًّا آخر يعرف بجمال الكفاة[٣٦].

---

٣٤ يذكر اليوسفي أنّ محاولة قتل النشو أثارت حفيظة السلطان وغضبه، وجمع الأمراء وهدّدهم وتوعدّهم بسوء العاقبة إذا مات النشو جراء هذه الحادثة، متّهمًا إيّاهم بتدبيرها، وأنّه قال لهم: «والله لأسمّرنّ الذي فعل هذا! وأنا أعرف أنّكم تبغضونه لأجل ما ترونه إلّا أنّ النشو سيتعافى من جراحه.» اليوسفيّ، نزهة، ٣٧٥–٣٧٦.

٣٥ الصفديّ، الوافي ٣٢٧/١٩، ابن حجر العسقلانيّ، الدرر الكامنة في أعيان المائة الثامنة، م٢، ص ٤٢٨–٤٢٩، المقريزيّ، السلوك، ٢/٢، ص ٥٠٥–٥٠٦.

٣٦ اليوسفيّ، المصدر ذاته، ص ٤٧٦–٤٨٦.

الخاتمة

يستفاد ممّا تقدّم، أنّ النظريّة السياسيّة للدولة الإسلاميّة لم تضع، منذ نشأتها، عقبات تذكر أمام ممارسة رعاياها من أهل الكتاب، حقوقهم الخاصّة والعامّة، بل أتاحت لهم حيزًا وافرًا للمشاركة في الحياة العامّة، فبرزت من بين أولئك شخصيّات مرموقة تولّت وظائف سامية في الدولة الإسلاميّة، في مشرق البلاد ومغربها.

وكان من الطبيعيّ ألاّ يشذّ سلاطين المماليك عمّا درج عليه أسلافهم من الحكام المسلمين، فاحتلّ أهل الكتاب عمومًا والمسيحيّون منهم خصوصًا، مركز الصدارة من الكثير من وظائف الدولة، ولاسيّما الوظائف المعنيّة بإدارة الشؤون الماليّة للدولة. ورغم ما ذكرته المصادر التاريخيّة من إبعاد الأقباط المصريّين أحيانًا عن وظائفهم ومصادرة أملاكهم وثرواتهم، فإنّ هؤلاء سرعان ما كانوا يعودون إلى ممارسة دورهم في البنية الإداريّة والماليّة لدولة المماليك.

أوضاع المسيحيّين في دمشق وحلب في العصر المملوكيّ

أندريه نصّار
باحث مستقلّ

يعود الوجود المسيحيّ في دمشق إلى بدء انتشار الديانة المسيحيّة. ثمّ امتدّت المسيحيّة إلى سائر أنحاء سورية منذ القرن الميلاديّ الأوّل. ودخلت مدينة حلب منذ عهد الرسل[1] وبسبب الانقسامات في الكنيسة أصبح المسيحيّون طوائف عدّة. وكانوا في أغلبيّتهم من الروم الملكيّين والسريان اليعاقبة.

أ) الروم الملكيّون: على أثر تهدّم أنطاكية على يد السلطان الظاهر بيبرس السنة ١٢٦٨/٦٦٦، انتقل البطاركة الملكيّون إلى دمشق. وفي القرن الرابع عشر اتّخذوها مركزًا للكرسيّ البطريركيّ الملكيّ. وكانت لهم أسقفيّات في قارا، يبرود، تدمر، الزبداني، صيدنايا، معلولا وزحلة[2].

---

[1] إغناطيوس ديك، الحضور المسيحيّ في حلب خلال الألفين المنصرمين، ج١، من نشأة المسيحيّة إلى الفتح العثمانيّ، حلب: ٢٠٠٢، ص ٣، ٤٨.

[2] إسحق أرملة، «الملكيّون، بطريركيّتهم الأنطاكيّة ولغتهم الوطنيّة والطقسيّة»، المشرق، ٣٤ (تمّوز.أيلول، ١٩٣٦) ٣٦١، ويذكر أنّ الملكيّين اتّخذوا دمشق مركزاً للكرسيّ البطريركيّ الملكيّ في العام ١٣٥٩، ولكنّ ابن كثير المعاصر للحدث يذكر في حوادث العام ٧٦٧هـ ما يأتي: «وحضر عندي في يوم الثلاثاء تاسع شوّال (١٩ حزيران ١٣٦٦م) البترك بشارة الملقَّب بميخائيل، وأخبرني أنّ المطارنة بالشام بايعوه على أن جعلوه بتركاً بدمشق عوضاً عن البترك بأنطاكية، فذكرت له أنّ هذا أمر مبتدع في دينهم، فإنّه لا تكون البتاركة إلاّ أربعة بالإسكندريّة وبالقدس وبأنطاكية وبرومية، فنقل بترك رومية إلى اسطنبول وهي القسطنطينيّة، وقد أنكر عليهم كثير منهم إذ ذاك، فهذا الذي ابتدعوه في هذا الوقت أعظم من ذلك. لكن اعتذر بأنّه في الحقيقة هو عن أنطاكية، وإنّما أذن له في المقام بالشام الشريف...»، البداية والنهاية، ط٧، بيروت: منشورات مكتبة المعارف ١٤٠٨هـ/١٩٨٨م، ج١٤، ٣١٩–٣٢٠، الأب يوسف الشمّاس المخلّصيّ، خلاصة تاريخ الكنيسة الملكيّة، راجعه وزاد عليه الأب إلياس كويتر المخلّصيّ، جونيه لبنان: المطبعة البولسيّة ٢٠٠٢، ٢٨٦–٢٨٧، ٣٠٨–٣٠٩، المطران ميشيل يتيم والأرشمندريت إغناطيوس ديك، تاريخ الكنيسة الشرقيّة، ط٤، بيروت جونيه: منشورات المكتبة البولسيّة ١٩٩٩، ٢٣١.

ب) اليعاقبة: وكان لهم في العصر المملوكيّ بطريرك في دمشق وآخر في حلب[٣].

ومن الجماعات المسيحيّة الأخرى التي وجدت في دمشق الأرمن[٤] وضمّت حلب الموارنة الذين بدأوا بالظهور فيها اعتبارًا من السنة ١٤٨٩/٨٩٤[٥]، كذلك ضمّت الأرمن الذين تجمّع عدد كبير منهم فيها في أواخر عهد المماليك[٦] ولهم كنيسة الأربعين شهيدًا التي جُدِّدت السنة ١٤٤٨/٨٥٢، وكنيسة العذراء مريم المذكورة في مخطوطات من السنتين ١٤٢٩ و١٤٧٦. كما وجد فيها النساطرة (الكلدان)، إذ ارتبطت أبرشيّة حلب في العهد الصليبيّ بكرسيّ القدس، وكانت مقاطعة القدس النسطوريّة تضمّ أبرشيّات دمشق وحلب وطرسوس ومصّيصة وملطيّة وفي وقت لاحق قبرص[٧].

وقد شكّل المسيحيّون في حلب نصف سكّان المدينة حتّى أواخر القرن الحادي عشر. لكن ابتداءً من القرن الثاني عشر بدأ عددهم يتناقص، ورحل كثير منهم إلى بلاد الروم وإيطاليا[٨].

---

٣ القلقشندي، صبح الأعشى في صناعة الإنشا، شرحه وعلّق عليه وقابل نصوصه محمّد حسين شمس الدين، بيروت: دار الفكر، لا.ت، ج١٣، ٢٨١–٢٨٢، الخالدي، كتاب المقصد الرفيع المنشا الهادي إلى صناعة الإنشا، تحقيق خليل شحادة، أطروحة دكتوراه غير منشورة، بيروت: جامعة القدّيس يوسف ١٩٨٨، ٢٧٥، سمير خليل سمير، «ذكر مذهب النصارى لمؤتمن الدولة ابن العسّال (نحو ١٢٦٣م)»، المشرق، ٦٦، ج٢ (١٩٩٢)، ٤٨٩، «مقالة للفيلسوف نجم الدين عن فِرَق النصارى في رواية المؤتمن ابن العسّال، إعتقاد النساطرة واليعاقبة في المسيح وماهيّة الاتّحاد»، المشرق، ٦٧، ج٢ (١٩٩٩)، ٤١٤–٤١٦، ٤٣٥–٤٣٦، ديك، حضور، ج١، ١٤١–١٤٢، نقولا زيادة، دمشق في عصر المماليك، بيروت: مكتبة لبنان ١٩٦٦، ١٦٣–١٦٤، William Popper, *Egypt and Syria under the Circassian Sultans 1382–1468 A.D. Systematic notes to Ibn Taghrî Birdî's Chronicles of Egypt*, Berkeley and Los Angeles: 1955, 109, C. E. Bosworth, "Christian and Jewish Religious Dignitaries in Mamlûk Egypt and Syria: Qalqashandi's Information on their Hierarchy, Titulature and Appointment", *International Journal of Middle East Studies 3* (1972), Part II, 204.

٤ زيادة، دمشق، ١٣٣، يوسف نعيسة، مجتمع مدينة دمشق ١١٨٦.١٢٥٦هـ/١٧٧٢.١٨٤٠م، ط١، دمشق: دار طلاس، ١٩٨٦، ج١، ١٩٠–١٩١.

٥ جرجس منش المارونيّ، «موارنة حلب الشهباء»، المشرق (١٩٠٣)، ٣٦١، إيرا مارفين لابيدوس، مدن الشام في العصر المملوكيّ، نقله إلى العربيّة وقدّم له الدكتور سهيل زكّار، ط١، دمشق: دار حسّان للطباعة والنشر، ١٤٠٥هـ/ ١٩٨٥م، ١٤٣.

٦ ابن العبريّ، تاريخ الزمان، نقله إلى العربيّة الأب إسحق أرملة، قدّم له جان موريس فييه، بيروت: دار المشرق ١٩٨٦، ٣١٦، لابيدوس، مدن، ١٤٣.

٧ ديك، حضور، ج١، ١٤٨، ١٤٩، شوقي شعث، حلب تاريخها ومعالمها التاريخيّة، طبعة ثانية مزيدة، حلب: منشورات جامعة حلب ١٤١١هـ/١٩٩١م، ٩٢، عبد الله حجّار، معالم حلب الأثريّة، طبعة ثانية مزيدة ومنقّحة، حلب: مطابع مؤسّسة جورج ومتيلد سالم الخيريّة ١٩٩٧، ٥١، ٥٢، ويذكر مشاركة مطران حلب هوفاكيم الحلبيّ في المجمع المسكونيّ في فلورنسا السنة ١٤٣٩م، Henri Musset, *Histoire du Christianisme spécialement en Orient*, vol. 1, Harissa: Imprimerie Saint Paul 1948, 448, note 1.

٨ ديك، حضور، ج١، ٧٩، ٩٠–٩١، ٩٢، ٩٥.

وبعد الغزو المغوليّ بقيادة هولاكو السنة ١٢٦٠ أقفرت حلب وجوارها. ويقول ابن العبريّ في رسالته إلى بطريركه فليكسين السنة ١٢٨٣، وقد بلغه أنّ بعض الأساقفة عزا إليه حبّ الارتقاء إلى السدّة البطريركيّة، لم تكن له رغبة في البطريركيّة. أوّلاً لأنّه قد شبع من الرئاسة. ثانيًا لأنّه فائز بالراحة هنا (في المناطق الشرقيّة تحت حكم المغول). ثالثًا وعلى فرض أنّه كان يتمنّى البطريركيّة اقتداءً بالذين سلفوه، فاليوم علام يتمنّاها وقد أمست أبرشيّات المغرب (أي سورية) قاعًا صفصفًا؟ هل يتوق إلى أبرشيّة حلب أو منبج أو قلنيقس (الرقّة) أو الرها أو حرّان وقد أقفرت برمّتها؟[٩]»

وبسبب الحروب المتواصلة وانعدام الأمن فرغ ريف حلب شيئًا فشيئًا من سكّانه المسيحيّين[١٠].

وعلى أثر الغزو المغوليّ بقيادة تيمورلنك السنة ١٤٠٠، نُهبت حلب وأُحرقت وفرغت من جميع سكّانها على أيدي جنوده، باستثناء ألفي رجل توجّهوا إلى مشهد الحسين في سفح جبل الجوشن[١١] فكان والحالة هذه أن يتركها المسيحيّون أيضًا. ولكنّهم ما لبثوا أن عادوا إليها بعد الانسحاب المغوليّ منها. ويقول البطريرك مكاريوس ابن الزعيم (القرن السابع عشر): «وأخيرًا بعد زمن طويل لمّا خلت باطن حلب من النصارى ثمّ عمّرت ورجع إليها أهلها المؤمنون صار عليها أسقف حلب اسمه غريغوريوس (١٥٤٠ – ١٥٨٠)[١٢]».

ونال المسيحيّون في دمشق نصيبهم أيضًا، إذ أكّد تيمورلنك للقضاة الأربعة الذين اجتمع بهم بعد احتلاله المدينة أنّه سيناضل لتحريرهم من نِير المسيحيّين، ومن الرِّبْقة السيّئة للسلطان المملوكيّ وشعبه حتّى لو كانوا مسيحيّين، لأنّ السلطان والمسيحيّين المرائين لا أساس لهم في الشريعة[١٣] ويقول ابن عربشاه إنّ رجال تيمورلنك فتكوا وسبوا، «وصالوا على المسلمين وأهل الذمم، صولة الذئاب الضواري على ضواني

٩ ابن العبريّ، التاريخ الكنسيّ، نشره أبيلوس ولامي، لوفان: ١٨٧٢–١٨٧٧، ج١، ٤٥٦، وج٢، ٤٥٧–٤٥٩، نقلاً عن ديك، حضور، ج١، ١٣٠.

١٠ ديك، حضور، ج١، ٩٥–٩٦.

١١ ابن عربشاه، عجائب المقدور في نوائب تيمور، تحقيق أحمد فايز الحمصيّ، ط١، بيروت: مؤسّسة الرسالة ١٩٨٦، ٢٢٠.

١٢ ديك، حضور، ج١، ١٤٠.

١٣ Walter J. Fischel, "A New Latin Source on Tamerlane's Conquest of Damascus (1400/1401) (B De Mignanelli's "Vita Tamerlani" 1416)" *ORIENS*, Vol. 9, n° 2, (1956), 218.

الغنم...[١٤]» ولم يسلم من الحريق إلاّ بعض بيوت المسيحيّين من أتباع الزنّار في الناحية الشرقيّة من المدينة[١٥].

أوّلاً – أماكن وجود المسيحيّين في دمشق وحلب:

أقام المسيحيّون في دمشق بحيّ خاصّ بهم عُرف باسم حارة النصارى في الزاوية الشماليّة الشرقيّة من المدينة على مقربة من باب توما خارج الأسوار[١٦] وأقاموا في حلب بحارة النصارى، «وهي المعروفة بالجُدَيْدة بالتصغير» في المنطقة الشماليّة الغربيّة خارج أسوار المدينة أيضًا[١٧] واحتلّ الأرمن والموارنة أحياء فيها[١٨].

وكان المسيحيّون في دمشق يدفنون موتاهم في مكان قريب من الأسوار يُسمّى مقابر اليهود والنصارى، وفي مقابر باب بستان النصارى[١٩] ويقول الرحّالة دي فارتيما إنّهم كانوا يدفنون موتاهم في الموضع الذي يقال إنّ السيّد المسيح تراءى فيه للقدّيس بولس[٢٠].

١٤ ابن عربشاه، عجائب، ٢٨١.

١٥ Fischel, "A New Latin Source", 299.

١٦ ابن طوق، التعليق يوميّات شهاب الدين أحمد بن طوق مذكّرات كتبت بدمشق في أواخر العهد المملوكيّ ٨٨٥–٩٠٨هـ/١٤٨٠–١٥٠٢م، تحقيق جعفر المهاجر، دمشق: المعهد الفرنسيّ للدراسات العربيّة ٢٠٠٢، ج٢، ٦٠٢، ١٠٠٧، ابن طولون، مفاكهة الخلاّن في حوادث الزمان، نشره محمّد مصطفى، القاهرة: ١٩٦٢–١٩٦٤، ج١، ١٢٤، ١٥٣، ج٢، ١٢٢–١٢٣، زيادة دمشق، ١٣١، أكرم العلبي، دمشق بين عصر المماليك والعثمانيّين ٩٠٦–٩٢٦هـ/١٥٠٠–١٥٢٠م (لا كما ورد خطأ ٩٠٦–٩٢٢/١٥٠٠–١٥٢٠)، ط١، دمشق: الشركة المتّحدة للتوزيع ١٩٨٢، ٦٣، ٨١، ووجدت في دمشق حارة عرفت باسم حارة الكنيسة، ولم يرد في المصادر ما إذا كان سكّانها من المسيحيّين، ابن طوق، التعليق، ج٢، ٦٣٧.

١٧ ابن الشحنة، محمّد، الدرّ المنتخب في تاريخ حلب، وقف على طبعه وعلّق حواشيه يوسف بن إليان سركيس الدمشقيّ، بيروت: المطبعة الكاثوليكيّة للآباء اليسوعيّين ١٩٠٩، ٢٤٢، حجّار، معالم، ٤٩

١٨ لابيدوس، مدن، ١٤٣.

١٩ ابن طوق، التعليق، ج١، دمشق ٢٠٠٠، ٥٢٤، وج٢، ٩٥٢، ولعلّ باب بستان النصارى هو باب كيسان كما ورد عند العلبي، دمشق، ٨٩.

٢٠ لودوفيكو دي فارتيما، رحلات فارتيما (الحاجّ يونس المصريّ)، ترجمة وتعليق عبد الرحمن عبد الله الشيخ، القاهرة: الهيئة المصريّة العامّة للكتاب ١٩٩٤، ٢٩ القلقشنديّ، **صبح**، ج٦، ١٦٤–١٦٥، ج١٢، ٢٨٩.

ثانيًا – أوضاع المسيحيّين:

تزوّدنا المصادر الإسلاميّة بمعلومات متقطِّعة عن أوضاع المسيحيّين في دمشق وحلب في العصر المملوكيّ. ولا تأتي على ذكرهم إلاّ لمامًا، ولا سيّما خلال الإجراءات أو التدابير المتَّخذة بحقّهم. ولكنّ هذا التقاطع لا يحول دون تكوين صورة عن أوضاعهم وإلقاء الضوء عليها وعلى واقع الحال العامّ. فكيف كان وضعهم في العصر المملوكيّ؟

أطلقت على المسيحيّين، تسمية أهل الذمّة والنصارى والملّة المسيحيّة والطائفة العيسويّة[٢١] وخضعوا لشروط أهل الذمّة التي أوجبها الشرع، واختلف وضعهم تبعًا لنزوات الحاكم وأحداث الحياة اليوميّة للسلطنة[٢٢].

والذمّة في اللغة تعني الأمان والعهد. «وأهل الذمّة هم المعاهدون من النصارى وغيرهم ممّن يقيم بدار الإسلام. وجاء في الحديث الشريف: «يسعى بذمَّتهم أدناهم». وقد فسَّر الفقهاء «ذمَّتهم» بمعنى الأمان. وعلى هذا يمكن القول إنّ عقد الذمَّة بمقتضاه يصير غير المسلم في ذمَّة المسلمين أي في عهدهم وأمانهم على وجه التأبيد، وله الإقامة بدار الإسلام على وجه الدوام[٢٣]».

ولا يُعَدُّ هذا العقد معاهدة بالمعنى الصحيح بل رابطة تنعقد بين دولة ورؤساء قاعدة شعبيّة... تنشىء واجبات تجاه الدولة الإسلاميّة وتجاه كلّ مسلم على حدة وكلّ ذمّيّ أو كتابيّ. وبهذا فإنّ لها مفعول القانون. لذلك حين يخالفها الذمّيّ يتحمّل وحده نتيجة المخالفة لا طائفته كلّها[٢٤].

وفُرِضَت على أهل الذمّة في دمشق وحلب الشروط العمريّة، وهي تقسم إلى قسمين: مستحقّ ومستحبّ. ويضمّ المستحقّ ستّة شروط هي: عدم ذكر الله بطعن فيه أو تحريف له. عدم ذكر الرسول بتكذيب له ولا ازدراء. عدم ذكر الإسلام بذمّ له ولا قدح فيه. ألّا يصيبوا مسلمة بزنا ولا باسم نكاح. ألّا يفتنوا مسلمًا عن دينه ولا يتعرّضوا لماله ولا دينه. ألّا يعينوا أهل الحرب.

---

٢١ القلقشنديّ، صبح، ج٦، ١٦٤–١٦٥، ج١٢، ٢٨٩

٢٢ M. Gaudefroy-Demombyne, *La Syrie à l'époque des Mamelouks d'après les Auteurs Arabes*, Paris 1923, XLIX.

٢٣ شفيق يمّوت، أهل الذمّة في مختلف أطوارهم وعصورهم، ط١، بيروت: الشركة العالميّة للكتاب ١٩٩١، ٤٩.

٢٤ Antoine Fattal, *Le statut légal des Non-Musulmans en pays d'Islam*, Beyrouth: Imprimerie catholique 1958, 7.

وهذه الشروط ملزمة، فإذا نقضوها نُقِض عهدهم[٢٥].

أمّا الشروط المستحبّة فشملت أيضًا ستّة بنود هي: شدّ الزنّار ولبس الغيار، أي الملابس المغايرة للون ملابس المسلمين لتمييزهم عنهم. ألّا تعلو أبنيتهم فوق أبنية المسلمين. ألّا تعلو أصوات نواقيسهم وتلاوة كتبهم. ألّا يجاهروا بشرب الخمر وإظهار صلبانهم وخنازيرهم. أن يُخفوا دفن موتاهم ولا يجاهروا بندب عليهم ولا نياحة. أن يُمنعوا من ركوب الخيل ولا يمنعوا من ركوب البغال والحمير.

وهذه الشروط المستحبّة لا تلزم بعقد الذمّة، ولا يكون ارتكابها نقضًا للعهد[٢٦].

١. على الصعيد الدينيّ:

أ) أرباب الوظائف الدينيّة:

خضع المسيحيّون دينيًا في العصر المملوكيّ لأرباب الوظائف الدينيّة، وقد ذكرت المصادر الإسلاميّة تسلسلهم بالشكل الآتي:

البطريرك، وهو القائم بأمور الدين، الأسقف، وهو نائب البطريرك، المطران، وهو القاضي الذي يفصل في الخصومات بينهم، القسّيس، وهو القارىء الذي يقرأ عليهم الإنجيل والمزامير وغيرها، الجاثليق، وهو صاحب الصلاة، الشمّاس، وهو قيّم الكنيسة، الراهب، وهو الذي يحبس ذاته على العبادة في الخلوة[٢٧].

بالنسبة إلى الملكيّين فإنّه بعد انتقال البطريركيّة من أنطاكية إلى دمشق، انتقل إلى الدمشقيّين حقّ انتخاب البطريرك، لأنّه صار بمقام مطرانها الخاصّ، وأضحت أبرشيّتها تخضع له مباشرة كما كانت تخضع له كذلك أبرشيّة أنطاكية سابقًا. لكنّ هذا الانتخاب لم يكن يتمّ إلاّ بمشاركة المطارنة أصحاب الأبرشيّات التابعة للبطريركيّة الأنطاكيّة وموافقتهم. فقد كانوا يتولّون تنصيب البطريرك الجديد في كرسيّه وتسليمه صولجان البطريركيّة في الكنيسة المريميّة إذا كان المنتخَب مطرانًا. ويتولّون رسامته الأسقفيّة على الكاتدرا البطريركيّة إذا كان كاهنًا أو شمّاسًا. وفي حال لم يحضروا كلّهم، كان لا بدّ من موافقتهم على الانتخاب مع حضور بعضهم لمن تيسّر له ذلك. وكان الغالب

---

٢٥ الماورديّ، الأحكام السلطانيّة والولايات الدينيّة، بيروت: دار الكتب العلميّة، لا. ت، ١٨٤–١٨٥.

٢٦ المصدر ذاته، ١٨٥.

٢٧ القلقشنديّ، صبح، ج٥، ٤٤٣–٤٤٥، وج١٣، ٢٧٧، الخالدي، المقصد، ٢٦٦–٢٦٥، Bosworth, "Christian and Jewish", I, 68–70، أمّا الترتيب الصحيح فهو: البطريرك، الجاثليق، المطران، الأسقف، القسّيس، الراهب، الشمّاس.

أن يتولّى الرسامة ورئاسة حفلة تنصيب البطريرك مطران صور وصيدا أوّل المطارنة المتقدّم في كراسيهم، أو مطران حوران في غيابه (وكانت إقامتهما غالبًا بدمشق) بحضور الأساقفة المجاورين لدمشق أي أساقفة صيدنايا والزبداني وبعلبك ومعلولا وقارا ويبرود[٢٨].

أمّا بطريرك اليعاقبة فقد كان نائب البطريرك في مصر، «وشرطه أن يكون لاحقًا بصفته وشرطه اللازم له، ولا يكتب توقيعه إلاّ بعد إذن البطريرك بالقاهرة بالكتابة له، وتوقيعه في العادة[٢٩]».

وارتبط إقرار البطريرك في منصبه بموافقة السلطان الذي كان يبعث برسالة توقيع بذلك، غالبًا ما تضمّنت سلسلة من النصائح للبطريرك الجديد حول كيفيّة مباشرته مهامّه ومعاملته الرعيّة، والطلب بالمقابل إلى المسيحيّين أن يمتثلوا أوامر بطريركهم بالطاعة والإذعان، والخضوع للشروط العمريّة[٣٠]. أمّا أصحاب الرُتب الأخرى فلم يكن لأحد منهم ولاية من الأبواب الشريفة[٣١]. وكان البطريركان الملكيّ واليعقوبيّ مسؤولَيْن أمام نائب السلطنة، وشمل اختصاص كلّ منهما المسيحيّين التابعين له. وكان في ما يتعلّق بهذه الناحية يأتي تحت السلطان مباشرة[٣٢].

وتضمّنت بعض الرسائل تهديدات مبطّنة قضت بأنّ على البطريرك ألّا «يؤوي إليه من الغرباء القادمين عليه من يريب أو يكتم عن الإنهاء إلينا (السلطان) مشكل أمر ورد عليه من بعيد أو قريب، ثمّ الحذر من إخفاء كتاب يرد إليه من أحد الملوك، ثمّ الحذر من الكتابة إليهم أو المشي على مثل هذا السلوك، وليتجنّب البحر وإيّاه من اقتحامه فإنّه يغرق[٣٣]».

وأطلقت على البطريرك ألقاب عديدة منها: بطرك النصارى، المحتشم، المبجَّل، العارف، الحبر، العالم بأمور دينه، المعلِّم لأهل ملّته، ذُخر الملّة المسيحيّة، كنز

٢٨ قسطنطين باشا المخلّصيّ، لمحة تاريخيّة في الرهبانيّة الباسيليّة المخلّصيّة، ق١، بيروت: المطبعة الأدبيّة ١٩٠٩، ٥٩–٦٠، الشمّاس، خلاصة، ٣٠٩.

٢٩ الخالديّ، المقصد، ٢٧٥.

٣٠ القلقشنديّ، صبح، ج١٢، ٤٢٢، ٤٢٦، Bosworth, "Christian and Jewish", II, pp. 202–203.

٣١ الخالديّ، المقصد، ص ٢٦٦.

٣٢ زيادة، دمشق، ١٦٣–١٦٤.

٣٣ ابن فضل الله العمريّ، التعريف بالمصطلح الشريف، دراسة وتحقيق سمير الدروبي، ط١، الكرك: منشورات جامعة مؤتة ١٤١٣هـ/ ١٩٩٢م، ٢٠٥–٢٠٦، القلقشندي، **صبح**، ج ١٢، ٤٢٤–٤٢٦.

الطائفة العيسويّة، المشكور بعقله عند الملوك والسلاطين[٣٤] ولم يُراع أحيانًا مقام البطريرك، وأطلقت عليه ألقاب مهينة منها «كنز الكفر» كما ورد السنة ١٤٨٨/٨٩٤ عند ابن طولون[٣٥] وقيل فيه ما لا يليق به، منها ما جرى لبطريرك الملكيّين في دمشق ميخائيل الأوّل السنة ١٣٦٦/٧٦٧، حين دخل مع ابن كثير في حوار حول نصوص ما يعتقده كلّ من الملكيّين واليعاقبة والنساطرة، فيقول ابن كثير: «فإذا هو يفهم بعض الشيء، ولكنّ حاصله أنّه حمار من أكفر الكفّار لعنه الله[٣٦]».

ومنع على المسيحيّين بناء كنائس جديدة، أو إعادة بناء الكنائس المهدّمة كما حصل السنة ١٣٥٣/٧٥٤ حين أفتى بعض المفتين بجواز إعادة بناء ما تهدّم من الكنائس، فغضب عليهم قاضي القضاة تقيّ الدين السبكيّ ولامهم بشدّة على ذلك، ومنعهم من الإفتاء، ووضع بسبب ذلك مصنّفًا يتضمّن المنع في ذلك سمّاه «الدسائس في الكنائس[٣٧]».

وتعرّضت الكنائس للحرق والتخريب نتيجة بعض التصرّفات الشاذة من قِبل المسيحيّين تجاه المسلمين. فعلى أثر الاحتلال المغوليّ لدمشق السنة ١٢٦٠/٦٥٨ من قبل هولاكو المتحالف مع هيثوم الأوّل ملك أرمينيا الصغرى وصهره بوهيمند السادس أمير أنطاكية وطرابلس، أساء المسيحيّون إلى المسلمين ودور عبادتهم، وخالفوا الشروط العمريّة من شرب الخمر وقرع الأجراس والجهر بالصلاة[٣٨] وبعد هزيمة المغول في معركة عين جالوت من السنة ذاتها، انتقم المسلمون من المسيحيّين، فخرّبوا لهم كنيسة مريم للروم الملكيّين وأحرقوها، كما أحرقوا جزءًا من كنيسة لليعاقبة، ونهبوا بيوتهم وأحرقوها أيضًا[٣٩].

وفي عهد السلطان الظاهر بيبرس (١٢٦٠–١٢٧٧) دخل شيخه خضر بن أبي بكر العدويّ كنيس مريم لليهود في دمشق ونهبه وحوّله إلى مسجد، وعمل به سماعًا ومدّ

---

٣٤ القلقشنديّ، صبح، ج٦، ١٦٤–١٦٥، ج١٢، ٢٨٩.

٣٥ ابن طولون، مفاكهة، ج١، ط. القاهرة، ١٠٠.

٣٦ ابن كثير، بداية، ج١٤، ٢٤٩.

٣٧ المصدر ذاته، ج١٤، ٣١٩–٣٢٠.

٣٨ ابن الورديّ، تاريخ ابن الورديّ، ط١، بيروت: دار الكتب العلميّة ١٩٩٦، ج٢، ٢٠٠، ابن كثير، بداية، ج١٣، ٢١٩–٢٢٠.

٣٩ ابن الورديّ، تاريخ، ج٢، ٢٢٠، ابن كثير، بداية، ج١٣، ٢٢١، العيني، عقد الجمان في تاريخ أهل الزمان عصر سلاطين المماليك (١) حوادث وتراجم ٦٤٨–٦٦٤هـ/١٢٥٠–١٢٦٥م، حقّقه ووضع حواشيه محمّد محمّد أمين، القاهرة: الهيئة المصريّة العامّة للكتاب ١٤٠٧هـ–١٩٨٧م، ٢٤٩–٢٥٠، ابن سباط، صدق الأخبار تاريخ ابن سباط، عني به وحقّقه عمر عبد السلام تدمريّ، ط١، طرابلس لبنان: جرّوس برسّ ١٤١٣هـ/١٩٩٣م، ج١، ٣٩٣.

به سماطًا وبنى فيه محرابًا[٤٠] وللشيخ خضر سوابق في التعدّي على دور العبادة المسيحيّة واليهوديّة، إذ سبق له أن ذبح قسّيس كنيسة القيامة وأباح لتلامذته نهب محتوياتها، ودخل كنيسة في الإسكندريّة ونهبها وصيّرها مسجدًا وسمّاها المدرسة الخضراء. «كلّ ذلك والسلطان موافق له على جميع ما يعتمده[٤١]».

ولكن هل هذا يعني أنّ عهد الظاهر بيبرس كان مجحفًا بحقّ المسيحيّين؟ فهو أبطل في عهده المظالم التي كانت تطال الناس، ومنها الجوالي المعجّلة[٤٢] وكان عادلاً مع المسيحيّين واليهود، وأنصفهم من أكابر الأمراء وأعيان الدولة وكفّهم عنهم، كما يقول مؤرّخ سيرته ابن شدّاد[٤٣].

ويعتبر الدكتور إلياس القطّار أنّ هذا الكلام يتناقض كلّيًا مع ما عُرف عن بيبرس من بطش ومجازر بحقّ المسيحيّين في أماكن عدّة، وهو قد يكون من باب تقرّب ابن شدّاد من السلطان[٤٤].

ب) التحوّل من المسيحيّة إلى الإسلام:

وشهد العصر المملوكيّ تحوّل بعض المسيحيّين إلى الدين الإسلاميّ إمّا مكرهين، وخصوصًا في ظلّ الشروط العمريّة، وإمّا بملء اختيارهم. ولا يستطيع من دخل الإسلام بملء اختياره العودة عن هذا القرار. فإذا قام بذلك تعرّض لتطبيق الحدّ عليه، وهذا يعني عقوبة الموت استنادًا إلى ما نصّت عليه الشريعة الإسلاميّة، إلاّ إذا تاب وعاد إلى الدين الإسلاميّ[٤٥].

---

٤٠ ابن شدّاد، تاريخ الملك الظاهر، باعتناء أحمد حطيط، النشرات الإسلاميّة ٣١، فيسبادن: فرانز شتاينر ١٤٠٣هـ/١٩٨٣م، ٥٩، ٢٧٣، اليونينيّ، ذيل مرآة الزمان، مج ٣، (من وقائع سنة ٦٧١ إلى سنة ٦٧٧ هجريّة)، ط١، حيدر آباد الدكن الهند: مطبعة مجلس دائرة المعارف العثمانيّة ١٣٨٠هـ/١٩٦٠م، ٦، النويري، نهاية الأرب في فنون الأدب، ج٣٠، تحقيق محمّد عبد الهادي شعيرة، مراجعة محمّد مصطفى زيادة، القاهرة: الهيئة المصريّة العامّة للكتاب ١٤١٠هـ/١٩٩٠م، ٣٧٨، ابن كثير، **بداية**، ج١٣، ٢٦٥.

٤١ ابن شدّاد، تاريخ، ٢٧٣–٢٧٤، النويري، نهاية، ج٣٠، ٣٧٨، ابن كثير، بداية، ج١٣، ٢٦٥، ٢٧٨.

٤٢ ابن عبد الظاهر، الروض الزاهر في سيرة الملك الظاهر، تحقيق ونشر عبد العزيز خويطر، ط١، الرياض: ١٣٩٦هـ/١٩٧٦م، ٧٧.

٤٣ ابن شدّاد، تاريخ، ٢٨١–٢٨٢.

٤٤ إلياس القطّار، نيابة طرابلس في عهد المماليك (٦٨٨–٩٢٢هـ/١٢٨٩–١٥١٦م)، بيروت: منشورات الجامعة اللبنانيّة ١٩٩٨، ٢٩٢.

٤٥ حسن الزين، الأوضاع القانونيّة للنصارى واليهود في الديار الإسلاميّة حتّى الفتح العثمانيّ، بيروت: دار الفكر الحديث ١٩٨٨، ٧٢–٧٣.

وتورد المصادر رفض بعض المتّهمين التوبة والعودة إلى الدين الإسلاميّ وعدم اللجوء إلى هذه الوسيلة لإنقاذ حياتهم، مفضّلين عقوبة الموت. ومنهم مسيحيّ اعتُقِل السنة ٨١٢/ ١٤٠٩، وادُّعي عليه بأنّه كان قد أسلم، وأقيمت البيّنة بذلك، فاعترف. ثمّ عُرِض عليه الإسلام، فامتنع، فضربت رقبته بين القصرين[٤٦].

ومن الشروط العمريّة المستحَقَّة التي حتّمت على المسيحيّين التحوّل إلى الإسلام عدم الازدراء برسول الله والإساءة إليه، أي الإساءة إلى كلّ ما يتعلّق بالدين الإسلاميّ. فكان المذنبون يحاكَمون بالإعدام أو يُمنحون حرّيّة الاختيار بين تغيير الدين أو الموت.

فقد شهدت في دمشق مجموعة من أهل السويداء ضدّ مسيحيّ سبّ النبيّ ثمّ كاتَبَ الأمير عسّاف بن أحمد بن حجّي ليجيره السنة ١٢٩٤/٦٩٣. لكنّ النائب عزّ الدين أيبك الحمويّ لم يهتمّ بالأمر مراعاة للأمير عسّاف. ثمّ اجتمع العامّة والفقهاء في الجامع وخرجوا مع الشيخين المفتيين تقيّ الدين ابن تيميّة وزين الدين الفارقيّ شيخ دار الحديث اللذين تحدّثا إلى النائب بشأنه، فأمر بإحضاره ومعاملته وفق الشرع الشريف. وخرج الشيخان شاكرين له يصحبهما جمع كبير من الناس. وكانت مجموعة قد رجمت المتّهم بالحجارة وأدمته وأثخنته جراحًا، ولم توفّر الأمير عسّاف. فما كان من النائب إلاّ العمل على تهدئة الوضع، فطلب الشيخين وضربهما، ورسم عليهما واعتقلهما في المدرسة العذراويّة مع بعض المشاغبين. ثمّ أرسل النائب أربعة عدول إلى السويداء ليشهدوا عليه بثبوت العداوة بين المسيحيّ وبين من شهد عليه، فلم يمكن ذلك، فأسلم المسيحيّ بحضورهم في زُرَع. وعقد النائب مجلسًا بسببه ضمّ القاضي الشافعيّ وبعض فقهاء الشافعيّة أجازوا حقن دمه بعد إسلامه، وأُفرِج عن الشيخين. ثمّ انعقد مجلس آخر في دار السعادة ضمّ النائب والفقهاء والقضاة الأربعة، «وأُخذت خطوط جماعة منهم في فُتيا بما رأوه على اختلاف العلماء والمذاهب، وانفصلوا من غير فصل.» وأحضر المتّهم إلى المدرسة العذراويّة ثمّ أطلق باهتمام الأمير شمس الدين الأعسر المشدّ الذي التزم للأمير عسّاف ذلك. وصنّف الشيخ تقيّ الدين ابن تيميّة في هذه الواقعة كتابه «الصارم المسلول على سابّ الرسول[٤٧]».

---

٤٦ ابن حجر، إنباء الغمر بأبناء العمر في التاريخ، ط٢، بيروت: دار الكتب العلميّة ١٤٠٦هـ/١٩٨٦م، ج٨، ٢٥٨.

٤٧ ابن الجزريّ، تاريخ حوادث الزمان وأنبائه ووفيّات الأكابر والأعيان من أبنائه، ط١، تحقيق عمر عبد السلام تدمريّ، صيدا بيروت: المكتبة العصريّة ١٤١٩هـ/١٩٩٨م، ج١، ٢٠٢–٢٠٤، ابن كثير، بداية، ج١٣، ٣٣٥–٣٣٦.

وادُّعي على عبد الله السكندريّ السنة ١٣٢٦/٧٢٦ بأنّه قال عن مؤذّني الجامع الأمويّ في دمشق «هؤلاء كفرة لأمور ما يمكن شرحها». فذكر أنّه اعترف بذلك عند قاضي القضاة الحنبليّ وأسلم على يده وقبل توبته[٤٨].

٢. على الصعيد الاجتماعيّ:

تأثّرت العلاقات بين المسيحيّين بالمجتمع بالعلاقات بين المماليك والعالم الخارجيّ. وانتظمت العلاقة بين المسيحيّين والمجتمع المملوكيّ بموجب الشروط العمريّة التي فُرضت وراوحت أحيانًا بين تطبيقها كاملة أو جزء منها. وأدّت روح الجهاد لقتال المغول والصليبيّين دورها في خلق تحرّكات معادية للمسيحيّين، ووصل مدّ الأدب الجدليّ الفقهيّ ضدّهم إلى ذروته ابتداء من النصف الثاني من القرن الثالث عشر. فقد كان الفقهاء ينبشون من حين إلى آخر قوانين إسلاميّة قديمة طُبِّقت قرونًا عديدة وتمّ نسيانها مدّة طويلة.

أ) الشروط العمريّة:

طُبِّق بعض الشروط العمريّة للمرّة الأولى السنة ١٢٩٠/٦٨٩ حين قضى مرسوم السلطان المنصور قلاوون بمنع استخدام أحد من اليهود والمسيحيّين في المباشرات الديوانيّة، فُصرفوا منها[٤٩]. وقد يكون سبب هذا القرار إمّا متعلّقًا باستعدادت السلطان لحصار عكّا، وخوفه من اتّصال الموظّفين المسيحيّين في الدواوين بالصليبيّين وإطلاعهم على رغبته في احتلال المدينة، وإمّا ردًّا على خرق الصليبيّين الهدنة المعقودة مع المماليك بقتلهم مجموعة من التجّار المسلمين.[٥٠] كذلك فُرض جزء من الشروط السنة ١٢٩٥/٦٩٤، وقد تمثّل بإلزام أهل الذمّة تغيير ألوان ملابسهم، والسماح لهم بركوب البغال فقط دون الخيل. ومُنح المسلمون الحقّ بسلب كلّ مخالف[٥١].

---

٤٨ ابن أبي الفضائل، المفضّل، النهج السديد والدرّ الفريد فيما بعد تاريخ ابن العميد حوادث الفترة بين سنتي ٧١٧ و٧٤١ هجريّة، نشرته
Samira Kortantamer, *Ägypten und Syrien zwischen 1317 und 1341 in der Chronik des Mufaddal b. Abi L-Fada'il*, Freiburg im Breisgau: 1975, 35.

٤٩ النويريّ، نهاية الأرب في فنون الأدب، ج٣١، تحقيق الباز العريني، مراجعة عبد العزيز الأهواني، القاهرة: الهيئة المصريّة العامّة للكتاب ١٤١٢هـ/١٩٩٢م، ١٧١.

٥٠ المصدر ذاته، ج٣١، ١٦٩، ١٧١.

٥١ مؤرّخ مجهول، تاريخ المسلمين، مخطوط في المكتبة الشرقيّة ببيروت، رقم ٧٦، ٤٩٦؛ ابن كثير، بداية، ج١٣، ٣٤٠.

ثمّ فُرضت الشروط العمريّة بشكل أشمل السنة ١٣٠١/٧٠٠. ويعزو بعض المصادر ذلك إلى وزير ملك مراكش في المغرب الذي وصل إلى القاهرة في طريقه إلى الحجّ، فانتقد الحرّيّة والتسامح اللذين كان يتمتّع بهما المسيحيّون واليهود في مصر، وخصوصًا في الملابس الفاخرة التي يرتدونها أو ركوبهم البغال والخيول المسوّمة، أو استخدامهم في المناصب العالية. وقد لقي كلامه آذانًا صاغية وأثّر في أرباب السلطنة، فأُلزِم المسيحيّون واليهود في مصر وبلاد الشام تغيير ملابسهم، فاعتمر اليهود عمائم صفراء، والمسيحيّون عمائم زرقاء، والسامريّون عمائم حمراء، وتميّزت نساؤهم بعلامات ظاهرة. ومنعوا من ركوب الخيل أو حمل الأسلحة، وسُمح لهم بركوب الحمير «بالأُكُف (البراذع) عرضًا من غير تزيين لها ولا قيمة»، أو منفلي الأرجل، أي أن يثني أحدهم رجله قدامه على الدابّة. وأجبروا على أن يتجنّبوا أوساط الطرق للمسلمين، وألاّ يرفعوا أصواتهم على أصوات المسلمين، وألاّ يشيّدوا أبنيتهم أعلى من أبنية المسلمين، وألاّ يحتفلوا بالشعانين أو يقرعوا أجراس كنائسهم، وألاّ ينصّروا مسلمًا ولا يهوّدوه، وألاّ يشتروا عبدًا ولا من سباه مسلم ولا من جرت عليه سهام المسلمين. وألاّ ينقشوا خواتمهم بالعربيّة، ولا يعلّموا أولادهم القرآن، ولا يستخدموا في أعمالهم الشاقّة مسلمًا، ولا يرفعوا النيران. وإذا زنى أحدهم بمسلمة قُتل، وإذا دخل الحمّام عَلَّق جرسًا في عنقه تمييزًا له عن المسلم. ومُنع استخدام كتّاب الدواوين وأرباب الأقلام منهم إلاّ إذا أسلموا[٥٢].

ويقول ابن حبيب الحلبيّ: «واستمرّ ذلك، واجتهدوا في إزالته وبذلوا أموالاً جمّة، فلم يقبل منهم شيء منها، وشرطت عليهم أشياء من التزام الذلّ والصَّغار، فأجابوا إليها[٥٣]».

---

[٥٢] ابن الحريريّ، كتاب منتخب الزمان في تاريخ الخلفاء والعلماء والأعيان، ط١، حقّقه عن نسخة يتيمة وعلّق عليه عبده خليفة، بيروت: دار عشتار ١٩٩٥، ج٢، ٣٧٧–٣٧٨. بيبرس المنصوري، مختار الأخبار تاريخ الدولة الأيّوبيّة ودولة المماليك البحريّة حتّى السنة ٧٠٢هـ، ط١، حقّقه وقدّم له ووضع فهارسه عبد الحميد صالح حمدان، القاهرة: الدار المصريّة اللبنانيّة ١٤١٣هـ/١٩٩٣م، ١١٦–١١٧. أبو الفداء، المختصر في أخبار البشر، ط١، علّق عليه ووضع حواشيه محمود ديّوب، بيروت: دار الكتب العلميّة ١٩٩٧، ج٢، ٣٨٥. النويريّ، نهاية، ج٣١، ٤١٧–٤١٨. ابن الوردي، تاريخ، ج٢، ٢٤٢. ابن كثير، بداية، ج١٤، ١٦. القلقشندي، صبح، ج١٣، ٣٧٧–٣٧٨. ابن قاضي شهبة، تاريخ ابن قاضي شهبة، حقّقه عدنان درويش، دمشق: المعهد العلميّ الفرنسيّ للدراسات العربيّة ١٩٩٤، مج٢، ج١، ١٨٥–١٨٦.

[٥٣] ابن حبيب الحلبيّ، تذكرة النبيه في أيّام المنصور وبنيه، ج١، حوادث وتراجم (٦٧٨–٧٠٨هـ/١٢٧٩–١٣٠٨م) مع نشر وتحقيق وثائق وقف السلطان قلاون، حقّقه ووضع حواشيه محمّد محمّد أمين، راجعه وقدّم له سعيد عبد الفتّاح عاشور، القاهرة: الهيئة المصريّة العامّة للكتاب ١٩٧٦، ٢٣٣.

ولكن ما تجدر ملاحظته أنّ فرض الشروط العمريّة على أهل الذمّة جاء بعدما احتلّ قازان المغوليّ مدينة دمشق السنة ٦٩٩ /١٣٠٠، بدعم مسيحيّ من قِبَل ملك أرمينيا الصغرى والكرَج، فنهبوا الصالحيّة والمزّة وداريّا وبعض المساجد ودور الحديث وأحرقوها، وسبوا عددًا كبيرًا من الأهالي. وفرض المغول مبالغ كبيرة من المال على الأسواق، ومصادرات وتراسيم وعقوبات على أكابر دمشق، وأخذوا أموال الأوقاف والمدارس. وضمنوا الخمّارات وحانات الزنا، وحوّلوا دار ابن جرادة خارج باب توما إلى خمّارة وحانة. وبعد تراجع المغول عن دمشق دُمِّرت الخمّارات والحانات، وعوقب أصحابها. وحلّت النقمة على المسيحيّين[٥٤].

وتكرّر فرض الشروط العمريّة طوال القرن الرابع عشر، منها السنة ٧٤٨ /١٣٤٧ عندما نودي في دمشق بمنع أهل الذمّة من ركوب الخيل والبغال. وفرح الناس بذلك[٥٥].

وقرئ مرسوم السلطان الصالح صلاح الدين بن الناصر محمّد بن قلاوون بجامع دمشق السنة ١٣٥٤/٧٥٥ وألزم أهل الذمّة التقيّد بالشروط العمريّة، والذلّة والصَّغار، وقضى بمنع استخدامهم في الدواوين السلطانيّة وغيرها، وألاّ تزيد عمامة أحد منهم على عشرة أذرع، وألاّ يركبوا الخيول والبغال، ولكن الحمير بالأُكُف (البراذع) عرضًا، وأن تكون قيمة الحمار دون المائة درهم، وألاّ يُكرَّموا في المجالس، وإذا مرّوا بمسلم جالس نزلوا وأظهروا المسكنة، وألاّ يدخلوا الحمّامات إلاّ إذا علّقوا صلبانًا في أعناقهم أو وضعوا خواتم نحاس أو رصاص. وألاّ تدخل نساؤهم الحمّامات مع المسلمات بل تكون لهنّ حمّامات خاصّة بهنّ. وإذا ارتدت المسيحيّة إزارًا يجب أن يكون من الكتّان الأزرق، واليهوديّة أصفر، والسامريّة أحمر، وأن يكون أحد خفّيها أسود والآخر أبيض. كما فُرِض أن يكون حكم مواريثهم وفق الأحكام الشرعيّة[٥٦].

---

٥٤ الذهبيّ، دول الإسلام، بيروت: منشورات مؤسّسة الأعلمي للمطبوعات ١٤٠٥هـ/١٩٨٥م، ٣٩٤، ابن كثير، بداية، ج ١٤، ٨، ٩، ١٠، ١١.

٥٥ القلقشنديّ، صبح، ج١٣، ٣٧٨–٣٨٧، ابن قاضي شهبة، تاريخ، مج ٢، ج١، ٥٠٨.

٥٦ ابن كثير، بداية، ج١٤، ٢٥٠، ابن دقماق، الجوهر الثمين في سير الملوك والسلاطين، تحقيق محمّد كمال عزّ الدين علي، بيروت: منشورات عالم الكتب ١٩٨٣، ج٢، ٢٠٤–٢٠٥، ويعيد تاريخ المرسوم إلى العام ٧٥٤هـ/١٣٥٣م، ابن الشحنة، محبّ الدين أبو الوليد، روض المناظر في أخبار الأوائل والأواخر، ط١، تحقيق سيّد محمّد مهنّى، بيروت: دار الكتب العلميّة ١٤١٧هـ/ ١٩٩٧م، ٢٨٤، ابن قاضي شهبة، تاريخ، مج ٣، ج٢، دمشق: ١٩٩٤، ٦٠–٦١، ٢٨٢، ولكنّه في الصفحة ٤٨ يذكر أنّ المرسوم طُبِّق في العام ٧٥٤هـ/١٣٥٣م، البطريرك إسطفان الدويهيّ، تاريخ الأزمنة، ط٣، نظر فيها وحقّقها الأباتي بطرس فهد، بيروت: دار لحد خاطر، لا.ت، ٣١٨-٣١٩.

أمام قساوة هذه الشروط أسلمت مجموعة طوعًا وكرهًا. وفعلوا بمصر أعظم ممّا فُعِل بالشام، وهدموا كنيسة بشبرا كان يعظّمها المسيحيّون كثيرًا. ورسم السلطان بأنّ مَنْ كان في بلده رزق لكنيسة أو دير يأخذه. وقد بلغ ما أُخذ أكثر من عشرين ألف فدّان[٥٧].

وتجدّدت تلك الشروط في دمشق وبقيّة النيابات في بلاد الشام السنة ١٣٦٣/٧٦٥[٥٨].

وردًّا على الهجوم البحريّ الذي شنّه بطرس الأوّل ملك قبرص على الإسكندريّة السنة ٧٦٧ /١٣٦٥ وأحرق أبوابها وقتل عددًا من رجالها وأسر بعض نسائها وأطفالها، نودي في دمشق بمنع النساء المسيحيّات من دخول الحمّامات مع المسلمات، بل يدخلن حمّامات خاصّة بهنّ. كما فُرض على الواحدة منهنّ أن تنتعل حذاءين بلونين مختلفين أحدهما أبيض والآخر أصفر. أمّا الرجال فإذا دخلوا الحمّامات مع المسلمين فيعلّقون الأجراس في أعناقهم، ويضعون خواتم من النحاس أو الرصاص لتمييزهم من غيرهم[٥٩].

وحين زار برتراندون دي لابروكيير دمشق في ثلاثينيّات القرن الخامس عشر، كان ما يزال محرَّمًا على المسيحيّين مثلاً ركوب الخيل في شوارع المدينة واعتمار القبّعة والعمامة البيضاء[٦٠].

وفي السنة ٨٩٣ /١٤٨٨ أمر نائب دمشق بأن يربط رجال أهل الذمّة حبالاً على أوساطهم إذا دخلوا الحمّامات، أمّا النساء فيعلّقن أجراسًا. كذلك منعوا من ركوب الدوابّ داخل المدينة[٦١].

وقد حاول بعض العاملين في الجهاز الإداريّ المملوكيّ تخفيف القيود التي فُرضت على أهل الذمّة، ولكنّها اصطدمت بمعارضة بعض الفقهاء المتشدّدين، ومنهم ابن تيميّة الذي رفض السنة ٧٠٩/ ١٣٠٩ سعي الوزير ابن الخليليّ للسماح للذمّيّين باعتمار العمائم البيضاء مقابل مبلغ من المال يلتزمونه للديوان علاوة على الجزية التي يدفعونها[٦٢].

---

٥٧ ابن قاضي شهبة، تاريخ، مج ٣، ج٢، ٦٠–٦١، ٢٨٢.

٥٨ القلقشنديّ، صبح، ج١٣، ٢١–٢٣، ابن كثير، بداية، ج١٤، ٣٠٥–٣٠٦، ابن قاضي شهبة، تاريخ، مج٣، ج٢، ٩٧، ٢٤٣.

٥٩ ابن كثير، بداية، ج١٤، ٣١٤–٣١٥، ٣١٧، ابن قاضي شهبة، تاريخ، مج ٣، ج٢، ٢٧٠–٢٧١.

٦٠ محمود زايد، «رحلة برتراندون دي لابروكيير إلى فلسطين ولبنان وسورية (١٤٣٢م)»، الأبحاث، السنة ١٥، ج٣ (١٩٦٢)، ٣١٣، ٣٢٦.

٦١ ابن طوق، التعليق، ج٢، ٧٤٨، ٧٥٥، ابن طولون، مفاكهة، ج١، ط. القاهرة، ٨٧.

٦٢ السيوطيّ، تاريخ الخلفاء، ط٣، تحقيق محمّد يحيى الدين، القاهرة: ١٩٦٤، ٤٨٥.

تظهر هذه الإجراءات المتّخذة بحقّ المسيحيّين الاضطهاد الذي كانوا يعانونه من قِبل المماليك، والحدّ من حرّيّاتهم. وقد جاء بعضها نتيجة الصراعات المملوكيّة المغوليّة الصليبيّة كما في السنتين ١٣٠١ و١٣٦٥. ولم يكن للمسيحيّين في دمشق وحلب أي علاقة مباشرة بها.

ولكنّ السؤال الذي يطرح ذاته: هل التكرار في إصدار المراسيم غير المرتبطة بالصراعات والقاضية بتطبيق الشروط العمريّة، دليل على التهاون في تطبيقها، أم أنّها كانت لتذكير أهل الذمّة بالدونيّة؟ يبقى الباب مفتوحًا أمام النقاش.

رغم قساوة الشروط العمريّة وانعزال المسيحيّين في أحياء خاصّة بهم خارج الأسوار، فقد انخرطوا في الحياة الاجتماعيّة، ولم يكونوا طارئين على المجتمع بل في صلبه. وربطتهم بالمسلمين علاقات متنوّعة، وتبادلوا الزيارات، وتناولوا الطعام إلى موائدهم، وشرب بعضهم الخمر معهم، وساد بينهم نوع من الأمانة والوفاء، واقترضوا منهم الأموال. وتمتّعوا أيضًا بحقّ شراء الأراضي وامتلاكها بموجب صكوك يوقّعها القضاة[٦٣].

كذلك شاركوا المسلمين في مواجهة الكوارث التي ضربتهم، ورفعوا الصلوات إلى جانبهم، وحملوا الإنجيل وصاموا وتضرّعوا إلى الله لينجّيهم منها، كما حصل السنة ١٣٤٨/٧٤٩ حين اجتاح الطاعون بلاد الشام[٦٤].

وفي المقابل استُبعِد المسيحيّون عن المشاركة في بعض المناسبات بأمر من السلطات المملوكيّة. فقد مُنعوا في حلب السنة ١٣٣٠/٧٣١ من الخروج مع الأمراء والناس للاحتفال بوصول مياه نهر الساجور إلى حلب[٦٥].

ب) الأعياد:

أمّا على صعيد الأعياد، فقد احتفل المسيحيّون بالأعياد الخاصّة بهم. ومنها عيد البربارة[٦٦] وعيد الميلاد. ويقول عنه شيخ الربوة الدمشقيّ: «وعيد الميلاد هو اليوم الذي ولد فيه المسيح. يقولون إنّه ولد يوم الاثنين. يجعلون عشيّة الأحد ليلة الميلاد، وهم

---

٦٣ ابن طوق، التعليق، ج١، ٢٤٠، ٢٦٧، ٤١٦، ٤٣٠، ٤٤٧، ج٢، ٦٤٢، ٨٨٧، ٩٠٧.

٦٤ ابن كثير، بداية، ج١٤، ٢٢٦، ابن بطّوطة، رحلة ابن بطّوطة، ط١، إعتنى به وراجعه درويش الجويدي، صيدا بيروت: المكتبة العصريّة ١٤٢٤هـ/٢٠٠٣م، ج١، ٩٢–٩٣، ابن قاضي شهبة، تاريخ، مج٢، ج١، ٥٤٦–٥٤٧.

٦٥ ابن الشحنة، روض، ٢٧٧.

٦٦ عبد الودود برغوت «جوانب اجتماعيّة من تاريخ دمشق في القرن الخامس عشر من مخطوطة أحمد بن طوق»، في: المؤتمر الدولي لتاريخ الشام، بيروت: الدار المتّحدة للنشر ١٩٧٤، ٤١٠–٤١١.

يقدون فيها المصابيح في الكنائس، وولد ببيت لحم بقرية يهودا من عمل أورشليم، وهي بيت المقدس[٦٧]» ويمكن معرفة طريقة الاحتفال به كما أوردها في حماة: «وفي هذه الليلة يوقد أهل حماة كبيرهم وصغيرهم وجليلهم وحقيرهم وجندهم وأميرهم من القناديل فوق الأسطحة، ومن القنّب والشيح عظيمًا، ويوقدون من البارود والنفط أنواعًا شتّى[٦٨]».

كذلك احتفلوا بعيد الختان، وكانوا يسمّونه الميلادة الصغيرة، «ويقولون إنّ المسيح خُتن في هذا اليوم وهو الثامن من الميلاد»[٦٩] كما احتفلوا بالغطاس[٧٠].

وتورد المصادر أنّ المسيحيّين في دمشق كانوا يصومون ثمّ يحتفلون بالعيد الكبير أي الفصح، وكان يطلق عليه «عيد النصارى[٧١]»، أمّا في حلب فكانوا يتوجّهون إلى حماة للاحتفال به. وترك لنا شيخ الربوة الدمشقيّ صورة عن الاحتفال، فيقول: «وفي هذا العيد تبطل أهل حماة مدّة ستّة أيّام أوّلها الخميس الكبير وهو خميس العهد (خميس الأسرار) وآخرها يوم الثلاث ثالث الفصح، وتنتقش فيه النساء وتلبس فيه الكساوى الفاخرة ويصبغون فيه البيض، ويعملون الأقراص والكعك، والمسلمون أكثر من النصارى. ويرد إلى حماة أهل سائر البلاد المجاورة لها مثل حمص وشيزر وسلميّة وكفرطاب وأبو قُبَيْس ومصياف والمعرّة وتِيزين والباب وبُزاعة والفُوعة وحلب ويطلعون جميعًا إلى العاصي ويضربون لهم أهل حماة على شطوطه خيامًا ويركبون في المراكب بالمغاني ويرقصون في المراكب النساء والرجال على الشطوط حتّى تتهتّك الخلائق ويمضي لهم ستّة أيّام لا يرى في الوجود مثلها، وكذلك يبطلون أوّل يوم صوم النصارى ويقولون قد طلعوا يلتقون الراهب...[٧٢]».

واحتفلوا بعد عيد الفصح بخميس الصعود أو خميس الأربعين وكانوا يسمّونه السلاّق. ويقول شيخ الربوة: «وهو الأربعون من الفطر ويزعمون أنّ المسيح تسلّق فيه بين تلاميذه إلى السماء بعد القيامة ووعدهم بإرسال البارقليط (كذا) وهو روح

---

٦٧ شيخ الربوة الدمشقيّ، كتاب نخبة الدهر في عجائب البرّ والبحر، نشره مهرن، لايبزغ: ١٩٢٣، ٢٨١

٦٨ المصدر ذاته، ٢٨١.

٦٩ المصدر ذاته، ٢٨٠–٢٨١، القلقشنديّ، صبح، ج٢، ٤٥٤–٤٥٥.

٧٠ برغوت، «جوانب»، ٤١٠–٤١١.

٧١ ابن طوق، التعليق، ج١، ٤١، ٥١، ١٢٣، ١٤٥، ٢٢٥، ٢٢٦، ٣٣٣، ٣٥١، ٤٤٠، ابن طولون، مفاكهة، ط١، وضع حواشيه خليل المنصور، ق١، بيروت: دار الكتب العلميّة ١٤١٨هـ/١٩٩٨م، ٧.

٧٢ شيخ الربوة، نخبة، ٢٨١.

القدس.» كما احتفلوا بعيد الخمسين أو العنصرة، وكانوا «يعملونه بعد خمسين يومًا من عيد القيامة. يقولون إنّ روح القدس حلَّت في التلاميذ شبه ألسنة ناريّة وتفرّقت عليهم ألسنة فتكلّموا بجميع الألسنة، وراح كلّ واحد منهم إلى بلاد لسانه الذي تكلّم به يدعوهم إلى دين المسيح[٧٣]».

ومن الأعياد أيضًا عيد في أوّل نيسان، وآخر يلي خميس البيض[٧٤] وعيد مولد السيّدة العذراء في ٨ أيلول، وعيد الصليب في ١٤ أيلول[٧٥].

واحتفل المسيحيّون في دمشق بهذه الأعياد في أحيائهم، إلاّ في خميس النصارى إذ كانوا يخرجون فيه إلى القابون. وقد شاركهم المسلمون في أعيادهم. وكانوا يهرعون للتفرّج على أعياد المسيحيّين الدينيّة التي كانوا يحتفلون بها عند مقابرهم في باب كيسان[٧٦].

ج) عدم التجاهر بشرب الخمر:

ومن الشروط المستحبّة التي فُرِضت على المسيحيّين عدم التجاهر بشرب الخمر علنًا. إذ قرن الشرع بين الخمر والميسر في التحريم، وأمر باجتنابها ومقاربتها بوجه، ولا يجوز اقتناؤها ولا شرب قليلها[٧٧].

وكان الظاهر بيبرس أوّل من أمر السنّة ٦٦٧/١٢٦٨–١٢٦٩ بإبطال الخمر والمسكرات، وأراق الخمور في دمشق[٧٨].

وكان الخمر يُعَدُّ من المحرّمات والمنكرات المتفشّية بين الناس، وشاع شربه بشكل واسع بين العامّة والمماليك، ووصل إلى داخل المساجد. وانتشرت الخمّارات بكثرة، وكان بعض النوّاب والأمراء يضمنونها ويحمونها ويؤمّنون نقل الخمر بحراسة الجنود. كما كانوا يسعون للحصول عليه بأيّ وسيلة. فقد نهب رجال حاجب دمشق السنة ٩١٧/١٥١١ بلدة قرب صرخد معظم سكّانها من المسيحيّين لأنّهم كانوا يشتهون

٧٣ المصدر ذاته، ٢٨٠–٢٨١، القلقشنديّ، صبح، ج٢، ٤٥٤–٤٥٥.

٧٤ شيخ الربوة، نخبة، ٢٨٠–٢٨١، برغوت، «جوانب»، ٤١٠–٤١١.

٧٥ ابن قاضي شهبة، تاريخ، مج١، ج٣، دمشق ١٩٧٧، ٥٩٠، ابن طوق، التعليق، ج١، ٧٨.

٧٦ ابن طوق، التعليق، ج٢، ٦٠٢، برغوت، «جوانب»، ٤١٠–٤١١، العلبي، دمشق، ٨٨–٨٩.

٧٧ عزيز العظمة، ابن تيميّة، ط١، بيروت، رياض الريّس للكتب والنشر ٢٠٠٠، ١٩٨.

٧٨ العبّاسيّ الصفديّ، نزهة المالك والمملوك في مختصر سيرة من ولي مصر من الملوك، ط١، تحقيق عمر عبد السلام تدمريّ، صيدا بيروت: المكتبة العصريّة ١٤٢٤هـ/٢٠٠٣م، ١٥٤، ابن دقماق، النفحة المسكيّة في الدولة التركيّة من كتاب الجوهر الثمين في سِيَر الخلفاء والسلاطين، ط١، تحقيق عمر عبد السلام تدمريّ، صيدا بيروت: المكتبة العصريّة ١٤٢٠هـ/١٩٩٩م، ٦١.

الخمر. وأمر بعض السلاطين بإراقة الخمور والتشديد في تنفيذ الأوامر. وحاول الصوفيّون وبعض العامّة الحدّ من انتشاره ومكافحة شربه وإقفال الخمّارات. وكثرت النداءات المطالبة بإبطاله والسعي لإزالته وخصوصًا من قبل رجال الدين. وجُرِّدت الحملات للتخلّص من الخمّارات، وصودر أصحاب الخمور بأموال طائلة، وتسبّبت بوقوع المشاكل بين رجال الدين ومسؤولي الطبقة الحاكمة. ودُهِمت بيوت المسيحيّين ووقعت صراعات نتيجة مكافحة تعاطي الخمر أسفرت عن جرحى وقتلى[٧٩].

وعوقب المتّهمون بشرب الخمر إمّا بالسجن كما حصل مع الرحّالة دي لا بروكيير، وإمّا بالموت أحيانًا كما حصل مع بدر الدين ابن القسّيس النفيس القبطيّ كاتب الأمير سيف الدين كجكل في دمشق السنة ١٢٨٨/٦٨٧، بعدما دُهِمَ بيته في شهر رمضان ووجد برفقة امرأة مسلمة يعاقران الخمر، فأمر نائب دمشق حسام الدين لاجين بإحراقه رغم المال الذي بذله للعفو عنه وتدخّل مخدومه[٨٠] وإذا جلس أحدهم في حانوت كان «يحفر له حفيرة يجلس فيها ولا يصدِّر[٨١]».

د) الضرائب والمصادرات:

دفع المسيحيّون عددًا من الضرائب، في طليعتها الجزية أو الجوالي، وهي إجباريّة تقرّها الشريعة الإسلامية التقليديّة، وتخوّلهم حقّ الحصول على الاعتراف بحقوقهم العامّة والخاصّة. وعرف المسؤول عن جبايتها باسم ناظر الجوالي أو متكلّم الجوالي، وكان يعيّنه النائب بموجب توقيع شريف[٨٢] وترتّب على الرجال البالغين دفعها دون النساء والصبيان والرهبان والعبيد والمجانين. ولم تجبَ من المسكين الذي يُتصدَّق عليه.

---

٧٩ ابن كثير، بداية، ج١٤، ٣١٧، ابن قاضي شهبة، تاريخ، مج٣، ج٢، ٢٧٣، ابن حجر، إنباء، ج٦، ٢٢٦، ج٨، ص ١٤٩، البصروي، تاريخ البصروي صفحات مجهولة من تاريخ دمشق في عصر المماليك من سنة ٨٧١هـ لغاية ٩٠٤هـ، ط١، تحقيق ودراسة أكرم حسن العلبي، دمشق: دار المأمون للتراث ١٩٨٨، ٢٠٤، ٢٠٥، ابن طوق، التعليق، ج١، ٢٣٧، ٢٤٠، ٤٢٢، ج٢، ٦٣٧، ٨٣٧، ٨٤٥، ٨٥٩، ١٠٠٧، ابن طولون، مفاكهة، ط. القاهرة، ج١، ٢١، ٣٠، ٣٢، ٨٤، ١٠٩، ١٥٣–١٥٤، ١٥٨، ٢٠٣، ٢٠٥، ٢١٠، ٢١٥–٢١٦، ٢٣٠، ٢٤٨–٢٤٩، ٣٠٣، ٣١٤، إعلام الورى بمن ولي نائباً من الأتراك بدمشق الشام الكبرى، ط٢، تحقيق محمّد أحمد دهمان، دمشق: دار الفكر ١٤٠٤هـ/١٩٨٤م، ١١٦–١١٧، ١٨٦، ١٨٨، ٢٠٣.

٨٠ حوادث الفترة بين سنتي ٦٨٢ و٦٨٧ هجريّة كما دوّنها شمس الدين محمّد بن ابرهيم الجزري في كتابه (حوادث الزمان) وأبو بكر بن عبد الله بن أيبك الدواداريّ في كتابه (كنز الدرر وجامع الغرر)، نشرهما وعلّق عليهما أولرخ هارمن، فرايبرج: ١٩٦٩، ١١٤، زايد، «رحلة»، ٣٢٦.

٨١ إ بن طولون، مفاكهة، ط. القاهرة، ج١، ٢٨٨، إعلام، ١٨٨.

٨٢ القلقشنديّ، صبح، ج٣، ٥٣٠–٥٣١، ج١٢، ٣٠٦–٣٠٧، ابن طوق، التعليق، ج٢، ٨٥٠، ابن طولون مفاكهة، ط. القاهرة، ج١، ١٦.

وكانت تُستخرَج أوّلا في شهر محرّم، ثمّ تحوّلت إلى ذي الحجّة، فمعجَّلة في رمضان في القرن الخامس عشر[٨٣].

وكانت الجزية تؤخذ من أهل الذمّة على قدر طبقاتهم، وحدّدتها كتب الحسبة المملوكيّة التي تعود إلى القرنين الثالث عشر والرابع عشر وبعض مصادر القرن الخامس عشر بدينار على الفقير، ودينارين على المتوسّط وأربعة دنانير على الغنيّ.[٨٤] وقد اشتُطّ أحيانًا في استخراجها كما حدث السنة ١٣٤١/٧٤٢ حين شرع نائب دمشق قُطْلُبُغا الفخريّ في تحصيل الأموال لتجهيز طُلْب السلطان، واستخرج من اليهود والنصارى جوالي ثلاث سنين معجَّلة[٨٥].

ونودي في دمشق السنة ٨٨٥ /١٤٨٠–١٤٨١ عن عُمَر بن الصابوني ناظر الجوالي: «مَنْ ظُلِم من اليهود والنصارى عليه بالأبواب الشريفة[٨٦]» وكان عبء الجزية ثقيلاً على المسيحيّين، لذلك لجأ بعضهم إلى اعتناق الإسلام[٨٧].

وإلى جانب الجزية فُرِضت ضرائب أخرى منها ضريبة الخفر لحماية القوافل التي كان يرافقها جنود مسلّحون. وكان يؤخذ من المسيحيّين واليهود مبلغ أكبر من المسلمين، وضريبة الخمر التي فُرضت على استهلاك الخمر وإنتاجه وتسويقه في العشر الثاني من القرن ١٥م. وكان الهدف من فرضها الحدّ من انتشاره بين أهل الذمّة. وضريبة الإرث التي خضعت للشرع الإسلاميّ، إذ كان الورثة يأخذون الحصَّة المقرَّرة لهم بحسب هذا الشرع، في حين يذهب الباقي إلى بيت المال. وفي حال لم يترك المتوفّى ورثة تذهب الأموال والملكيّة كلّها إلى بيت المال، وهو ما عُرف باسم المواريث الحشريّة. كما

---

٨٣ ابن مماتي، كتاب قوانين الدواوين، ط١، جمعه وحقّقه عزيز سوريال عطيّة، القاهرة: مكتبة مدبولي ١٤١١هـ/١٩٩١م، ٣١٧–٣١٩، القلقشندي، صبح، ج٣، ٥٣٠.

٨٤ ابن الإخوة، معالم القربة في أحكام الحسبة، تحقيق محمود شعبان، القاهرة: ١٩٧٦، ٩٩، ١٠٠، ابن بسّام، نهاية الرتبة في طلب الحسبة، تحقيق حسام الدين السامرّائي، بغداد: ١٩٦٨، ٢٠٧، ٢٠٨، ولم تختلف قيمة الجزية عن تلك التي حدّدها الشيزري في العصر الأيوبيّ، أنظر كتاب نهاية الرتبة في طلب الحسبة، ط٢، تحقيق ومراجعة السيّد الباز العريني، بيروت: دار الثقافة ١٤٠١هـ/١٩٨١م، ١٠٧، ابن حجر، **إنباء**، ج٧، ٧٣، العيني، عقد الجمان في تاريخ أهل الزمان الحوادث والتراجم من سنة ٨١٥هـ إلى سنة ٨٢٤هـ، ط١، نشره عبد الرازق الطنطاوي القرموط، لا دار نشر ١٤٠٦هـ/١٩٨٥م، ١٤٩.

٨٥ شمس الدين الشجاعيّ، تاريخ الملك الناصر محمّد بن قلاوون الصالحيّ وأولاده، حقّقته وترجمته إلى الألمانيّة برباره شيفر، القسم الأوّل، النصّ العربيّ، فيسبادن: فرانز شتاينر ١٣٩٨هـ/١٩٧٨م، ١٩٤، ابن قاضي شهبة، تاريخ، مج٢، ج١، ٢٣١، وقد ورد في كلا المصدرين «حوالي» بدلاً من «جوالي»، وهو خطأ، إذ إنّ صفة المعجّلة وردت في المصادر في معظم الأحيان ملازمة لكلمة الجوالي، راجع ابن عبد الظاهر، الروض، ٧٧ والقلقشنديّ، صبح، ج٣، ص ٥٣٠، ابن كثير، بداية، ج١٤، ص ١٩٨.

٨٦ ابن طولون، مفاكهة، ط. القاهرة، ج١، ١٦.

٨٧ ابن طوق، التعليق، ج١، ص ١١٧.

كانت هناك ضريبة على شكل هديّة تسمّى «ضيافة القدوم» وتعطى لأحد الموظفين عند دخوله مكان وظيفته[٨٨].

ولم يسلم أهل الذمّة والمسلمون في العهد المملوكيّ من مصادرة الأملاك وفرض الغرامات وسوء المعاملة من قبل السلطنة لأسباب مختلفة. وكانت في معظمها مخالفة للشرع الإسلاميّ، وفُرضت في حالات طارئة أو في الأزمات.

وتفيد المصادر بأنّ بعض الكتّاب المسيحيّين وغيرهم تسبّبوا باندلاع النيران في دمشق السنة ١٣٤٠/٧٤٠ واحتراق جزء من الجامع الأمويّ وأوقافه، وما حوله من قيساريّات ومدارس وأسواق، وبعض الأملاك. واتّهموا بالتواطؤ مع راهبين من القسطنطينيّة يدعيان ملاني وعازر يتقنان صناعة كعكعات من النفط، على إحراق ما يمكن من أماكن المسلمين في دمشق ردًّا على ما أُحرِق من كنيستهم. وأمّن لهما عامل الجيش ما يحتاجان إليه. فأنجزا المهمّة ثمّ أرسلهما المسيحيّون متنكّرَيْن إلى بيروت ومنها إلى القسطنطينيّة[٨٩].

ويقول شمس الدين الشجاعيّ: «إنّ النصارى بدمشق غرّهم الشيطان وحملهم الطغيان واجتمعت جميعهم (كذا) منهم كتّاب وغيرهم واتّفقوا على أن يرموا النار بدمشق خفية ويكيدوا المسلمين بمكيدة[٩٠]».

وبعدما تحرّى تنكز، نائب دمشق، عن حقيقة الأمر وموجبه، تبيّن له أنّ عددًا من كتّاب الدواوين المسيحيّين وغيرهم هم الذين أشعلوا النار. فقبض على نحو ستّين من رؤوس النصارى، من بينهم الرشيد سلامة كاتب سنجر البشمقدار، والمكين يوسف بن يحيى عامل الجيش، والمكين جرجس بن أبي الكرم كاتب الحوطات، والمكين يوسف كاتب بهادر آص، والعلم عامل بيروت، وسمعان أخو بشارة الكركيّ، وجزّاران وجرائحيّ وشخص يُعرف بسبيل الله وعلى مجموعة أخرى. وفرض على أربعة منهم مليونًا ومايتي ألف درهم. وأمر بصلب أحد عشر

---

٨٨ Abraham David, “The Jewish Settlement in Palestine in the Mamluk Period (1260–1516)”, in: The Jewish Settlement in Palestine 634–1881, eds. Alex Carmel, Peter Schäfer, and Yossi Ben-Artzi, Wiesbaden: 1990, 57–59.

٨٩ الشجاعيّ، تاريخ، ٧٤–٧٥، ابن الوردي، تاريخ، ج٢، ٣١٨، ابن كثير، بداية، ج١٤، ص ١٨٦، ابن قاضي شهبة، تاريخ، مج٢، ج١، ١١٥–١١٦، والحاشية رقم ١ في الصفحتين المذكورتين، ابن سباط، صدق، ج٢، ٦٥٩–٦٦٠،
M. Perlman, “Notes on Anti-Christian Propaganda in the Mamlûk Empire”, *Bulletin of the School of Oriental Studies*, Vol.X, (1940–1942), 854.

٩٠ الشجاعيّ، تاريخ، ص ٧٤.

من أعيان الكتبة المسيحيّين والدوران بهم في دمشق، وأحرقهم حتّى صاروا رمادًا، وسجن قسمًا من المعتقلين، في حين أسلم بعضهم. وأفتى فقهاء المذاهب الأربعة بانتقاض عهد من مالأ على هذه الكائنة منهم، أي أنّهم خالفوا أحد الشروط العمريّة المستحقّة المتمثّل في عدم إعانة أهل الحرب، بما أنّ المماليك كانوا في صراع مع البيزنطيّين في تلك الفترة، ورُسم ألّا يستخدموا في شيء من الدواوين. ثمّ اطّلع النائب على ما احترق من أملاك المسلمين ونظر في ما يقوم بعمارتها. فصادر بقيّة مسيحيّي دمشق واستخلص منهم بالضرب والمقارع والعقوبات مبلغًا كبيرًا من المال، وأمر بصرفه في إعادة بناء ما أحترق من الأملاك. ووصل إلى السلطان ما فعله نائب دمشق بالمسيحيّين، فأنكر عليه أخذ أموال المسيحيّين، وأنّ ذلك يؤدّي إلى إساءة معاملة المسلمين في القسطنطينيّة بسبب ما فعله مع المسيحيّين. وأمره بأن يرسل إليه ما استخلصه من الأموال، وبأن يتمّ بناء ما احترق من وقف الجامع من أوقافه، وكلّ من له مُلك يعمّره من ماله. فلم يرسل تنكز شيئًا واستمرّ في البناء، فغضب السلطان لذلك[٩١].

وفي رمضان السنة ٧٤١/ شباط آذار ١٣٤١ اكتمل بناء مئذنة الجامع الأمويّ الشرقيّة من أموال المسيحيّين بعدما احترقت وسقطت كلّها.[٩٢] ثمّ أمر بَرَصْبُغا الحاجب الذي قدم من مصر مع مجموعة من الأمراء لتجديد البيعة للسلطان بإطلاق سراح مَنْ سُجن من المسيحيّين المتّهمين باندلاع الحريق[٩٣].

وتورد المصادر أنّه في السنة ٧٦٧ /١٣٦٥ احتيط على الفرنج في دمشق وأُودعوا سجون القلعة ردًّا على الهجوم البحريّ الذي شنّه بطرس الأوّل ملك قبرص على الإسكندريّة وأحرقها وقضى على عدد من رجالها وأسر بعض نسائها وأطفالها. وتلقّى نائب دمشق سيف الدين منكلي بغا مرسومًا سلطانيًّا، يأمره بإمساك المسيحيّين وبأخذ ربع أموالهم لبناء ما تهدّم في الإسكندريّة ولبناء مراكب لغزو الصليبيّين القبارصة. امتثل النائب للأوامر، وأهين المسيحيّون وطلبوا من بيوتهم بعنف من دون أن يفهموا ما يراد بهم، وخافوا من أن يُقتَلوا، فهربوا[٩٤].

---

٩١ الشجاعيّ، تاريخ، ٧٤–٧٦، ابن الوردي، تاريخ، ج٢، ٣١٨، ابن كثير، بداية، ج١٤، ١٨٦، ابن ابي الفضائل، نهج، نشر كورتنتمر، ٨٣–٨٥، ابن قاضي شهبة، تاريخ، مج٢، ج١، ١١٦–١١٧، وتتمّة الحاشية رقم ١، ١١٥، البصروي، تاريخ، ٨٩–٩٠.

٩٢ ابن قاضي شهبة، تاريخ، مج٢، ج١، ١٢٧.

٩٣ المصدر ذاته، مج٢، ج١، ١١٥–١١٧.

٩٤ ابن كثير، بداية، ج١٤، ٣١٤–٣١٥، ابن قاضي شهبة، تاريخ، مج٣، ج٢، ٢٧٠، ٢٧١.

ويذكر الدويهيّ أنّ السلطان غضب على المسيحيّين وأمر بإمساك أساقفتهم وسجنهم في دمشق، فاختفى بعضهم، وهرب بعضهم الآخر كالأسقف حنين (أي يوحنّا) إلى قبرص، وقُبض على بعضهم الثالث وسُجن، وكان منهم يعقوب مطران إهدن، لكنّه هرب من السجن[٩٥].

وصادر يلبغا الناصريّ جميع المسيحيّين والرهبان في مصر والشام ووضع يده على جميع ما في الأديار من أموال، حتّى يقال إنّه اجتمع عنده من ذلك اثنا عشر ألف صليب، منه صليب ذهب وزنه عشرة أرطال مصريّة[٩٦].

ويعترف ابن كثير المعاصر للحدث بأنّ هذا الأمر لم يكن شرعيًّا، ولا يجوز اعتماده مع المسيحيّين. لذلك، حين طلبه نائب دمشق للاجتماع به في ١٦ صفر/٢ تشرين الثاني من تلك السنة، ذكر له ذلك، فقال له النائب إنّ بعض فقهاء مصر أفتى بذلك للأمير الكبير يلبغا الناصريّ، فقال له ابن كثير إنّ هذا لا يسوَّغ شرعًا، ولا يجوز لأحد أن يفتي بهذا. وما داموا على الذمّة ويؤدّون الجزية ملتزمين الذلّة والصَّغار، وأحكام الملّة قائمة، فلا يجوز أن يؤخذ منهم الدرهم الواحد الفرد زيادة عمّا يؤدّونه من الجزية. فتعلّل النائب بأنّه لا يستطيع مخالفة المرسوم. ولكنّ ابن كثير الذي حاول التخفيف عن مسيحيّي دمشق، ذكر له أمورًا كثيرة يمكن اعتمادها للاقتصاص من القبارصة، وأنّه يجوز ذلك وإنْ لم يفعل ما يتوعّدهم به، فاقتنع النائب، وأرسل مطالعة إلى مصر. ثمّ ورد مرسوم السلطان وفيه أمر ببناء الشواني والمراكب لغزو قبرص. وفي صباح الأحد الأوّل من شهر ربيع الأوّل/١٦ تشرين الثاني طلب النائب المسيحيّين الذين اجتمعوا في كنيستهم، وكانوا نحو أربعمئة شخص، وحلّفهم على كمّيّة أموالهم وألزمهم أداء الربع. وقد أُمِر الولاة بإحضار مَنْ في معاملتهم، وقصد والي البرّ القرى بسبب ذلك، وجُرِّد أمراء إلى النواحي لاستخلاص الأموال من المسيحيّين في القدس وغيره[٩٧].

---

٩٥ الدويهيّ، تاريخ، ٣٢٢–٣٢٣.

٩٦ ابن حجر، الدرر الكامنة في أعيان المائة الثامنة، ط١، ضبطه وصحّحه الشيخ عبد الوارث محمّد علي، ج٤، بيروت: دار الكتب العلميّة ١٤١٨هـ/١٩٩٧م، ٢٧١، حبيب الزيّات، سمات «أهل الكتاب» في المصنّفات العربيّة، إعداد وتحقيق الدكتور يوسف قزما الخوري، ط١، بيروت: دار الحمراء ١٩٩٢، ٣٥، الصليب في الإسلام، قدّم له وأعدّ فهارسه الدكتور وسام كبكب، ط٢، جونيه لبنان: منشورات المكتبة البولسيّة ٢٠٠٥، ٤٣، ٧٧.

٩٧ ابن كثير، بداية، ج١٤، ٣١٥، ابن قاضي شهبة، تاريخ، مج٣، ج٢، ٢٧١، ٢٧٢.

ثمّ ورد مرسوم سلطانيّ في أوائل ربيع الآخر/كانون الأوّل بإرجاع كلّ ما أُخِذ من النساء المسيحيّات مع الجباية «وإن كان الجميع ظلمًا (كذا)، ولكنّ الأخذ من النساء أفحش وأبلغ في الظلم...[٩٨]».

ووصل من مصر إلى دمشق السنة **١٤٨٩/٨٩٥** خاصكيّ يحمل مرسومًا بمصادرة أهل الذمّة، فصادرهم. ثمّ عاد إلى القاهرة التي كانت تستعدّ لإرسال حملة ضدّ العثمانيّين أنفق فيها السلطان الأشرف قايتباي على الأمراء والجنود نحو خمس مئة ألف دينار[٩٩].

ووردت أحيانًا مراسيم سلطانيّة تطالب بعدم الإجحاف في جباية الضرائب والإعفاء من بعض الغرامات والموجبات[١٠٠] منها مثلاً إبطال عمر السفّاح صاحب ديوان الإنشاء الشريف في حلب أخذ موجب ما يجلبه مسيحيّو قارا من القماش والثمار السنة ١٤٤٢/٨٤٦.[١٠١] وقضى مرسوم صادر السنة ١٤٦٠/٨٦٤ بإعفاء المسلمين وأهل الذمّة من مشاهرة الحسبة، ومشاهرة الدباغة التي برسم البشمقداريّة. ومرسوم أخر يعفي الحدّادين والمسيحيّين من طرح الفولاذ[١٠٢].

هـ) استخدام المسيحيّين في وظائف السلطنة:

يجوز اشتراك الذمّيّين في تحمّل أعباء الدولة وإسناد الوظائف العامّة إليهم التي هي دون البطانة في المركز والأهمّيّة، ما داموا ثقة أكفّاء. وقد دلّ على ذلك الكتاب والسنّة[١٠٣].

وعمل المسيحيّون في الوظائف الإداريّة كالدواوين والمباشرات والجهات والأعمال كما يتبيّن عبر المراسيم الصادرة في السنوات **١٢٩٠/٦٨٩** و**١٣٠١/٧٠٠** و**١٣٥٤/٧٥٥** و**١٣٥٦/٧٥٧** **١٣٥٩–١٣٦٠** و**١٣٦٣/٧٦٥**. فقد طالبت تلك المراسيم بمنع استخدام أهل الذمّة في الوظائف، ووضع بعضها الإسلام شرطًا لقبولهم،

---

٩٨ ابن كثير، بداية، ج١٤، ٣١٧.

٩٩ ابن طولون، مفاكهة، ط. القاهرة، ج١، ١٢٨، ١٣٠، ابن إياس، بدائع الزهور، ج٣، الهيئة المصريّة العامّة للكتاب، القاهرة: ١٤٠٤هـ/١٩٨٤م، ٢٧٠.

١٠٠ ابن طولون، مفاكهة، ط. القاهرة، ج١، ١٩٨.

١٠١ شعث، حلب، ٨٨.

١٠٢ Jean Sauvaget, "Décrets Mamlouks de Syrie", *Bulletin D'Études Orientales*, T II, Fascicule I, (1932), 41–42, 51.

١٠٣ يموت، أهل الذمّة، ١٠٤–١٠٧.

فأسلم عدد منهم طوعًا وكرهًا كما حدث السنة ١٣٥٤/٧٥٥[١٠٤].

وقرئ في دمشق السنة ٧٠٧/١٣٠٧–١٣٠٨ مرسوم يدعو إلى محاربة المغول والكتّاب المسيحيّين[١٠٥].

ولم تستطع السلطنة الاستغناء عنهم بعد أن أصبحت الحاجة ماسّة إلى وجودهم في الدواوين[١٠٦]، رغم المحاولات التي قادها ضدّهم القضاة والفقهاء المسلمون، كابن النقّاش في «المذمّة في استعمال الذمّة»، والأسنويّ في «الكلمات المهمّة في مباشرة أهل الذمّة[١٠٧]».

ومن الأسماء التي زوّدتنا بها المصادر في القرنين ٨ و ١٤/٩ و ١٥، الرشيد سلامة كاتب سنجر البشمقدار، والمكين يوسف بن يحيى عامل الجيش، والمكين جرجس بن أبي الكرم كاتب الحوطات، والمكين يوسف كاتب بهادر آص، والعلم عامل بيروت[١٠٨] وبدر ابن القسّيس النفيس القبطيّ كاتب الأمير سيف الدين كجكل[١٠٩] وموسى بن سمعان النصرانيّ الكركيّ كاتب الأمير سيف الدين قطلوبك الجاشنكير[١١٠] وكاتب مسيحيّ كان يعمل في خدمة القاضي الشافعيّ في دمشق السنة ١٤٨٧/٨٩٢[١١١].

استخدام المسيحيّين في الدواوين وفي غيرها من الوظائف يعني أنّهم كانوا أصحاب خبرة وكفاية، ودليل على مشاركتهم إلى حدٍّ ما في حياة البلاد السياسيّة، وتهيئة سبيل

---

١٠٤ مؤرّخ مجهول، تاريخ، ٥٣٠، ابن الحريريّ، **منتخب**، ج٢، ٣٧٧–٣٧٨، بيبرس المنصوريّ، مختار، ١١٦–١١٧، أبو الفداء، مختصر، ج٢، ٣٨٥، النويريّ، نهاية، ج٣١، ١٧١، ٤١٧–٤١٨، ابن الوردي، تاريخ، ج٢، ٢٤٢، الصفدي، صفيّ الدين الحلّيّ، تحقيق عدنان درويش، ط١، دمشق: منشورات وزارة الثقافة ١٩٩٥، ١٢٦، ابن كثير، بداية، ج١٤، ١٦، ٢٥٠، ٣٠٥–٣٠٦، ابن حبيب، تذكرة، ج١، ٢٣٣، ابن دقماق، جوهر، ج٢، ٢٠٤–٢٠٥، ابن الشحنة، روض، ٢٨٤، القلقشندي، صبح، ج١٣، ٢١–٢٣، ٣٧٧، ابن قاضي شهبة، تاريخ، مج٢، ج١، ١٨٥–١٨٦، مج ٣، ج٢، ٤٨، ٦٠–٦١، ٩٧، ٢٤٣، ٢٨٢، ابن سباط، صدق، ج٢، ٦٦١، ٧١١، الدويهي، تاريخ، ٣١٨–٣١٩، ٣٧٩.

١٠٥ Perlman, "Notes", 843, note 3.

١٠٦ العينيّ، عقد الجمان في تاريخ أهل الزمان، ج٣، حقّقه ووضع حواشيه محمّد محمّد أمين، القاهرة: الهيئة المصريّة العامّة للكتاب ١٤١٠هـ/١٩٩٠م، ١٨٣.

١٠٧ عن الأسنوي أنظر Perlman, "Notes", 843–861, Ibid, "Asnawi's Tract Against Christian Officials", in *Ignaz Goldziher Memorial Volume*, eds. S. Löwinger and J. Somogy, Budapest: 1948–1958, vol. II, 172–208.

١٠٨ الشجاعيّ، تاريخ، ٧٥، البصروي، تاريخ، ٨٩.

١٠٩ الجزريّ، حوادث، ١١٤.

١١٠ النويريّ، نهاية الأرب في فنون الأدب، ج٣٢، تحقيق فهيم محمّد علي شلتوت، مراجعة عبد العزيز الأهواني وسعيد عبد الفتّاح عاشور، القاهرة: مطبعة دار الكتب المصريّة ١٩٩٨، ٢١٥، ابن حجر، إنباء، ج٢، ١٣٩.

١١١ ابن طوق، التعليق، ج٢، ٦٨٢–٦٨٣.

التمتّع بقوّة مميّزة دفعت عنهم خطر العزل الذي كثيرًا ما كان يتهدّد مصيرهم. كما أنّه دليل على أنّهم كانوا طبقة متعلّمة، وإن كانت المصادر تغفل ذكر المدارس التي تعلّموا فيها. لكن من المؤكّد أنّهم لم يعدموا أيّة طريقة لتحصيله. ومن الأمثلة على ذلك أنّه في بدء العصر المملوكيّ كان يعيش في دمشق نحويّ لغوّي ضرير يدعى ابن نجا (توفّي السنة ١٢٦٢/٦٦٠) كان متبحّرًا في علوم كثيرة، وكان يجتمع في بيته السنة والشيعة والمسيحيّون واليهود والسامريّون ليدرسوا علم الأوائل (علوم الإغريق)[١١٢].

٣. على الصعيد القضائيّ:

كان المسيحيّون يلجأون إلى المحاكم الكنسيّة في القضايا الدينيّة. وتورد المصادر الإسلاميّة أنّ المطران هو القاضي الذي كان يفصل في الخصومات بينهم[١١٣] ولكن يتبيّن في نسخة التوقيع للبطريرك من قبل السلطان أنّ هذا الأخير كان يطلب إليه أن يحكم بين أبناء رعاياه «بمقتضى مذهبه... ويفصل بينهم بحكم مذهبه في موارثهم وأنكحتهم...» وأن يقدّم المصالحة بين المتحاكمين إليه قبل الفصل في القضايا[١١٤].

كذلك لجأ المسلمون إلى رجال الدين المسيحيّين في خلافاتهم مع المسيحيّين. فقد لام ابن فطين شيخ سوق الجوخيّين والخلعيّين بائع جوخ مسيحيًّا لأنّه خدعه في البيع السنة ١٤٨٨/٨٩٤، ثمّ شكاه إلى «كنز» رئيس الطائفة أي البطريرك[١١٥] ولكنّ المماليك تولّوا في بعض الحالات معاقبة المتّهمين المسيحيّين من دون محاكمة وبغياب القضاة. منها قطع قجماس نائب دمشق رأس مسيحيّ مع ستّة متّهمين السنة ١٤٨٥/٨٩٠، وعدم الرأفة به حتّى بعد أن أشهر إسلامه[١١٦] كذلك أمر نائب دمشق قانصوه اليحياويّ بتوسيط اللحّام إسحق السنة ١٤٩٣/٨٩٩ لأنّه قتل زوجته بعد أن فرضت عليه دراهم[١١٧].

أمّا معظم المسيحيّين الذين مثلوا أمام القضاة فكانوا إمّا قد ارتدّوا بعدما اعتنقوا الإسلام وإمّا خالفوا الشريعة الإسلاميّة أو أحد الشروط العمريّة. وتورد المصادر العديد من الحالات. منها ارتداد توما بن عبد الله في دمشق السنة ١٣٢٦/٧٢٦، بعد إسلامه

---

١١٢ الكتبيّ، فوات الوفيّات، ج١، بولاق، ١٢٩٩هـ، ١٣٤–١٣٥، ابن كثير، بداية، ج١٣، ٢٣٥، E. Strauss, "L'inquisition dans l'Etat Mamlouk", *Revista degli Studia Orientalia*, Vol. XXV, (1950) 11–12.

١١٣ القلقشنديّ، صبح، ج٥، ٤٤٤، الخالدي، المقصد، ٢٦٦، زيادة، دمشق، ١٥٦.

١١٤ القلقشنديّ، صبح، ج١٢، ٤٢٣، ٤٢٥.

١١٥ ابن طولون، مفاكهة، ط. القاهرة، ج١، ١٠٠.

١١٦ ابن طوق، التعليق، ج١، ٤٥٣–٤٥٤.

١١٧ ابن طولون، مفاكهة، ط. القاهرة، ج١، ١٥٣.

على يدي الشيخ ابن تيميّة، ومجاورته بالمئذنة الشرقيّة في جامع دمشق، وقوله إنّ القرآن ثلثه من التوراة وثلثه من الإنجيل. وحين قامت البيّنة عليه بذلك عند قاضي القضاة شرف الدين المالكيّ، حكم بإراقة دمه وقتله، فقُطِع رأسه. وحكم القاضي ذاته السنة ١٣٣٠/٧٣٠ بإراقة دم مسيحيّ كان قد أسلم ثمّ ارتدّ، فضُرِبتْ عنقُه بسوق الخيل، ثمّ أحرقه العامّة حتّى صار رمادًا، وذرّوه في نهر بردى[١١٨].

وحكم قاضي القضاة جمال الدين المالكيّ في دمشق السنة ١٣١٤/٧١٤ بقتل موسى بن سمعان الكركيّ كاتب الأمير سيف الدين قطلوبك الجاشنكير إذ تجرّأ على رسول الله، بعدما استمال رجلاً مسلمًا من ضعفاء العقول والقلوب ونصّره ووشم على يده صليبًا[١١٩].

وسُجِن الرحّالة دي لا بروكيير في دمشق السنة ١٤٣٢ بأمر من القاضي بعدما أُلقي القبض عليه بتهمة أنّه سقى أحد العرب خمرًا[١٢٠].

وكان بعض المرتدّين يتوجّهون بأذاتهم إلى المسؤولين ليعلنوا لهم أنّهم مذنبون بسبب ارتدادهم عن الإسلام. ولا نعلم إن كان دافعهم السعي وراء هالة الشهادة. منهم مسيحيّ حضر أمام القاضي الشافعيّ في دمشق السنة ١٣٨٣/٧٨٥ واعترف له بأنّه أسلم ثمّ ارتدّ، وطلب إليه أن يضرب عنقه، فهمّ بذلك. ولكنّه تاب وأسلم، فأطلق سراحه. ثمّ ارتدّ ثانية، فحكم القاضي المالكيّ بضرب عنقه[١٢١].

ولمّا كان المسلمون يكرّمون أنبياء العهد القديم، فقد عوقب كلّ من أساء بحقّهم. ويورد ابن حجر أنّ مسيحيًّا «وقع في حقّ داود عليه السلام» السنة ١٤٣٢/٨٣٥، فأودع السجن مدّة ليعتنق الدين الإسلاميّ، ولكنّه رفض، فقُتِل[١٢٢].

ولكن في بعض المحاكمات أنصف القضاةُ المسيحيّين، وأعادوا إليهم حقوقهم وعاقبوا المعتدين عليهم[١٢٣] وتمّت تبرئة المتّهمين، منهم مثلاً كاتب كان يعمل في خدمة القاضي

---

١١٨ النويريّ، نهاية الأرب في فنون الأدب، ج٣٣، تحقيق مصطفى حجازي ومحمّد مصطفى زيادة، القاهرة: مطبعة دار الكتب المصريّة ١٩٩٧، ٢١٠–٢١١، ٣١٣، ابن الجزري، حوادث، ج٢، ١٠٨، ٤٠٠، الذهبي، دول، ٤١٧، ابن الوردي، تاريخ، ج٢، ٢٧٠، ابن طولون، مفاكهة، ط. القاهرة، ج١، ١٥٣.

١١٩ ابن حجر، إنباء، ج٢، ١٣٩، Strauss, “L’Inquisition”, 21–22.

١٢٠ زايد، «رحلة»، ٣٢٦.

١٢١ ابن حجر، إنباء، ج٤، ٤، ج٨، ٢٥٨، ابن إياس، بدائع الزهور، ج١، ق٢، حقّقها وكتب لها المقدِّمة محمّد مصطفى، فيسبادن: فرانز شتاينر ١٣٩٤هـ/١٩٧٤م، ٣٢٨.

١٢٢ ابن حجر، إنباء، ج٦، ١٧٢.

١٢٣ النويريّ، نهاية، ج٣٣، ٢٨٥.

الشافعيّ في دمشق السنة ١٤٨٧/٨٩٢، بعد ادّعاء رفعه ضدّه جلال الدين بن الطّماجي متّهمًا إيّاه بأنّه صدم والده بدابّة فمات. ثمّ ثبت في مجلس الشهود أنّ المسيحيّ لا يستحقّ حقًّا ولا ديّة ولا قصاصًا ولا إرثًا ولا عمدًا ولا شبهًا ولا حقًّا من سائر الحقوق الشرعيّة، وذلك بعد ورود مرسوم شريف بذلك. وثُبّتت البراءة في بيت القاضي المالكيّ[١٢٤].

لم توجد في السلطنة المملوكيّة محاكم خاصّة تنظر في القضايا المعادية للدين. ولكن ما يمكن ملاحظته أنّ معظم القضايا المتعلّقة بهذه النقطة كانت في أغلب الأحيان تُرفع إلى قضاة المذهب المالكيّ نظرًا إلى خطورة الاتّهمات الدينيّة. وكان القضاة الملكيّون متشدّدين ويطلقون أحكامًا قاسية. كما يتبيّن من الحالات التي أوردناها. ويمكن أن نعزو الأمر إلى أنّ التصرّف بقساوة حيال القضايا المتعلّقة بالدين كان مطلوبًا. ففي حالة المساس بشخصيّة الرسول مثلا يفرض القضاء المالكيّ عدم الأخذ بمبدأ التوبة على عكس ما تتّجه إليه بقيّة المذاهب الأخرى.

وكانت أحكام القضاة تُنفَّذ مباشرة ومن دون أيّ تأخير، ولم يُمنَح المتَّهم فرصة الاستئناف إذا جاز التعبير.

٤. على الصعيد الاقتصاديّ:

امتلك المسيحيّون في دمشق مخازن ومحالّ كثيرة غصّت بالملابس والحرير والسُّنْدُس أو الأطلس Satin والمخمل والأواني النحاسيّة والبضائع المطلوبة كلّها[١٢٥] وكانت لهم حوانيت في جوار خان السلطان تجاه سوق النقليّة من جهة الفواخرة، في سوق جقمق داخل باب الجابية، وفي سوق البزوريّة، تعرّضت للسرقة في بعض الأحيان[١٢٦].

وانطلاقًا من علاقات المسيحيّين بالسلطنة والمجتمع الإسلاميّين، فقد كانوا أحرارًا في ممارسة جميع المهن والحِرَف، فكان منهم البنّاء، والقشّاط، والفعَلَة، والفلاّح، والحدّاد، والجرائحيّ، واللحّام أو الجزّار وبائع الجوخ[١٢٧] وعملوا في بعض المهن جنبًا إلى جنب مع المسلمين، كما عملوا لدى المسلمين وتقاضوا بدل أتعابهم. منهم مثلا صدقة بن نصر الله فلاح المؤرّخ ابن طوق[١٢٨].

---

١٢٤ ابن طوق، التعليق، ج٢، ٦٨٢–٦٨٣.

١٢٥ دي فارتيما، رحلات، ٣٢.

١٢٦ ابن طوق، التعليق، ج١، ٤٨، ٤٧٠، ابن طولون، مفاكهة، ط. دار الكتب العلميّة، ج١، ٣٥، ٥٩.

١٢٧ ابن طوق، التعليق، ج١، ٥٠، ٨٨، ٣٥٤، ج٢، ٨٩٣، ابن طولون، مفاكهة، ط. القاهرة، ج١، ١٠٠، ١٥٣، Sauvaget, “Décrets”, T II, Fasc. I, 51.

١٢٨ ابن أبي الفضائل، نهج، نشر كورتنتمر، ٨٤، ابن طوق، التعليق، ج١، ٥٠، ٨٨.

حرّيّة ممارسة المهن والحِرف كانت مفيدة جدًّا سواء بالنسبة إلى السلطنة المملوكيّة أو المجتمع، وخصوصًا أنّها كانت تتيح للمسيحيّ التمكّن من دفع الضريبة المتوجّبة عليه لخزينة السلطنة ليستمرّ في الحصول على حقّ ممارسة حقوقه.

خاتمة:

بعد هذا العرض السريع لأوضاع المسيحيّين في دمشق وحلب، يتبيّن أنّ الشروط العمريّة هي الإطار الذي حدّد طبيعة وجودهم وعلاقاتهم بالمجتمع. وما إصدار المراسيم المتكرّر للمطالبة بتنفيذها إلاّ للتذكير بضرورة التزامها، وإن اختلفت الظروف التي حتّمت إصدارها.

أصبحت تلك الشروط مصدرًا دائمًا للإجراءات التعسّفيّة التي تطلّ كلّما ظهرت أسباب تدعو إلى ذلك. كما استُعمِلت كمبرّر قانونيّ لمبادرات الحكّام في هذا المجال. ولكنّ اللجوء إلى تطبيق مضمونها كان يقتصر على فترات الاضطهاد القليلة المتباعدة في الزمن والقصيرة في المدّة. وكان الرجوع السريع عن الإجراءات التعسّفيّة وعدم امتدادها في الزمن يعودان إلى اعتبارات متعدِّدة كانت تؤدّي دورًا معاكسًا فتنتزع من الإجراءات التعسّفيّة قوّتها التنفيذيّة بعد مدّة قليلة من بدئها. ويمكن ملاحظة ذلك في موضوع عزل الموظّفين من أهل الذمّة، إذ كانت تُتَّخذ إجراءات متتالية في هذا المجال يبدو أنّها لم تكن تعرف سبيلاً إلى التنفيذ.

ولكنّ الشروط العمريّة لم تحل دون انخراط المسيحيّين في المجتمع رغم التزامهم تطبيقها. فقد كانوا جزءًا لا يتجزّأ منه يتفاعلون معه ويؤثّرون فيه ويتأثّرون به، وإن كانوا يتمتّعون بحرّيّة مقيّدة أو محدودة. ولكن من جهة أخرى فإنّ أيّ حرّيّة لن تكون فعّالة من دون المشاركة في النظام السياسيّ. وكان المسيحيّون مستبعدين عن هذه المشاركة تمامًا، ولو أنّ بعضهم قد وصل إلى مراكز إداريّة في السلطنة.

وقد حافظ المسيحيّون على حقوقهم العامّة من طريق دفع الجزية والخضوع للسلطات الإسلاميّة. وأنصفهم القضاء في قضايا حاول بعضهم استغلالها ضدّهم.

ولكن يبقى أنّ الحكم النهائيّ على أوضاع المسيحيّين في دمشق وحلب مرتبط بدراسة شاملة لأوضاعهم في بلاد الشام ومقارنتها بأوضاعهم في مصر طوال العصر المملوكيّ، ثمّ بأوضاعهم في العصر الأيّوبيّ. على أمل أن تتمكّن البحوث المستقبليّة من توضيح هذه النقطة.

لائحة المصادر والمراجع

المصادر:

- ابن أبي الفضائل، المفضّل، **النهج السديد والدرّ الفريد فيما بعد تاريخ ابن العميد الفترة بين سنتي ٧١٧ و٧٤١ هجريّة**، نشرته Samira Kortantamer, *Ägypten und Syrien zwischen 1317 und 1341 in der Chronik des Mufaddal b. Abi L-Fada'il*, Freiburg im Breisgau: 1975
- ابن الأخوّة، **معالم القربة في أحكام الحسبة**، تحقيق محمود شعبان، القاهرة، ١٩٧٦
- ابن إيّاس، **بدائع الزهور في وقائع الدهور**، ج١، ق٢، حقّقها وكتب لها المقدِّمة محمّد مصطفى، فرانز شتاينر فيسبادن، ١٣٩٤هـ/١٩٧٤م، ج٣، الهيئة المصريّة العامّة للكتاب، القاهرة ١٤٠٤هـ/١٩٨٤م
- ابن بسّام، **نهاية الرتبة في طلب الحسبة**، تحقيق حسام الدين السامرّائي، بغداد، ١٩٦٨
- ابن بطّوطة، **رحلة ابن بطّوطة المسمّاة تحفة النظّار في غرائب الأمصار وعجائب الأسفار**، ج١، إعتنى به وراجعه د. درويش الجويدي، المكتبة العصريّة، صيدا بيروت ١٤٢٤هـ/٢٠٠٣م
- ابن الجزري، **تاريخ حوادث الزمان وأنبائه ووفيّات الأكابر والأعيان من أبنائه**، الجزءان ١و٢، تحقيق د.عمر عبد السلام تدمريّ، ط١، المكتبة العصريّة، صيدا بيروت ١٤١٩هـ/١٩٩٨م

حوادث الفترة بين ٦٨٢ و٦٨٧ هجريّة كما دوّنها شمس الدين محمّد بن ابراهيم الجزري في كتابه (حوادث الزمان) وأبو بكر بن عبد الله بن أيبك الدواداريّ في كتابه (كنز الدرر وجامع الغرر)، نشرهما وعلّق عليهما أولرخ هارمن، فرايبرج ١٩٦٩

- ابن حبيب الحلبيّ، **تذكرة النبيه في أيّام المنصور وبنيه**، ج١، حوادث وتراجم (٦٧٨–٧٠٨هـ/١٢٧٩–١٣٠٨م) مع نشر وتحقيق وثائق وقف السلطان قلاوون، حقّقه ووضع حواشيه د. محمّد محمّد أمين، راجعه وقدّم له د. سعيد عبد الفتّاح عاشور، الهيئة المصريّة العامّة للكتاب، القاهرة ١٩٧٦

- ابن حجر، **إنباء الغمر بأبناء العمر في التاريخ**، الأجزاء ٢، ٤، ٦، ٧، ٨، ط.٢، دار الكتب العلميّة، بيروت ١٤٠٦هـ/١٩٨٦م
- **الدرر الكامنة في أعيان المائة الثامنة**، ج٤، ضبطه وصحّحه الشيخ عبد الوارث محمّد علي، ط١، دار الكتب العلميّة، بيروت ١٤١٨هـ/١٩٩٧م
- ابن الحريريّ، **كتاب منتخب الزمان في تاريخ الخلفاء والعلماء والأعيان**، ج٢، حقّقه عن نسخة يتيمة وعلّق عليه عبده خليفة، ط١، دار عشتار، بيروت، ١٩٩٥
- ابن دقماق، **الجوهر الثمين في سير الملوك والسلاطين**، تحقيق محمّد كمال عزّ الدين علي، ج٢، منشورات عالم الكتب، بيروت ١٩٨٣

النفحة المسكيّة في الدولة التركيّة من كتاب الجوهر الثمين في سير الخلفاء والسلاطين، تحقيق أستاذ دكتور عمر عبد السلام تدمريّ، ط١، المكتبة العصريّة، صيدا بيروت ١٤٢٠هـ/١٩٩٩م

- ابن سباط، **صدق الأخبار تاريخ ابن سباط**، جزءان، عني به وحقّقه الدكتور عمر عبد السلام تدمري، ط١، جرّوس برسّ، طرابلس لبنان ١٤١٣هـ/١٩٩٣م
- ابن الشحنة، محمّد، **الدرّ المنتخب في تاريخ حلب**، وقف على طبعه وعلّق حواشيه يوسف بن إليان سركيس الدمشقيّ، بيروت في المطبعة الكاثوليكيّة للآباء اليسوعيّين، بيروت، ١٩٠٩
- ابن الشحنة، محبّ الدين أبو الوليد، **روض المناظر في علم الأوائل والأواخر**، تحقيق سيّد محمّد مهنّى، ط١، دار الكتب العلميّة، بيروت ١٤١٧هـ/ ١٩٩٧م
- ابن شدّاد، **تاريخ الملك الظاهر**، باعتناء أحمد حطيط، النشرات الإسلاميّة ٣١، فرانز شتاينر بفيسبادن، ١٤٠٣هـ/١٩٨٣
- ابن طوق، **التعليق يوميّات شهاب الدين أحمد بن طوق مذكّرات كتبت بدمشق في أواخر العهد المملوكيّ ٨٨٥–٩٠٨هـ/١٤٨٠–١٥٠٢م**، جزءان، تحقيق الشيخ جعفر المهاجر، المعهد الفرنسيّ للدراسات العربيّة بدمشق، دمشق ٢٠٠٠–٢٠٠٢
- ابن طولون، **مفاكهة الخلاّن في حوادث الزمان**، نشره محمّد مصطفى، جزءان، القاهرة ١٩٦٢–١٩٦٤، وطبعة دار الكتب العلميّة، ق١، وضع حواشيه خليل المنصور، بيروت ١٤١٨هـ/١٩٩٨م

إعلام الورى بمن ولي نائبًا من الأتراك بدمشق الشام الكبرى، تحقيق محمّد أحمد دهمان، ط٢، دار الفكر، دمشق ١٤٠٤هـ/١٩٨٤م

- ابن عبد الظاهر، **الروض الزاهر في سيرة الملك الظاهر**، تحقيق ونشر عبد العزيز خويطر، ط١، الرياض ١٣٩٦هـ/١٩٧٦م

- ابن العبريّ، **تاريخ الزمان**، نقله إلى العربيّة الأب إسحق أرملة، قدّم له الأب الدكتور جان موريس فييه، دار المشرق، بيروت ١٩٨٦
- **التاريخ الكنسيّ**، ج١وج٢، نشره أبيلوس ولامي، لوفان ١٨٧٢–١٨٧٧
- ابن عربشاه، **عجائب المقدور في نوائب تيمور**، تحقيق أحمد فايز الحمصي، ط١، مؤسّسة الرسالة، بيروت ١٩٨٦
- ابن فضل الله العمري، **التعريف بالمصطلح الشريف**، دراسة وتحقيق د. سمير الدروبي، ط١، منشورات جامعة مؤتة، الكرك ١٤١٣هـ/ ١٩٩٢م
- ابن قاضي شهبة، **تاريخ ابن قاضي شهبة**، أربعة مجلّدات، حقّقه عدنان درويش، المعهد العلميّ الفرنسيّ للدراسات العربيّة بدمشق، دمشق ١٩٧٧–١٩٩٧
- ابن كثير، **البداية والنهاية**، ج١٣و١٤، منشورات مكتبة المعارف، ط٧، بيروت ١٤٠٨هـ/١٩٨٨م
- ابن مماتي، **كتاب قوانين الدواوين**، جمعه وحقّقه عزيز سوريال عطيّة، ط١، مكتبة مدبولي، القاهرة ١٤١١هـ/١٩٩١م
- ابن الورديّ، **تاريخ ابن الورديّ**، ج٢، دار الكتب العلميّة، ط١، بيروت ١٩٩٦
- أبو الفداء، **المختصر في أخبار البشر**، ج٢، علّق عليه ووضع حواشيه محمود ديّوب، ط١، دار الكتب العلميّة، بيروت ١٩٩٧
- البصرويّ، **تاريخ البصروي صفحات مجهولة من تاريخ دمشق في عصر المماليك من السنة ٨٧١هـ لغاية ٩٠٤هـ**، تحقيق ودراسة أكرم حسن العلبي، ط١، دار المأمون للتراث، دمشق ١٩٨٨
- بيبرس المنصوريّ، **مختار الأخبار تاريخ الدولة الأيّوبيّة ودولة المماليك البحريّة حتّى السنة ٧٠٢هـ**، حقّقه وقدّم له ووضع فهارسه د. عبد الحميد صالح حمدان، ط١، الدار المصريّة اللبنانيّة، القاهرة ١٤١٣هـ/١٩٩٣م
- الدويهيّ، البطريرك إسطفان، **تاريخ الأزمنة**، نظر فيها وحقّقها الأباتي بطرس فهد، ط٣، دار لحد خاطر، بيروت، لا.ت
- دي فارتيما، لودوفيكو، **رحلات فارتيما (الحاجّ يونس المصريّ)**، ترجمة وتعليق د. عبد الرحمن عبد الله الشيخ، الهيئة المصريّة العامّة للكتاب، القاهرة ١٩٩٤
- الذهبيّ، **دول الإسلام**، منشورات مؤسّسة الأعلمي للمطبوعات، بيروت ١٤٠٥هـ/ ١٩٨٥م
- السيوطيّ، **تاريخ الخلفاء**، تحقيق محمّد يحيى الدين، ط٣، القاهرة، ١٩٦٤

- شحاده، خليل، **تحقيق كتاب المقصد الرفيع المنشا الهادي إلى صناعة الإنشا**، أطروحة دكتوراه غير منشورة، جامعة القدّيس يوسف، بيروت، ١٩٨٨
- شيخ الربوة الدمشقيّ، **كتاب نخبة الدهر في عجائب البرّ والبحر**، نشره مهرن، لايبزغ ١٩٢٣
- شمس الدين الشجاعيّ، **تاريخ الملك الناصر محمّد بن قلاوون الصالحيّ وأولاده**، حقّقته وترجمته إلى الألمانيّة بربارة شيفر، القسم الأوّل، النصّ العربيّ، فرانز شتاينر فيسبادن ١٣٩٨هـ/١٩٧٨م
- الشيزريّ، **كتاب نهاية الرتبة في طلب الحسبة**، تحقيق ومراجعة د. السيّد الباز العريني، ط٢، دار الثقافة، بيروت ١٤٠١هـ/١٩٨١م
- الصفديّ، **صفيّ الدين الحلّيّ**، تحقيق د.عدنان درويش، ط١، منشورات وزارة الثقافة، دمشق ١٩٩٥
- العبّاسيّ الصفديّ، **نزهة المالك والمملوك في مختصر سيرة من ولِّي مصر من الملوك**، تحقيق الدكتور عمر عبد السلام تدمري، ط١، المكتبة العصريّة، صيدا بيروت ١٤٢٤هـ/٢٠٠١م
- العينيّ، **عقد الجمان في تاريخ أهل الزمان عصر سلاطين المماليك (١) حوادث وتراجم ٦٤٨–٦٦٤هـ/١٢٥٠–١٢٦٥م**، حقّقه ووضع حواشيه الدكتور محمّد محمّد أمين، الهيئة المصريّة العامّة للكتاب، القاهرة ١٤٠٧هـ–١٩٨٧م، **(٣) حوادث وتراجم ٦٨٩–٦٩٨هـ/١٢٩٠–١٢٩٨م**، حقّقه ووضع حواشيه د. محمّد محمّد أمين، الهيئة المصريّة العامّة للكتاب، القاهرة، ١٤١٠هـ/١٩٩٠م، **الحوادث والتراجم من السنة ٨١٥هـ إلى السنة ٨٢٤هـ**، نشره د. عبد الرازق الطنطاوي القرموط، ط١، لا دار نشر، ١٤٠٦هـ/١٩٨٥م
- القلقشنديّ، **صبح الأعشى في صناعة الإنشا**، الأجزاء ٢، ٣، ٥، ٦، ١٢، ١٣، شرحه وعلّق عليه وقابل نصوصه محمّد حسين شمس الدين، دار الفكر، بيروت، لا.ت.
- الكتبيّ، **فوات الوفيّات**، ج١، بولاق ١٢٩٩هـ
- الماورديّ، **الأحكام السلطانيّة والولايات الدينيّة**، دار الكتب العلميّة، بيروت، لا. ت.
- مؤرّخ مجهول، **تاريخ المسلمين**، مخطوط في المكتبة الشرقية ببيروت، رقم ٧٦
- النويريّ، **نهاية الأرب في فنون الأدب**، ج٣٠، تحقيق د. محمّد عبد الهادي شعيرة، مراجعة د. محمّد مصطفى زيادة، الهيئة المصريّة العامّة للكتاب، القاهرة ١٤١٠هـ/

١٩٩٠م، ج**٣١**، تحقيق د. الباز العريني، مراجعة د. عبد العزيز الأهوانيّ، الهيئة المصريّة العامّة للكتاب، القاهرة **١٤١٢**هـ/**١٩٩٢**م، ج**٣٢**، تحقيق فهيم محمّد علوي شلتوت، مراجعة د. عبد العزيز الأهوانيّ ود. سعيد عبد الفتّاح عاشور، مطبعة دار الكتب المصريّة بالقاهرة، **١٩٩٨**، ج**٣٣**، تحقيق مصطفى حجازي ومحمّد مصطفى زيادة، مطبعة دار الكتب المصريّة بالقاهرة، **١٩٩٧**

- اليونينيّ، **ذيل مرآة الزمان**، مج٣، (من وقائع السنة ٦٧١ إلى السنة ٦٧٧ هجريّة)، الطبعة الأولى، مطبعة مجلس دائرة المعارف العثمانيّة، حيدر آباد الدكن الهند ١٣٨٠هـ/١٩٦٠م

المراجع:

- باشا، قسطنطين المخلّصيّ، **لمحة تاريخيّة في الرهبانيّة الباسيليّة المخلّصيّة**، ق١، المطبعة الأدبيّة، بيروت **١٩٠٣**
- حجّار، عبد الله، **معالم حلب الأثريّة**، طبعة ثانية مزيدة ومنقّحة، مطابع مؤسّسة جورج ومتيلد سالم الخيريّة، حلب **١٩٩٧**
- ديك، الأرشمندريت إغناطيوس، **الحضور المسيحيّ في حلب خلال الألفين المنصرمين**، ج١، من نشأة المسيحيّة إلى الفتح العثمانيّ، حلب **٢٠٠٢**
- الزيّات، حبيب، **سمات «أهل الكتاب» في المصنّفات العربيّة**، إعداد وتحقيق الدكتور يوسف قزما الخوري، ط١، دار الحمراء، بيروت **١٩٩٢**
- **الصليب في الإسلام**، قدّم له وأعدّ فهارسه الدكتور وسام كبكب، ط٢، منشورات المكتبة البولسيّة، جونيه لبنان **٢٠٠٥**
- زيادة، نقولا، **دمشق في عصر المماليك**، مكتبة لبنان، بيروت **١٩٦٦**
- الزين، حسن، **الأوضاع القانونيّة للنصارى واليهود في الديار الإسلاميّة حتّى الفتح العثمانيّ**، دار الفكر الحديث، بيروت **١٩٨٨**
- شعث، شوقي، **حلب تاريخها ومعالمها التاريخيّة**، طبعة ثانية مزيدة، منشورات جامعة حلب ١٤١١هـ/١٩٩١م
- الشمّاس، يوسف المخلّصيّ، **خلاصة تاريخ الكنيسة الملكيّة**، راجعه وزاد عليه الأب إلياس كويتر المخلّصيّ، المطبعة البولسيّة، جونيه لبنان **٢٠٠٢**
- العظمة، عزيز، **ابن تيميّة**، ط١، رياض الريّس للكتب والنشر، بيروت **٢٠٠٠**

- العلبي، أكرم، **دمشق بين عصر المماليك والعثمانيّين ٩٠٦-٩٢٦هـ/١٥٠٠-١٥٢٠م** (لا كما ورد خطأ ٩٠٦-٩٢٢/١٥٠٠-١٥٢٠)، ط١، الشركة المتّحدة للتوزيع، دمشق ١٩٨٢
- القطّار، إلياس، **نيابة طرابلس في عهد المماليك (٦٨٨-٩٢٢هـ/١٢٨٩-١٥١٦م)**، منشورات الجامعة اللبنانيّة قسم الدراسات التاريخيّة ٤٣، بيروت ١٩٩٨
- لابيدوس، إيرا مارفين، **مدن الشام في العصر المملوكيّ**، نقله إلى العربيّة وقدّم له الدكتو سهيل زكّار، ط١، دار حسّان للطباعة والنشر، دمشق ١٤٠٥هـ/ ١٩٨٥م
- نعيسة، يوسف، **مجتمع مدينة دمشق ١١٨٦-١٢٥٦هـ/١٧٧٢-١٨٤٠م**، ج١، دار طلاس، ط١، دمشق ١٩٨٦
- يتيم، المطران ميشيل، وديك، الأرشمندريت إغناطيوس، **تاريخ الكنيسة الشرقيّة**، ط٢، منشورات المكتبة البولسيّة، بيروت جونيه ١٩٩٩
- يمّوت، شفيق، **أهل الذمّة في مختلف أطوارهم وعصورهم**، ط١، الشركة العالميّة للكتاب، بيروت، ١٩٩١

المقالات:

- أرملة، إسحق، «الملكيّون، بطريركيّتهم الأنطاكيّة ولغتهم الوطنيّة والطقسيّة»، **المشرق**، ٣٤، (تمّوز.أيلول، ١٩٣٦)، ص ٣٦١-٣٩٤
- برغوت، عبد الودود، «جوانب اجتماعيّة من تاريخ دمشق في القرن الخامس عشر من مخطوطة أحمد بن طوق»، **المؤتمر الدوليّ لتاريخ الشام**، الدار المتّحدة للنشر، بيروت (١٩٧٤)، ص ٣٩٩-٤١٥
- زايد، محمود، «رحلة برتراندون دي لابروكيير إلى فلسطين ولبنان وسورية (١٤٣٢م)»، **الابحاث**، الالسنة ١٥، ج٣ (١٩٦٢)، ص ٢٩٩-٣٣٥
- سمير، سمير خليل، «ذكر مذهب النصارى لمؤتمن الدولة ابن العسّال (نحو ١٢٦٣م)»، **المشرق**، ٦٦، ج٢ (١٩٩٢)، ص ٤٨١-٤٩١ و«مقالة للفيلسوف نجم الدين عن فِرَق النصارى في رواية المؤتمن ابن العسّال، اعتقاد النساطرة واليعاقبة في المسيح وماهيّة الاتّحاد»، **المشرق**، ٦٧، ج٢ (١٩٩٩)، ص ٤٠٤-٤٤١
- جرجس منش المارونيّ، «موارنة حلب الشهباء»، المشرق (١٩٠٣)، ص ٣٦١

المراجع الأجنبيّة:

- FATTAL, Antoine, **Le statut légal des Non-Musulmans en pays d'Islam**, Imprimerie Catholique, Beyrouth, 1958
- GAUDEFROY-DEMOMBYNE, M., **La Syrie à l'époque des Mamelouks d'après les Auteurs Arabes,** Paris, 1923
- MUSSET, Henri, **Histoire du Christianisme spécialement en Orient,** vol.1, Imprimerie Saint Paul, Harissa, 1948
- POPPER, W., **Egypt and Syria under the Circassian Sultans 1382–1468 A.D. Systematic notes to Ibn Taghrî Birdî's Chronicles of Egypt**, Berkeley and Los Angeles, 1955

المقالات الأجنبيّة:

- BOSWORTH, C.E., "Christian and Jewish Religious Dignitaries in Mamlûk Egypt and Syria: Qalqashandi's Information on their Hierarchy Titulature and Appointment" in **IJMES** vol 3, (1972), Part I, pp. 59–74, Part II, pp. 199–216
- DAVID, Avraham, "The Jewish Settlement in Palestine in the Mamluk Period (1260–1516)", in **The Jewish Settlement in Palestine 634–1881**, Ed. by Alex CARMEL, Peter SCHÄFER and Yossi BEN-ARTZI, Dr. Ludwig REICHERT, Wiesbaden, (1990), pp. 40–85
- FISCHEL, Walter J., "A New Latin Source on Tamerlane's Conquest of Damascus (1400/1401) (B. De Mignanelli's "Vita Tamerlani" 1416)", in **ORIENS**, vol. 9, n° 2, (1956), Leiden, E. J. BRILL, pp. 201–232
- PERLMAN, M., "Notes on Anti-Christian Propaganda in the Mamlûk Empire", in BSOS, vol. X, (1940–1942), pp. 843–861, and "Asnawi's Tract Against Christian Officials", in **Ignaz Goldziher Memorial Volume**, ed. S. Löwinger and J. Somogy (Budapest, 1948–1958), vol. II, pp. 172–208
- SAUVAGET, Jean, "Décrets Mamlouks de Syrie", in **BEO**, T II, Fascicule I, Damas, (1932), pp. 1–52
- STRAUSS, "L'inquisition dans l'Etat Mamlouk", in **RSO**, vol. XXV, (1950), pp. 11–12

المحور الثاني

مجالات الإنتاج الثقافيّ:
الفنّ

الفنّ المسيحيّ في
بلاد الشام والحقبة المملوكيّة

إلياس الزيات
باحث مستقلّ

يتعلّق الموضوع بفنون الشكل arts de la forme ou arts plastiques كما هو «بجملته» ويمكننا أن نطرح تساؤلين، فأوّلاً: هل هناك فنّ مسيحيّ؟... أقول: هناك مفردات مسيحيّة، لاهوتيّة أو طقسيّة..، فإذا ما اقتضت الحاجة إلى أن يُعبَّر عنها فنّيًّا، فيُستدعى الفنّ كأداة للتعبير. وهذه الأداة تكون مرحليّة، أي أنّها تعتمد على فنّ المرحلة التاريخيّة للمجتمع الذي يمارس هذا الفنّ، ويكون الفنّ عندئذٍ متناسبًا مع تنامي الوعي الفكريّ في هذا المجتمع.

ويلاحظ دارس تاريخ الفنّ المسيحيّ في بلاد الشام، في المرحلة بين القرنين الثالث الميلاديّ والثالث عشر، المرحلة الممتدّة من ظهور هذا الفنّ في بلادنا إلى الزمن المملوكيّ – أنّ الفنّان المسيحيّ في البدء استخدم فنّ المرحلة أي فنّ تدمر ودورا أوروبّس.

وفي الحقبة الأمويّة التي جاءت بعد، تأثّر الفنّ الإسلاميّ بالفنّ الهلنستيّ السوريّ. وفي الحقبة العبّاسيّة عمل الفنّان المسيحيّ بالمشاركة مع الفنّان المسلم وأسّس كلاهما مدرسة عربيّة – سريانيّة – إسلاميّة هي مدرسة الموصل وبغداد كما سنرى.

وهكذا نجد أنّ الفنّ المسيحيّ في بلاد الشام، في مراحل مهمّة من تاريخه، قد التحم في نسيج الفنّ العامّ في هذه المنطقة من الشرق، بديناميّة التبادل الحضاريّ الذي حصل فيها.

وأمّا التساؤل الثاني فهو: أين موقع الحقبة المملوكيّة من تاريخ بلاد الشام؟.. ألم يكن وجود العنصر المملوكيّ المقاتل عنصرًا معتمدًا من الحكم العباسيّ منذ القرن التاسع الميلاديّ، أي من قَبل استيلاء المماليك فعليًّا على الحكم في مصر وبلاد الشام

في العام ١٢٥٠م، وكانوا، أي المماليك، في محبّة الحياة مؤهّلين لاقتباس الذوق الفنّيّ ممّن تربّوا على أيديهم من عبّاسيّين وأيّوبيّين، حتّى تقولب الذوق الفنّيّ في الزمن المملوكيّ بصيغة فنّيّة مملوكيّة أسّست للعثمانيّة في ما بعد؟!...

بهذا المنظور، كما أوردته في التساؤلين السابقين، فليُسمح لي بأن أناقش، في ما يلي، موضوعنا هذا:

لم تكن الحقبة المملوكيّة هي الوحيدة التي قام فيها حكم لا عربيّ في المنطقة العربيّة الإسلاميّة بعد دولة بني أميّة. فالدولة العبّاسيّة التي تلت الأمويّة في العام ٧٥٠م واستمرّت حتّى منتصف القرن الثالث عشر العام ١٢٥٨م، بدأ الخلفاء فيها بالعزوف عن العصبيّة العربيّة في القرن التاسع الميلاديّ، فاستمرّت بذلك «خيمة كبيرة» استظلّ بها الطولونيّون والأخشيديّون والفاطميّون والسلاجقة والأيّوبيّون.

ذاك الزمن العبّاسيّ الذي دام حوالى خمسة قرون لم يخلُ من فترات هدوء وسلم نسبيّ، وفترات انتفاض وتحوّل، لكنّه في شموله كان منفتحًا بقابليّة على حضارات العالم القديم: الكلدانيّة والمصريّة واليونانيّة والفارسيّة والهنديّة والصينيّة، بقدرةٍ في الاستيعاب فسحت في المجال للابتكار في علوم الطبّ والتجريد الرياضيّ وتطبيقاته التجريبيّة وفي الفنون، وجاء تطويع اللغة العربيّة آنذاك متناسبًا مع انفتاح الفكر وغدونا نلمس شكل التطويع اللغويّ في الأدب والشعر العبّاسيّين وفي الكتب العلميّة.

وكانت للسريان مساهمة كبيرة في النقل من اليونانيّة إلى العربيّة عبر السريانيّة في الحقبة العبّاسيّة، وذلك بسبب معرفتهم الوثيقة بالعلوم اليونانيّة، تلك المعرفة التي أهّلت العلماء السريان التمكّن من تلك العلوم والابتكار فيها بما يتلاءم مع المرحلة العربيّة[1]. ونذكر من العلماء عائلة بختيشوع التي توارثت الطبّ في بلاط الخلافة، كما نذكر من أولئك في زمن المأمون، «٨١٤–٨٣٣»، و«بيت الحكمة» الذي أنشأه: حنين بن إسحق ويحيى بن البطريق ويوحنّا بن ماسويه، وفي ما بعد، في القرن الثالث عشر، ابن العبريّ «١٢٢٦–١٢٨٦».

وكما في العلوم والابتكار فيها وتطويعها بما يتلاءم مع المرحلة، فإنّ الزمن العبّاسيّ شهد تطويع الفنون والابتكار فيها ومنها فنّ المنمنمات الذي رافق نصوص الكتب العلميّة والدينيّة والأدبيّة، ذلك بأنّ مدرسة فنّيّة «عبّاسيّة» قدّ تشكّلت على أيدي الخطّاطين والرسّامين والمصوّرين السريان والمسلمين ألا وهي مدرسة الموصل[2].

---

١ جورج صليبا: الفكر العلميّ العربيّ، نشأته وتطوّره، جامعة البلمند ١٩٩٨، ٦٢–٧٢.

٢ شاكر لعيبي: الفن الإسلاميّ والمسيحيّة العربيّة، بيروت، رياض الريس للكتب والنشر، ٢٠٠١، ٩٧–١٠١.

مدرسة الموصل، وقد سمّاها البعض مدرسة بغداد بسبب تقارب إنتاج الفنّانين في هاتين المدينتين، تمثّل أسلوبًا ساد في القرنين الثاني عشر والثالث عشر الميلاديّين، ويظهر هذا الأسلوب في نسخ المخطوطات المزدانة بالرسوم التوضيحيّة والزخارف الهندسيّة والنباتيّة، فيتجلّى باعتماده الرسم بالخطّ الداكن وتلوين المساحات التي يشكّلها هذا الخط بألوان صريحة مسطّحة ومن دون ظلال. وقد ترافق ذاك الرسم الملوّن مع النصّ المكتوب فهو يصوّر موضحًا حادثة مركزيّة فيه أو يجاريه في حرفيّته وفي إدراك للحدث الذي يمثّل فتخاله شريطًا مسلسلاً، ناهيك عن تأكيد شخصانيّة أبطال النصّ ومجريات الحياة اليوميّة فيه. وكلّ ذلك بتلقائيّة في الرسم واختزال الموضوع في عناصر أساسيّة فحسب من دون تفاصيل تجميليّة لا لزوم لها.

هذا وإنّ مدرسة الموصل في تزويق المخطوطات هي مدرسة عربيّة، تعدّت أوّلاً المنطقة الرافديّة إلى بلاد الشام ومصر إذ عُرف فيهما مصوّرون اشتغلوا بهذا الأسلوب عينه، وثانيًا فقد حمل الأسلوب جماليّة خاصّة به تختلف مورفولوجيًّا عمّا نراه في أساليب المخطوطات المعاصرة أو السابقة من بيزنطيّة[٣] وفارسيّة، أي من حيث البناء الفنّيّ بجانبيه الهندسيّ والتعبيريّ.

وإن كان القرن الثالث عشر هو الزمن الذي بقي لنا منه أجمل مخطوطات الأناجيل السريانيّة المصوّرة ومثلها مخطوطات العلوم والآداب العربيّة، وكلّها تعبّر عن فنّ المرحلة، تلك المرحلة الموافقة لأوج النهضة السريانيّة[٤]، وذاك الفنّ المتمثّل بأسلوب مدرسة الموصل، فقد بحث الباحثون في مسألة جذور هذا الفنّ: فرغم ويلات الحروب والتدمير التي أخفت الكثير من معالم الحضارة والفنّ في بلاد الرافدين والشام، فإنّ مقاربة فنّ مدرسة الموصل بما بقي من آثار الفنّ الجداريّ في «سامرّاء» من القرنين التاسع والعاشر الميلاديّين[٥]، وبصور سقف كنيسة «قصر باليرمو» وأسلوبها الفاطميّ من القرن الثاني عشر[٦]، وحتّى إذا ما أردنا الغوص بعيدًا في التراث القديم لبلاد المشرق والمغرب العربيّين، فتنبئ هذه المقاربة عن فنّ مدرسة الموصل وتفرّده، وذلك بسبب من إدماج الفنّان في إنتاجه فيه تلقائيًّا بعض موروثه المحلّيّ.

---

٣ Jules Leroy, *Les Manuscrits Syriaques à Peintures*, Paris 1964, 100.

٤ Allexandre Papadopoulo, *L'Islam et l'Art Musulman*, Paris: Mazenod 1976, 34.

٥ Richard Ettinghausen, *La Peinture Arabe*, SKIRA 1962, 47.

٦ "Ibid", 44.

دور المماليك

إذا كانت بحوث التاريخ قد حدّدت الحقبة المملوكيّة في ما بين استيلاء المماليك على الحكم في مصر وبلاد الشام في الفترة من ١٢٥٠م وبين سقوط دولتهم في السنة ١٥١٦، فإنّ العنصر المملوكيّ المقاتل نراه في الزمن العبّاسيّ منذ أواسط القرن التاسع الميلاديّ. فمنذ تلك الفترة وبعدها في القرن العاشر بخاصّة، عندما اشتدّ صراع القوى المحلّيّة والإقليميّة في الزمن العبّاسيّ وانعكس ذلك على المجتمع في تحوّلات إثنيّة ومذهبيّة، وتناقضت الحياة العامّة تناقضًا ما عرف شدّته المسلمون (والعرب)، كما يقول طه حسين[٧]، الأمر الذي أرّق الخلفاء العبّاسيّين بالإضافة إلى ضعف العنصر العربيّ المقاتل؛ فدعا خوف هؤلاء الخلفاء على سلطتهم إلى التهافت على تدعيمها بالعنصر المملوكيّ التركيّ وحمايتها به.

هذا، ومن ناحية أخرى فقد حصلت تغييرات اجتماعيّة جذريّة وسلميّة في المراكز المدنيّة العربيّة منذ منتصف القرن الثامن الميلاديّ، فصعدت طبقة التجّار والصنّاع وأصحاب المهن الفنّيّة لتشكّل طبقة متوسّطة في مجتمعات تلك المراكز كما تشكّلت طوائف الحرفيّين وتقنّنت، فتطوّرت بذلك فنون الأقمشة والسجّاد والمعدن والفخار وتزويق المخطوطات واحتازت، تلك الأصناف، في قوافل التجّار البرّيّة والبحريّة باتّجاه الشرق الآسيويّ والغرب الأوروبيّ[٨].

أوّل من اعتمد على العنصر التركيّ بشكل أساس حتّى أصبح الحرس المملوكيّ التركيّ دعامة الخلافة أيّام حكمه، هو الخليفة العبّاسيّ المعتصم «٨٣٣–٨٤١».

كذلك فعل أحمد بن طولون (حكم الطولونيّون مصر وسورية في أيّام الدولة العباسيّة من ٨٦٨ إلى ٩٠٤م). وقد نهجت الدولة الأخشيديّة (٩٣٥–٩٦٥ م)، التي خلفت الطولونيّة نهج هذه في الاعتماد على المماليك، وكذلك اعتمد عليهم الفاطميّون حين استولوا على مصر (٩٧٣–١١٧١م).

وكان السلاجقة قد اعتمدوا على المماليك ودُعي هؤلاء بالأتابكة وهم الذين تربّوا في البلاط السلجوقيّ، واشتهر منهم الأتابك عماد الدين الزنكيّ «ت ١١٤٦م» الذي ولّى نجم الدين أيّوب حاكميّة بعلبك، ونجم الدين هذا هو والد صلاح الدين الأيّوبيّ» ١١٣٧ ؟–١١٩٣» الذي رافق عمّه أسد الدين في حملة إلى مصر العام ١١٦٤م، للحؤول دون احتلالها من قبل مملكة بيت المقدس الصليبيّة، على رأس جيش تألّف

---

٧ عادل العوّا، مقال «إخوان الصفا» في: الموسوعة العربيّة، ج١، دمشق ١٩٨٨، ٥٦٠.

٨ R. Ettinghausen, *Peinture Arabe*, 54.

في غالبيّته من المماليك. ولمّا تولى صلاح الدين الأيّوبيّ وزارة مصر من قبل الخليفة الفاطميّ العاضد «ت.١١٧١م» راودته فكرة تأسيس دولة أيّوبيّة في مصر فعمل على إسقاط الدولة الفاطميّة فيها، وتمّ له ذلك السنة ١١٧٤م. وأمر صلاح الدين بالخطبة في المساجد للخليفة العبّاسيّ المستضيء، وضرب العملة باسمه كي يبقى المركز الرمزيّ لديار الإسلام في بغداد ويبقى الخليفة العبّاسيّ مرجع السلطة الدينيّة الوحيد.

وبعد خمس عشرة سنة من حكم صلاح الدين وتوحيد صفوف المسلمين، نجح في استرجاع بيت المقدس من يد الصليبيّين منتصرًا في معركة حطين «٤ تموز ١١٨٧م».

ولمّا كانت فئات المماليك قد اشتركت في مختلف المعارك، أخذ نفوذها يزداد في الإمارات الإسلاميّة في السنوات الأخيرة من القرن الثاني عشر الميلاديّ والسنوات الأولى من القرن الثالث عشر. وقد استغلّ المماليك الخلاف الذي دبّ بين أبناء البيت الأيّوبيّ بعد وفاة صلاح الدين فأخذوا يعملون على عزل وتولية من يشاؤون من الأيّوبيّين، وكان السلطان الأيّوبيّ الناصر أيّوب «١٢٤٠–١٢٤٩م» قد أدخل جحافل من المماليك في الجيش، فبعد وفاته استولى هؤلاء على الحكم في السنة ١٢٥٠م، بعد أن قتلوا ابن الناصر أيّوب وولي عهده[٩].

والجدير بالذكر أنّ السلالة الأيّوبيّة قد ذهبت من مصر وبلاد الشام بعد حوالى ثلاثة أرباع القرن من نشوئها وقد تركت آثارًا مهمّة في الثقافة والفنّ والعمارة[١٠].

وأمّا حكم المماليك فقد دام حوالى قرنين ونصف في مصر وبلاد الشام وبعض بلاد الرافدين، وتولّى فيه على التوالي فئتان من المماليك: البحريّة «١٢٥٠–١٣٨١» والبرجيّة «١٣٨٢–١٥١٧».

وكان زمن المماليك عصرًا اندفعت إليه حضارات ما قبله، بما تحمله من علم وثقافة وفنّ، وذهبت إلى ما بعده وتبوتقت فيه في صيغة «مملوكيّة» في أمبراطوريّةٍ شاسعة تتماس وتتجاذب حدودها في الشمال مع بيزنطية وأرمينية وآسية الصغرى ومنها نزولاً إلى سورية بلاد الشام وبعدها مصر فالحجاز واليمن. وتأتي تلك الحدود من الشرق، فتتماس مع بلاد فارس دخولاً في بلاد الرافدين، وهكذا حتّى حوض المتوسّط في الغرب، حيث تتجاذب بضائع الشرق وفنونه وبضائع الجزر الأوروبيّة حتّى الأندلس.

---

[٩] عن دور المماليك انظر: محمد سهيل طقّوش، تاريخ المماليك في بلاد الشام ومصر، بيروت ١٩٩٧، ١٦–٤٣.

[١٠] Sophie Makariou, "L'Orient de Saladin", in: *L'Orient de Saladin, l'art des Ayyoubides*, Catalogue de l'Exposition… à l'IMA: Paris, Gallimard 2001, 11–13.

والفنُّ... ماذا عنه؟..

إن كنت حاولت، في ما سبق، عرض بعض المعطيات حول صراع القوى في بلاد الشام والرافدين ومصر وما تمخّض عنها من جدلٍ اجتماعيّ، إثنيّ أو مذهبيّ، فما ذلك إلا تمهيدًا لبحث أحوال فنون الشكل وتصرّف أهل صناعتها في الحقبة المملوكيّة وعلاقتها بما سبقها من أيّوبيّة وعبّاسيّة؛ خصوصًا وأنّ هذه الحقب الزمنيّة قد خلّفت لنا فنونًا أصبحت اليوم تراثًا نعتزّ به.

وهنا تجدر الإشارة إلى أنّه قد تلازم في فنوننا التراثيّة المعنى البصريّ visuel مع المعنى الاستعماليّ usuel، الأمر الذي أعطى القدرة الجماليّة لفنون الشكل arts de la forme عندنا من حيث إنّها بصريّة واستعماليّة بآن، فكان أن أدّت فنون الشكل تلك دورًا مهمًّا في زخرفة الأبنية العامّة والخاصّة وفي حياة الناس اليوميّة، وكان لعليّة القوم فنون متميّزة عن فنون العامّة.

فمن تلك الفنون ما ظهر مسطّحًا، كما في فنّ الكتاب (المخطوطات والمنمنمات والتجليد) والفنّ الجداريّ والحياكة. ومنها ما ظهر مجسّمًا كما في الأواني والأدوات والصياغة، وكذلك في الحفر على الخشب والحجر وإدخال اللون عليهما. وهكذا كانت فنوننا التراثيّة فنّ الحياة اليوميّة، ووسيلة التواصل بين الناس.

ولأنّ الفنّ مرتبط بالإنسان وحياته الاجتماعيّة وتطلّعاته المادّيّة والروحيّة، فهو «عامل أساس في الإنسان، كما يقول رنيه هويغ[١١]، لازم للأفراد كما للجماعات، أكّد نفسه كضرورة منذ النشأة الأولى. والفنّ والإنسان لا ينفصمان، فلا فنّ بدون إنسان وأيضًا، وربّما، لا إنسان بلا فنّ [....] إنّه نوع من تنفّس روحيّ شبيه بالتنفّس الطبيعيّ الذي لا غنى لجسدنا عنه. والفرد أو الحضارة اللذان لا يرقيان إلى الفن مهدّدان باختناق فكريّ خفيّ وباضطراب معنويّ».

وإذا كان تاريخ الفنّ يسير بمحاذاة الأحداث السياسيّة إلا أنّ خصائص الفنّ لا تتبدّل بتبدّلات الحكم في حيّز جغرافيّ معيّن، لأنّ جغرافيّة الفنّ لا تلتزم بالحدود الجغرافيّة الوضعيّة، بل تتماشى مع الأسلوب الفنّيّ ومدى انتشاره في المكان والزمان العائد إليهما. قابليّة أسلوب فنّيّ ما للحياة تكمن في قابليّته للتطوّر حسب معادلة بيانيّة ترسم ارتباطه بأسلوب مرحلة سابقة له زمانيًّا تمهيدًا لمرحلة لاحقة؛ وهذه الجدليّة يعسر التحكّم بها أو تقنينها لأنّ خصائص الأسلوب الفنّيّ تبقى «في كمون» لدى الجماعة

[١١] رنيه هويغ، الفنّ تأويله وسبيله، ج١، ترجمة صلاح برمدا، دمشق: وزارة الثقافة ١٩٧٧، ١١.

التي تُنتج الفنّ أو تتمتّع بالمُنتَج الفنّيّ في جغرافيّة معيّنة، حتّى إذا أتتها موجة فنّيّة وافدة عليها، فتعتدل تلك الخصائص بالقدر الذي تكون فيه القدرة الإبداعيّة للفنّان المحلّيّ قابلة للتمازج مع التيّار الوافد، الذي غالبًا ما يسوقه المدّ الفكريّ والتبادل التجاريّ أو تحمله الانزياحات السكّانيّة[١٢]. هذا وإنّ الخصائص الفنّيّة لأسلوب ما، هي في ارتقاء أو انحدار تبعًا للذوق العامّ للجماعة الممارسة وإمكاناتها المادّيّة والعرض والطلب للمُنْتَج الفنّيّ.

وقبل أن نحاول تطبيق ما أسلفنا عن الأسلوب الفنّيّ وخصائصه على الفنّ في الزمن المملوكيّ، فمن دون أن نغوص في دراسة فئات الناس المُستهلِكة للفنّ وتشكّلها الإثنيّ وتوضّعها الاجتماعيّ وأوضاعها الحياتيّة في ذاك الزمن، يجدر بنا أن نأخذ في الاعتبار أنّ الحكّام المماليك وقادة الجيش الذين استولوا على الحكم في مصر وبلاد الشام في السنة ١٢٥٠م، وكانوا تعوّدوا دعم الحكومات المتوالية على العراق وبلاد الشام ومصر منذ أوائل القرن التاسع الميلاديّ كما رأينا، قد عُرف أنّهم كانوا على درجة عالية من التدرّب القتاليّ إضافة إلى الحنكة والدهاء وإلى محبّة الرفاه أيضًا، الأمر الذي قادهم إلى الاقتداء بمعلّميهم، الذين تربّوا عندهم، في الاستمتاع بآثار الفنّ وفي العمارة وزخرفتها والأثاث وما إليه من أقمشة وطنافس وأدوات استعماليّة بالإضافة إلى اقتناء نُسخ الكتب المزيّنة بالصور.

أضف أنّ اهتمام حكّام المماليك بالمباني الدينيّة وصحائف القرآن النفيسة، كان من شأنه تأكيد نصرتهم للإسلام، تجاه طبقات الشعب من أئمة وقضاة والناس في المدن وفي الريف حسب الإقطاعيّات التي كان يوليها السلطان المملوكيّ لأمرائه.

ولمّا كان المماليك مسلمين من أصول قوميّة مختلفة (قد يكون فيها عنصر مسيحيّ)، أو أنّهم ولدوا مسلمين في البلاد التي خدم فيها آباؤهم، فهم، أي المماليك، تاليًا عنصر صار متعايشًا مع العناصر العربيّة والمحلّيّة. وأمّا فنون زمانهم فقد استمرّت بأسلوب «اتباعيّ» قد جهد صنّاعُه (الفنّانون) في العمل على ملاءمته مع الطلب وتطويره حسب الرغبة... وكان من الطبيعيّ أن تكون منتجات الفنّ راقية لعليّة القوم وشعبيّة متواضعة للعامّة.

---

١٢ ما سقناه من جدل حول الأسلوب الفنّيّ ينطبق على فنون الشكل في الزمن المملوكيّ الذي ندرس والتي هي بصريّة استعماليّة كما رأينا، كما يمكن تطبيقه اليوم على الفنون التشكيليّة بمفهومها الحديث والمعاصر حسب التيّارات المتتالية التي ظهرت منذ ما بين الحربين العالميّتين في أوروبا وتركت آثارًا مهمّة حتّى اليوم في مسيرة الفنّ. وأمّا الفنّ الموجّه الذي فرضته بعض الأنظمة التوتاليتاريّة في أوروبا في القرن العشرين فمسيرته كانت تبعًا للتوجيه الفكريّ الأحاديّ في تلك الأنظمة.

والآن نعود إلى السؤال: ما هو أسلوب الفنّ الذي أخذت به الفئات الحاكمة وتلتها فئات الناس في استمرائه في الحقبة المملوكيّة؟.. هو أسلوب يحاكي أسلوب الفنّ في الحقبة الأيّوبيّة السابقة، وهذا الفنّ الأيّوبيّ حمل ما حمل من الأسلوب العبّاسيّ الذي سبقه وواكبه بآن.

وبمزيد من التخصيص أقول إنّ وجود المسيحيّين، سريان وروميّين وأقباطًا مع وافدين من أرمن وكرج وصقالبة في المحيطات الشاميّ والرافدينيّ والمصريّ، وبقاء هذا الوجود في زمن أمبراطوريّة المماليك، ما يُحتّم استمرار فنٍّ ذي صبغة مسيحيّة إلى جانب الفنّ الإسلاميّ.

واستمرّ الحكم المملوكيّ، كالأيّوبيّ من قبله، في التعاطي مع القوى المسيحيّة في الخارج، وفي تولية الرعايا المسيحيّين في الداخل العارفين بأمور اللغة العربيّة وكتابتها مهامًا علمانيّة في دواوين الدولة إلى جانب المسلمين[١٣].

وبناءً على ما تقدّم نستشفّ أنّ المماليك اعتمدوا صنّاعًا (فنّانين) مسيحيّين أيضًا، إن لم يكن في نَسْخ القرآن الكريم والكتب الدينيّة الإسلاميّة وتزيينها، ففي الصناعات الفنّيّة التقليديّة وفَنّ العمارة. وكان لنسخ الكتب المسيحيّة الدينيّة وزخرفتها نصيب من عمل هؤلاء الفنّانين المسيحيّين الذين أتقنوا فنّ المرحلة الفنّيّ[١٤]حتّى إنّ تأثير العيش المشترك بين المسلمين والمسيحيّين قد آل بالذوق المملوكيّ إلى تمييز عمارة الكنائس المسيحيّة، بما فيها من مقرنصات وخزفيّات وأيقونسطاسات خشبيّة محفورة أو مصابيح ومشكاوات زجاجيّة[١٥]، وكذلك الفنون في دور السكن المسيحيّة وفنّ المخطوطات والمنمنات. وقد استمرّ ذلك في الزمن العثمانيّ في ما بعد. ولذا نستطيع القول إنّ الفنّ المسيحيّ في الحقبة المملوكيّة هو عبور من الأيّوبيّ تمهيدًا للعثمانيّ.

---

١٣ فضل الله بن أبي الفخر الصقاعيّ، تالي كتاب وفيّات الأعيان، تحقيق: جاكلين سوبلة، دمشق، المعهد الفرنسيّ للدراسات العربيّة ١٩٧٤، XV.

١٤ Sophie Makariou, “L’Orient de Saladin”, in: *L’Orient de Saladin, l’art des Ayyoubides*, Catalogue de l’Exposition… à l’IMA: Paris, Gallimard 2001, 11–13.

١٥ Esin Atil, *Renaissance of Islam: Art of the Mamluks*, Washington D.C.: Smithsonian Institution Press 1981, 205–207.

الفنّ المسيحيّ في بلاد الشام

حتّى نفهم استمرار الفنّ في الزمن المملوكيّ، لا بدّ من العودة إلى الجذر في الفنّ العبّاسيّ/ الفاطميّ ثمّ الأيّوبيّ في النحاسيّات والخزفيّات والخشب[١٦] وما سوى ذلك من حياكة ورنوك وخطّ عربيّ وعمارة... ومقارنة ما بقي من النماذج المسيحيّة مع ما رافقها من نماذج إسلاميّة، وهذا مجال واسع، لذلك سأقتصر على دراسة عيّنتين من فنّ مسيحيّ بامتياز وهو «الفنّ السريانيّ» في المخطوطات السريانيّة الكنسيّة المصوّرة أوّلاً ثمّ في جداريّات دير مار موسى الحبشيّ، وذلك في النماذج التي صارت في فترة زمنيّة تماشت مع الزمن المملوكيّ في بلاد الشام أو مهّدت له، أي الفترة التي تبدأ بالقرنين الثاني عشر والثالث عشر الميلاديّين.

المخطوطات السريانيّة الكنسيّة المصوّرة[١٧]

ونلاحظ في دراستها ما يلي:

١. ترجع مخطوطات القرنين الثاني عشر والثالث عشر في روحيّة أسلوبها، إلى مخطوطات سريانيّة من فترات سابقة لها تصل إلى مخطوط رابولا في القرن السادس الميلاديّ[١٨].

٢. ما يلفت النظر بوضوح هو انتساب مجموعة من المخطوطات السريانيّة، في القرنين الثاني عشر والثالث عشر، إلى مدرسة التصوير العبّاسيّ، ألا وهي مدرسة الموصل التي سبقت الإشارة إليها.

وأيضًا من مخطوطات هذه الفترة ما له طابع شعبيّ يتمادى في التعبيريّة حتّى يقارب بعض طروحات الفنّ المعاصر في المحيطين الغربيّ والعربيّ.

---

١٦ "Ibid": 50, 118, 146, 195, 223, 250.

١٧ J. Leroy, *Manuscrits Syriaques à Peintures*, Paris, 1964, 93–139.

١٨ Kurt Weitzman: *Late Antique and Early Christian Book Illumination*, New York, Braziller: 1977, plates 34–38.

J. Leroy, *Manuscrits syriaques à Peintures*, Paris 1964, Album: Planche 50.

Mahmoud Zibawi, *Orients Chrétiens*, Paris: Desclée de Brouwer, 1995, Planches 4,5.

٣. نجد في الفترة المشار إليها مخطوطات سريانيّة قد تمازج أسلوبها الفنّيّ بفنّ المخطوطات البيزنطيّة. (الصورة ٥)

٤. هناك مخطوطات سريانيّة مؤرّخة تدخل حصرًا في فترة الحكم المملوكيّ. (الصورة ٦)

٥. دارس المخطوطات الكنسيّة السريانيّة يجد تعدّدًا منها وافرًا نسبيًّا في زمن المماليك البحريّة «١٢٥٠ – ١٣٨١»، بينما تقلّ تلك المخطوطات في ما بعد في زمن المماليك البرجيّة «١٣٨٢ – ١٥١٧». وأرى ذلك عائدًا إلى وضع الأديار السريانيّة والكنائس في شمال المنطقة الرافدينيّة/ السوريّة؛ ففي الزمن الأوّل، أي زمن المماليك البحريّة، كانت تلك الأديار شبه محميّات ولا تشكّل هاجسًا سياسيًّا للمماليك، بخاصّة أنّ الصراع آنذاك مع الصليبيّين كان على أشدّه في منطقة بعيدة عن تلك الأديار، أي في غرب بلاد الشام وسواحلها الجنوبيّة، الأمر الذي لم يدم في ما بعد إذ يزحف المغول التيموريّون من الشمال، في مطلع القرن الخامس عشر، ويدمّرون ملطيّة وغيرها من المناطق السريانيّة ويتوغّلون إلى حلب ودمشق[١٩]، وذلك ما تسبّب في هجر السريان مناطقهم، حاملين معهم مخطوطاتهم التي تبعثرت، فما فقد منها لم يعد تعويضه ممكنًا. ومعلوم أنّ تيمور المغول أخذ معه من بلاد الشام إلى سمرقند، في مطلع القرن الخامس عشر، صفوة الصنّاع الضالعين في مختلف الفنون والحرف وكان منهم خطّاطون ورسّامون مصوّرون[٢٠].

الجداريّات الكنسيّة السريانيّة

(أنموذجًا جداريّات كنيسة دير مار موسى الحبشيّ شرق النبك)[٢١]

كشفت أعمال الصيانة والترميم التي أجريت على جداريّات دير مار موسى الحبشيّ عن ثلاث طبقات من التصوير الجداريّ رُسمت فوق بعضها البعض.

عملت عاديات الزمن عملها في تلك الطبقات فسقطت أجزاء منها بشكل عشوائيّ، الأمر الذي أدّى إلى بيان نماذج من كلّ واحدة من تلك الطبقات الثلاث، وذلك ما شكّل مادّة علميّة/ فنيّة وساعد على الدراسات العلميّة والنظريّة التي أجريت عليها.

---

١٩ طقّوش: تاريخ المماليك، بيروت، دار النفائس ١٩٩٩، ٤١٨–٤٣٠.

٢٠ "Ibid": 431.

٢١ باولودا لوليو، «تاريخ دير ما موسى الحبشيّ ووصف الرسوم الجداريّة فيه»، في: ترميم دير ما ر موسى الحبشيّ، دمشق، وزارة الثقافة السوريّة ووزارة الخارجيّة الإيطاليّة ١٩٩٨، ١١–٢٣.

حدّد الدارسون أزمان الطبقات المشار إليها بناءً على الكتابات البائنة على الجدار الحجريّ من تحت الطينة المصوّرة والكتابات الظاهرة على بعض الصور كالتالي[٢٢]:

الطبقة الأولى: من منتصف القرن الحادي عشر بعد العام ١٠٥٨م وهو تاريخ بناء الكنيسة.

الطبقة الثانية: من نهاية القرن الحادي عشر في العام ١٠٩٥م.

الطبقة الثالثة: من مطلع القرن الثالث عشر في العام ١٢٠٨م.

وعليه فلا تدخل جداريّات دير مار موسى حصرًا في الحقبة المملوكيّة بل تنضوي، تاريخيًّا، تحت الحقبتين العبّاسيّة والأيّوبيّة. لكن الطبقة الثالثة من تلك الجداريّات، أعني السطحيّة، هي من العام ١٢٠٨م أي من بدء القرن الثالث عشر، وقد عمدنا في بحثنا هذا، إلى مقاربة فنّ هذه الفترة بما يخصّ ذوق الأسلوب المملوكيّ. ويكفي أن نجري مقاربة مورفولوجيّة بين صورة القدّيس يوحنّا المعمدان من تلك الطبقة الثالثة وبين صورة المسيح في مخطوط سريانيّ من القرن الثاني/الثالث عشر حتّى نتبيّن التشابه الأسلوبيّ بين الصورتين كما نتبيّن انتماء كلتيهما إلى الفنّ السريانيّ (الصورة ٧)، وانظر أيضًا (الصورة ٨).

٢٢ M. Zibawi, *Orients Chrétiens*, Paris, 1995, Planches: 12, 13, 14a, 14b, 15.

المحور الثالث

مجالات الإنتاج الثقافيّ:
الأدب والتاريخ

التجديد في منهج تقي الدين أحمد المقريزيّ (٧٦٦–٨٤٥/١٣٦٤–١٤٤٢)

أنطوان ضومط
الجامعة اللبنانيّة

أوّلاً: البيئة السياسيّة والدينيّة والثقافيّة للتأريخ في القرن التاسع/الخامس عشر

في العهد المملوكيّ شغل معظم المؤرّخين وظائف ديوانيّة مثل كتابة السرّ، والحسبة والتوقيع بديوان الإنشاء... ما سمح لهم بالاطلاع على دقائق سجلات هذه الوظائف، وعلى ركائز النظامين العسكريّ والإقطاعيّ المملوكيّين فازدهرت كتب الإدارة مثل مسالك الأبصار للعمريّ، ونهاية الأرب للنويريّ، وصبح الأعشى للقلقشنديّ، والمواعظ والاعتبار للمقريزيّ، وزبدة كشف الممالك للظاهريّ... إضافة إلى التواريخ العامّة، التي لم يقتصر حضورها على السياسيّ والعسكريّ بل تعدّاهما إلى النشاطات الاجتماعيّة والاقتصاديّة والإداريّة. فاكتملت بذلك صورة التاريخ بأبهى حلّة، وأروع رؤية، وصارت المؤلّفات تنبض بالحياة وتتحدّث عن الخاصّة والعامّة معًا بعد أن كانت حكرًا على الأولى.

تجاه هذا الازدهار المنقطع النظير للمؤلّفات في ميدان التاريخ على تنوّع مواضيعه، نلاحظ انحطاطًا مخيفًا ومربكًا في بقيّة العلوم على مدى العصر المملوكيّ. وقد يكون مردّ ذلك إلى وعي المؤرّخين للدينيّ المرتبط بالسياسيّ الناتج من احتضان المماليك للشرعيّة الدينيّة السنّيّة الوحيدة، فصارت بنظرهم دولة المماليك وحدها الدولة الشرعيّة في العالم الإسلاميّ، وتحوّلت الدول الأخرى غير الخاضعة للخلافة العبّاسيّة إلى دولٍ عاقّة، ما جعل التاريخ المحلّيّ أو الإقليميّ يزدهر بامتياز، بحيث قلّما تجاوزت مضامين مؤلّفات المؤرّخين المشرقيّين حدود الدولة التي يعيشون في كنفها اللهم إلا ابتهاجًا بفتح إسلاميّ، أو نجاة المسلمين من هجوم الفرنجة.

وبذلك، غابت عن الساح التأريخيّة مؤلّفات التاريخ العام الشامل، وإن أطلقنا على بعضها هذه الصفة لأنّ حضورها اقتصر على التاريخ الإقليميّ الخاضع أصلا لنفوذ سياسيّ محدّد، ما عكس الانقسام السياسيّ على الفكر الدينيّ وعلى الوضعين الاجتماعيّ والاقتصاديّ. ولم يعدّ العالم الإسلاميّ كلّه مسرحًا لأقلام المؤرّخين المسلمين، بل تقوقع التوجّه، خلال الحقبات التي نضجت فيها المناهج التأريخيّة عمومًا، ليحدّد السمات العامّة للمراحل الأخيرة من العصور الوسطى. وقد حرمنا هذا المنظور السياسيّ الدينيّ الضيّق من كنوز كثيرة لأنّه لو توفّر للمقريزيّ وبعض زملائه المبدعين، بما تمتّعوا به من نفاذ البصيرة والحسّ الاجتماعيّ، الاطلاع على أخبار الدول الإسلاميّة الأخرى ودوّنوا أخبارها لربّما كانت المكتبة العربيّة قد اغتنت بمادّة علميّة تاريخيّة قلّ نظيرها، ولكن مع الأسف الشديد اقتصر حضورهم التأريخيّ على دولة المماليك خصوصًا أنّ بعض المؤرّخين شغل وظائف ديوانيّة، ما جعلهم قريبين من القرار السياسيّ، ومطّلعين على معلومات كان متعذّرًا على غيرهم الوصول إليها، ومدركين بدقّة بنية المؤسّسات المملوكيّة بسلبيّاتها وإيجابيّاتها.

ثانيًا: حياة المقريزيّ ومؤلّفاته

١. **حياته:** هو تقي الدين أحمد بن علي العبيدي المقريزيّ[١]، وهذه الشهرة الأخيرة تعود إلى إحدى حارات بعلبك التي عاشت في كنفها أسرته، قبل انتقال جدّه لأبيه من بعلبك إلى دمشق[٢]. ولد المقريزيّ في القاهرة في حارة برجوان العام ١٣٦٤/٧٦٦ في أسرة اشتهرت بتحصيل العلوم؛ فجدّه لأبيه نشأ في بعلبك وتثقّف على عدد وافر من العلماء والفقهاء[٣] ثمّ انتقل إلى دمشق حيث ولد ابنه علي والد المقريزيّ. بعد دمشق ارتحل إلى القاهرة واستقرّ فيها حيث تقلّب في وظائف ديوانيّة عدّة[٤].

---

١ ابن تغري بردي (جمال الدين يوسف)، النجوم الزاهرة في ملوك مصر والقاهرة، تحقيق إبراهيم علي الطرخان، الهيئة المصريّة العامّة للتأليف والنشر، ج١٥، ص ٤٩٠ و السخاوي، الضوء اللامع لأهل القرن التاسع، ج٢، ص٢٢.

٢ كثيرون ترجموا لجدّي المقريزيّ لأمّه ولأبيه، ومنهم المقريزيّ نفسه، السلوك لمعرفة دول الملوك،، ج٢، ق١، ص ٣٦٥.وابن حجر العسقلاني (احمد بن علي)، الدرر الكامنة في أعيان المائة الثامنة، دار الجيل، بيروت، دون تاريخ، ج٢، ص ٣٩١.

٣ لمزيد من الاطلاع انظر: عز الدين علي (محمد)، أربعة مؤرّخين وأربعة مؤلّفات، الهيئة المصريّة العامّة، القاهرة، ١٩٩٢، ص ١٦١–١٦٣ حيث أسهب في ذكر تراجم الأشخاص الذين تثقف عليهم.

٤ المقريزيّ، السلوك، ج٢، ق١، ص ٣٦٥.

وقد يكون جدّه لأمّه، الذي احتضن المقريزيّ، أكثر ثقافة من جدّه لأبيه[٥]. درس مؤرّخنا في الأزهر على الكثير من العلماء والفقهاء بلغ عددهم ستّمائة[٦] من أبرزهم: شمس الدين بن الصائغ جدّه لأمّه، وأبو إسحق التنوخيّ، وسراج الدين البلقينيّ، والعماد الحنبليّ، وابن خطيب الناصريّة المؤرّخ المعروف، وابن خلدون بعد أن استقرّ في القاهرة منذ العام **١٣٦٤/٧٨٤**، وقد تأثّر به كثيرًا ولا سيّما بمقدّمته المشهورة. كما أجازه عدد من أعلام عصره نذكر منهم: العماد ابن كثير (+ **١٣٧٣/٧٧٤**، وأبا البلقاء السبكيّ (+ **١٣٧٥/٧٧٧**) وأبا الفضل النويريّ (+ **١٣٨٤/٧٨٦**)[٧].

كان المقريزيّ على اتصال وثيق بالسلطان برقوق، وبابنه السلطان فرج، وبالأمير يشبك الدوادار، ما سمح له باشتغال وظائف حكوميّة عدّة. وكان مقرّبًا جدًّا من الناصر فرج الذي تمنّى عليه أن يكون رسوله إلى تيمورلنك لكنّه اعتذر.[٨]

ثمّ ما لبث أن اعتزل الوظيفة العامّة لينصرف إلى تدوين مؤلّفاته جاعلاً من بيته موئلاً لأهل العلم من تلاميذه وأصدقائه. ولربّما يكون قد وجد في هذا السلوك السلوى والسلوان عمّا آلت إليه أوضاع البلاد من انحطاط اقتصاديّ وفساد إداريّ ورعب عسكريّ، وعمّا فقده من وظائف، وعزاء ذاتيًّا لفقدانه ابنته فاطمة التي توفّيت بالطاعون العام **١٤٢٣/٨٢٦** وذهب هو نفسه ضحيّة الوباء عينه العام **١٤٤١/٨٤٥** مخلّفًا ثروة علميّة ضخمة، ومدرسة تأريخيّة خاصّة.

٢. **مؤلّفاته:** ترك المقريزيّ عددًا كبيرًا من المؤلّفات في مختلف ميادين العلوم الإنسانيّة أربت على المائتين على ما ذكر السخاويّ[٩]، ويبدو أنّ معظمها قد ضاع، وما بقي طبع معظمه، وسنكتفي بذكر بعضها:

- اتعاظ الحنفاء بأخبار الأئمة الفاطميّين الخلفاء.
- إغاثة الأمّة بكشف الغمّة، هو كتيّب اقتصاديّ اجتماعيّ يعتبر من أجلّ الدراسات الاجتماعيّة والاقتصاديّة خلال العصور الوسطى.
- الأوزان والأكيال الشرعيّة، وهو يتمّم الكتاب السابق، وباعتقادي أنّ المقريزيّ وضعه بعد تجربته المريرة في وظيفة الحسبة.

---

٥ وقد توسّع عز الدين علي بالترجمة لمن أخذ عنهم العلم، المرجع السابق، ص ١٦٤–١٦٨.

٦ أنظر حول ترجمة المقريزيّ: السخاويّ، الضوء اللامع، ج٢، ص ٢١–٢٤، ابن تغري بردي، المنهل الصافي، ج١، ٣٩٤–٣٩٩.

٧ عز الدين علي، أربعة مؤرّخين، ص١٧٢.

٨ أنظر حول وظائف المقريزيّ الحاشية رقم ٧ ولا سيّما السخاويّ، الضوء اللامع، ٢٢/٢.

٩ السخاويّ، الضوء اللامع، ٢٢/٢.

- التاريخ الكبير المقفّى في تاريخ أهل مصر والواردين عليها، وهو تراجم لأكابر المصريّين ومن دخل إلى مصر من العلماء والمشاهير، مرتّب على حروف المعجم. صدر منه حتّى الآن ستة عشر مجلّدًا، ويبدو أنّ المقريزيّ أراد له أن يكون في حوالى ثمانين مجلّدًا على حدّ تعبير السخاويّ وابن تغري بردي[١٠].
- درر العقود الفريدة في تراجم الأعيان المفيدة[١١].
- شذور العقود في ذكر النقود، منشور.
- المنتقى من أخبار مصر لابن ميسّر، منشور
- المواعظ والاعتبار بذكر الخطط والآثار
- كتاب السلوك لمعرفة دول الملوك، وهو موضوع هذا البحث.

وهناك العديد من المؤلّفات ذكرها السخاويّ، وابن تغري بردي، وأعطى الدكتور محمد كمال الدين عز الدين علي معلومات عنها وتوسّع بمضمون بعضها خصوصًا المخطوط منها الذي تمكّن من الاطلاع عليه.[١٢]

ثالثًا: التجديد في منهجه في كتاب السلوك لمعرفة دول الملوك

التجديد هو إبداع يتجسّد في الخروج عن المألوف جزئيًّا أو كليًّا، وتاليًا اعتماد نمط جديد قد يغدو لاحقًا نموذجًا يحتذى. ويتمظهر التجديد في التأريخ في المنهج على مستويين: الشكل، والمضمون. ونعني بمنهج المضمون موقف المؤرّخ من الحدث الذي يؤرّخ له، أي كيفيّة استقراء جزئيّاته ومن ثمّ إعادة تركيبها بما يوضح مدى عمق رؤيته العموديّة. ويُظهر الجهدَ الذي بذله للوصول إلى أكبر قدر ممكن من الحقيقة التاريخيّة التي هي مطلقة في الأساس. ويمكن إطلاق مصطلح: «النظرة التاريخيّة» على مجمل هذه الجهود.

ويرتبط أسلوب التجديد في العصور الوسطى بمقدار خروج المؤرّخ على الصورة التقليديّة للخبر التاريخيّ، لأنّ الخبر استمرّ بوجه عامّ مستقلاً بذاته ولذاته عند معظم مؤرّخي العصور الوسطى الإسلاميّة، وقلّما أسّس لخبر جديد، أو استند إلى خبر آخر سابق لينفذ إلى أعماق الحدث الكلّيّ. فبراعة المؤرّخ تتجلّى بمقدار إخراجه الأحداث

---

١٠ السخاويّ، الضوء اللامع، ٢/٢٢، المنهل الصافي، ١/٣٩٧.

١١ أنظر الحاشية السابقة.

١٢ أنظر ترجمة المقريزيّ في الضوء اللامع، والمنهل الصافي، وأربعة مؤرّخين وأربعة مؤلّفات، ص ١٢٧–٢١٨.

التي تتداخل بعض وجوهها أو تتقاطع في سياق شامل ومترابط تتجلّى فيه كليّة الحدث المقصود.

وعلى هذا سندرس نظرة المقريزيّ التاريخيّة على كلّ المستويات التي أرّخ لها، كما سنبيّن مدى خروجه على الصورة التقليديّة للخبر أو وفائه لها.

I – نظرته التاريخيّة في السلوك:

المقريزيّ أوّل المؤرّخين الذين نظروا إلى الاجتماع الإنسانيّ نظرة عامّة شاملة غير تنظيريّة في المطلق، بل حكمتها ركائز من ذاتيّته غدت قوانين خاصّة به، وعامّة لمؤرّخين آخرين مثل ما طرحه ابن خلدون في مقدّمة كتاب «العبر وديوان المبتدأ والخبر». فجاءت نظرة معرفيّة نابعة من خبرة التعاطي في الشأن العامّ، ومراقبة الأحداث وتطوّرها، ومن رؤيته الإنسانيّة العامّة المتأثّرة، من دون شكّ، بنظريّات أستاذه ابن خلدون ومحاولته تطبيقها في التأريخ. وهي نظرة هادفة، غايتها تبديل سلوك الحكّام نحو الأفضل علّ الخلف يتّعظ من السلف.

وتكمن أهمّيّة نظرته بمعالجتها نواحٍ متعدّدة من النشاطات الإنسانيّة في المجتمع المملوكيّ: سياسيّة، وعسكريّة، وإداريّة، واقتصاديّة، وعمرانيّة، واجتماعيّة بمختلف أبعادها شأن الأوبئة والأمراض، والجرائم، والحرائق... وتأثيراتها المتبادلة.

أ) نظرته إلى الوضع العسكريّ: شكّل الصراع بين فئات المماليك على اختلاف مستوياتهم وتنوّع انتماءاتهم محورًا رئيسًا في حياة المماليك منذ تأسيس دولتهم وحتّى العام ١٤٤١/٨٤٤ الذي تتوقّف عنده أخبار « السلوك ». وتستوقفنا في هذا المدى محطّات صراعيّة بارزة، أخصّ منها ما حدث في سلطنتي الناصر محمد بن قلاوون الأولى والثانية. لكنّ المشهد يبدو أكثر اضطرابًا في عهود أبناء الناصر محمّد بن قلاوون وأحفاده بحيث صوّر المقريزيّ المجتمع المملوكيّ مجتمعًا دمويًّا غادرًا تلفّه المؤامرات والفتن.[١٣] ويستمرّ المشهد عينه على امتداد معظم العهد الجركسيّ، وفق محطّات أو مفاصل، قد يكون من نماذجه النافرة ما حصل في البدء بين برقوق ومنافسيه، ثمّ في معظم عهد الناصر فرج بن برقوق[١٤]: كالصراعات بين منطاش وشيخ المحموديّ ونوروز الحافظيّ، وبين جقمق واينال[١٥]...

---

١٣ المقريزيّ، السلوك، ٢ ق٣/٥٦٧–٥٨٠.

١٤ المصدر السابق، ٣، ق٣/٩٦٠ وما بعد ولا سيما ١١٣٦ وما يليها.

١٥ المقريزيّ، السلوك، ٤، ق٣ /١٠٧٢–١٠٨١.

لم يحصر المقريزيّ آثار ما كان يحصل بالمماليك فقط، بل تناول تداعياته المدمّرة على كلّ فئات المجتمع بقوله: «وحلّ بالقاهرة ومصر خوف شديد بسبب اختفاء الأشرفيّة -نسبة إلى السلطان الأشرف برسباي- وتطلّبهم، فإذا دخل المماليك جهة من الجهات للبحث عنهم حلّ بسكّانها أنواع البلاء ما لا يوصف من النهب والهدم والعقوبة والغرامة وجد فيها أشرفية أم لم يوجد. وكان يتبعهم بهجومهم غوغاء العامّة فحلّ بالنساء بلاء لا يوصف، فهدمت بعض المدارس ونهب بعضها الآخر...[١٦]»

ولكي تتبلور الصورة العسكريّة، وهي من معالم التجديد في نظرته التاريخيّة، وصف الفنون القتاليّة وطرائقها، والخطط الحربيّة، وأنواع الأسلحة المستخدمة. فتناول في حصار آمد العام ١٤٣٤/٨٣٧ المدفع النحاسيّ المستخدم فيه الذي بلغت زنته مائة وعشرين قنطارًا مصريًّا، وزنة قذيفته ٥٧٠ رطلا مصريًّا[١٧]. ووصف في هذا الإطار أنواع السفن الإفرنجيّة، والسفن المملوكيّة وسبل استخدامها[١٨].

وفي المسار عينه أرّخ المقريزيّ لعلاقة العربان العدائيّة بالسلطة المملوكيّة الناتجة أصلاً من ظلم الحكّام[١٩]. ويتقاطع هذا الموضوع مع نواحٍ أخرى متعدّدة تتكامل جميعها معًا، لتجعل المشهد العسكريّ تامًا بأحداثه وتفاعلاته بما يفرز من نتائج أو تداعيات حدّدت أبرز محطّات التجديد في نظرته.

ب) موقفه من الاقتصاد: يحتلّ الاقتصاد منزلة تأريخيّة مهمّة جدًّا في «السلوك»، فهو المحرّك الأساس لكلّ نشاطات الدولة والمجتمع، ولكلّ الصراعات الداخليّة. وانطلاقًا من هذه الحركيّة كان الحكّام المماليك يتوسّلون ظلم الشعب. ولعلّ هذا ما جعل المقريزيّ يدرس مجمل الركائز الاقتصاديّة أفقيًّا وعموديًّا مستخلصًا منها العبر.

١. **النقود:** يعتبر النقد العصب الأساس في كلّ عمليّة اقتصاديّة، والوضع النقديّ يعتبر مقياسًا لتطوّر الحالة الاقتصاديّة أو لركودها. لذلك ركّز المقريزيّ على قيمة النقود من حيث جودتها وغشّها، مظهرًا دور الغش في إفقار الناس[٢٠]. ما دفعه إلى دراسة

---

١٦ المقريزيّ السلوك، ٤، ق٣ / ١١٢٧.

١٧ المقريزيّ، السلوك، ٤، ق٢/٩٠٦.

١٨ شيني أيّ سفن كبيرة، قرقورة وهي سفن كبيرة تستخدم بتموين الأسطول، الغراب لأنّ رأس السفينة يشبه الغراب وهو يحمل المقاتلين ويسير بالقلع، وطريدة وهي مركب خفيف وسريع، وشختورة وهي سفينة ضخمة. المقريزيّ السلوك، ق١/١٤٩.

١٩ أنظر نماذج عنها في: السلوك، ١ ق٣/٩٢٠-٩٢٢ و٢، ق٣/٨٠٤، ٩١٧، و٤، ق١/٣١٩، ٣٩٦...

٢٠ المقريزيّ، السلوك، ٢، ق١/٢٠٥، ٢، ق٣ /٦٦٩ وغيرها كثير جدًّا.

تطوّر النقود منذ العهد الأيوبيّ وحتّى أيّامه ذاكرًا أسباب غشّها وتداعياته على الأسعار والحياة الاجتماعيّة، دارسًا بطريقة تركيبيّة نظريّة متكاملة للتضخّم النقديّ[٢١]، وهي لعمري خطوة سبقت عصره بل نظريّة الاقتصاديّين العالميّين. وهي تزداد وضوحًا كلّما اقترب بالتأريخ من عصره بسبب وفرة المعلومات؛ فقد درس تطوّر الرواتب، وازدياد أرباح التجّار وانعكاس هذين الأمرين على النظام الزراعيّ عمومًا، محمّلاً المماليك المسؤوليّة:« وكلّ ذلك من سوء نظرة ولاة الأمور [٢٢]». وتكتمل نظريّة التضخّم النقديّ بدراسته أسبابه؛ إذ يرجعه إلى كثرة ما كان يتوجّب على الدولة من جوامك (رواتب شهريّة) للمماليك السلطانيّة، محدّدًا مقاديرها النقديّة والعينيّة من لحم وكسوة وعليق للدواب[٢٣]. مبرزًا سوء تصرّف المماليك السلطانيّة من أجل الحصول عليها وعلى علاوات جاعلاً منه أبرز أسباب إفساد إدارات الدولة، «وإلى خراب إقليم مصر وزوال نعم أهله[٢٤]».

ولفهم عمليّة غشّ النقود وأثرها على التضخّم النقديّ قارن بين النقود الذهبيّة المملوكيّة ومثيلاتها الأوروبيّة المستخدمة في الديار المملوكيّة محدّدًا مستواها وإقبال الناس عليها: الأوّل هو الهرجة وقد قلّ بأيدي الناس، والثاني يقال له الأفرنتيّ والأفلوريّ أي «الفلوران الهولنديّ» والبندقيّ أو الدوكة، وقد وصفها جميعها. والثالث الدينار الذهبيّ الناصريّ. كما تحدّث عن جميع أنواع الفلوس[٢٥]. وبذلك، يكون المقريزيّ أوّل مؤرّخي العصور الوسطى الذين أحاطوا بأحوال النقود الإيجابيّة والسلبيّة، وتناولوا تداعياتها على مجمل مناحي الحياة الاجتماعيّة والاقتصاديّة والعسكريّة.

٢. **الرسوم والضرائب:** واستكمالاً لنظرته الاقتصاديّة تحدّث عن عمليّات الطرح والتحكير، والاحتكارات، والرشوة، والمصادرات، والرسوم، وهي جميعها ضرائب استثنائيّة باتت بنظره عاديّة لكثرة ما فرضت. وتناول أيضًا الغلاء ومسبّباته، وتطوّر

---

٢١ المقريزيّ، السلوك،٣، ق١١٣١/٣–١١٣٢.

٢٢ المقريزيّ، السلوك، ٤، ق٢٧/١–٢٩.

٢٣ المقريزيّ، السلوك، ٤، ق٢٧/١–٢٩.

٢٤ المكان عينه.

٢٥ المقريزيّ، السلوك ٤، ق٣٠٥/١–٣٠٦. ويعلّق على غشّ النقود وعلى عدم التداول بها بأنّ الإدارة لم تكن تثبت على أمر فحينا تمنع أمرًا ما ثمّ لا تلبث أن تتغاضى عن المنع ضاربًا مثلا على النقود الأشرفيّة: «فلما نودي بالمنع منها عاد الامر كما كان، فخسر الناس عدة خسارات، وأخذت الباعة وغيرها بجمعها – أي الأشرفيّة – لتتربص بها مدة، ثمّ تخرجها شيئًا فشيئًا، **لعلمهم أنّ الدولة لا تثبت على حال وأنّ أوامرها لا تمضى.**» السلوك، ٤، ق٢/ ٨٥٢.

الأسعار. كما تحدّث عن الرسوم من حيث أصنافها، وكيفيّة فرضها، وتأثيرها على الناس[٢٦]. وشرح بعض المصطلحات كالطرح وهو أن يشتري الوزير أو الاستادار سلعًا بأسعار بخسة أو يصادر سلعًا تحت عناوين جائرة متنوّعة، ثمّ يعيد بيعها من التجار بأسعار مرتفعة جدًّا. وازداد هذا النهج سوءًا في العهد الجركسيّ حتى بات إحدى سماته النافرة[٢٧]. جعل من المصادرات عنوانًا سيّئًا في سجلّ المماليك المثقل بالمظالم فأبان مساوئها وتداعياتها على التجّار وأرباب الحرف وكبار الإداريّين، وعلى تطوّر الحياة السياسيّة والعسكريّة والإداريّة المملوكيّة[٢٨]. كانت الرسوم والضرائب تثقل كاهل الناس حتى بلغ بعضهم مستوى الفقر والبعض الآخر ما دونه. وكان غشّ النقود يسبّب غلاء بالأسعار وحالاً من الفوضى الاقتصاديّة، وللغلاء عند المقريزيّ أسباب أخرى؛ مثل قلّة فيضان النيل أو شدّته، وإن جاء الأمران شديدي الوطأة كان الجوع والمرض يعمّان حتّى:«أكل الناس من شدّة الجوع الميتات والقطط والكلاب والحمير، وأكل بعضهم لحم بعض[٢٩]»، بالإضافة إلى الجراد الذي كان يأتي على المزروعات[٣٠]، والمطر المتساقط قبل الأوان الذي تعقبه فترة من الحرّ الشديد كان يخرج دودًا كثيرًا يتلف المزروعات[٣١].

٣. **نتائج السياسة الاقتصاديّة:** لم تكن نظرته مركّزة على الوضع الاقتصاديّ المتردّي فحسب، وإن كان الأكثر تعبيرًا عن سوء أحوال الناس الذين يقنعون بالفتات[٣٢]، ولم تكن تنظيريّة نابعة من فراغ، بل أمدّنا باستمرار، وكلّما توفرت له المعلومات، بأسعار السلع ارتفاعًا أو هبوطًا مقارنًا أحيانًا بما كانت عليه أسعارها

---

[٢٦] أبرز الرسوم التي ذكرها هي: ساحل الغلة، نصف السمسرة، مقرّر الحوائص والبغال، مقرّر السجون، طرح الفراريج، مقرّر الفرسان، مقرر الاقصاب والمعاصر، رسوم الأفراح، حماية المراكب، حقوق القينات، وشد الزعماء، حقوق النوبة والسودان، متوفر الجراريف، مقرّر المشاعلية، ثمن العبى التي كانت تستأدى من البلاد، مقرّر الاقبان، زكاة الرجالة. السلوك، ٢، ق١/١٥٠–١٥٢.

[٢٧] المقريزيّ، السلوك، ٢،ق٢/٤٣٩، ٤٤٤، و٣، ق٢/٥٥، و ٤، ق٢/٨٠١، ٤، ق٣/١١٢٧ وغيرها.

[٢٨] المقريزيّ، السلوك، ٢، ق٢/٣٥٨، ٣٦١، ٣٧٠، ٣٨٤، ٤٣١. وقد طالت هذه المصادرات مباشري المعاصر والدواليب بحجّة زغل السكّر والعسل ٢،ق٢/٤١٩ وأموال الأيتام وتمّت معاقبة القضاة الذين كانوا يدافعون عن أموال الأيتام السلوك،٢، ق٢/٤٣٢، كما كانت المغنيات تصادر بذرائع متنوّعة السلوك، ٢، ق٢/٨٣٦، وكان كبار الأمراء يصادرون بدورهم بسبب تآمرهم أو غير ذلك كما كانوا سيغرّمون أموالا وهذا الأمر يعتبر مصادرة، السلوك، ٣، ق٣/١١٤١.

[٢٩] المقريزيّ، السلوك،١، ق٣/٨١٠، ٨١٤.

[٣٠] المقريزيّ، السلوك،٢، ق٣/٧٠٢.

[٣١] المصدر السابق، ٤، ق٣/١٠٩٨.

[٣٢] المقريزيّ، السلوك، ١، ق١/١٣٠–١٣٤، ٢٠٠.

وكيف صارت.[٣٣]ودرس غلاء الأسعار أحيانًا بشكل بيانيّ من دون أن يجد سببًا موضوعيًّا لارتفاعها سوى فساد الإدارة المملوكيّة[٣٤]. ولعلّ من أبرزها دراساته تطوّر سعر أردب القمح: فإنّه كان ينقص نصف سدسه بسبب كلفة سفره وأجرة السمسرة، وحمولته، وغربلته، وطحنه[٣٥].

واعتبر الاحتكار أحد أبرز أسباب الغلاء ولا سيّما في عهد برسباي، الذي فرض على التجّار شراء السكّر من المتجر السلطانيّ فقط، كما حظّر على المزارعين زراعة السكّر لتبقى احتكارًا سلطانيًّا[٣٦]. وتعدّى الأمر السكّر، الذي هو إنتاج محلّيّ، إلى احتكار الفلفل المستورد إذ: «أوقعت الحوطة سنة **١٤٣٢/٨٣٥** على فلفل التجّار بالقاهرة ومصر والإسكندريّة... ورسم بأن يكون الفلفل مختصًّا بمتجر السلطان.[٣٧]» وفي هذا الإطار درس أحيانًا موازنة الدولة كما في عهدي اسماعيل بن الناصر محمّد بن قلاوون[٣٨]، وبرقوق[٣٩]. وهي لعمري دراسة ماليّة متقدّمة جدًّا، تنمّ عن وعي تامّ للوضع الاقتصاديّ والفساد الإداريّ.

استنزاف المماليك للطاقات الاقتصاديّة من جراء فرض الرسوم والضرائب الجائرة، وطرح السلع على التجّار، ومصادرة ممتلكات أرباب الاقتصاد والإدارة وأموالهم جعل أرباب المعرفة بالاقتصاد، يأنفون من تولّي المناصب الإدارية الاقتصاديّة كالوزارة وديواني الخاصّ والمفرد، والاستاداريّة[٤٠]. والمقريزيّ، إلى ذلك، درس بجلاء بنية الاقتصاد المملوكيّ المتردّي محذّرًا من أنّ استمراره سيؤدّي إلى إضعاف الدولة وسقوطها.

ج) موقفه من الإدارة: خبر المقريزيّ الإدارة المملوكيّة عن كثب، إذ تولّى الحسبة والقضاء، وأدرك مدى اهتراء أهل الرأي في الإدارة، ومدى تردّدهم

---

٣٣ المصدر السابق، ١، ق٢/٤٤٦ وق٣/٧١٧–٧١٨.

٣٤ المعلومات وفيرة حول هذه الناحية وإليك بعض الصفحات:السلوك، ٣، ق٣/٩٨٢، و١١٠٠، ١١٣٣–١١٣٥.

٣٥ المقريزيّ، السلوك، ٣، ق٣/١١٣٢–١١٣٥.

٣٦ المقريزيّ، السلوك، ٤، ق٢/٦٤٧، ٦٥٤، ٧٦٦.

٣٧ المقريزيّ، السلوك، ٤، ق٢/٨٦٩.

٣٨ المقريزيّ، السلوك، ٢، ق٣/٦٦٥، ٦٧١.

٣٩ فذكر فيها مقدار الذي تركه حين وفاته، وقيمة ومقدار المخزون عنده من مختلف الاصناف، وعدد الخيول والجمال في اصطبلاته، ومقدار جوامك مماليكه الشهريّة، وعليق خيولهم، السلوك، ٣، ق٢/٩٣٨.

٤٠ المقريزيّ، السلوك، ٢، ق٣/٩١٨–٩١٩.

باتخاذ القرارات المسؤولة، ومن ثمّ التراجع عنها إكرامًا لهذا الأمير أو ذاك، أو تقرّب السلطان من مسبّبي القلق السياسيّ في دولته، علّه بهذا الإكرام يتّقي شرهم.

وما عاد معظم أصحاب الوظائف الديوانيّة أو المتعمّمين على اختلاف مراتبهم بمن فيهم قضاة القضاة، والقضاة يمارسون وظائفهم بنزاهة، بل صاروا في خدمة السلطان وكبار أمرائه، لأنّ وظائفهم صارت تشرى بمال حتّى باتت الرشوة عنوان العهد الجركسيّ[٤١]. وساهمت معرفة بعض السلاطين الجركسة المتواضعة بالعلوم الدينيّة في إفساد النظام القضائيّ كما حصل في المجلس الذي عقده المؤيّد شيخ لقضاة القضاة الأربعة ومشايخ العلم، وقد تندّر به المقريزيّ قائلا: «فكان مجلسًا بغاية القبح، من إهانة الهروي وبهدلته[٤٢]». وهو يسوق مثالاً على هذه الأوضاع الشاذّة إسناد الحسبة العام ١٤٠٦/٨٠٨ إلى أحد باعة السكّر، معلّقًا على ذلك: «فكان هذا من أشنع القبائح وأقبح الشناعات».[٤٣] ويروي أنّ أقبغا الجمالي «سعى في الاستداريّة على أن يحمل عشرة آلاف دينار[٤٤]». وأضاف السلطان العام ١٤٣٢/٨٣٥ إلى كاتب السرّ الصاحب كريم الدين عبد الكريم ابن كاتب المناخ الوزارة ويعلّق على هذه الحادثة متحسّرًا :«ولم يقع مثل ذلك في الدولة التركيّة... وباشر مع بعده عن صناعة الإنشاء وقلّة دربته بقراءة القصص والمطالعات الواردة من الأعمال. غير أنّ الكفاءة غير معتبرة في زماننا، بحيث إنّ بعض السوقة ممن نعرف ولّي كتابة السرّ بحماه على مال قام به[٤٥]».

د) المجتمع: ١. المجتمع القلق: لربّما يكون مؤرّخنا قد ركّز على هذا المجتمع غير المطمئن لشدّة الصراعات الدامية بين طوائف المماليك وأمرائهم ما كان يؤدّي إلى غلاء في الأسعار، وإغلاق للأسواق ونهبها، وخطف الناس من الطرقات، والتعدّي

---

٤١ المصدر السابق، ١، ق٥٣٨/٢–٥٤٠، ٥٤٢، و٢، ق٤٣٩/٢–٤٤٣.

٤٢ وقد حضر هذا المجلس ابن مغلي قاضي قضاة الحنابلة الذي سأل قاضي قضاة الشافعي عن أربع مسائل وهو يجيبه فيقول له أخطأت، وتدخل قاضي قضاة الحنفية لصالح الأوّل وراح يشتم الهروي قاضي قضاة الشافعيّة ثمّ قال: « يا مولانا السلطان أشهدك على اني حجرت عليه الاّ يفتي.» السلوك، ٤، ق٤٧٩/١–٤٨٥.

٤٣ المقريزيّ، السلوك، ٤، ق١١/١.

٤٤ المقريزيّ، السلوك، ٤، ق٢/ ٨٦٦–٨٦٧.

٤٥ المقريزيّ، السلوك، ٤، ق٢/ ٨٧٠–٨٧١.

على الرجال والنساء في الحمامات[٤٦]. وكثيرًا ما كان سبب الفتنة تافهًا كإشاعة كاذبة، أو خلاف مؤقّت بين أميرين لا يلبثان أن يتصالحا[٤٧]. ولم يكن لذلك المجتمع القلق هويّة فكانت أحداثه ومظاهره متشابهة في كلّ مكان: في القاهرة أو حلب أو دمشق، رغم تغيّر الظروف في كلّ منها. وكان المقريزيّ شديد الحساسيّة تجاه هذه التصرّفات الخارجة على الأطر الدينيّة والأخلاقيّة، التي كانت تهدّد حياة الناس ومصالحهم في كل وقت وتقضّ مضاجعهم، من دون أن يعمل المماليك على حلّها جذريًّا، لأنّهم كانوا مسبّبيها.

وشكّلت الحرائق إحدى عوامل القلق الاجتماعيّ والأمنيّ لما كانت تسبّبه من أضرار بالغة من دون أن يُعرف إجمالاً مسبّبوها[٤٨]. وكذلك كانت حال المناسر التي تشتدّ أحيانًا[٤٩]. وعرض مؤرّخنا للأوبئة والأمراض ومسبّباتها ونتائجها، ذاكرًا بعض أسماء النباتات والفواكه المستخدمة كأدوية في معالجتها، محدّدًا أسعارها، متحسّرا بسبب عجز عدد وافر من الناس عن شرائها[٥٠]. وكان الطاعون الأشدّ فتكا بين الأوبئة. وصوّر حالة الناس وأرباب الدولة عندما كان الوباء يشتدّ فيعجز الأطبّاء عن الحدّ من انتشاره وعن شفاء المرضى، فكانوا أمام هذا العجز يلوذون بالصلاة والصيام مدّة ثلاثة أيّام، أو يخرجون للصلاة في الصحراء[٥١].

٢. الملابس: واستكمالاً للنظرة الكلّيّة إلى مجتمع لم يغفل عن وصف الملابس، محدّدًا مستوى ملابس كلّ فئة من فئات المجتمع المملوكيّ وأنواعها، ذاكرًا أسباب منع ارتداء بعض الأزياء واستبدالها بأخرى فتصبح (موضة)[٥٢]. ويمكن للباس أن يشكّل بطاقة هويّة لبعض الموظّفين. فإذا كانت للمماليك على اختلاف مراتبهم ألبسة محدّدة لكلّ فئة ومنزلة، فإنّه كان لكلّ درجة من المتعمّمين لباسها المميّز: «خلع على شمس الدين محمّد الهروي واستقر قاضي للقضاة... فغيّر زيّه، وهذه المرّة الرابعة في تغيير زيّه، فإنّه كان أوّلًا يتزيّا بزيّ العجم، فلبس عمامة عوجاء

---

٤٦ المصدر السابق، ١، ق٣٨/٢.

٤٧ المصدر السابق، ٣، ق١٠١٨/٣ والنماذج كثيرة.

٤٨ ٣، ق٢٧/١–٢٨، ٤، ق٨٩٢/٢.

٤٩ تخوّف الناس من منسر انعقد بالقاهرة، وكان أعضاؤه يكتبون أوراقًا يطلبون فيها أموالاً من الأغنياء: «ومتى لم تبعث لنا ذلك كنا ضيوفك» السلوك، ٢، ق٦٤٤/٣، ٩٠١–٩٠٢.

٥٠ السلوك، ٣، ق١١٢٤/٣–١١٢٦.

٥١ المقريزيّ، السلوك، ٤، ق٤٨٧/١.

٥٢ المصدر السابق، ٢، ق٨١٠/٣–٨١١.

بعذبة عن يساره. فلمّا ولّي القضاء لبس الحبة، وجعل العمامة كبيرة، وأرخى العذبة بين كتفيه، فلما ولّي كتابة السرّ تزيّا بزيّ الكتاب وترك زيّ القضاة وضيّق أكمامه، وجعل عمامته صغيرة مدوّرة ذات أضلاع، وترك العذبة، وصار على عنقه طوق ولبس الذهب والحرير[٥٣]».

٣. **اللهو والاحتفالات:** تناول «السلوك» أنواع اللهو[٥٤]، والاحتفالات الدينيّة والدنيويّة التي كان يعبق بعضها بالفسق والفساد[٥٥]، من دون أن يهمل المغنّين ونشاطاتهم[٥٦]. ومدّنا بنماذج عن مهر الزواج[٥٧]. واعتبر أنّ الخمرة من المساوئ الاجتماعيّة متحدّثًا عن أسباب إبطال الخمّارات وإهراق الخمور[٥٨].

هـ) **موقفه من الذمّيّين:** لم يقتصر مجتمع المقريزيّ على حياة المسلمين فقط إنّما أرّخ أيضًا لعلاقة أهل الذمّة بالمسلمين عمومًا وأركان الحكم خصوصًا. وكان ينحاز إلى جانبهم عندما يظلمون، ويهاجمهم عندما كانوا يخطئون، مبديًا ملاحظات قيّمة حول علاقاتهم الاجتماعيّة. فذكر أنّ الشروط العمريّة طبّقت عليهم مرّات عديدة[٥٩]، ومنعوا مرّات كثيرة من شغل الوظائف الحكوميّة أو التي طردوا منها، متطرّقًا إلى الأسباب الموجبة، وهي برأيه غير مطلقة بسبب تضارب مواقف الفقهاء منها بين مؤيّد ومعارض[٦٠]. ويأسف لهدم عدد كبير من الكنائس لأنّه كان يتمّ مرارًا، من دون مبرّر

٥٣ المصدر السابق، ٤، ق٦٧٠/٢–٦٧١.

٥٤ بحديثه عن لهو السلطان شعبان يتناول حضير الحمام (تربيتها وكشّها)، والصراع، والتثاقف، والشباك، وجري السعاة، والنطاح بالكباش، ومناقرة الديوك والقماري.السلوك، ٢، ق٧٣٩/٣.

٥٥ ويتحدّث المقريزيّ عن أحد الشيوخ الذي عمل المولد العام ٧٩٠ وقد حدث فيه أنواع الفساد: «وفي هذه الليلة عمل الشيخ... المولد على عادته في زاويته... فكان فيه من الفساد ما لا يوصف، إلا أنّه وجد من الغد في المزارع مائة وخمسون جرّة فارغة من جرار الخمر التي شربت تلك الليلة، سوى ما حكي عن الزنا واللياطة.» ٣، ق٥٧٦/٢. ويذكر أنّ المراكب منعت من عبور خليج الحاكميّ لكثرة ما كان يحصل هناك من فساد والتظاهر بالمنكر، وتبرّج النساء وجلوسهن مع الرجال مكشوفات الوجوه... وشربهن الخمر ٢، ق٢٩/١، وتتبع محتسب القاهرة اماكن الفساد بنفسه فمنع النساء من النياح على الأموات، ومنع أيضًا التظاهر بالحشيش، وكفّ البغايا عن الوقوف لطلب الفاحشة في الأسواق ومواضع الريب» السلوك، ٤، ق٧٩٠/١.

٥٦ المقريزيّ، السلوك، ٣، ق٥٧٦/٢ أبرز المقريزيّ الشهرة التي كان يحظى بها أحد المغنّين، وتاليًا يمكّننا عبر السلوك التعرّف إلى مشاهير المغنّين والموسيقيّين٢، ق٧١٥/٣.

٥٧ المقريزيّ، السلوك، ٢، ق٣٣٣/٢.

٥٨ المصدر السابق، ق٥٣/١–٥٤، ٢١١، ٤،ق٤٨٦/١ وغيرها.

٥٩ المقريزيّ، السلوك، ١، ق٩٠٩/٣–٩١٣، ٢، ق٩٢١/٣–٩٢٧، وذكر أنّ الشروط العمريّة طبّقت على أهل الذمّة من دون ذكر السبب، السلوك، ٣، ق١٠٤٠/٣.

٦٠ المقريزيّ، السلوك، ١، ق٩٠٩/٣–٩١٣، ٢،ق٢٢٦/١–٢٢٨.

دينيّ أو مسوّغ قانونيّ[٦١]. وتحدّث عن بعض المسيحيّين ممّن تحوّل إلى الإسلام قسرًا، وبعض الذين ارتدّوا مجدّدًا إلى المسيحيّة تكفيرًا عن ذنوبهم غير آبهين بالمصير المحتوم الذي ينتظرهم[٦٢].

وهكذا نلاحظ أنّ نظرة المقريزيّ إلى التاريخ تناولت معظم جوانب الحياة السياسيّة والعسكريّة، والإداريّة، والاقتصاديّة، والاجتماعيّة؛ قبيحها وجيّدها. فيتبدّى لك مجتمع المماليك في «السلوك» مجتمعًا متحرّكًا نابضًا بالحياة. وقد يكون لرصيد ثقافة المقريزيّ الدينيّة، وحسّه الاجتماعيّ المرهف، وأخلاقه الحميدة ما جنّبه الانجرار في مسار الفساد الجارف الذي ساد عصره، لا بل غدا أبرز سماته السيّئة. ولست أغالي إذا اعتبرت أنّ هذا الرصيد برز في موقفه من ثقافة المماليك العامّة في مختلف الميادين، ومن نقده اللاذع لممارساتهم غير المبرّرة دينيًّا وإنسانيًّا. واعتقد أنّه تناول كلّ ذلك من أجل تقويم المفاسد والمساوئ، لأنّ في التاريخ عبرًا.

ي) موقفه من المماليك: لعلّ محور نظرته تركّز على موقفه من المماليك سلطانًا وأمراء وأجنادًا، فقد أنصفهم عندما كانوا يستحقّون الإنصاف، وهاجمهم في غالب الأحيان لأنّه اعتبرهم مصدر المساوئ الإداريّة والاجتماعيّة والاقتصاديّة بسبب سوء تصرّفاتهم، وشرههم للمال، وتصارعهم على المناصب الرفيعة، وإهمالهم الرعيّة. وتعبيرًا عن موقفه هذا، وسمهم بشتّى أنواع النعوت غير الحميدة، وسأكتفي بالإشارة إلى بعضها: فقد ذكر في حوادث السنة ١٢٥١/٦٤٨: «كثر ضرر المماليك البحريّة بمصر، ومالوا على الناس وقتلوا ونهبوا الأموال، وسبوا الحريم، وبالغوا بالفساد، حتّى

---

٦١ أفتى الفقيه نجم الدين بن رفعة بنهب الكنائس وبوجوب هدمها فعارضه فقيه آخر، وكان تمّ هدم بعض الكنائس والبيوت في الإسكندريّة وبقيت الكنائس في مصر مغلقة مدّة سنة كاملة، ولم يتمّ فتحها إلا بشفاعة ملك أرغونة ١، ق٩٥٠/٣، كما ذكر الأعمال الاحتياليّة من قبل بعض المتعصّبين لهدم الكنائس ما أدّى إلى هدم عدد كبير منها وكأنّه، على حدّ تعبيره، أمر سلطانيّ ٢، ق٢١٦/١–٢١٨. وأمر السلطان برقوق بهدم كنيسة بوالنمرس لأنّ نواقيسها أزعجت احد المسلمين على حد تعبير المقريزيّ وحوّلها إلى مسجد. السلوك، ٣، ق٣٤٠/١–٣٤١.

٦٢ بضغط من العامّة وتعصّبهم تحوّل عدّد من المسيحيّين إلى الإسلام خوفًا على أنفسهم على حدّ تعبيره، السلوك، ٢، ق٢٢٦/١–٢٢٨، وروى أنّ بعض المسلمين كان يشتكي للسلطان من أنّ المسيحيّين استجدّوا بعض الكنائس فيأمر بهدمها، فيستغل هؤلاء الموضوع لنهب الكنائس والأديار وهدم بعضها الآخر وإن كان غير مستجدّ، ووجه المقريزي لومًا للسلطان وغيره من أرباب الدولة على هذا التصرّف الأخرق. وكانت هذه الأعمال تؤدّي إلى تحويل بعض المسيحيّين إلى الإسلام قسرًا. السلوك، ٢، ق٩٢١/٣–٩٢٧. وروي أيضًا عن قدوم جماعات من المسيحيّين ممّن كانوا تحوّلوا قسرًا إلى الإسلام يشهرون ارتدادهم إلى المسيحيّة تكفيرًا عن ذنوبهم لأنّهم كانوا قد ارتدّوا عنها، فعرض عليهم الإسلام ولمّا رفضوه قتلوا مع النساء المرافقات لهم. السلوك، ٣، ق٣٧٢/١–٣٧٣.

لو ملك الفرنج ما فعلوا فعلهم[٦٣]». وتعليقاته على سوء تصرّف المماليك كثيرة جدًّا، وقد اعتبرها غضبًا من عند الله ليتمّ أمره فيهم، كقوله بالأمير يلبغا الجوباتي إبّان صراعه مع الأمير برقوق العثمانيّ (السلطان لاحقًا): «وكان الأمير يلبغا لأمر يريده الله قد شحّت نفسه، وساءت أخلاقه... [٦٤]».

وتحوّلت كثرة الفتن ومحاولة إخمادها وبالاً على سكّان المحلّة أو المنطقة التي كانت مسرحًا لها: إذ كانت تنهب القرى نهبًا قبيحًا، ويسطى على المواشي، ويتمّ التعدّي على النساء، وتعذيب من يظفر به المماليك حتّى يطلعهم على ما عنده من علف وغيره[٦٥].

ويغتنم المقريزيّ كلّ فرصة سانحة ليعبّر عن سوء تصرّف أيّ سلطان أو أمير فيوجّه إليه أشدّ النقد قساوة، شأن تعليقه على موت السلطان الناصر فرج بن برقوق الذي طرح على مزبلة، عاريًا إلا من سروال يستر عورته: «وغوغاء العامّة تعبث بلحيته ويديه ورجليه طوال نهار السبت، نكالاً من الله، فإنّه كان مستخفًّا بعظمة الله سبحانه، فأراه الله قدرته فيه[٦٦]». وأضاف مقوّمًا عهده السيّىء قائلاً: «وكان الناصر هذا أشأم ملوك الإسلام، فإنّه خرّب بسوء تدبيره جميع أراضي مصر والشام... وَطرق ديار مصر الغلاء من سنة ست وثمان مائة، فبذل أمراء دولته ومدبّروها جهدهم في ارتفاع الأسعار... وأفسدوا مع ذلك النقود بإبطال السكة الإسلاميّة من الذهب... ورفعوا سعر الذهب حتى بلغ إلى مئتين وأربعين كلّ مثقال بعدما كان بعشرين درهمًا... وأخذت على نواحي مصر مغارم تجبى من الفلاحين في كلّ سنة، وأهمل عمل جسور أراضي مصر... وأكثر وزراؤه من رمي البضائع على التجّار... بأغلى الأثمان... هذا مع تواتر الفتن واستمرارها بمصر والشام... [٦٧]». واعتقد أنّ رأيه هذا يحدّد بكلّ دقّة نظرته إلى المماليك.

وعليه، جاءت نظرته أفقيّة من جهة لأنّها تناولت معظم النشاطات الإنسانيّة في المجتمع المملوكيّ من دون أن تتعامى عن المساوئ، وعموديّة تحليليّة من جهة ثانية لأنّه درس حالات متعدّدة للموضوع الواحد قبل إصدار حكمه أو رأيه به. ما أعطاه فرادة بين مؤرّخي العصور الوسطى ليكون رائد مدرسة جديدة في التاريخ الاجتماعيّ والاقتصاديّ المرتبط عضويًّا بالتاريخ السياسيّ والعسكريّ.

---

٦٣ المقريزيّ، السلوك، ١، ق٣٨/٢.

٦٤ المصدر ذاته، ٣، ق١٣٠/١.

٦٥ المقريزيّ، السلوك، ٤، ق١ /١٠٥.

٦٦ المقريزيّ، السلوك، ٤، ق١/ ٢٢٤.

٦٧ المقريزيّ، السلوك، ٤، ق١/ ٢٢٥–٢٢٦.

II – أسلوبه التأريخيّ:

أ) التأريخ الحوليّ وموقف المقريزيّ من الخبر:

١. وفاؤه لصورة الخبر التقليديّة: جريًا على منهج التأريخ ظلّ المقريزيّ غالبًا وفيًّا للمفهوم التقليديّ للخبر، فحصره ضمن أجزائه السنويّة الموزّعة على أيّام أو أسابيع وربّما شهور تبعًا لمقتضى المدّة الزمنيّة للحادثة–الخبر. وإذا لم يكن تامًّا ضمن مدد وجيزة قطّعه إلى أجزاء خصوصًا إذا تجاوز السنة الواحدة، رابطًا بين هذه الأجزاء بالمصطلحات التقليديّة: « وفيها حدث كذا » أو « ورد الخبر من عكا [٦٨] »، أو « في اليوم كذا من شهر كذا فوّض القضاء إلى [٦٩] »... لإتمام الخبر عينه من دون أن يربطه سببيًّا بما كان قد حدث إلا في حالات يعود إليه وحده أمر تقديرها، إمّا لأنّها ترتبط بحدث مهمّ جدًّا، أو تتعلّق ببعض الأمور الاقتصاديّة، كما سيتّضح لاحقًا.

٢. عطف الخبر على ما سبقه: رغم وفاء المقريزيّ بوجه عامّ للصورة التقليديّة للخبر فإنّه عطفه على خبر سابق أو أكثر، ذاكرًا أحيانًا أسبابه البعيدة، كما في ذكر دوافع هجوم السلطان قلاوون على عكا: خرق الصليبيّون المعاهدة التي كانوا قد وقّعوها مع السلطان بيبرس، وقتلوا التجّار المسلمين وصادروا بضائعهم [٧٠].

ويزداد هذا المنهج وضوحًا باقتراب المقريزيّ من التأريخ لعصره، لأنّ الصورة، على ما أعتقد، باتت أكثر جلاء في ذهنه والأحداث في متناول يده يتابعها عن كثب، إمّا بالاطلاع الشخصيّ المباشر، أو بأخذها من شهود عيان موثوقين.

٣. ونجد في «السلوك» نمطًا آخر من التدوين كالخبر كالمستقل بذاته والهادف إلى رؤية أحاديّة متكاملة لموضوع محدّد بأسبابه البعيدة ونتائجه المباشرة، كما في تعداده الأسباب التي دفعت السلطان الناصر محمّد بن قلاوون إلى عزل الأمير تنكز نائب الشام وما ترتّب عليها من مصادرة أمواله[٧١]. أو تلك التي أدّت إلى خلع السلطان أحمد بن محمّد بن قلاوون: ومنها أنّ صحبه ورسله كلّهم كانوا من أوباش الكرك، جاؤوا معه إلى القاهرة، وأكثروا من أخذ البرطيل، وتسلّطوا على الوزير، وحجبوا السلطان عن الأمراء. ومنها أيضًا جمعه الأغنام من الصيد بطريقة مريبة وتلك التي كانت لوالده ولبعض الأمراء؛ واستيلاؤه على الحيوانات النادرة من الحوش السلطانيّ،

---

٦٨ المقريزيّ، السلوك، ١، ق٢/٤٤٧.

٦٩ المصدر ذاته، ١، ق٢/٤٤٨.

٧٠ المصدر ذاته، ١، ق٣/٧٥٣–٧٥٤.

٧١ المقريزيّ، السلوك، ٢، ق٢/٥٠٩.

واستيلاؤه أيضًا على ذهب وفضّة من شعائر السلطنة ومن اللجم... وسلبه ما كان لجواري والده من ذهب ومصاغ؛ ومصادرة نساء الأمراء الذين أمر بقتلهم[٧٢]. وهناك أمثلة كثيرة على هذا النمط من التأريخ منتشرة على صفحات «السلوك» مثل أسباب مقتل غرلو شاد الدواوين[٧٣]...

٤. **تعليل الحوادث:** رغم تفتيته الخبر على الطريقة التقليديّة إذا تجاوز اليوم الواحد، فإنّه حلّل بعض الحوادث وعلّلها، كما في تأريخه لضَيَاع المماليك السلطانيّة بعد عودة الناصر محمّد إلى العرش للمرّة الثانية: قويت البرجيّة بقيادة بيبرس الجاشنكير الاستادار، وكانت تقابلها الأشرفيّة والمنصوريّة بقيادة نائب السلطنة الأمير سلار، وشاركهما الأمير برلغى الذي التفّت الأشرفيّة حوله، فأصبح للمماليك السلطانيّة ثلاثة معسكرات متناقضة ما سمح للناصر محمّد بالعودة إلى الحكم[٧٤]. والأمثلة عديدة على هذا النمط كما في تعليله التضخّم النقديّ.

ويتكرّر هذا المنهج التحليليّ الاستنتاجيّ بوضوح عند المفاصل التاريخيّة المهمّة كما في التحليل الرائع لشخصيّة الأمير برقوق العثمانيّ وأسلوبه بالتمهيد لاعتلاء العرش[٧٥]. وانظر في السياق عينه تحليله الرائع لتصرّفات الناصر فرج بن برقوق السيّئة، وموقفه منها[٧٦]. واعتمد هذا النمط لإبراز نتائج الأحداث المهمّة، من دون أن يذكر أنّها نتائج، فأتت مكمّلة للحدث بل جزءًا منه، وهي نتائج اقتصاديّة، وعسكريّة، وإداريّة وسياسيّة، واجتماعيّة، كما في كلامه على تطوّر معركة وادي الخازندار[٧٧].

ويحتلّ التحليل والتعليل منزلة مهمّة في الحوادث التي عاصرها المقريزيّ، خصوصًا تلك التي كان يستاء منها، وتؤذي الناس، من أجل توضيح الصورة السيّئة للعهد الجركسيّ لأنّ الإيجابيّات المملوكيّة قليلة في «السلوك»؛ ما جعل منهجه فذًّا على هذا المستوى.

---

٧٢ المقريزيّ، السلوك، ٢، ق٣/٦١٨–٦١٩.

٧٣ المصدر ذاته، ٢، ق٣/٧٣٥–٧٣٧.

٧٤ المقريزيّ، السلوك، ١، ق٣/٨٧٥–٨٧٦.

٧٥ «وخلا الجو للأمير الكبير، ورأى أنّه قد أمن، فإنّه لما أخذ الإمرة في أيّام أينبك كان معه في ضيق، لأنّ نفسه تريد منه ما لا يؤهل له. فلما زالت دولة اينبك... وصار هو والامير بركة يتنازعان الأمور، ولا يقدر على عمل شيء إلا بمراجعة بركة حتّى كان من أمره ما ذكر، فصارت المماليك الأسياد يريدون التوثب عليه وهو يداريهم جهده، حتّى وثب بهم، وأخذهم، فلم يبق له معاند، وصار له من المماليك الجراكسة عدد كبير... فرقّاهم إلى ما لم يخطر لهم ببال، وأنعم على جماعة بامريات المقريزيّ، السلوك، ٣، ق٢/٤٧٤.

٧٦ المقريزيّ، السلوك، ٣، ق٣/١١٧٦–١١٧٨.

٧٧ المقريزيّ، السلوك، ١، ق٣/٨٩٧–٩٠٤.

٥. التركيز على وحدة الموضوع: نجد في السلوك نمطًا آخر من التأريخ الحوليّ، المبني على وحدة الموضوع حيث تضطرد الأحداث بشكل متلاحم وتتلاقى فيها الأسباب بالنتائج؛ فتجاوز المقريزيّ هكذا المنهج الحوليّ التقليديّ الذي يمزّق الخبر بالاستطرادات المتكرّرة الناجمة عن ذكر الحوادث اليوميّة[٧٨]. ومن أبرز نماذجه أخبار الناصر محمّد بن قلاوون منذ خروجه من مصر وتنازله عن العرش، وحلول بيبرس الجاشنكير مكانه، وحتّى عودته إلى العرش، ونتائج هذه العودة. ويبيّن هذا النمط مهارة المقريزيّ التأريخيّة[٧٩]. ويشكّل تأريخه للفيداويّة، من حيث علاقتهم بالسلطان الناصر محمّد بن قلاوون ونوّابه، نموذجًا صارخًا لتماسك المعلومات وتمحورها حول موضوع واحد متماسك من دون أن يتوزّع على الأيّام والشهور[٨٠].

٦. تقويم الحالة العامّة في البلاد: وبدءًا بالعام ٧٥٥ صار المقريزيّ يستهلّ أخبار السنة الجديدة بذكر السلطان القائم وأكابر رجال دولته، ليعود إلى متابعة الأحداث التي كان قد بدأها في السنة المنصرمة خلافًا لما كان قد درج عليه بإتمام الخبر عينه في السنة الجديدة، من دون أن يستهلّها بذكر السلطان القائم وكبار رجال دولته.

ومن معالم التجديد البارزة عند المقريزيّ تقويمه الحالة العامّة في الدولة في مستهلّ بعض السنوات، وهي ميزة رائعة لا نجدها عند سواه. وتنمّ في الوقت عينه عن تمرّد نفسيّ على الحكّام المماليك وتقريظ لهم لشدّة ظلمهم وسوء تدبيرهم، كما استهلّ أخبار السنة ٨٢٨/ ١٤٢٥:« وأسواق القاهرة ومصر ودمشق في كساد، وظلم ولاة الأمر من الكشاف والولاة فاش، ونوّاب القضاة قد شنعت قالة العامّة فيهم من تهافتهم. وأرض مصر أكثرها بغير زراعة، لقصور مدّ النيل في أوانه، وقلّة العناية بعمل الجسور، فإنّ كشّافها، إنّما دأبهم، إذا خرجوا لعملها أن يجمعوا مال النواحي لأنفسهم وأعوانهم. والطرقات بمصر والشام مخوفة من كثرة عبث العربان والعشير. والناس على اختلاف طبقاتهم قد غلب عليهم الفقر. واستولى عليهم الشحّ والطمع، فلا تكاد تجد إلا شاكيًا مهتمًّا لدنياه. وأصبح الدين غريبًا لا ناصر له. [٨١]». وكان يستهلّ بعض الأشهر بتقويم

---

[٧٨] أنظر مثلا مقتل الأشرف خليل وتتابع الأحداث حتّى إعلان سلطنة الناصر محمّد بن قلاوون، السلوك، ١، ق٣/٧٨٨–٧٩٨، وانظر أيضًا في السياق عينه سلطنة لاجين فهروبه حتّى اعتلاء كتبغا العرش، المصدر ذاته، ١، ق٣/٨٢٠–٨٢٧.

[٧٩] المقريزيّ، السلوك، ٢، ق١/٥٣ وما بعد.

[٨٠] المصدر ذاته، ٢، ق٣/٥٥٤–٥٥٨.

[٨١] المقريزيّ، السلوك، ٤، ق٢ /٦٧٨، وانظر نماذج أخرى: المصدر ذاته، ٤، ق٢/ ٧٠٥، ٧٣٤...

الوضع العامّ ولا سيّما الأسعار التي كانت تشكّل بنظره معيارًا لسلبيّات الحكم أو إيجابيّاته مظهرًا تداعياتها على الفقراء[٨٢].

ويشكّل اختتام المقريزيّ بعض السنوات بتقويم عامّ ميزة جديدة بل فرادة اختصّ بها، كما ختم العام **٨٣٣/ ١٤٣٠**: «كانت ذات مكاره عديدة من أوبئة شنيعة، وحروب وفتن، فكان بأرض مصر وبالقاهرة... وباء... وغرق ببحر القلزم... وغرق بالنيل... وكان ببلاد المشرق بلاء عظيم وهو أنّ شاه رخ بن تيمور... وكان ببلاد السراي والدشت وصحارى القبجاق... قحط شديد... وكان ببلاد الحبشة بلاء لا يمكن وصفه... أمّا بلاد المغرب... [٨٣]».

ب) التراجم: كان يتوسّع بترجمة السلاطين الذين أحسنوا إدارة الدولة من أمثال الناصر محمّد بن قلاوون، حتّى باتت ترجمته تختصر عهده الزاهي[٨٤]. وترجم للسلطان برقوق متحدّثًا عن حسناته، وأشاد به لأنّه ألغى الكثير من المكوس، ولتقديره الفقهاء ورجال الدين عمومًا، ولإكثاره من المنشآت العمرانيّة. ولشدّة إعجابه به تناول موازنة الدولة في عهده، وقوّم موجوداته[٨٥]. ولم تمنعه تلك الإشادة من ذكر سيّئاته وتداعياتها كشدّة نهمه للمال حتّى حذا كبار أمرائه حذوه وصار البرطيل عرفًا، بل عنوان عهده؛ وأبرز انتشار لواط الغلمان الذي أصبح عادة في عهده حتّى تشبّهت بهم البغايا[٨٦].

واللافت للانتباه أنّه لم يفرد لبعض السلاطين ترجمة خاصّة بهم في نهاية عهد كلّ منهم، بل ذكرها باقتضاب بين تراجم وفيّات العام الذي توفيّ فيه كلّ واحد منهم، وقد تكون ترجمة السلطان برسباي أبرز هذا النمط الجديد. ولعلّ مردّ ذلك إلى الصفات السيّئة التي اتّصف بها بسبب احتكاراته وبخله:« كان له في الشحّ والبخل والطمع، مع الجبن والجور وسوء الظنّ ومقت الرعيّة... وسرعة التقلّب بالأمور وقلّة الثبات أخبار لم نسمع بمثلها. وشمل مصر وبلاد الشام في أيّامه الخراب، وقلّت الأموال بها، وافتقر الناس، وساءت سيرة الحكّام والولاة... [٨٧]». ويعكس مجموع هذه التراجم الحياة الاجتماعيّة والاقتصاديّة والسياسيّة والعسكريّة في عصر المماليك، وتشكّل تاريخًا مختصرًا للحقبة التي تناولها «السلوك».

---

٨٢ المصدر السابق، ٤، ق٢/٨٠٤ وغيرها كثير.

٨٣ المصدر ذاته، ٤، ق٢/ ٨٣٦–٨٤١.

٨٤ المقريزيّ، السلوك، ج٢، ق٢، ص٥٢٤–٥٤٨.

٨٥ المقريزيّ، السلوك، ٣، ق٢ /٩٣٧–٩٤٧.

٨٦ المقريزيّ، السلوك، ٣، ق٢/ ٦٢٦–٦١٨.

٨٧ المقريزيّ، السلوك، ٤، ق٣/ ١٠٦٦.

منهج تقي الدين أحمد المقريزيّ من أكثر مناهج المؤرّخين المسلمين تنوّعًا من حيث الشكل، فقد تمتّع بخصائص طبعت «السلوك» وميّزته عن غيره من مؤلّفات العصر المملوكيّ. وتلاءمت إجمالاً مع نظرته التاريخيّة التي شكّلت لبّ منهجه، وقد تفوّق بها عمومًا على ما عداه من مؤرّخي العصور الوسطى، ما أعطاه فرادة بينهم تنمّ عن عمق في التفكير قلّما نجد له نظيرًا، وشغفٍ بالنواحي الاقتصاديّة بمحاولات دؤوبة صوّرت واقع الحياة الاجتماعيّة. وقد قال فيه تلميذه ابن تغري بردي: «هو أعظم من رأيناه وأدركناه في علم التاريخ ودروبه، مع معرفتي لمن عاصره من علماء المؤرّخين، والفرق بينهم ظاهر، وليس في التعصّب فائدة»[٨٨].

٨٨ ابن تغري بردي، نجوم، ٤٩١/١٥.

المحور الرابع

مجالات الإنتاج الثقافيّ:

العلوم

تطوّر التحصينات العسكريّة بين الفترتين الصليبيّة والمملوكيّة على الساحل اللبنانيّ
التطوّر المدُنيّ في طرابلس عبر دراسة تحصينات المدينة

أنيس شعيا
جامعة القدّيس يوسف

دراسة التحصينات العسكريّة موضوع تصعب معالجته في مؤتمر عنوانه: «عصر المماليك ازدهار أم انحطاط، تسامح أم اضطهاد؟»

لذلك تجدر الإشارة إلى أنّنا سنعالج في مداخلتنا هذه بعض المسائل المتّصلة بتطوّر شبكة التحصينات في مدينة طرابلس بين الفترتين الصليبيّة والمملوكيّة.

في أواخر القرن الحادي عشر كان الساحل اللبنانيّ يعتبر إداريًّا وسياسيًّا من أعمال الخلافة الفاطميّة في مصر[١]. ولكن مع ضعف سلطتهم، تحوّلت السلطة الإداريّة والفعليّة في هذه المنطقة إلى عائلات إقطاعيّة ولّيت سابقًا على بعض هذه المناطق مثل: عائلة بني عمّار في طرابلس والمنطقة المحاذية لها[٢].

أيضًا في القرن الحادي عشر، أدّت مجموعة من المعطيات والأحداث السياسيّة والاقتصاديّة والاجتماعيّة في أوروبا إلى تبلور فكرة إرسال حملات عسكريّة إلى بيت المقدس[٣].

---

١ Ducellier, Alain, Kaplan, Michel et Martin, Bernadette, *Le Proche-Orient Médiéval*, Paris: Hachette 1978; Bianquis, Thierry, *Damas et la Syrie sous la domination Fatimide (969–1076): Essai d'interprétation de chroniques arabes médiévales*, 2 tomes, Damas: IFD 1986–1989.

٢ Ibn Shaddād, *al-A'lāq al-khaṭira (Topographie historique d'Ibn Shaddād: Liban, Jordanie, Palestine)*, éd. S. Dahan, Damas : IFD 1963; al-Balādhurī, *Kitāb Fūtūḥ al-Buldān*, traduit par K. Hitti, *The Origins of the Islamic State*, Beyrouth: 1966.

٣ Riley-Smith, Jonathan, *The First Crusade and the Idea of Crusading*, London: 1986.

وصول ما يعرف بالحملات الصليبيّة إلى الشرق سيضع القادمين الجدّد بمواجهة مباشرة على أكثر من صعيد مع حضارات الشرق: العالم البيزنطيّ (حضارة الإمبراطوريّة الرومانيّة الشرقيّة الأرثوذكسيّة) و العالم العربيّ – الإسلاميّ (الحضارة العربيّة).

وقد عرف الشرق بين نهاية القرنين الحادي عشر والثالث عشر تطوّرات وأحداثًا سياسيّة وعسكريّة متتاليّة وضعت كامل المشرق في حالة صراع وتصادم[٤].

عند وصول الصليبيّين في أواخر القرن الحادي عشر وبدء القرن الثاني عشر، كانت مدينة طرابلس والتي كانت قائمة منذ حقب الحضارات القديمة في محلّة الميناء حاليًا محصّنة جدًّا[٥].

بعد سقوط مدينة القدس بأيدي الفرنجة وقيام مملكة بيت المقدس[٦]، تحوّل نظر قادة الحملة الصليبيّة الأولى إلى المناطق الساحليّة التي عبروها باتجاه الأراضي المقدّسة. وقد باشروا محاولة إخضاع هذه المناطق وبناء دويلات لهم فيها. وتوجّه «ريمون دي سان جيل» /كونت تولوز (في فرنسا) – أحد قادة الحملة الصليبيّة الأولى – إلى منطقة طرابلس لإخضاع المدينة وتأسيس إمارة يحكم هو عليها[٧].

ويفيدنا المؤرّخون أنّ قوّة تحصينات طرابلس أجبرت «ريمون دي سان جيل» إلى وضع حصار حول المدينة وذلك بقطع طرق التموين والمواصلات عبر بناء حصن خارج المدينة لتمكينه من إحكام قبضته على طرق التموين والتعزيزات[٨]. ويرى بعض الباحثين في موقع قلعة طرابلس على الطرف الشماليّ لتلّة أبو سمرا أنّه هو المكان الذي كان يقوم فيه حصن سفيان الأزدريّ[٩].

---

٤ Cahen, Claude, *Orient et occident au temps des croisades*, Paris: Aubier 1983; Nicolle, David, *The Crusades. Essential Histories*, Oxford: Osprey Publishing 2001.

٥ Diodore de Sicile, XVI, 41; Salamé-Sarkis, Hassān, "Histoire de Tripoli. 1. Des origines à l'époque franque", *Les cahiers de l'Oronte* 10 (1972), 81–102; Salamé-Sarkis, Hassān, "Wahlia- Mahallata- Tripoli?", *MUSJ* 49 (1975–6), 551–563.

٦ Grousset, René, *Histoire des croisades et du Royaume Franc de Jérusalem*, 3 vol., 2ème éd., Paris: Perrin 1991; Lobrichon, Guy, *1099 Jérusalem conquise*, Paris: Ed. du Seuil 1998.

٧ Deschamps, Paul, *Les châteaux des croisés en Terre Sainte: III. La défense du Comté de Tripoli et de la Principauté d'Antioche*, 2 tomes, Paris: BAH 1973.

٨ Abou al-Maḥāsen, *Les étoiles brillantes*, in: *Recueil des Historiens Orientaux des Croisades*, 3, Paris: 1884, 477; Ibn al-Qalaniṣi, *Suite à l'histoire de Damas*, trad. Roger Le Tourneau, Damas: IFD 1952, 49 et 59.

٩ عمر عبد السلام تدمريّ، تاريخ طرابلس السياسيّ والحضاريّ عبر العصور، طرابلس: مطابع دار البلاد ١٩٧٨، ٦٨.

Salamé-Sarkis, Hassān, *Contribution à l'histoire de Tripoli et de sa région à l'époque des croisades*, Paris: BAH 1980, 24–25.

هناك مصادر تاريخيّة عديدة تأتي على ذكر حصن منيع مع مربض شيّدا في بدء الفتح العربيّ (في القرن السابع للمسيح) على يد سفيان بن مجيب الأزدريّ وهو أحد قادة العسكر لدى معاوية بن أبي سفيان لمّا كان هذا الأخير آمر جند دمشق في عهد الخليفة عثمان بن عفان[١٠]. وتذكر المصادر أنّ الهدف من بناء هذا الحصن كان حصار مدينة طرابلس البيزنطيّة[١١].

كما توجد مصادر تاريخيّة أخرى من القرن العاشر تأتي على ذكر ربض[١٢] خارج مدينة طرابلس تعرّض للحرق على يد الإمبراطور البيزنطيّ نقفور فوكاس Nicéphore Phocas (٩٦٣–٩٦٩م) وذلك لمّا لم يتمكّن هذا الأخير من دخول المدينة خلال حملته العسكريّة على المنطقة السنة (٣٥٨هـ/٩٦٨م).

وهناك مصدر تاريخيّ آخر يأتيّ على ذكر ربض يقع شرق مدينة طرابلس تعرض السنة ٩٨٠م خلال حملة الإمبراطور البيزنطيّ باسيل الثاني (٩٧٦–١٠٢٥م) للهجوم والخراب[١٣].

من هنا يمكن الاستنتاج أنّ لدى وصول الصليبيّين إلى طرابلس كانت توجد على تخوم المدينة من جهة الشرق بقايا حصن سفيان الأزدريّ والذي من المرجّح أن يكون قد تمّ استعماله خلال الحقب التاريخيّة اللاحقة.

يشكّل الطرف الشماليّ لتلّة أبو سمرا موقعًا استراتيجيًّا لبناء حصن أو قلعة[١٤] يشرف ويتحكّم بالجسر الموجود على نهر أبو علي (نهر قاديشا) والذي يفصل السهل الساحليّ الذي كانت تقوم على طرفه الغربيّ مدينة طرابلس عن الامتداد الشماليّ المؤدّي إلى منطقة البدّاوي وسهل عكار (خريطة رقم ١).

---

١٠ البلاذري، فتوح البلدان، القاهرة: ١٩٠١، ١٣٣؛ إبن الأثير، الكامل في التاريخ، ٢، بيروت: ١٩٦٥، ٤٣١؛ Salamé-Sarkis, *Contribution à l'histoire de Tripoli...*, 16–17.

١١ و التي كانت قائمة أيضًا في منطقة محلّة الميناء حاليًّا.

١٢ Yaḥya Bin Sa'id al-Anṭāki, "Histoire", in : *Corpus Scriptorum Christianorum Orientalium. Scriptores Arabici*, 51:7, eds. Louis Cheikho s.j., Réimpression Louvain, Beyrouth: 1909; Ibn al-'Adim, *Histoire d'Alep*, 1, éd. S. Dahan, Damas: IFD, 1951, 158.
الحمدانيّ، تكملة تاريخ الطبريّ، الطبعة الثانية، بيروت: منشورات أ. كنعان ١٩٦١، ٢٠١؛ إبن الأثير، الكامل في التاريخ، ٥٩٦.

١٣ يحيى بن سعيد الأنطاكيّ، صلة كتاب سعيد بن بطريق، الأب شيخو اليسوعيّ، بيروت: ١٩٠٩. Al-Anṭāki, "Histoire", 161.

١٤ Salamé-Sarkis, *Contribution à l'histoire de Tripoli*..., 24–27.

نذكر هنا أنّ موقع مدينة طرابلس، كان منذ الحقب التاريخيّة القديمة وحتّى بدء الحقبة المملوكيّة[١٥]، في الطرف الغربيّ للسهل الساحليّ في منطقة رأس طبيعيّ داخل البحر الأبيض المتوسّط ما يشكّل له حماية طبيعيّة من ثلاث جهات: الغرب، الجنوب والشمال. تستند قاعدة هذا السهل الساحليّ من جهة الشرق إلى أولى مرتفعات جبال لبنان مع نهر أبو علي الذي يجري في هذا السهل من جهة الجنوب باتّجاه الشمال ويشكّل فاصلاً طبيعيًّا لهذا السهل المثلّث الشكل(خريطة رقم ١).

مجرى نهر أبو علي بعد خروجه من مساره في أودية جبال لبنان يتّجه نحو مصبّه شمال مدينة طرابلس، ويمرّ بين تلّة أبو سمرا من جهة الغرب وتلّة القبّة من جهة الشرق حيث يتراوح ارتفاعهما بين علو ستّين وثمانين مترًا فوق مستوى البحر.

موقع تلّة أبو سمرا يقع غرب نهر أبو علي الذي يشكّل خطًا عازلاً طبيعيًّا بين شمال السهل الساحليّ وجنوبه. كما أنّ تضاريس التلّة تنحدّر تدريجيًّا من الجنوب باتّجاه الشمال والغرب بنسبة توازي خمسًا وأربعين درجة بينما من الجهة الشرقيّة الانحدار حادّ ووعر بدرجة انحدار تتراوح نسبته من سبعين إلى خمس وسبعين درجة (خريطة رقم ٢).

الطريق من الشمال إلى الجنوب كان يمرّ في المكان الأنسب لعبور نهر أبو علي وهذا المكان يقع في أسفل تلّة أبو سمرا لجهة الشمال في موقع حيث إمكانيّة بناء جسر يؤمّن التواصل بين الضفّتين كان سهلاً، وهو موقع الجسر القديم قرب المدرسة البرطاسيّة قبل فيضان نهر أبو علي وبناء البولفار على طول مجرى النهر (خريطة رقم ٢).

هذا الطريق يمرّ في ما بعد بمحاذاة تلّة أبو سمرا من جهة الغرب في أسفل مدرّجات التلّة في موقع سوق الخضار الحاليّ ويتّجه جنوبًا (خريطة رقم ٢).

تظهر الزيارة الميدانيّة للمدينة القديمة بعض المعالم في النسيج المدنيّ والتي تشكّل دراستها مدخلاً لاكتشاف مراحل التمدّد المدنيّ في مدينة طرابلس بالإضافة إلى بعض ما عرفته المدينة من تحصينات.

في نصف الطريق النازل من قلعة طرابلس (صورة رقم ١) باتّجاه الأسواق والذي يلاقي مباشرةً الطريق المارّ بمحاذاة التلّ والذي يصل الشمال بالجنوب (طريق الأسواق المذكور سابقًا)، يفاجئنا وجود بقايا بوّابة ضخمة في وسط النسيج العمرانيّ القديم (صورة رقم ٢). لا نجد أيّ شرح لدور هذه البوّابة لدى أيّ من الباحثين.

دراسة تضاريس التلّ وموقع البوّابة (صورة رقم ٣ و٤) يظهر لنا أنّ هذه البوّابة مبنيّة في مكان تتحوّل فيه نسبة انحدار الطريق. إنّ نسبة الانحدار في الجزء العلويّ من هذا

---

[١٥] Salamé-Sarkis, "*Contribution à l'histoire de Tripoli*...".

الطريق أقوى منها في الجزء السفليّ. وعند نقطة تغيّر نسبة الانحدار تمّ بناء البوّابة (التي أتينا على ذكرها) على شكل قنطرة مرتفعة (خريطة رقم ٢ و٣).

دراسة هذه البوّابة مع تحليل وجودها في هذا المكان تعطي عددًا من المعلومات التي توضح جزءًا من تاريخ المدينة وتطوّر بنائها وتمدّدها العمرانيّ.

إغلاق البوّابة يتمّ باتجاه الجزء السفليّ؛ بمعنى أنّ الواجهة الداخليّة هي لجهة الجزء العلويّ أيّ من جهة الشرق. أمّا الجزء الخارجيّ فهو الجزء السفليّ أي لجهة الغرب.

- يظهر ذلك عبر قواعد تثبيت البوّابة (صورة رقم ٥) وهي تظهر من الجهة الشرقيّة للبوّابة (من الجهة العلويّة).
- وجود بقايا سقاطات (Machicoulis) عدّة تظهر قواعدها على الواجهة الخارجيّة لجهة الغرب والتي تطلّ على الجهة السفليّة من الطريق (صورة رقم ٦)

دراسة شكل قنطرة البوّابة والسقاطات تساعدنا على وضع تاريخ بناء هذه البوّابة الدفاعيّة وذلك استنادًا إلى المقارنة ودراسة تاريخ فنّ العمارة والهندسة المعماريّة العسكريّة.

مقارنة قنطرة البوّابة مع عدد من أشكال القناطر المعروفة وعبر دراسة طريقة بنائها مع عدم وجود مفتاح للقنطرة وإنّما هناك بدل ذلك حجران متلاصقان عموديًّا ومتوازيان كمفتاح، يتبين لنا أنّها مشابهة لعدد من القناطر والبوّابات في منطقة كونتيّة طرابلس والتي تعود إلى القرن الثاني عشر. نذكر منها على سبيل المثال: البوّابة الشماليّة في البرج الأساس في قلعة طرابلس (صورة رقم ٧) والبوّابة في السور الشرقيّ للحصن الأوّل لقلعة طرابلس والموجود حاليًّا داخل أسوار القلعة (صورة رقم ٨ و٩)، بالإضافة إلى البوّابات وعدد من القناطر والمداخل في قلعة حصن الأكراد (Crack des Chevaliers).

نذكر في هذا المجال أنّ الفرنجة الذين استقرّوا في منطقة طرابلس كانوا بإمرة «ريمون دي سان جيل» – كونت مدينة «تولوز» – وعائلته الذين قدموا من جنوب فرنسا. المقارنة مع بعض معالم العمارة العسكريّة في منطقة «تولوز» من تلك الحقبة تظهر لنا في قلعة «كاركاسون» «Carcassonne» وبالأخص في أجزائها السفليّة القديمة العناصر الهندسيّة ذاتها في العمارة وفي بناء القناطر والبوّابات، والتي تعود بتاريخها إلى القرنين الحادي عشر والثاني عشر[١٦].

أمّا في ما خصّ السقاطات (صورة قم ٤ و٦)، فهي عناصر دفاعيّة في الهندسة المعماريّة العسكريّة تستعمل لتأمين دفاع عموديّ لقاعدة الجدران والبوّابات أو مداخل

---

١٦ Grimal, François, *Cité de Carcassonne*, Paris: Caisse nationale des monuments historiques 1966.

الحصون و القلاع والمدن. تجدر الإشارة إلى أنّ هذه السقاطات مطابقة بشكلها إلى السقاطات التي كانت موجودة في البرج الأساس في قلعة جبيل والتي يعود تاريخها إلى بدء القرن الثاني عشر.

موقع هذه البوّابة في وسط الطريق المؤدّي إلى أسفل التلّ (نحو الغرب) في مكان تتحوّل فيه درجة الانحدار بشكل ملحوظ، يعطي البوّابة موقعًا مشرفًا واستراتيجيًّا على الطريق الذي يمرّ بمحاذاة أسفل التلّ بالإضافة إلى إمكانيّة مراقبته وقطعه عند الاقتضاء (خريطة رقم ٢؛ صورة رقم ٢ و٣).

استنادًا إلى ما تقدّم، يمكننا تحديد تاريخ بناء هذه البوّابة في بدء القرن الثاني عشر. وهي الفترة التي شهدت تأسيس كونتيّة طرابلس عبر بناء قلعة سان جيل لتقوية الحصار ضد بني عمّار – حكّام مدينة طرابلس حينها.

شمال البوّابة من الجهة الداخليّة ينطلق زقاق بمحاذاة امتداد جدار البوّابة نحو الشمال (صورة رقم ١٠ و١١). لدينا هنا بعض الأجزاء من سور يحصّن الجزء العلويّ من التلّ حيث توجد القلعة. بمعنى آخر القلعة في الحقبة الصليبية كانت موجودة داخل منطقة محصنة تمتدّ على جزء كبير من شمال تلّة أبو سمرا مع منحدراتها من ثلاث جهات: الغرب، الجنوب والشرق (خريطة رقم ٣).

عبر بقايا هذا السور والبوّابة بالإضافة إلى عدد من المكتشفات المتفرّقة مع دراسة تضاريس المنحدرات في محيط التلّ، يمكن إعادة رسم مخطّط موقع السور من الجهة الغربيّة لتلّة أبو سمرا حيث يمتدّ شمالاً انطلاقًا من البوّابة بخطٍ متوازٍ للطريق الذي يصل الشمال بالجنوب والذي يمرّ بمحاذاة أسفل التلّ. أغلب الظنّ أنّ السور كان يكمل ويستدير مع شكل التلّ على المستوى ذاته فيلتفّ لجهة الشرق لتأمين الحماية من جهة الشمال ثمّ يلتفّ مجدّدًا جنوبًا ليشكّل حاجز حماية من جهة الشرق على مستوى عالٍ ضدّ أيّة أخطار عسكريّة وبخاصّة عوامل فيضان النهر (خريطة رقم ٣)

أمّا جنوبًا فالسور كان يمتدّ حوالى عشرة أمتار على امتداده الشماليّ ذاته ثمّ يرتفع مستواه باتجاه أعلى التلّ بموازاة الطريق الحالي الصاعد –الطريق المعروف بطلعة الرفاعيّة– حتّى نصفه ثمّ يتبع خطّ طريق مشاة و درجًا ضيّقًا باتجاه الجنوب–الشرقيّ ودليلنا على ذلك أنّه في سياق أعمال تمديدات قنوات للهاتف و للصرف الصحّيّ في طلعة الرفاعيّة تمّ اكتشاف نفق مبنيّ باتّجاه شرق–غرب وهو ممرّ/سرداب بعلو يناهز ١٢٠ سنتم يصل بين أعلى التلّة و الجزء السفليّ منها (خريطة رقم ٣). يعود هذا النفق إلى القرنين الثالث عشر والرابع عشر، وذلك استنادًا إلى مكتشفات لقى كسر من الفخار وجدت في أتربة الردميّات المستخرجة.

أمّا من الجهة الجنوبيّة فيبقى تحديد مكان مرور هذا السور غير أكيد وذلك لعدم توفّر أيّ دليل حسيّ[١٧]. من المرجّح أنّه كان يمرّ بشكل مباشر جنوب كنيسة مار يوحنّا الصليبيّة باتّجاه السور الذي كان موجودًا جهة الشرق؛ منطلقًا من طرف الدرج المتفرّع صعودًا من طلعة الرفاعيّة عابرًا وسط تلّة أبو سمرا المكان الذي يتحوّل فيه انحدار الأرض باتّجاهي الغرب والشرق. يمرّ السور جنوب كنيسة مار يوحنّا ليلاقي السور الشرقيّ بالقرب من مجرى نهر أبو علي (خريطة رقم ٣).

بناءً على ما تقدّم، فإنّ شمال تلّة أبو سمرا مع القلعة القائمة عليه كان محصّنًا في بدء الحقبة الصليبيّة على غرار صافيتا[١٨] البرج الأبيض(Castel Blanc) التي تشرف على النهر الشماليّ الكبير من جهة الشمال وهي من أعمال كونتيّة طرابلس.

من هنا نرى أنّ الجزء الشماليّ من تلّة أبو سمرا كان محصّنًا بأسوار تحوط بمربض في وسطه قلعة سان جيل/قلعة طرابلس مع كنيسة مار يوحنّا نحو الجنوب–الغربيّ (خريطة رقم ٣).

تلتقي المصادر على أنّ الفرنجة قاموا ببناء حصن و بأسفله[١٩] مربض حوالى السنة ٤٩٧هـ/١١٠٣م وذلك بهدف حصار مدينة طرابلس للاستيلاء عليها. كما أنّهم لم يتمكّنوا من احتلالها إلاّ السنة ٥٠٣هـ/١١٠٩م. ولكنّهم تمكّنوا من بسط سيطرتهم تدريجيًّا على كامل المدن و القلاع والأبراج المحيطة بطرابلس شمالاً وجنوبًا.

بين ١١٠٣ و١١٠٩م قام الفرنجة بتشديد قبضتهم على الساحل في محيط طرابلس وذلك باحتلالهم تدريجيًّا مختلف المدن والقلاع شمال طرابلس وجنوبها وشرقها: جبيل، البترون، عرقا، عكار العتيقة، حصن الأكراد[٢٠]... كانت عمليّة الحصار تشتدّ حينًا و تلتغي أحيانًا على طرابلس إلى حين تمّ تنظيم هجوم كامل على المدينة السنة ١١٠٩م.

خلال كلّ الفترة الممتدّة من ١١٠٣ حتّى ١١٠٩م، أدّت قلعة طرابلس، ومربضها، دورًا مهمًّا حيث سيكون مركز الثقل السياسيّ في كونتيّة طرابلس. هذه الأهمّيّة السياسيّة

---

١٧ نظرًا إلى التمدّد العمرانيّ خلال القرن العشرين مع وجود نسبة كبيرة من الأبنية الحديثة المقامة في هذه المنطقة بالإضافة إلى عدد من الشوارع.

١٨ Deschamps, *La défense du Comté de Tripoli*.

١٩ يمكن أن كلمة «أسفله» اعتمدت في المصادر القديمة لأنّ كلّ من يرتاد الطريق الآتي من الشمال باتّجاه الجنوب أو الطريق القادم من جهة مدينة طرابلس التي كانت تقع على الساحل لجهة الغرب، يرى الجهتين الشماليّة والغربيّة من المربض اللتين تظهران بأسفل القلعة. المربض يمتدّ اسفل القلعة من الجهتين الشماليّة والغربيّة، أمّا من الجهتين الشرقيّة والجنوبيّة فمستوى المربض أعلى من مستوى المكان الذي تقوم عليه القلعة.

٢٠ Deschamps, *La défense du Comté de Tripoli*.

شكّلت عامل جذب سكّانيّ لهذا الموقع. وبعد أن تمكّن الصليبيّون من السيطرة على مدينة طرابلس، أبقوا على الدور العسكريّ المهمّ للقلعة، بينما شهد المربض المحيط بالقلعة تطوّرًا وتمدّدًا سكانيًّا نحو أسفل تلّة أبو سمرا من جهتي الشمال والغرب.

من البديهيّ التذكير بأنّ القلعة كانت في تواصل مستمرّ مع مختلف المواقع والقلاع المحيطة بها، من هنا أهمّيّة وضع تصوّر لإمكانيّات التواصل إن بريًّا أو بواسطة إشارات وعلامات بين مختلف المواقع المطلّة على بعضها البعض.

موقع قلعة طرابلس يضعها في تواصل مباشر مع عدد من المواقع المحصّنة:

- منطقة البدّاويّ
- برج نهر أبو علي
- برج نهر البحصاص
- منطقة الجبال الداخليّة من جهة الجنوب–الشرقيّ الموازي لمجرى نهر أبو علي (قاديشا) و ذلك حتّى أعالي جبال لبنان وتحديدًا منطقة إهدن حتّى حردين.

في نهاية القرن الثالث عشر، لم يتمكّن المماليك من احتلال كونتيّة طرابلس إلاّ على مراحل، وذلك على غرار الصليبيّن. بين ١٢٦٧ و١٢٨٩م قام السلطان بيبرس وبعده السلطان قلاوون بتشديد القبضة تدريجيًّا على كامل المنطقة عبر احتلال جميع المواقع المحصّنة في محيط طرابلس ومن ثمّ تمكّنوا من الاستيلاء على المدينة.

تجدر الإشارة إلى أنّ المماليك أبقوا على نفوذ غربيّ في مدينة جبيل حتّى السنة ١٣٠٤م، وذلك عبر معاهدة تعاون تجاريّ واقتصاديّ تترك لنفوذ العائلات الإيطاليّة تدبير الشؤون التجاريّة والداخليّة لمدينة جبيل مقابل الاعتراف بسلطة المماليك و دفع الجزية لهم[٢١].

سيطر المماليك تدريجيًّا على المنطقة كما يلي:

- قلعة طرابلس مع المربض و محيطهما مع السلطان بيبرس السنة ١٢٦٧م؛
- أغلبيّة القلاع في منطقة عكار مع السلطان بيبرس حوالى السنة ١٢٦٧م؛
- مناطق واسعة من الجبال العالية –قسم من جبّة بشري– مع السلطان بيبرس السنة ١٢٨٣م؛
- وأخيرًا مدينة طرابلس القديمة القائمة على الشاطئ مع السلطان قلاوون السنة ١٢٨٩م.

ولدينا هنا بعض الدلائل على أنّه تمّت المحافظة على طريقة التنظيم المدنيّ ذاتها مع تراتبيّة خطوط الدفاع عينها في الفترة المملوكيّة : القلعة ضمن مربض محصّن ثمّ المدينة المملوكيّة.

---

٢١ Riley-Smith, Jonathan, *Atlas des croisades*, Paris: Autrement, 1996.

يوجد عدد من الدلائل الأثريّة والمعماريّة التي تدلّ على وجود بقايا أبنية من الحقبة الصليبيّة استعملها المماليك داخل خط أسوار المربض الأوّل وهي موجودة في حمى أسوار خط الدفاع الأوّل و التي يمكن دراستها مثل:

- المساقط المعلميّة لمسجد الأويسيّة مع دراسة مختلف حقب البناء في جدرانه حيث تظهر قناطر تعود إلى حقبة البوّابة المذكورة أعلاه عينها (صورة رقم ١٢ و١٣)؛
- منازل عدّة شمال وشمال–غرب البوّابة الصليبيّة والتي تظهر دراسة تقاسيمها مع ما تحتويه من زخرفات ومقرنصات. نحن أمام منزل كبير غنيّ أو قصر مملوكيّ لأحد أعيان المدينة.

يمكن تصوّر تطوّر العدّد السكّانيّ في المربض ومحيطه قرب القلعة خلال كلّ هذه الفترة، الشيء الذي دفع بالسكّان والسلطات الحاكمة إلى التوسّع في السكن نحو أسفل تلّة أبو سمرا وتأسيس إحياء مع دور عبادة وأبنية مختلفة. وجود عدد من الأبنية خارج المنطقة المذكورة أعلاه تحتوي على عدد من المعالم التي تعود إلى الفترة الصليبيّة، يظهر تطوّر تمدّد السكن والمخطّط المدنيّ في هذه المنطقة خارج أسوار المربض الأوّل العائد إلى الفترة الصليبيّة والتي استعملت في ما بعد خلال الفترة المملوكيّة.

هذا التوسّع كان نواة ما سيصبح في ما بعد مدينة طرابلس المملوكيّة (خريطة رقم ٤).

من هنا يمكن تفهّم قرار قلاوون بنقل المدينة من الساحل إلى محيط تلّة أبو سمرا –موقع مدينة طرابلس المملوكيّة– حيث كان يوجد هناك مجمّع سكنيّ متكامل يؤلّف نواة مدينة صغيرة يستعمله المماليك منذ احتلالهم القلعة ومحيطها السنة ١٢٦٧م[٢٢] وحتّى ١٢٨٩[٢٣] تاريخ سقوط مدينة طرابلس الصليبيّة في يد المماليك. من هنا كان عدم جدوى المحافظة على مدينة طرابلس الساحليّة، بخاصّة مع تخوّف السلطان قلاوون من عودة الفرنجة في حملة جديدة واستعمالهم المدينة الساحليّة كرأس جسر.

---

٢٢ المقريزيّ، كتاب السلوك لمعرفة دول الملوك، جزءين، القاهرة: مصطفى زيادة ١٩٥٦، ٧٣ و١٩٥٧، ٥٦٦.

Salamé-Sarkis, *Contribution à l'histoire de Tripoli*..., 34.

٢٣ المقريزيّ، كتاب السلوك... ١٩٣٩، ٧٤٧.

Abū-l-Fidā, *Résumé de l'Histoire*, in: *Recueils des Historiens Orientaux des Croisades*, Paris: 1872, 1–165.

Salamé-Sarkis, *Contribution à l'histoire de Tripoli*..., 37–34.

المحور الخامس

الدولة والإدارة والعلاقة بالمجتمع

الحسبة في العصر المملوكيّ
بين التوظيف الدينيّ والسياسيّ والإدارة المدنيّة

أحمد عبد السلام
باحث مستقل

الحسبة هي أمر بالمعروف إذا ظهَرَ تركُهُ ونَهيٌ عن المنكر إذا أُظهِرَ فعلُهُ.[١] هكذا عرّف الإمام الماورديّ الحسبة في مؤلّفه الأحكام السلطانيّ في منتصف القرن الخامس الهجريّ وعلى دربه سار الفقهاء إلى يومنا هذا. وكذا اكتسبت الحسبة ونعني بها هنا الإشراف على الأسواق ومتابعة أهل الصنائع صفة وظيفة دينيّة.

وقد لازمتها هذه الصفة أو ألزمها إيّاها رجال الدين. فرغم تأكيد الماورديّ على التمييز بين المحتسب المعيّن من قبل الحاكم والفرد المتطوّع نجده يعدّ ولاية المحتسب إحدى الولايات الدينيّة التي تستمدّ شرعيّتها من تفويض الرعيّة وليَ الأمر لتنفيذ أحكام الشرع ثمّ انتداب وليُ الأمر المحتسبَ لإدارة شؤون الحسبة. وهو يقدّم بذلك مبرّرًا الشرعيّة ممارسات السلطة ممثّلة في مؤسّسة الحسبة ويقيّد في الوقت ذاته حرّيّة الفرد في أداء التكليف الشرعيّ ليضحى الاحتساب بذلك فرض عين على المحتسب المندوب بحكم الولاية، ومن نافلة أعمال المتطوّع التي له أن يتشاغل عنها بعدما كان الاحتساب فرض كفاية على الكافّة.[٢]

عرض الماورديّ للحسبة كوظيفة (function) يعدّ أوّل تنظير لها كمؤسّسة (institution) من مؤسّسات إدارة الحكم/الدولة (administration). وذلك في إطار نظريّة عامّة تفسّر العلاقة بين الفرد والسلطة الحاكمة والدين. ولقد قام بعرض نظريّته في كتابين. أوّلهما «تسهيل النظر وتعجيل الظفر في أخلاق الملك وسياسة الملك» ويشتمل

---

١ أبو الحسن الماورديّ، الأحكام السلطانيّة والولايات الدينيّة، بيروت: دار الكتب العلميّة [١٩٩٢]، ص ٢٩٩.

٢ المرجع السابق، ص ٥ و٢٩٩–٣٠٠.

على الطرح النظريّ وفلسفته. أمّا الثاني فهو «كتاب الأحكام السلطانيّة والولايات الدينيّة» وفيه يعرض تصوّره لما يجب أن تنظّم عليه إدارات الحكم، والتي ميّزها بين ولايات دينيّة وأحكام سلطانيّة بناءً على طرحه المسبق.[٣]

الدين عند الماورديّ هو أس المُلك وتوأمه والمَلك هو الحارس لهذا الأساس فلا يستقرّ كيان لأحدهما من دون الأخر.[٤] فمشروعيّة الحكم عند الماورديّ لا تكمن في دين الحاكم ولكن في قيامه بحراسة الدين وسياسة الدنيا عقب تفويض الأمور إليه من قبل الأمّة استجابة لحكم الشرع.[٥] وقد أقرّ الغزاليّ رأي الماورديّ باقتباسه الجملة ذاتها معنى ولفظًا في مؤلّفه الاقتصاد في الاعتقاد[٦]. وإن اختلف معه في ما يختصّ بالحسبة.[٧] ولقد سبقه في ذلك إمام الحرمين الجويني.[٨] فوفقًا لهما يكتسب التكليف بمجرّد الإيمان فلا حاجة للمرء إلى تفويض أو إذن من الحاكم لممارسة الحسبة. كما إنّه لا ينتقص من حقّهم في أدائها انتداب الحاكم من ينتدب فيها إنّما كلّ وقدرته.[٩]

لقد ربط الفقهاء بين لازمة مدنيّة حضريّة من لوازم اجتماع البشر في المجتمعات الإنسانيّة كافّة، بغضّ النظر عن مرجعيّتها الدينيّة، ألا وهي الإشراف على الأسواق – حيث كان يسمّى المندوب إليها حتّى العصر الأمويّ بعامل السوق – وبين تكليف دينيّ عامّ بالأمر بالمعروف والنهيّ عن المنكر، حكمه فرض كفاية، عبر إطلاق مسمّى الحسبة على كليهما. توافق هذا التطوّر والخطاب السياسيّ لبني العبّاس الذين ادّعوا أنّهم من قال الله تعالى فيهم {والذين إن مكّناهم في الأرض أقاموا الصلاة وآتوا الزكاة وأمروا بالمعروف ونهوا عن المنكر}[١٠]، [١١] فعدّت الحسبة من الوظائف الدينيّة التابعة للولايات السلطانيّة.

---

٣ قارن أحمد محمّد البغداديّ، شرعيّة السلطنة الأيّوبيّة: تطوّر مصادر الشرعيّة – الشرعيّة ونظام الجند – الفقهاء وشرعيّة السلطنة، القاهرة: دار النهضة العربية ٢٠٠٤، ص ٦٨–٧٢.

٤ أبو الحسن الماورديّ، تسهيل النظر وتعجيل الظفر في أخلاق الملك وسياسة الملك، تحقيق رضوان السيّد، بيروت: المركز الإسلاميّ للبحوث ١٩٨٧، ص ٢٠١–٢٠٢.

٥ الماورديّ، الأحكام، ص ٥.

٦ أبو حامد الغزاليّ، الإقتصاد في الإعتقاد، بغداد: مكتبة الشرق الجديد، ص ١٣٥.

٧ See also Ahmed Abdelsalam, "The Practice of Violence in the ḥisba-Theories", *Iranian Studies* 38,4 (2005), 551.

٨ أبو المعالي الجوينيّ، الإرشاد إلى قواطع الأدلة في أصول الاعتقاد، القاهرة، ص ٣٦٨.

٩ أبو حامد الغزاليّ، إحياء علوم الدين، الجزء ٢، القاهرة: دار إحياء الكتب العربية [١٩٩٢]، ص ٣٣٩ و٣٤٢؛ الجوينيّ، الإرشاد، ص ٣٦٨؛.قارن محمد كمال الدين إمام، أصول الحسبة في الإسلام – دراسة تأصيليّة مقارنة، الإسكندريّة: منشأة المعارف ١٩٨٦، ص ٦٨–٧٠.

١٠ سورة الحج، الآية ٤١.

١١ الرواية في الإحياء للغزاليّ عن الخليفة العبّاسيّ المأمون،الجزء ٢، ص ٣٤٥.

وإذ اعتبرت مهمة السلطان حراسة الدين كما سبق ذكره والحسبة وظيفة دينيّة فلا جرم إن صار اهتمام الحاكم أيًّا كان مسمّاه بولاية الحسبة وتوليته إيّاها عالمًا مشهورًا بورعه أو شدّته في حاضرة ملكه إشارة لإسلاميّة حكومته وتاليًا ادّعاءً لشرعيّتها في مواجهة العلماء والعامّة. بخاصّة حين يعتبر الفقهاء أنّ مقصود جميع الولايات في الإسلام هو أمر بمعروف أو نهي عن منكر.[١٢] بذلك أصبح تعيين الحاكم لمحتسب ما رسالةً موجّهة إلى رجال الدين أوّلاً وجمهور الرعيّة من أهل السنّة على وجه الأخصّ ثانيًا رسالة تعبّر عن رغبته في تأكيد سلطات حكومته المركزيّة وشرعيّة مطالبه. أي يمكن اعتبارها خطابًا بحسن النيّات، بخاصّة عند تأسيس أو محاولة ترسيخ نظام حكم جديد. وقد أشار (Axel Havemann) إلى إتباع كلّ من عماد الدين زنكي وصلاح الدين الأيّوبيّ لتلك السياسات في بلاد الشام.[١٣] كما أنّ الفاطميّين مارسوا تلك السياسة حينما فتحوا الديار المصريّة وكانت شرعيّة حكمهم محلّ تساؤل فاهتمّوا بالحسبة وفاعليّة أجهزتها في تنظيم إداريّ مركزيّ حذا حذوه الأيّوبيّون والمماليك. لكنّ الفاطميّين أهملوها بعد ذلك فصار يشرف عليها الوالي أو القاضي أو صاحب الشرطة.[١٤] وانعكس ذلك على سياستهم حين ضمّوا إلى ملكهم بلاد الشام فلا نجد في المصادر ما يشير إلى وجود محتسب فاطميّ ذي سلطة هناك بل العكس.[١٥]

اكتسبت ولاية الحسبة الدلالة على شرعيّة الحكم وإسلاميّته رغم ما تؤكّده المصادر التاريخيّة من استمرار وظيفة المحتسب في الممالك المسيحيّة في الديار الشاميّة كجهة إداريّة تعنى بالرقابة على الأسواق وأصحاب الصنائع وذلك من دون أيّة تحفّظات مذهبيّة بالإضافة إلى رسوخ فكرة مسؤوليّة الدولة عن مراقبة الأسواق وأصحاب الصنائع في النظام

١٢ أنظر أحمد بن تيميّة، الحسبة في الإسلام، تحقيق إبراهيم رمضان، بيروت: دار الفكر اللبناني ١٩٩٢، ص ١٠؛ أحمد بن تيميّة، السياسة الشرعيّة في إصلاح الراعي والرعيّة، تحقيق محمد الشبراويّ، بيروت: دار الكتب العلمية ١٩٨٨، ص ٧٢–٧٣.

١٣ See Axel Havemann, *Ri'āsa und Qaḍā': Institutionen als Ausdruck wechselnder Kräfteverhältnisse in syrischen Städten vom 10. bis zum 12. Jahrhundert,* Freiburg: Schwarz 1975, 151–153; compare Claudia Kickinger, *Städtische Märkte des Nahen Ostens*, Europäische Handschriften, Frankfurt: Peter Lang Verlag 1997, 77.

١٤ كان أبو جعفر الخراسانيّ أوّل محتسب فاطميّ في مصر وذلك قبل قدوم المعزّ ثمّ تلاه بعد أشهر قليلة سليمان بن عزة إثر وفاة الأوّل؛ المقريزيّ، إتعاظ الحنفاء بأخبار الأئمة الفاطميّين الخلفاء، تحقيق محمّد حلمي محمّد أحمد، الجزء ١، القاهرة: وزارة الأوقاف، المجلس الأعلى للشؤون الإسلاميّة ١٩٩٦، ص ٣٤.

١٥ Compare Kickinger, *Städtische Märkte*, 75; see Ahmed Abd-Elsalam, *Das mamlukische muḥtasib-Amt – Eine islamische Institution im Kontext sozio-politischen Wandels* (Unpublished MA thesis, Halle 2004), 50–54.

الإداريّ البيزنطيّ حتّى قبل الإسلام.[١٦] ولا أدّعي بهذا أنّ المسلمين أخذوا عن البيزنطيّين وظيفة عامل السوق وهي المسمّى الأوّل للمحتسب فذلك ممّا يفتقد للدليل التاريخيّ وقد وضّح ذلك (Benjamin Foster)[١٧] وإنّما أرغب في الإشارة إلى أنّ الرقابة على الأسواق من مستلزمات تنظيم المجتمع ومسؤوليّات الدولة إسلاميّة كانت أو مسيحيّة، قديمة أو حديثة، ملكيّة أو جمهوريّة.[١٨] وهو ما يدعونا إلى أن ننفي عن الحسبة وصفها كوظيفة دينيّة كما يشير ذلك إلى أنّ هذا الوصف ما كان إلا توظيفًا لها لخدمة الخطاب السياسيّ لرجال الدين والخطاب الدينيّ لرجال السياسة في المشرق العربيّ. هذه الجدليّة تتجلّى بوضوح في العصر المملوكيّ. ونعزو هذا التجلّي إلى توافر مصادر المعلومات عن ذلك العصر وتنوّعها ولا نعزوه إلى تميّز سياسات تلك الدولة عن سابقتها وإن أدّت سيطرة العنصر المملوكيّ على أجهزة إدارة الدولة في عهود سلاطين الشراكسة، كما سنرى، دورًا هامًا في إبراز محاور التحوّل في تعامل الدولة مع مؤسّسة الحسبة وتحديد هويّتها الوظيفيّة.

تعدّدت الدراسات الحديثة للحسبة في العصر المملوكيّ تعدّد مصادر المعلومات المتاحة وروافدها من آثار ذلك العصر. ويمكن تقسيم المصادر على النحو التالي:

أوّلاً: الرسائل الفقهيّة في الحسبة والأمر بالمعروف كرسالة الحسبة لابن تيميّة والطرائق الحكميّة لابن قيّم الجوزيّة وكالمدخل لابن الحاج وحتّى تناول ابن خلدون للحسبة في مقدّمته يمكن إدراجه القسم ذاته. ربّما عكست هذه التناولات الفقهيّة للحسبة جانبًا من تطوّر الخطاب الدينيّ في شقّه السياسيّ خلال العصر المملوكيّ إذ لا تخلو آراؤهم من إتباع إحدى مدرستي الحسبة وأعني بذلك وجهتي النظر غير المتوائمتين للماورديّ والغزاليّ.[١٩] ولا تعكس تلك الرسائل بحال الكيفيّة التي مورست بها الحسبة في عصرهم. إلا في حالات قليلة ينتقد فيها الفقيه أداء المحتسب مدّعيًا عدم التزامه بالمفروض عليه شرعًا. فنعلم بذلك ما لم يدخل في اختصاص المحتسب أو ما لم يزاوله ومن ذلك مراقبة سلوكيّات الأفراد، أو التشديد على اتّباع الشروط العمريّة، المميّزة بين أتباع الطوائف الدينيّة أو وعظ أولياء الأمر من سلاطين وأمراء.

---

١٦ السيّد الباز العرينيّ، نهاية الرتبة في طلب الحسبة لعبد الرحمن بن نصر الشيزريّ، بيروت: دار الثقافة [١٩٦٩]، ملحق ٣، ص ١٢٥–١٢٩ وملحق ٤، ص ١٣٣.

١٧ See Benjamin Foster, "Agoranomos and Muhtasib", *Journal of the Economic and Social History of the Orient* XIII (1970), 128–144.

١٨ Compare Jonathan Berkey, "The Muḥtasib of Cairo under the Mamluks", in: *The Mamluks in Egyptian and Syrian Politics and Society*, eds. Michael Winter and Amalia Levanoni, Leiden: Brill 2004, 245–246.

١٩ See Abdelsalam, "Practice of Violence", 547 ff..

ثانيًا: كتب الحسبة كمعالم القربة لابن الإخوة ونهاية الرتبة لابن بسام التي ألّفت على نسق كتاب الشيزريّ نهاية الرتبة في طلب الحسبة لتكون معاونًا ومرشدًا لمن ولّي أمر الحسبة. وهي تجمع بين خبرات عمليّة خاصّة في مجال مكافحة الغشّ والتدليس في الأعمال والصناعات ونصائح بعضها ذو مرجعيّة دينيّة وأخرى ذو مرجعيّة أخلاقيّة. وكان للمحتسب أن يعوّل عليها مسترشدًا لا مُلزَما. وهي بهذا تختلف عن كتاب والي المدينة البيزنطيّ (The Book of the Prefect) من القرن العاشر الميلاديّ، والذي هو قواعد وقوانين يجب اتّباعها.[٢٠] وقد اعتمدت كتب الحسبة قاطبة في شقّها الفقهيّ على الجمع بين آراء كلّ من الماورديّ والغزاليّ رغم تعارضها، ما يعكس برجماتيّة في التناول تدعو إلى تمكين المحتسب من ممارسة مهامه وفقًا لواجبات افتراضيّة مثاليّة ذات خلفيّات أخلاقيّة دينيّة متغاضية في بعض الأحوال عن عدم توافق هذا التصوّر المثاليّ مع واقع الحال الذي يحدّد فيه الحاكم للمحتسب عند تعيينه حدود اختصاصاته وسلطاته، بما لا يتداخل مع اختصاصات الآخرين.[٢١] وتنبّه لهذا ابن تيميّة فنبّه إليها في رسالته في الحسبة. وكانت كتب الحسبة أولى بهذا التنبيه بافتراض طبيعتها كمرشد عمليّ لمتولّي الحسبة.

يقول ابن تيميّة:

عموم الولايات وخصوصها وما يستفيده المتولّي بالولاية يتلقى من الألفاظ والأحوال والعرف. ليس لذلك حدٌ في الشرع. فقد يدخل في ولاية القضاء في بعض الأمكنة والأزمنة ما يدخل في ولاية الحرب في مكان وزمان أخر وبالعكس، وكذلك الحسبة وولاية المال.[٢٢]

ويضيف:

وأمّا المحتسب فله الأمر بالمعروف والنهي عن المنكر ممّا ليس من خصائص الولاة والقضاة وأهلِ الديوان ونحوِهم. وكثير من الأمور الدينيّة هو مشترك بين ولاة الأمور. فمن أدّى فيه الواجب وجبت طاعته.[٢٣]

ثالثًا: الوثائق والمراسيم السلطانيّة المتّصلة بالحسبة والمحتسب وهي على ندرة المحقّق والمنشور منها حتّى الآن فهي مهمّة للتعرّف إلى طبيعة عمل المحتسب كمحصّل للرسوم والضرائب التجاريّة في الأسواق. وهي من أقدم مجالات اختصاصه

---

٢٠ العرينيّ، نهاية الرتبة، ملحق ٤، ص ١٣٣.

٢١ Compare Kickinger, *Städtische Märkte*, 55–72.

٢٢ ابن تيميّة، الحسبة، ص ١٤.

٢٣ ابن تيميّة، الحسبة، ص ١٥.

منذ كان بعد يُسمى عامل السوق كما تخبرنا بذلك روايات عدّة.[٢٤] ولقد أورد بعض هذه الوثائق أحمد عبد الرازق في كتابه البذل والبرطلة، زمن سلاطين المماليك نقلاً عن أحمد دراج ومقاله الحسبة وآثارها على الحياة الاقتصاديّة، والمنشور في المجلّة التاريخيّة المجلّد ١٤.[٢٥] وعلى خلاف المراسيم التي هي أوامر مباشرة من السلطان أو أحد نوّابه، للمحتسب واجبة الإعلان والتنفيذ بإلغاء أو إبطال ما كان مقرّرًا للمحتسب سابقًا تحصيله أو أداؤه فإنّ طابع الإنشاء الأدبيّ يغلب على سجلات ولاية الحسبة، أو بعبارة أخرى مراسيم الإقرار والتعيين التي ضمّنها القلقشنديّ كتابه صبح الأعشى.

وإذا كان (Ulrich Haarmann) قد شكّك في مصداقيّة كتابات مؤرخيّ العصر المملوكيّ لغلبة الإنشاء على المنهجيّة العلميّة للتأريخ (Literarisierung der Geschichtsschreibung) فمن باب أولى مراعاة ذلك البعد عند تناول هذه السجلات كمصدر للتأريخ للعصر المملوكيّ.[٢٦]

كما أنّه بالإضافة إلى غلبة الإنشاء على صياغة السجلات، فقد قام القلقشنديّ بالنقل عن سجلات سابقة لعهود حكم أسبق من دون مراعاة اختلاف الأبعاد الاجتماعيّة والسياسيّة باختلاف البعد الزمانيّ والمكانيّ. وعلى هذا تظلّ ديباجة سجلّ التعيين أو العزل الجزئيّة ذات الدلالة التاريخيّة في السجلّ. حيث كان يلزم على الكاتب تغيير الألقاب المستخدمة لتتفق، ومن قام بإصدار أمر العزل أو التعيين تبعًا لوظيفته الرسميّة وللألقاب الممنوحة لها، أو المتاح له استخدامها وفقًا لأعراف متّفق عليها وقد سردها القلقشنديّ جملةً وتفصيلاً في غير موضع من صبح الأعشى. فتتيح لنا تلك الديباجات إمكانيّة التعرّف إلى هيئة من خوّل لهم في العصر المملوكيّ إصدار أوامر العزل والتعيين في حقّ المحتسب، وبخاصّة في نيابات الديار الشاميّة. فيما كان ينفرد السلطان بتعيين محتسبي مصر والقاهرة كذلك نائبه في حال غيبته كما أجمعت على ذلك المصادر.

رابعًا: الكتابات التأريخيّة من العصر المملوكيّ. وتؤرّخ هذه الكتابات للدولة ولأولياء الأمر ولا تؤرّخ للمجتمع وتطوّره وفاعليّاته. فحركة المجتمع تُستقرأ ولا تُقرأ

---

٢٤ تناولت بعض هذه الروايات بالتحليل والنقد في دراسة سابقة لي كما أشار إليها (Buckley) في مقاله ("The Muḥtasib", *Arabica* 39 (1992), 59–60).

٢٥ أنظر أحمد عبد الرازق، البذل والبرطلة زمن سلاطين المماليك، القاهرة: الهيئة العامّة للكتاب ١٩٧٩، ص ٢١١ وما يليها.

٢٦ Compare Ulrich Haarmann, *Quellenstudien zur frühen Mamlukenzeit*, Freiburg: Robischon 1969, 159–181; see also Bernd Radtke, *Weltgeschichte und Weltbeschreibung im Mittelalterlichen Islam*, Beiruter Texte und Studien 51 (1992), Beirut: Orient-Institut der DMG, 185ff.

في الكتابات التأريخيّة المملوكيّة. وإنّه وإن كانت الحسبة مؤسّسة ذات علاقة وثيقة بحركة المجتمع المملوكيّ لما لها من أثر على الحياة اليوميّة لأفراد الشعب ولما يقود إليه اضطرابُ سياسات متولّيها من تذمّرات وتكدّرات شعبيّة ما تلبث أن تتحوّل إلى مظاهرات تلقي بظلالها على ساكني القلعة وتؤثّر على قراراتهم فقد اكتسبت أهمّيّة إضافيّة في العصر المملوكيّ من جرّاء موقع الحسبة في الخطاب الدينيّ السياسيّ والذي حاول كلّ من العلماء وأمراء المماليك توظيفه لمصلحتهم.

لذلك أرى اعتبار ذكر المؤرّخ المملوكيّ لمحتسب ما إشارة إلى ارتفاع أسهم أهمّيّة المنصب في السنة المذكور فيها أو أهمّيّة دور الشخص الذي تولاها لشخصه أو لسيرته فيها بالسلب أو الإيجاب. والعكس على عكس ذلك. فعدم ورود إشارة إلى المحتسب خلال فترة معيّنة قد يعني ضآلة دور المحتسب أو مؤسّسته خلال تلك الفترة. ولا بدّ للقيام بذلك من مراجعة عدد كبير من مؤلّفات مؤرخيّ العصر المملوكيّ سواء كانت سير ملوك وسلاطين، أو دول وحوليّات أو كتب رجال، أو وفيّات بحيث تغطي حياة مؤلّفي هذه الأعمال فترة حكم المماليك كاملة قدر الإمكان. ثمّ يعتدّ من كتاباتهم ما عاصروه منها. فإذا أهمل أحدهم ذكر محتسب معاصر له، كان ذلك دليلاً على إهمال شأن الحسبة وضعفها. أمّا إذا أهمل المؤرّخ ذكر محتسبه المعاصر له نتيجة لعداءٍ شخصيّ، وهذا وارد، فإنّ ذكر ذلك المحتسِب المهمل عداء في مؤلّفات مؤرّخين آخرين معاصرين أو لاحقين يفضح ذلك الغرض. وهذه القاعدة تلاحظ عند مقارنة أعمال كلّ من المقريزيّ والعينيّ وابن حجر للفترة ذاتها. هذا يعنيّ عدم كفاية الرجوع إلى مؤلَّف تأريخيّ واحد لدراسة المحتسب المملوكيّ من الناحية التاريخيّة والركون إلى ذلك.[٢٧]

وأخذت على عاتقي القيام بهذه المهمّة مستغرقًا قرابة العام في دراسة المراجع المملوكيّة ومقابلتها من كتب تأريخ ووفيّات وطبقات مسترشدًا بلائحة أسماء من تولّوا حسبة القاهرة في العصر المملوكيّ التي ألحقها أحمد عبد الرازق مقالَه (La Ḥisba et le Muḥtasib en Egypte au temps des Mamluks) في (*Annales islamologiques*, vol. 13 (1977), pp 115–178) وما أورده في كتابه البذل والبرطلة في عصر سلاطين المماليك. وقد اعتمد عبد الرازق بصورة أساسيّة على كتاب السلوك للمقريزيّ لجمع معلوماته.

وقد خلصت من هذه الدراسة إلى أنّه:

---

[٢٧] قارن عبد الرازق القرموط، مقدّمة كتاب عقد الجمان في تاريخ أهل الزمان لبدر الدين العينيّ، القاهرة: الزهراء للإعلام العربيّ ١٩٨٩، ص ٢٢–٣٣.

أوّلاً:

١. بالإضافة إلى ما هو مشتهر من وجود ثلاثة مناصب للمحتسب في مصر وهي محتسب القاهرة ومصر السفلى وهو أعلاهم شأنًا في دوائر الدولة السياسيّة والإداريّة ومحتسب مصر الفسطاط ومصر العليا ومحتسب الإسكندريّة، فقد كان لهؤلاء المحتسبة نوّاب يقومون بتعيينهم أو إقرارهم في أعمالهم.[٢٨] ويكاد يشكّل هؤلاء النوّاب أساس الجهاز الإداريّ الحقيقيّ لمؤسّسة الحسبة نتيجة لخبراتهم التي جمعوها، طيلة أعوام في خدمة العديد من المحتسبة، وخير مثال على ذلك بدر الدين بن الرشيد المصريّ الذي ظل نائبًا للحسبة على مدى أربعين عامًا ثمّ خلفه ابنه عماد الدين الذي سعى في ولاية حسبة القاهرة في العام ١٤١٧/٨٢٠ على أن يرمّم برجي القلعة بما قيمته ٥٠٠ دينار.[٢٩]

٢. يمكن مقارنة نوّاب الحسبة بنوّاب القضاء في العصر المملوكيّ من تبعيّتهم المباشرة للمحتسب الذي يجري عليهم أرزاقهم كما هو بين القاضي ونوّابه. كما كان لنائب الحسبة مباشرة القضاء في قضايا الحسبة نيابة عن المحتسب ممّا يستلزم تأهّله علميًا للقيام بذلك. فقد ذكر المقريزيّ في رثاء نائب له في الحسبة وهو شهاب الدين أحمد بن محمّد بن صلاح المعروف بابن المحمرة والمتوفّى العام ١٤٣٦/٨٤٠، والذي تولّى بعد ذلك قضاء قضاة الشافعيّة في دمشق، أنّه كان يجلس للأحكام على بابه أثناء ولاية المقريزيّ الثالثة لحسبة القاهرة من ٢٢ شوال إلى ٢١ ذي القعدة ٨٠٧ هجريًّا الموافق ١٤٠٥ ميلاديًّا.[٣٠] كما يذكر ابن حجر في وفيّات العام ١٣٧٦/٧٧٨ محمّد بن علي بن أبي رقيبة المجود والذي ناب في الحسبة وكان مؤدّبًا للملك الكامل شعبان ثمّ تولّى حسبة مصر.[٣١]

٣. كانت تلك الأرزاق تقتطع عادة مّما يقوم المحتسب بتحصيله من الباعة وأصحاب الصنائع من مكوس وضرائب أشهرها مقرّر الحسبة والمشاهرة والمجامعة.[٣٢]

---

٢٨ القلقشنديّ، صبح الأعشى في صناعة الإنشاء، طبعة بولاق، الجزء ٤، القاهرة، ص ٣٧.

٢٩ ابن حجر العسقلانيّ، إنباء الغمر بأبناء العمر، الجزء ٧، حيدر أباد الدكن: مجلس دائرة المعارف العثمانيّة ١٩٧٥، ص ٢٧٥.

٣٠ المقريزيّ، درر العقود الفريدة في تراجم الأعيان المفيدة، تحقيق محمد كمال الدين علي، الجزء ١، بيروت: عالم الكتب ١٩٩٢، ص ٢٦٩.

٣١ ابن حجر، إنباء الغمر، الجزء ١، ص ١٠٢.

٣٢ قارن بدر الدين العيني، عقد الجمان في تأريخ أهل الزمان، تحقيق عبد الرازق القرموطي، القاهرة: الزهراء للإعلام العربيّ ١٩٨٩، ص ١٢١.

٤. كانت جامكيّة المحتسب، أي راتبه، تصرف له في حال تولّيه الحسبة تكليفًا لا التزامًا من أموال الجوالي أي الجزية.[٣٣] ويعكس حرص هؤلاء المحتسبة على أن تصرف رواتبهم من عوائد الجزية لبيت المال اعتقادهم في عدم شرعيّة مقرّرات الحسبة. لذا يمكن الربط بين تولية الحسبة من طريق الالتزام وتحصيل ضرائب بعينها. والالتزام هو ضمان توريد مبالغ ماليّة محدّدة مسبقًا إلى الخزائن السلطانيّة في حال تسليم أعمال ولاية ما إلى الملتزم. وكانت هذه المبالغ تتحوّل في الغالب إلى مديونيّات شخصيّة واجبة الدفع حتّى وإن أخفق الملتزم في جمعها قبل عزله.[٣٤]

٥. لم يتوخّ المؤرّخون الدقّة في تحديد من تولّى الحسبة على سبيل الالتزام، ومن تولاّها من طريق البذل والبرطلة، وهما الرشوة لاستهجانهم بذل المال للحصول على المنصب، بل كان المقريزيّ يعيّب سعي العالم لنيل الولاية عمومًا ويعدّ بذل المال فيها فسادًا.

٦. تتعدّد الروايات في استخدام مسمّيات أخر في العصر المملوكيّ إلى جانب الحسبة كالنظر في جهات الأسواق والنظر في الأسواق والتحدّث في جهات الحسبة؛ وقد يستخدم أيضًا لفظ متكلّم عوضًا من متحدّث.[٣٥] ويفهم من تلك الروايات أنّ استخدام تلك المسمّيات يرتبط بتكليف أحد موظّفي الدولة من خارج دوائر العلماء بالإشراف على مهام المحتسب إلى جانب مهامه الأصليّة أو بصورة مؤقّتة من دون تسميته محتسبًا.[٣٦]

ثانيًا:

بحصر أسماء من تولّوا منصب الحسبة للقاهرة وهي حاضرة السلطنة، ومحتسبها له من السلطة والجاه ما يفوق أقرانه، وجدت أنّ منصب محتسب القاهرة تمّ شغله منذ اعتلاء الظاهر بيبرس عرش السلطنة وشروعه في ترسيخ حكم المماليك وإعادة ترتيب نظام الدولة في العام ١٢٦٥/٦٦٣ وحتّى سقوط دولة المماليك في العام ١٥١٧/٩٢٣، على الأقلّ ١٨٢ مرّة، أمكن حصرها

---

٣٣ المرجع السابق، ص ١٢١.

٣٤ المقريزيّ، إغاثة الأمّة بكشف الغمّة، القاهرة: الهيئة العامة للكتاب ١٩٩٩، ص ٧٣–٧٤؛ قارن عبد الرازق، البذل والبرطلة، ص ١٢٠.

٣٥ أنظر ابن إياس، بدائع الزهور في وقائع الدهور، تحقيق محمد مصطفى، Bibliotheca Islamica 5، القاهرة: مطبعة عيسى البابي الحلبيّ ١٩٣١–١٩٨٦، الجزء ١، القسم ٢، ص ٢٣٤ و٢٨٣ و٣٧٠ والجزء ٣، ص ١٦٠ و١٦٥ و٤١٠ والجزء ٥، ص ١٤٩ و٣٠٣؛ قارن المصدر، الفهارس ٢، ص ٣٤٩–٣٥٣.

٣٦ See Abd-Elsalam, *Das mamlukische muḥtasib-Amt*, 93–96.

وتعيين أسماء متولّيها. وبمراجعة ما ذكرته المراجع عن هؤلاء المحتسبة، وما تولّوا من مناصب وأعمال، قبل وبعد إسناد الحسبة إليهم، وتقويم معاصريهم لسيرتهم فيها، وبالربط تاريخيًّا بين تولّيهم المنصب والتطوّرات السياسيّة للدولة المملوكيّة، أمكن التمييز بين ثلاث مراحل تاريخيّة تغيّرت تبعًا لها رؤية النخبة الحاكمة المملوكيّة لوظيفة المحتسب وكيف يمكن توظيفها في خدمة أهداف الحاكم/الدولة. ولا يختلف هذا التقسيم كثيرًا في نتائجه عمّا ذهب إليه (Berkey) بالتمييز بين ستّ مراحل مختلفة لتطوّر مؤسّسة الحسبة في العصر المملوكيّ.

مراحل تطوّر مؤسّسة الحسبة في العصر المملوكيّ:

المرحلة الأولى مرحلة التأسيس والترسيخ (١٢٦٥/٦٦٣–١٣٨٧/٧٨٩):

تشمل هذه المرحلة فترة حكم المماليك البحريّة من **١٢٦٥/٦٦٣** إلى **١٣٨٧/٧٨٩**. وتمتاز بثبات مؤسّسة الحسبة عمومًا واستجابة السلاطين لتصوّر الفقهاء لمنصب الحسبة كإحدى الوظائف الدينيّة التي لا يتولاها إلا رجال الدين، مثلها مثل القضاء ووكالة بيت المال. وهو ما يؤكّد ما أشرت إليه سلفًا من توظيف الحسبة بغرض الاعتراف الضمنيّ بشرعيّة الحكم، من قبل العلماء، حيث غازل السلاطين وعلى رأسهم بيبرس رجال الدين بتوليتهم المناصب، وإسباغ مظاهر الجاه والسلطة عليها، مثل مشاركتهم في جلسات دار العدل والإنعام عليهم بالخلع السلطانيّة والسماح لهم بالسير في المواكب وركوب البغال النفيسة والخيول.

وقد تضمّنت هذه المرحلة تأسيس منظومة مؤسّسة الحسبة للعصر المملوكيّ على نهج تنظيمها إبّان عهد الفاطميّين. فتحدّثنا المصادر أنّ أوّل مرسوم بتعيين محتسب كان في العام **١٢٦٥/٦٦٣** من نصيب آخر وزراء الدولة الأيّوبيّة ومن خلف شيخ إسلام عصره العز بن عبد السلام في قضاء القضاة أعني ابن بنت الأعز عبد الوهاب بن خلف الأعلميّ. وقد ولّي حسبة مصر قاطبة قبل تقسيم أعمال المحتسب على ثلاثة أقاليم، وقضاء القضاة على المدارس الفقهيّة الأربع. وتصف المصادر ابن بنت الأعز بأنّه كان أعلم علماء عصره فكانت تولية الحسبة له إعلاء من شأنها لا من شأنه، بالإضافة إلى ذلك تذكر المصادر توليه ثلاث عشرة وظيفة بالإضافة إلى الحسبة.[٣٧] وقد خلفه في المنصب في العام ذاته أبو حفص شرف الدين عمر بن عبد الله بن صالح السبكي، قاضي

[٣٧] ابن إيّاس،بدائع الزهور، جزء ١، ص **٣٢٥**؛ ابن قاضي شهبة، طبقات فقهاء الشافعية، تحقيق محمد حامد الفقي، جزء ١، القاهرة: مطبعة السنة المحمدية [**١٩٥٥**]، ص **٤٥٩**–٤٦١.

قضاة المالكيّة، الذي كان وفقًا للمصادر أوّل من تولّى حسبة القاهرة. ثمّ خلفه القاضي علاء الدين أحمد بن ابن بنت الأعز في العام ٦٧٠/١٢٧١ لتنتقل الحسبة به وبعده إلى طور جديد في المرحلة ذاتها تتّضح فيه اختيار شخص المحتسب من دوائر العلماء، والعائلات القريبة من السلطان أو حاشيته، فيحدّثنا ابن حجر في تأريخه إنباء الغمر بأبناء العمر أنّ القاضي أبا الثناء جمال الدين العجميّ وهو نائب حكم قاضي قضاة الحنفيّة قد تولّى حسبة القاهرة أوّل مرّة في العام ٧٧٨/١٣٧٧ بترتيب من الأمراء طشتمر اللفاف أتابك العسكر والأميرين قرطاي وقرابغا.[٣٨] وهي ظاهرة يتعارف معاصرونا على تسميتها بالوساطة أو المحسوبيّة، لكنّها في العصر المملوكيّ كانت نظام رعاية (patronage) تحكمه مجموعة من المصالح المشتركة أو المتبادلة، بين أمراء المماليك وأفراد من طبقة العلماء. وقد أشار كلّ من (Michael Chamberlain) و(Anne Broadbridge) إلى انتشار هذه الظاهرة في القرن الخامس عشر.[٣٩]

ورغم شهرة علماء الطور الأوّل لهذه المرحلة لا تحدّثنا المصادر عن جهودهم الحسبويّة بل عن جهود بيبرس وأمرائه في القيام بفروض الحسبة سواء في تفسيرها كنهي عن منكر أو كصلاحيّاتها كجهة الإشراف على الطرق والمحال والنظام العامّ. هذا يدفعني إلى اعتبار تعيين أولائك المحتسبة تعيينًا شكليًّا من دون أن تكون لهم الإمكانات لمتابعة واجبات ولاياتهم وبخاصّة أنّهم قد جمعوا بين القضاء والحسبة أو نظر الأحباس أو غيرها من الوظائف. وربّما ساهم هؤلاء المحتسبة الثلاثة الأوائل في رسم ملامح العمل داخل مؤسّسة الحسبة ما كان له أثره في تمتّع الحسبة طوال فترة حكم البحريّة، بالاستقرار رغم الخلافات والاضطرابات السياسيّة. واستمرّ الكثير من المحتسبة في ولاياتهم رغم تغيّر الحكّام. وقد يعود ذلك إلى موقع هؤلاء المحتسبة في دوائر العلماء، وكونهم من وجهائهم أو منتمين عائليًّا إلى تلك الدوائر ذات التربيطات المعقّدة بدوائر الحكم. كما إنّهم كانوا أكفاء ومن ذوي الخبرة كما شهد لهم بذلك مؤرّخو عصرهم.

وقد أمكن حصر ثلاثين قرار تعيين لمحتسب على مدى مائة واثنين وعشرين عامًا لم تسجّل فيها المصادر أيّة حالات للفساد أو إساءة لمنصب المحتسب استدعت عزل المحتسب. والمؤرّخون أنصفوا ابن خطيب بيت الآبار رغم عزله عن ولاية الحسبة بتأثير الوزير النشو في العام ٧٣٨/١٣٣٧، وكان قد عيّن في العام السابق محتسبًا للقاهرة

---

٣٨ ابن حجر، إنباء الغمر، الجزء ٣، ص ٣٦٢–٣٦٤.

٣٩ See Anne F. Broadbridge, "Academic Rivalry and the Patronage System in Fifteenth Century Egypt", *Mamlūk Studies Review* 3 (1999), 85.

وفسطاط مصر، بعدما كان محتسبًا للأخيرة فقط حيث أشادوا بجهوده في مكافحة الغلاء إثر الأزمة الاقتصاديّة التي عصفت بمصر في ذلك الوقت في عهد الملك الناصر محمّد (الولاية الثالثة: ١٣١٠/٧٠٩–١٣٤١/٧٤١). وعاد ابن خطيب بيت الآبار لمنصب محتسب القاهرة بعد أربعة أعوام في ولاية الملك الأشرف كجك (١٣٤١/٧٤٢)، ليستقرّ فيها لمدّة ستّة أعوام رغم تغيّر الحكّام من أبناء الناصر وقصر ولاياتهم.

لكن مع تزايد نفوذ الأمراء الجراكسة وبخاصّة الظاهر برقوق (١٣٨٢/٧٨٤–١٣٨٩/٧٩١) و(١٣٩٠/٧٩٢–١٣٩٩/٨٠١) وتدخّلاتهم في أمور الحكم امتدّت يد الاضطراب لتشمل شتّى دوائر الدولة ومن ضمنها الحسبة. لتنتقل جدليّة العلاقة بين الحكّام والفقهاء إلى دور جديد. حيث طغت التربيطات الفرديّة بين أفراد من داخل وخارج دوائر العلماء وشخص الحاكم، أو أحد أمرائه أو أفراد حاشياته، على جدليّة المصلحة الجماعيّة، بين العلماء والنخبة الحاكمة وحلّت محلّها. لتبدأ بذلك المرحلة الثانية في تطوّر مؤسّسة الحسبة.

المرحلة الثانية، مرحلة عدم الاستقرار (١٣٨٩/٧٨٩–١٤١٣/٨١٦):

أؤرّخ لهذه المرحلة بتولية الملك الظاهر برقوق نجمَ الدين الطنبديّ حسبة القاهرة مقابل دفعه ٥٠،٠٠٠ درهم إلى السلطان في ٢٥ رمضان من العام ٧٨٩ هـ الموافق ١٣٨٩ م. تمتدّ هذه المرحلة حتّى العام ٨١٦ هـ الموافق ١٤١٣ م وتتميّز بقصر ولاية المحتسبة وفسادهم، حتّى إنّه تمّ شغل هذا المنصب في هذه الفترة القصيرة ٧٩ مرّة، منها ١٥ مرّة في ولاية الظاهر برقوق الثانية، والتي لم تزد عن التسعة أعوام و٢٨ مرّة في عهد ابنه الناصر فرج (١٣٩٩/٨٠١–١٤٠٥/٨٠٨)، أي ما يقلّ عن سبعة أعوام. وتذكر المصادر أنّ ابن شعبان الجابيّ تمكّن من شراء المنصب٢٠ مرّة، بعضها لم يتجاوز ثلاثة أيّام فتولّى حسبة القاهرة من ١١ إلى ١٣ ذي الحجّة من العام ١٤٠٥/٨٠٧.

وإن كان هناك ممّن تولّى منصب المحتسب في تلك المرحلة من لم تلحق به تهمة فساد كالمقريزيّ، وبدر الدين العينيّ، فإنّما تولاها لقربه أو تبعيّته لهذا الأمير أو ذلك السلطان، الذي يحظى بدعمه وحمايته. وكان لهذا مرتبطًا بنفوذ الأمير صاحب الرعاية (patron) وقربه من السلطان، كما كان أحيانًا سببًا لنقمة السلطان على المحتسب، إذا بدر بين السلطان وبين الأمير خلاف. وخير مثال على ذلك كلّ من المقريزيّ وبدر الدين العينيّ اللذين تولّيا الحسبة غير ذي مرّة في تلك المرحلة.[٤٠]

[٤٠] See Broadbridge, “Academic Rivalry”, 85ff.

كانت تولية الحسبة لأحد مشاهير العلماء بغير بذل أو برطلة أو من دون التزام تتمّ غالبًا في أوقات الأزمات الاقتصاديّة وارتفاع الأسعار التي تدفع العامّة إلى الخروج، والتظاهر ضدّ الغلاء والفساد مطالبين عادة بإقصاء المحتسب باعتباره المسؤول الأوّل في نظرهم عن أوضاع السوق. فكان السلاطين يلجأون في مثل هذه الأحوال إلى تعيين محتسب ذي قبول شعبيّ وقبول عند العلماء، وهم غالبًا من يحرّض العامّة على التظاهر. فإذا ما استكانت الأمور يتمّ عزل هذا المحتسب ليولّى من يقبل ضمان موارد الخزانة من طريق الضرائب والرسوم، وكانت لا تكفي لسداد قيمة الالتزام ومصاريف الأعوان ولا تحقّق له الثراء الذي يصبو إليه من طريق المنصب فيلجأ المحتسب بدوره إلى تعيين عمّاله ونوّابه من طريق الالتزام أيضًا ويغضّ طرفه عن ارتشائهم ومفاسدهم. ذلك إن لم يقم هو شخصيًّا بذلك لسداد التزاماته من هدايا ورشاوٍ لرعاته من أمراء المماليك لمعاونته على البقاء في المنصب.[٤١] وقد هاجم المقريزيّ وابن تغري بردي تلك السياسات وحمّلاها مسؤوليّة تردّي الوضع الاقتصاديّ للدولة.[٤٢] بل أنّ الطرسوسي من علماء القرن الرابع عشر طالب بإلغاء وظيفة المحتسب نتيجة لفسادها وابتعادها عن مقاصدها الشرعيّة.[٤٣]

وقد ذكرت المصادر ما يزيد على سبع وثلاثين حالة لتولّي منصب الحسبة من طريق الرشوة أو الالتزام أمكن تعيين عشرين منها على امتداد تلك المرحلة والمرحلة اللاحقة، ولقد أشار أحمد عبد الرازق في مقاله السابق الذكر و في كتابه البذل والبرطلة إلى العديد من هذه الحالات.

وإن كانت هذه المرحلة قد تميّزت عن لاحقتها بارتباط ولاية الحسبة بتلك الممارسات وتفشيّ الرشوة، حتّى كادت تكون إحدى لوازمها. فإنّه يجب علينا التمييز بين تولّي المنصب من طريق الرشوة وتطبيق نظام الضمان أو الالتزام. ذلك بأنّ نظام الالتزام لم يكن إحدى البدع المملوكيّة، كما لم يقتصر على ولاية الحسبة إذ يشير أبو الفداء في تاريخه إلى تولّي أبي العبّاس عبد الله بن الحسن بن أبي الشوارب قضاء القضاة في بغداد العام **٩٦١/٣٥٠** عن التزام قدره **٢٠٠** ألف درهم سنويًّا وذلك في أيّام معزّ الدولة بن بويه ثمّ تبع ذلك تضمين الحسبة والشرطة في بغداد أي توليتها وفق نظام الالتزام حسب روايته.

---

٤١ المقريزيّ، كتاب السلوك لمعرفة دول الملوك، تحقيق محمّد مصطفى زيادة، الجزء **٤**، القسم ١، القاهرة: لجنة التأليف والترجمة **١٩٥٧**، ص ٣٨٨–٣٨٩؛ ابن حجر، إنباء الغمر، الجزء ٦، ص ١٦.

٤٢ المقريزيّ، السلوك، الجزء ٤، القسم ١، ص٣٨٨–٣٨٩؛ ابن تغري بردي، النجوم الزاهرة في ملوك مصر والقاهرة، تحقيق محمد حسين شمس الدين، الجزء ٥، بيروت: دار الكتب العلمية **١٩٩٢**، ص ٢٧٤.

٤٣ أنظر عبد الرازق، البذل والبرطلة، ص ١١٨.

جدول حصريّ لمن تولّى حسبة القاهرة عن رشوة أو على سبيل الالتزام

	المحتسب	تاريخ ولايته	المبلغ	السلطان
١	نجم الدين محمّد بن عمر الطنبديّ	٢٥ رمضان ١٣٨٧/٧٨٩–١١ شوال ١٣٨٩/٧٩١	٥٠٠٠٠ درهم	الملك الظاهر برقوق (١٣٨٢/٧٨٤–١٣٨٩/٧٩١)
٢	بهاء الدين محمّد بن البرجيّ	٨ رمضان ١٣٩١/٧٩٣–٢٥ ربيع الثاني ١٣٩٢/٧٩٤	غير معلوم، دفعه إلى نائب الغيبة الأمير كمشبغا	الملك الظاهر برقوق (١٣٩٠/٧٩٢–١٣٩٩/٨٠١)
٣	نورالدين علي القور الجيزيّ	٤ صفر–٢٨ صفر ١٣٩٦/٧٩٨	غير معلوم، لم يستطع الوفاء بالمبلغ المعيّن عليه وعزل	الملك الظاهر برقوق (١٣٩٠/٧٩٢–١٣٩٩/٨٠١)
٤	شمس الدين محمّد بن الأنصاريّ البهنسيّ	٢٦ جمادى الآخر ١٣٩٦/٧٩٨–١٧ صفر ١٣٩٧/٧٩٩	غير معلوم	الملك الظاهر برقوق (١٣٩٠/٧٩٢–١٣٩٩/٨٠١)
٥	نجم الدين محمّد بن عمر الطنبديّ	٢ محرم–١٤ ربيع الثانى ١٤٠٠/٨٠٢	غير معلوم، دفعه على سبيل الالتزام	الملك الناصر فرج بن برقوق (١٣٩٩/٨٠١–١٤٠٥/٨٠٨)
٦	شمس الدين محمّد بن الشاذلي الإسكندرانيّ	١٨ ربيع الأول ١٤٠٢/٨٠٤–٣ جمادى الآخر ١٤٠٣/٨٠٥	غير معلوم	الملك الناصر فرج بن برقوق (١٣٨٢/٧٨٤–١٣٨٩/٧٩١)
٧	شمس الدين محمّد بن عمر بن شعبان الجابيّ	١٢ شعبان–١١ رمضان ١٤٠٣/٨٠٥	وفقًا للمصادر تولّى الحسبة ما يزيد على عشرين مرّة كلّها من طريق الرشوة ما بين ١٤٠٣/٨٠٥ و١٤٣٠/٨٢٣	الملك الناصر فرج بن برقوق (١٣٨٢/٧٨٤–١٣٨٩/٧٩١)
٨	تاج الدين محمّد بن أحمد بن علي المعروف بابن المكللة وابن جماعة	١٦–٢٤ ذي القعدة ١٤٠٧/٨٠٩	١٠٠٠ دينار	الملك الناصر فرج بن برقوق (١٣٨٢/٧٨٤–١٣٨٩/٧٩١)

٩	صدر الدين أحمد بن محمود بن محمّد العجميّ	١١ ربيع الأول–٢٨ ذي الحجة ١٤١٢/٨١٥	١٠٠٠ دينار على سبيل الالتزام، لم يستطع سدادها فعزل من منصبه مع السداد ممّا أضطرّه إلى بيع ممتلكاته ولم يقدر رغم ذلك سوى على سداد مبلغ ٣٠٠ دينار منها	الملك المؤيّد شيخ (١٤١٢/٨١٥–١٤٢١/٨٢٤)
١٠	شمس الدين محمّد بن عمر بن شعبان الجابيّ	٢٨ ذي الحجة ١٤١٢/٨١٥–١١ جمادى الأولى ١٤١٣/٨١٦	٥٠٠ دينار وتم عزله وجلده ٣٠٠ جلدة في حضرة السلطان	الملك المؤيّد شيخ (١٤١٢/٨١٥–١٤٢١/٨٢٤)
١١	شمس الدين محمّد بن عمر بن شعبان الجابيّ	١٤ ربيع الأول–٢٢ رجب ١٤١٦/٨١٩	٥٠٠ دينار رشوة لكاتب السرّ الباريزيّ	الملك المؤيّد شيخ (١٤١٢/٨١٥–١٤٢١/٨٢٤)
١٢	شمس الدين محمّد بن يعقوب الدمشقيّ التبانيّ البهنسيّ	٢٦ محرم–٢١ جمادى الأخر ١٤١٧/٨٢٠	قدّم هدايا للسلطان قدّرت قيمتها بعشرة ألاف دينار	الملك المؤيّد شيخ (١٤١٢/٨١٥–١٤٢١/٨٢٤)
١٣	عماد الدين بن بدر الدين بن الرشيد	٢١ جمادى الأخر–٢٤ ذي الحجة ١٤١٧/٨٢٠	كان محتسبًا على الفسطاط فسعى في حسبة القاهرة إلى أن يعمّر برجي القلعة بقيمة ٥٠٠ دينار	الملك المؤيّد شيخ (١٤١٢/٨١٥–١٤٢١/٨٢٤)
١٤	صارم الدين إبراهيم بن محمّد بن الحسام لاجين الصقريّ	٢٠ رجب ١٤٢٠/٨٢٣–١٤ محرم ١٤٢١/٨٢٤	١٠٠٠ دينار على سبيل الالتزام	الملك المؤيّد شيخ (١٤١٢/٨١٥–١٤٢١/٨٢٤)
١٥	علاء الدين علي بن محمّد بن أقبرس	٢٢ ذي الحجة ١٤٤٨/٨٥٢–٤ جمادى الأول ١٤٤٩/٨٥٣	غير معلوم	الملك الظاهر جقمق (١٤٣٨/٨٤٢–١٤٥٣/٨٥٧)

١٦	علي بن نصر الله العجميّ الخراسانيّ الشهير بيار وعلي الطويل	٢٩ جمادى الأولى ١٤٥٠/٨٥٤–٢٧ ذي القعدة ١٤٥٣/٨٥٧	ألزم نفسه بسداد ٢٠٠٠ دينار شريطة بقائه في منصبه وعدم عزله.	الملك الأشرف إينال (١٤٥٣/٨٥٧–١٤٦١/٨٦٥)
١٧	علي بن أحمد الكاشف	٢٩ ذي القعدة ١٤٥٣/٨٥٧–تاريخ عزله غير معلوم. لكنه لم يمكث في منصبه سوى بضعة أشهر.	٣٠٠٠ دينار	الملك الأشرف إينال (١٤٥٣/٨٥٧–١٤٦١/٨٦٥)
١٨	صلاح الدين أحمد بن محمّد المكينيّ	٢٧ ذي القعدة ١٤٥٦/٨٦١–١٨ جمادى الأول ١٤٥٧/٨٦٢	٣٠٠٠ دينار	الملك الأشرف إينال (١٤٥٣/٨٥٧–١٤٦١/٨٦٥)
١٩	سيف الدين تنم بن عبد الله من عبد الرزاق المؤيّدي المعروف بالرصاص	٦ صفر ١٤٦٠/٨٦٥ حتّى مقتله في ٧ ذي الحجة ١٤٦٤/٨٦٧	غير معلوم	الملك المؤيد أحمد (١٤٦١/٨٦٥) الملك الظاهر خوشقدم (١٤٦١/٨٦٥–١٤٦٧/٨٧٢)
٢٠	مماي الصغير	ربيع الأول – ربيع الثاني ١٥١٦/٩٢٢	١٥٠٠٠ دينار	الملك الأشرف قنصوة الغوريّ (١٥٠١/٩٠٦–١٥١٦/٩٢٢)

المرحلة الثالثة: الحسبة إدارة مدنيّة لا دينيّة (١٤١٣/٨١٦–١٥١٧/٩٢٣):

المرحلة الثالثة لتطوّر مؤسّسة الحسبة في العصر المملوكيّ، كان قد أطلق عليها أحمد عبد الرازق، في مقاله المذكور، مرحلة المحتسبة الأمراء في تمييزه محتسبة الدولة المملوكيّة بين محتسبة أمراء أي من المماليك ومحتسبة فقهاء. وكنت قد عمدت في السابق إلى اعتماد تلك التسمية ثمّ خلصت إلى عدم دقّتها لأنّ محتسبة هذه المرحلة لم يكونوا جميعًا من المنتمين للعنصر المملوكيّ بل كان يميّزهم ويجمع بين أغلبيّتهم خبراتهم الإداريّة. وقد خلص إلى ذلك أيضًا (Berkey) وإن قسم هذه المرحلة إلى أربعة أطوار.[٤٤]

[٤٤] يقسم (Berkey) هذه المرحلة إلى طور إصلاح المؤسّسة في عهد المؤيّد شيخ وطور الاستقرار من ١٤٢٢/٨٢٥ إلى ١٤٣٨/٨٤١ وهي فترة حكم الأشرف برسباي ثمّ طوّر سيطرة العنصر الشركسيّ على مؤسّسة الحسبة من ١٤٣٨/٨٤١ إلى ١٥٠٥/٩١٠ وأخيراً ولاية الزينيّ بركات بن موسى حتّى نهاية دولة المماليك في العام ١٥١٧/٩٢٣؛ See Berkey, "The Muḥtasib of Cairo", 253–258.

تبدأ هذه المرحلة في عهد السلطان الملك المؤيّد شيخ (١٤١٢/٨١٥–١٤٢١/٨٢٤) وذلك في ٢٠ رجب من العام ٨١٦هـ الموافق ١٤١٣ م حينما ضجّ من فساد الأوضاع في السلطنة، وأراد إعادة ترتيبها بالركون إلى أهل الثقة من رجال الإدارة فولّى الحسبة أحد كبار المماليك الكتابيّة وهو مناكلي بغا العجميّ. وكان مشهورًا عنه اهتمامه بالفقه. إلا إنّه لم يثبت جدارته في المنصب فعزله في ٢٩ شوال ٨١٧ هـ الموافق ١٤١٤ م وسجنه لأيّام عدّة. وكان قد استقرّ بذلك في ولايته للحسبة ما يربو عن العام. ثمّ ولّى إيّاها خلفًا له والي القاهرة تاج الدين السويكيّ القزانيّ. إلا أنّ حزم وشدة المؤيّد شيخ دفعت بالسويكيّ إلى عزل نفسه حينما فقد السيطرة على الأسعار، خوفًا من بطش السلطان. وتكرّر هذا الموقف ما دفع بالسلطان للإشراف على الحسبة بنفسه قرابة شهر ثمّ ولاها البدر العينيّ محتسبًا يسانده فيها الأمير إينال متحدّثًا في شؤون الحسبة أي مشرفًا على تنفيذ أوامر العينيّ وسياساته، وذلك خوفًا من العينيّ، من بطش العامّة به واشتداد الأزمة. بعد أن هدأت الأمور عادت حاشية السلطان إلى قبول الرشوة للترشيح للمناصب، وعاد السلطان إلى نظام الامتياز، لكن في حالات معدودة وليس بحدّة المرحلة السابقة. وأدّت سياسات المؤيّد شيخ الإصلاحيّة وركونه إلى تولية منصب المحتسب إلى أهل الثقة من ذوى الخبرة الإداريّة، بغضّ النظر عن كونهم من الفقهاء، أهل القلم، أو العسكر من أهل السيف، إلى إعادة اكتشاف هويّة الحسبة كمؤسّسة إداريّة مدنيّة ذات طبيعة اقتصاديّة لا دينيّة تولّى لذوي الخبرة ولو على سبيل الالتزام ولم يبق من مظاهرها الدينيّة سوى لقب قاضٍ إن كان من رجال القلم كما كان الحال مع أخر محتسبة دولة المماليك الزيني بركات بن موسى. لقد سار على درب المؤيّد شيخ من خلفه من سلاطين وأنهوا بذلك احتكار رجال الدين لها، والاعتراف بحقوقهم فيها، ما أدّى إلى استقرار الحسبة وسمح للعنصر الشركسيّ بتولّيها من دون حرج يذكر، إلا في كتابات العلماء المترحّمين على أيّام كانت الحسبة فيها لا تولّى إلا لفقيه.

فهرس الأعلام والأماكن

الصورة ١: في الأعلى: تفصيل من صفحة في مخطوط عربيّ (مقامات الحريريّ) للواسطي من العام ١٢٣٧. باريس، المكتبة الوطنية.

في الأدنى: صفحة في إنجيل سرياني من حوالى العام ١٢٢٠. مكتبة الفاتيكان

قارن بين رسم الديك في المخطوطين ورسم الوجوه.

الصورة ٢: صفحة من مخطوط سريانيّ من حوالى العام ١٢٢٠م. مكتبة الفاتيكان.

الصورة ٣: صفحتان من مخطوطين سريانيّين من حوالى العام ١٢٢٠. لندن، المتحف البريطاني (أعلى)، مكتبة الفاتيكان (أدنى).

الصورة ٤: صفحتان من مخطوط سريانيّ من فترة القرنين ١٣/١٢. لندن، المتحف البريطاني.

الصورة ٥: صفحة من مخطوط سريانيّ من العام ١٢٢٧. كنيسة مار سوبو في حاح، طور عابدين.

الصورة ٦: صفحتان من مخطوط سريانيّ من فترة القرنين ١٤/١٣. كنيسة مار جاورجيوس في قرقوش قرب الموصل.

الصورة ٧: مقارنة بين رسم المسيح (يسار) من مخطوط سريانيّ من فترة القرنين ١٢/١٣م. في المتحف البريطاني وبين صورة جداريّة للقدّيس يوحنّا المعمدان (يمين) من دير مار موسى الحبشيّ من العام ١٢٠٨. من كنيسة دير مار موسى الحبشي، النبك، سوريا.

الصورة ٨: صورة جداريّة من صور صدر الهيكل في كنيسة دير مار موسى الحبشيّ من العام ١٢٠٨.

صورة رقم ١

صورة رقم ٢

صورة رقم ٣

صورة رقم ٤

صورة رقم ٥

صورة رقم ٦

صورة رقم ٧

صورة رقم ٩

صورة رقم ٨

صورة رقم ١٠

صورة رقم ١١

صورة رقم ١٢

صورة رقم ١٣

الطريق بين الشمال والجنوب
موقع البوابة
جزء من سور المربض
قلعة طرابلس
Nahr Abu Ali
Éch. 1/5000
كنيسة مار يوحنا
مكان اسوار تحصينات المربض الأول
موقع السرداب المكتشف

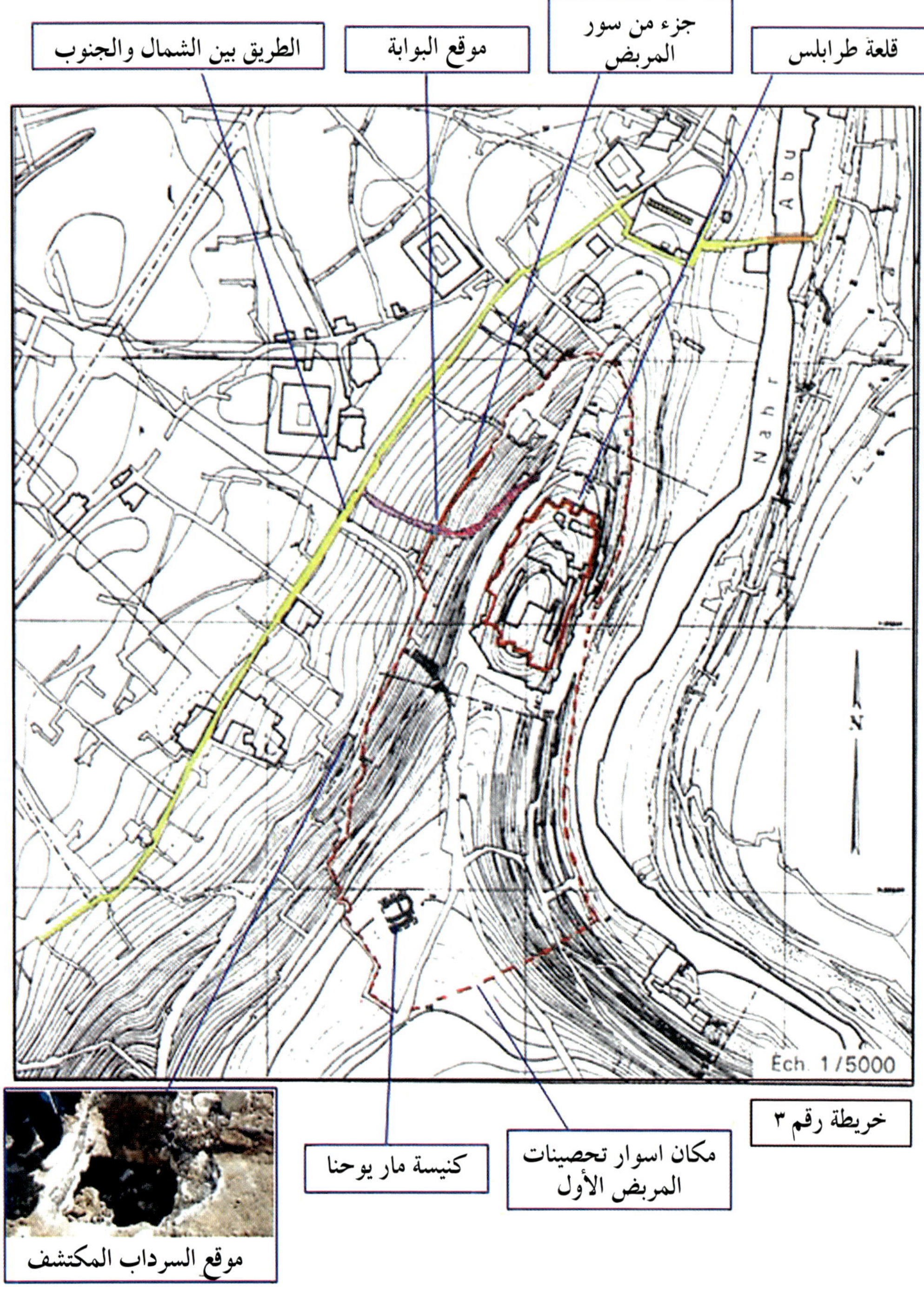

خريطة رقم ٣

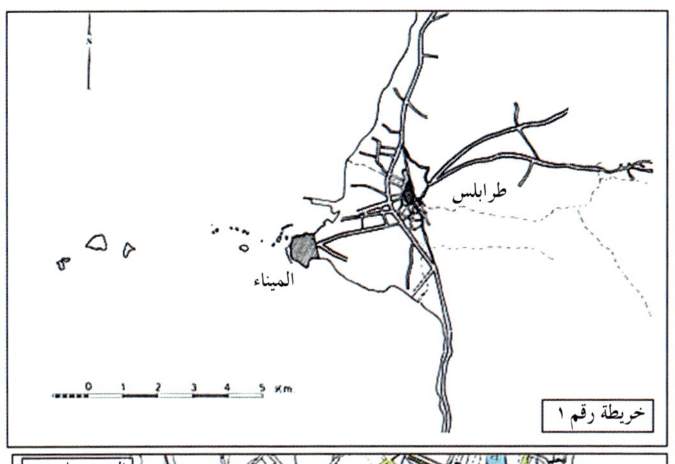
طرابلس
الميناء
0 1 2 3 4 5 Km
خريطة رقم ١

الجسر على نهر أبو علي
الطريق بين الشمال والجنوب
موقع البوابة
قلعة طرابلس
نهر أبو علي
خريطة رقم ٢

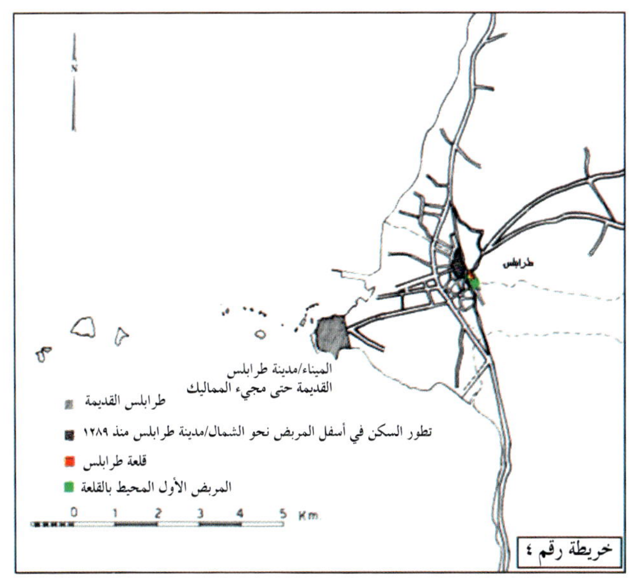
طرابلس
الميناء/مدينة طرابلس
القديمة حتى مجيء المماليك
طرابلس القديمة
تطور السكن في أسفل المربض نحو الشمال/مدينة طرابلس منذ ١٢٨٩
قلعة طرابلس
المربض الأول المحيط بالقلعة
0 1 2 3 4 5 Km
خريطة رقم ٤

Figs. 11a and b. Qarṭāwiyya Madrasa, façade and detail.

Figs. 9a and b. al-Nāṣiriyya Madrasa, portal and detail

Figs. 10a and b. Jāmiʿ al-ʿAṭṭar, portal and detail.

Figs. 8a and b. Great Mosque, portal and detail.

Figs. 7a and b. Khātūniyya Madrasa, portal and detail.

Figs. 5a and b. Portals of Jāmiᶜ Ṭaynāl and Burṭāsī, detail.

Figs. 6a and b. Qarṭāwiyya Madrasa, portal and detail.

Figs. 4a and b. Jāmiʿ Ṭaynāl, inner portal and detail.

Figs. 3a and b. The ʿAjamiyya madrasa, façade and detail.

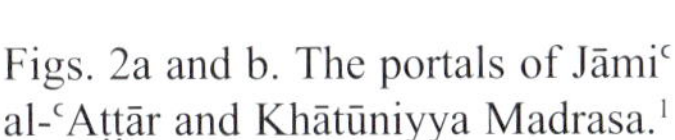

Figs. 2a and b. The portals of Jāmiʿ al-ʿAṭṭār and Khātūniyya Madrasa.[1]

---

1 Source for images number 2a and b, 4a and b, 9a and b, and 11a and b is El-Bizri, Amin (ed.) *Arabic Calligraphy in Architecture: Islamic Monuments Inscriptions in the City of Tripoli during the Mamluk Period* (Beirut, 1999).

Figs.1a and b. The Saqraqiyya Madrasa, façade and detail

Pl. 14. Lectern from the Church of Ḥārat al-Rūm; Coptic Museum, Cairo

Pl. 15. Central ciborium of Al-Muᶜallaqa

Pl. 12. Central sanctuary screen of Al-Muᶜallaqa

Pl. 13. Detail of the geometric decoration; screen of Al-Muᶜallaqa

Pl. 10. Detail of the geometric decoration; screen of Ḥārat Zuwaylah

Pl. 11. Detail of the door; screen of Ḥārat Zuwaylah

Pl. 8. Wall painting; Dayr Anbā Būlā

Pl. 9. Detail of the geometric decoration; screen of Abū Sargā

Pl. 5. St George; Dayr Ḥammāṭūra

Pl. 7. Bishop on south wall; Chapel of the Prophet Elijah, Maʿarrat Ṣaydnāyā

Pl. 6. Virgin and Child; Chapel of the Prophet Elijah, Maᶜarrat Ṣaydnāyā (Bas ter Haar Romeny)

Pl. 3. St Sergius; Church of St Sergius and St Bacchus, Qārah (B. ter Haar Romeny)

Pl. 4. Ascension of Elijah; private collection (after Van Rijn, Icons, pl. on 80).

Pl. 1. Donor; Church of Mār Tādrus, Biḥdaydāt

Pl. 2. St Bacchus; Dayr Mār Mūsā

Fig. 1. Map of Lebanon (by M. Immerzeel)

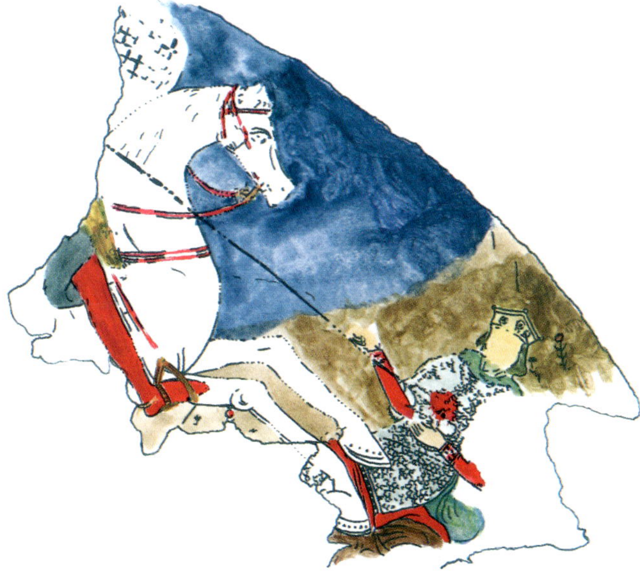

Fig. 2. St George; Dayr Ḥammāṭūra (reconstruction M. Immerzeel)